A CULTURAL HISTORY OF LAW

VOLUME 3

A Cultural History of Law
General Editor: Gary Watt

Volume 1
A Cultural History of Law in Antiquity
Edited by Julen Etxabe

Volume 2
A Cultural History of Law in the Middle Ages
Edited by Emanuele Conte and Laurent Mayali

Volume 3
A Cultural History of Law in the Early Modern Age
Edited by Peter Goodrich

Volume 4
A Cultural History of Law in the Age of Enlightenment
Edited by Rebecca Probert and John Snape

Volume 5
A Cultural History of Law in the Age of Reform
Edited by Ian Ward

Volume 6
A Cultural History of Law in the Modern Age
Edited by Richard K. Sherwin and Danielle Celermajer

A CULTURAL HISTORY OF LAW
IN THE EARLY MODERN AGE

Edited by Peter Goodrich

BLOOMSBURY ACADEMIC
LONDON • NEW YORK • OXFORD • NEW DELHI • SYDNEY

BLOOMSBURY ACADEMIC
Bloomsbury Publishing Plc
50 Bedford Square, London, WC1B 3DP, UK
1385 Broadway, New York, NY 10018, USA
29 Earlsfort Terrace, Dublin 2, Ireland

BLOOMSBURY, BLOOMSBURY ACADEMIC and the Diana logo
are trademarks of Bloomsbury Publishing Plc

First published in Great Britain 2019
Paperback edition published in 2023

Copyright © Bloomsbury Publishing Plc, 2019

Peter Goodrich has asserted his right under the Copyright, Designs and
Patents Act, 1988, to be identified as Editor of this work.

Cover image: Hieroglyphica, sive, De sacris Aegyptiorvm literis commentarii
© Getty Research Institute, Los Angeles (2856–226)

All rights reserved. No part of this publication may be reproduced or transmitted in
any form or by any means, electronic or mechanical, including photocopying, recording,
or any information storage or retrieval system, without prior permission in writing
from the publishers.

Bloomsbury Publishing Plc does not have any control over, or responsibility for,
any third-party websites referred to or in this book. All internet addresses given in this book
were correct at the time of going to press. The editor and publisher regret any inconvenience
caused if addresses have changed or sites have ceased to exist, but can accept no
responsibility for any such changes.

A catalogue record for this book is available from the British Library.

A catalog record for this book is available from the Library of Congress.

ISBN:		
	PB set:	978-1-3503-6891-0
	HB:	978-1-4742-1264-9
	PB:	978-1-3503-6867-5
	ePDF:	978-1-3500-7929-8
	eBook:	978-1-3500-7930-4

Series: The Cultural Histories Series

Typeset by Integra Software Services Pvt. Ltd.
Printed and bound in Great Britain

To find out more about our editors and books visit www.bloomsbury.com
and sign up for our newsletters.

CONTENTS

LIST OF FIGURES — vi
NOTES ON CONTRIBUTORS — x
SERIES PREFACE — xii

Introduction: The Great Dialogue — 1
Peter Goodrich

1 Justice — 17
   Valérie Hayaert

2 Constitutions — 39
   Susan Byrne

3 Codes: Redressing London—Sumptuary Laws and the Control of Clothing in the Early Modern City — 65
   Sophie Pitman

4 Agreements — 87
   Laurent de Sutter

5 Arguments: The Visual Mediation of Arguments in the Renaissance — 99
   Piyel Haldar

6 Property and Possession — 121
   Thanos Zartaloudis and Richard Braude

7 Wrongs — 137
   Chloë Kennedy and Lindsay Farmer

8 The Legal Profession: Tudor Lawyers in an Age of Litigation — 155
   Dominique Goy-Blanquet

NOTES — 171
BIBLIOGRAPHY — 210
INDEX — 254

LIST OF FIGURES

INTRODUCTION

0.1 Servitus (libera), from Piero Valeriano, *Hieroglyphica sive de sacris Ægyptorum literis commentarii* (Basle, 1550) 237 recto. — 2

0.2 Servitus libera, Ottavio Scarlattini, *Homo et eius partes* (1695 edn) 80. — 3

0.3 Servitus libera, Claude Paradin, *Devises heroiques* (1551) at 78. — 5

0.4 Title page, Jan David, *Veridicus Christianus* (1601). — 8

0.5 Woodcut, Richard Hooker, *Of the Lawes of Ecclesiastical Politie* (1617) at 1. — 13

0.6 Alciato, *In vitam humanam, Emblemata* (1584) at 208. — 13

JUSTICE

1.1 *The Judgement of Cambyses*, Dirck Vellert, 1542, glass roundel, d. 29.4 cm. — 19

1.2 Johann Theodor de Bry, Dirck Volckertsz Coornhert and Maarten van Hermskerck, *Emblemata saecularia varietate seculi huius mores ita experimentia*, 1611, engraving, h 94 mmm x w 105 mm. — 21

1.3 Christoph Haunold, *Controversiarum de Justitia et Jure privatorum universo nova et theorica methodo, tomus primus*, Ingolstadt, Joannes Simon Knab, 1671, frontispiece. — 22

1.4 Juan de Solorzano Pereira, *Emblemata centum regio politica in centuriam unam redactam*, Madrid Garcia Morràs, 1653, emblema LXII "Statera Regum". — 24

1.5 *Justitia*, part of a series of the seven virtues, workshop of Jacob de Gheyn (II), 1591–1595, engraving, d 148 mm. — 29

1.6 Crispijn van de Passe (II), Frontispiece for the edition of the *Corpus Juris Civilis*, by Denis Godefroy, Paris, Antoine Vitré, 1627, engraving, h 347 mm x w 212 mm. — 29

1.7 Workshop of Claes Jansz Visscher (II), Satire on Oliver Cromwell and the Protectorate suggesting that he aimed to become king, published by Rombout van den Hoeye, 1653–1654, engraving, h 402 mm x w 458 mm. — 30

LIST OF FIGURES   vii

1.8   Peeter van der Borcht, *The Broom of Justice*, Antwerp, 1578, published by Adriaen Huybrechts (I), engraving, h 298 mm x w 220 mm.   32

1.9   Heinrich Oraeus, *Viridarium hieroglyphico-morale: in quo virtutes et vitia ... illustrantur*, Francfort, Jacques de Zetter, 1619, pp. 52–53.   34

1.10   Bartolomeo Del Bene, "Domus Injustitiae" (Temple of Injustice) in *Civitas veri sive morum, Aristotelis de moribus doctrinam carmine et picturis complexa, et llustrata commentariis Th. Marcilii*, Paris, Ambroise et Jérôme Drouart, 1609, p. 165.   35

1.11   Bartolomeo Del Bene, "Domus Justitiae" (Temple of Justice) in *Civitas veri sive morum, Aristotelis de moribus doctrinam carmine et picturis complexa, et llustrata commentariis Th. Marcilii*, Paris, Ambroise et Jérôme Drouart, 1609, p. 166.   36

CONSTITUTIONS

2.1   "First sonnet." In *Tratado de los juicios* by Antonio Peña.   50

2.2   "Famous attorney" Valencia. Allegation of rights of the king to appoint a non-native viceroy in Aragon, 1590.   53

2.3   Pedro Luis Martínez. Response to king's defense, 1591.   55

2.4   Cover page. *Quaderno de Cortes, Valladolid.* 1523.   56

2.5   *The Politician*, 1771, with picture of Don Quixote battling a windmill in the background.   61

2.6   *Captain Bun Quixote attacking the oven*, 1778.   62

2.7   Isaac Cruikshank. *Aristocratic crusade*, 1791, with Edmund Burke as Don Quixote.   63

CODES

3.1   Mor's Gentleman was clearly of noble enough status to proudly wear such stuffed hose in his portrait. Their style, size, and shape might have been similar to those worn and removed from the servant Richard Walweyn. Antonis Mor, Netherlandish, (1519–1576), *Portrait of a Gentleman*, 1569, oil on canvas, 119.7 x 88.3 cm.   66

3.2   Even for the illiterate population, these tables showed clearly that clothing and social status were hierarchical. "The brief content of certayne Actes of Parliament" from 16 February 1577 Proclamation Enforcing Statutes of Apparel (London: R. Jugge, 1577).   70

3.3   Doublet and Trunk Hose with Canions, uncut silk velvet on a voided satin ground, English, *c.* 1604, Grimsthorpe and Drummond Castle Trust. Pencil drawings by Janet Arnold.   73

3.4	This large ruff is marked with the initials 'CY' in small red silk stitch, probably to ensure its safe return from the laundry. Ruff, c. 1615–1635, linen, h3cm x c38cm, l1950cm x w13cm.	78
3.5	Knitted cap, sixteenth century, English, wool, 23.5 cm wide.	80
3.6	Piece of woolen velvet, sixteenth century, Flemish, 27.9 x 30.5 cm. The Metropolitan Museum of Art, Rogers Fund, 1909, 09.50.1075. Courtesy www.metmuseum.org.	84

AGREEMENTS

4.1	*The village bride or The village agreement*, 1761, by Jean-Baptiste Greuze (1725–1805), oil on canvas, 92x117 cm.	96
4.2	*Mariage à la mode—The settlement*.	97
4.3	Watteau, *Marriage contract*.	97

ARGUMENTS

5.1	*Anatomy of Melancholy*, Frontispiece.	105
5.2	Guillaume de La Perrière, *Theatre bon engines*.	108
5.3	Pierre Le Moyne, *De L'Art Des Devices*.	109
5.4	Jean-Jacques Boissard, *Finis Coronat Opus*.	114
5.5	Pierre Cousteau *In Rabulis et Operarios Lingua Ce Lexi ponatur celeri custodia linguae, / Saepe loqui nocuit, sed tacuisse iuvat."*	115
5.6	Alciato, *Garrulum et Gulosum*.	116

WRONGS

7.1	The spiritual warfare.	138
7.2	Newes from Scotland, declaring the damnable life of Doctor Fian [i.e. John Cunningham], a notable sorcerer, who was burned at Edenbrough in Ianuarie last, 1591 [for practising sorcery against King James I. A reprint of the ed. printed in London probably in 1591. Edited by Sir George H. Freeling].	142
7.3	Joseph Glanvill's *Saducismus Triumphatus: Or, Full and Plain Evidence Concerning Witches and Apparitions* (1681).	144
7.4	Woman wearing a scold's bridle. Ralph Gardiner, *England's Grievance Discovered* (1655).	150

THE LEGAL PROFESSION

8.1 Drawings by Robert Beale in his official report on "the trial and execution of Mary Queen of Scots." 168

8.2 Another drawing in Beale's report, "The execution." 169

8.3 Anonymous colored woodcut, is entitled "The Seven Ages of Man, From a Black Print in the British Museum" colored woodcut, originally inserted in a printed copy of Nicolaus de Lyra's *Moralia super Bibliam*, c. 1460, reproduced under the title "The Seven Ages of Man" in *Archæologia*, vol. XXXV, 1853, plate XVII, p. 188. 170

NOTES ON CONTRIBUTORS

Richard Braude studied medieval history, law, and architecture at Cambridge University, the Warburg Institute and Birkbeck College, University of London. His doctoral thesis was on medieval English building contracts and class struggle. He works as a translator and interpreter in Palermo, Italy.

Susan Byrne is Professor of Hispanic Studies and Chair of the Department of World Languages and Cultures at the University of Nevada, Las Vegas. She is the author of three books: *Ficino in Spain* (University of Toronto Press, 2015), *Law and History in Cervantes'* Don Quixote (University of Toronto Press, 2012), and *El Corpus Hermeticum y tres poetas españoles* (Juan de la Cuesta, 2007), as well as of a number of articles in various venues. Her research interests include the history of ideas as expressed in, and altered by, creative letters; Italo-Hispanic exchanges in the Early Modern period; law and literature; philosophy in, and of, literature.

Lindsay Farmer is Professor of Law at the University of Glasgow.

Peter Goodrich is Professor of Law, and Director of the Program in Law and Humanities at Cardozo School of Law, New York and Visiting Professor, School of Social Science, New York University Abu Dhabi. *Schreber's Law: Jurisprudence and Judgment in Transition* was published in Fall 2018.

Dominique Goy-Blanquet is Professor Emeritus at the University of Picardie, a member of the editorial board of *En attendant Nadeau* (formerly *La Quinzaine littéraire*), a contributor to *Books* and to the *Times Literary Supplement*, president of the Société Française Shakespeare 2009–2015. Her works include *Côté cour, côté justice: Shakespeare et l'invention du droit* (Classiques Garnier, 2016), essays for *Shakespeare Survey, Cambridge Companion, Literary Encyclopedia, Europe, Moreana, Law and Humanities*. Her latest book, *Shakespeare in the Theatre: Patrice Chéreau* (Arden/Bloomsbury) is due out in 2018.

Piyel Haldar is Lecturer in Law, Birkbeck College, University of London where he teaches legal history, equity, and the laws of evidence. He is currently writing, or not writing, a monograph provisionally titled "Curatorialism and other half forgotten functions of equity."

Valérie Hayaert is a classicist, historian, and humanist researcher of the Early Modern tradition. Her research interest lies in the emblem tradition and its links with legal mindsets and culture. Her recent work has looked at the aesthetics of justice in courthouses from the Early Modern period until today. She is Research Fellow at the Käte Hamburger Kolleg / Center for Advanced Study in the Humanities "Law as Culture", University of Bonn.

Chloë Kennedy is Lecturer in Criminal Law at the University of Edinburgh. She holds a Ph.D. and LLM from the University of Edinburgh and an LLB (Hons) from the University of Glasgow. Her research is mainly focused on criminal law, legal theory, legal history, and the relationship between these areas. She is also interested in the critical potential of legal history and the interrelations between law and religion. Her work has appeared in the *Oxford Journal of Legal Studies, Edinburgh Law Review*, and *Jurisprudence*. She is currently working on the Scottish Feminist Judgments Project, of which she is a co-editor.

Sophie Pitman is a Lecturer in History and a postdoctoral researcher on the Making and Knowing Project at the Center for Science and Society at Columbia University, New York. She received her PhD in History from Cambridge University in 2017.

Laurent de Sutter is Professor of Legal Theory at Vrije Universiteit, Brussels. He is the author of a dozen books on pornography, Gilles Deleuze, cinema, kamikaze, drugs, prostitution, art, police and law, translated into several languages. He also is the Managing Editor of the Perspectives Critiques series at Presses Universitaires de France, and the Theory Redux series at Polity Press.

Thanos Zartaloudis is a Reader in Legal Theory and History at the University of Kent, Kent Law School and the Architectural Association, London. His latest book is *The Birth of Nomos* (Edinburgh University Press, 2018).

SERIES PREFACE

The six volumes in *A Cultural History of Law* present a panorama of law's cultural significance over the span of several centuries, especially as it relates to the place of law in the arts and humanities. Each volume focuses on a distinct time period from antiquity to modernity and in each volume a chapter is devoted to one of eight legally significant themes: "Justice," "Constitution," "Codes," "Agreements," "Arguments," "Property and Possession," "Wrongs," and "The Legal Profession." The collection does not seek to provide encyclopedic coverage, but rather to present cultural case studies that highlight how particular cultural artifacts express and explore the key legal—and inevitably the key political and social—concerns of their time. The authors have picked flowers from their field of expertise—a play, a painting, a mosaic, a book, a film—which bring into close focus the cultural and legal flourishing of the time. The volume editors are internationally distinguished scholars with a passion and deep appreciation for the law and culture of their chosen period. Together with the experts that they have assembled to contribute chapters on the eight themes, they are reliable guides not merely to the facts about each period but to the feel of each period. Every volume has an ethos and a style that immerses the reader in the distinctive quality of its era. The series is indebted to the archivist's concern to discover and catalog historical materials, but what sets it apart is its concern to show how the materials of history are materially meaningful. In this way, our retrospective of more than 2,000 years continues to have relevance for lawyers and for all culturally concerned citizens today.

Sometimes we find that artifacts have lost the cultural meanings that first produced them. Likewise, we sometimes we find that artifacts are culturally meaningful today in ways that they were not at the time of their creation. Take the example of Magna Carta—The Great Charter of King John of England sealed at Runnymede on the Thames in 1215. Today, in the United States in particular, Magna Carta has been hoisted to totemic heights in the cultural imagination. It might therefore seem strange to us that William Shakespeare's play *King John* makes no reference at all to this great artifact. The reason for its omission is that for Shakespeare and his early modern contemporaries, the most dramatic historical event in the reign of King John was his surrender of the crown to the papal legate and his receiving it again as a papal vassal. The modern significance of Magna Carta is largely a post-Enlightenment invention and its principal promoters were the great myth-makers who framed the American Constitution and created the idea of the United States. It is some proof of this that the Magna Carta memorial which stands at Runnymede today was erected by the American Bar Association. The small-scale temple, like the much larger Jefferson Memorial in Washington DC, has become a place of secular pilgrimage; a sanctuary to the values of political freedom and human rights under law.

In 2015, to mark the 800th anniversary of the sealing of Magna Carta, sculptor Hew Locke's "The Jurors" was installed at Runnymede. It comprises twelve bronze chairs, each of which (according to the official narrative) "incorporates symbols and imagery representing concepts of law and key moments in the struggle for freedom, rule of law and equal rights." In this respect, it performs a similar function to the eight bas relief panels by sculptor John Donnelly Jnr that adorn the great bronze doors of the United States Supreme Court in Washington DC. Shakespeare would have appreciated the performative purpose of these "solemn temples" but he would surely be surprised to see today how much has been made of Magna Carta. The rise of Magna Carta as an artifact of cultural history would certainly have amazed the landed aristocrats who first compelled King John to set his seal to the charter in the culturally Christian, monarchal, and feudal context of the High Middle Ages. The narrative accompanying "The Jurors" alerts us to the license that the sculptor has taken with the history of law. We are told that it is "not a memorial, but rather an artwork that aims to examine the changing and ongoing significance and influences of Magna Carta." It is, in short, a cultural reworking of an artifact that owes its great status to creative cultural appropriation. The actual provisions of Magna Carta that survive in law are impressively few, but the three survivors are perhaps all the more significant for their small number. Much is still made of the survival of the right to trial by jury. Rather less is made, nowadays, of the provisions that preserve the "liberties of the English Church" and the "privileges of the City of London." One of the most important contributions we can make to the appreciation of history is to show where cultures are selective in what they present as fact. The artifacts of history are always presented in the cabinets of culture.

The word "fact" comes, in fact, from the Latin *facere* ("to make") and it can be helpful to think of historical facts as things that are produced by the action of culture and as things which, in turn, produce cultures. Even where a society is collectively in error in its understanding of historical fact, a commonly held mistake inevitably becomes part of the cultural history of that society. The story becomes the history. One of the mistakes we often make, as the shifting status of Magna Carta indicates, is to suppose that the modern commentator can claim a monopoly in the present moment to determine "true" history from "false." Today's official history is only ever the history of the present. The past had its own histories. Cultural history allows an appreciation of the cultural stories that give meaning to societies in time and across time. From a cultural perspective, myths can be more meaningful, and in that cultural sense more "true," than many a cold matter of fact.

Another great and oft-repeated mistake that this book series seeks to remedy is the supposition that law can be meaningfully separated from the culture in which it exists. In *Law as Culture*, Lawrence Rosen observes that law:

> never stands apart from life—some refined essence of professional inquiry or arcane speech. Rather, it forms the conscious attention we give to our relationships. Like art and literature, through law we attempt to order our ties to one another … However it is displayed, however it is applied, we can no more comprehend the roles of legal institutions without seeing them as part of their culture than we can fully understand each culture without attending to its form of law.[1]

There is an historical aspect to this understanding of law as culture. Pierre Legrand writes, for example, that:

> French law is, first and foremost, a cultural phenomenon, not unlike singing or weaving. The reason why the French have the *chanteurs* they have lies somewhere in their history, their Frenchness, in their identity. Similarly, the reason why the French have the legislative texts or the judicial decisions they have, say, on a matter of sales law, lies somewhere in their history, their Frenchness, in their identity.[2]

There are obvious limits to the mechanistic metaphor by which we talk of cultural history as something manufactured or fabricated. Human hands fashion historical artifacts, but legal artifacts grow out of a culture in a way that makes it hard to know where the artifact starts and the culture ends. It might be better to take the "culture" metaphor seriously and to suggest that laws grow out of a society organically and that the artificial intervention of human hands are like those of the gardener—taming, tending, and ordering wild growth. Thus the cultural history of law becomes something like a horticultural history. This is not such a strange thought when one considers that the English word for the "court" of law is derived from the Latin *hortus* (garden). Malcolm Andrews has suggested that "one could write an illuminating, if oblique, history of a nation's cultural development by examining its changing conception of the garden's scope, design and function."[3] The gardening metaphor may be especially useful in helping us to understand the cultural history of law, given the complex relation between natural justice and artificial laws in human society. Dress is another artificial creation of human craft which, as a cultural outworking of the complex relation between nature and human ordering, serves well as a way to understand the artificial and creative nature of law's contribution to culture. Laws are produced in society in much the same way that gardens, dress, and other products of complex cultural systems are produced in society. When we have completed our journey through the six volumes of this series we may conclude that the chief legislator across the ages has been no parliament nor any body of the people politically represented, but that the great lawmaker has always been the deep, rich, and creative power of human culture.

Gary Watt, Professor of Law,
University of Warwick, UK

Introduction:

The Great Dialogue

PETER GOODRICH

The nose is a portent of good judgment, the sign of equilibrium, and an omen of wisdom in the humanistic disciplines, as equally in law. Thus Piero Valeriano in his highly influential *Hieroglyphica* begins his chapter *De naso* under the heading *Sagacitas* and postulates immediately that the proboscis, whether large or small a matter of indifference, is the instrument of wisdom and the guide to higher things.[1] A clean nose—*emunctæ naris*—is a mark of great prudential skill, and to this he adds, drawing on the early discipline of *oneirocriticism*, that when someone appears in a dream with a large nose (*magno naso*) it signals a promise of extraordinary sanctity and dexterity in decision making. Erasmus, in his *Ciceronianus*, makes a similar point in inverted form when he has Bulephorus observe "that there is a kind of madness that does not take away the whole mind, but affects only one part in such an extraordinary degree that the victims believe that they are … burdened with long noses."[2] The olfactory organ may well lead by smell, by scent and sense, by intuition but it is singular and needs a means of balance and hence, and this, may it please your honors, is my point, the extraordinary importance of the ears precisely because, as Valeriano is quick to point out, our chosen symbol and nasal index of wisdom, sits between the auditory oracles and is the median between the eyes (Figure 0.1).

The juridical nose, the prodromus and prow of the person, leads the way and through smell in particular can both follow, as Montaigne might put it, the scent of our pilgrimage as ordained by the *nomos* of nature, while equally helping to avoid the foul stench of bad laws and ill-begotten prose. For common lawyers, laboring as they did with what was technically an unwritten law, it was less immediately the civilian's parchment proboscis than the keen ear for an oral and auditory tradition of the customs and conversations of the community that needed their listening attention. These became the common eruditions (*eruditiones*) of the Bar and, over time, made up the maxims and other rules of life and law that defined both the office of the lawyer and the medium of their practice. It is a question of hearing and of hearings, of audition and auditory attention that the legal subject seeks to convey. Thus, to take an example from the very beginning of our early modern period, to give a sense of the auricular trajectory of our era of *oyer et terminer*, of hearing and deciding cases, according to what amounts to a learned version of word of mouth, we can witness Chief Justice Bryan dispensing with argument on a point, because he had heard otherwise previously: "he did not want to hear him argue this notion, because it is one that is clearly against our ancient common learning which is now a question of principle."[3] If every such point was to be so argued, he proceeds, and here I will continue to translate for ease of exposition, "we would have to change (*transposer*) all of our ancient *presidentes*." Not reason, one might illate, and the early modern sages are at one on this, but authority is the law.

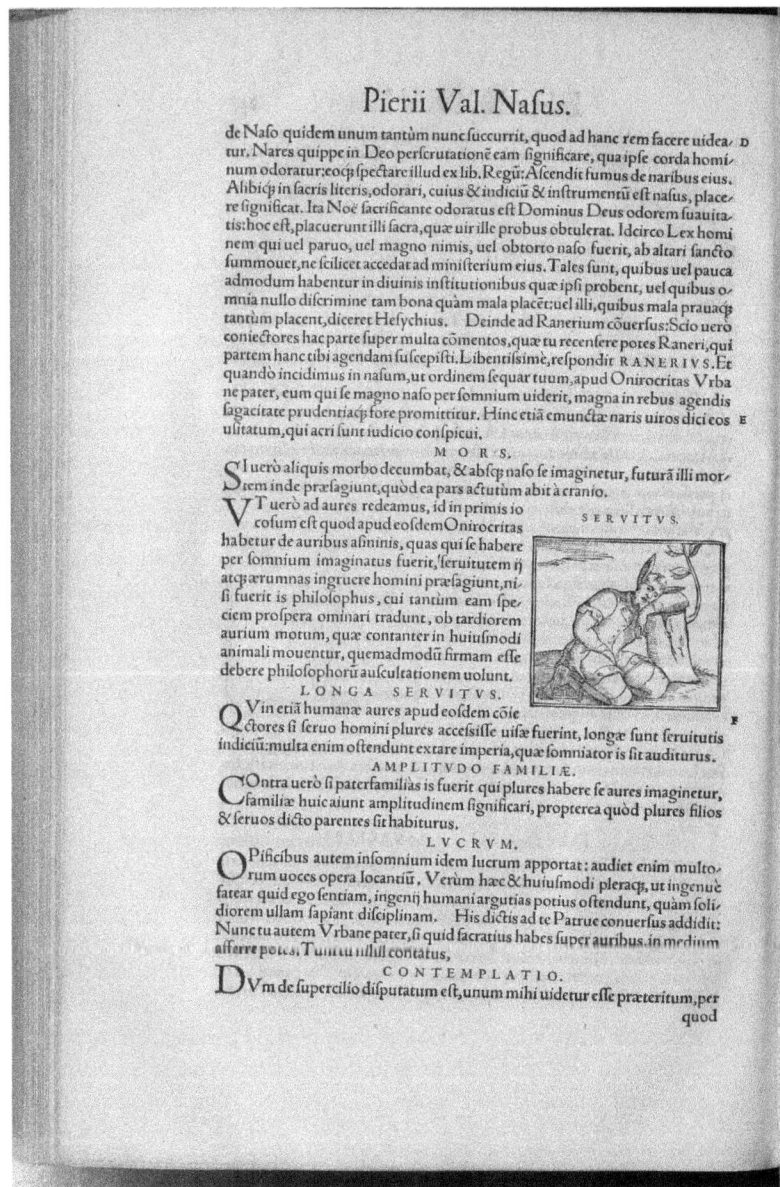

FIGURE 0.1 Servitus (libera), from Piero Valeriano, *Hieroglyphica sive de sacris Ægyptorum literis commentarii* (Basle, 1550) 237 recto. Source: Getty Images

So we start with the ear, *auris* in the Latin of the time, as the locus of memory, and borrowing from Scarlattini's later work on the hieroglyphs of man, we can note that in the humanistic lexicon, the ear is "the sense of the disciplines" and most apt for the carriage of all communication.[4] More than that, reverting to Valeriano, the ear is the index not simply of memory, of precedent, and common opinion, of the age and priority of the "somesays" and other storehouses of law, but it is equally and for the same reason

FIGURE 0.2 Servitus libera, Ottavio Scarlattini, *Homo et eius partes* (1695 edn) 80. Source: Mannheim University Library, Sch 106/283–1/2.

the *indicium* of the future, in that it provides the formulas through which propinquity and the next step are determined. Time then, enough by way of prolegomenon, to attend to the ear of the law and specifically to the dictate of justice, that the case be heard. The question to be posed, throughout, then as now, is what is it that is implied in the drawing together, the *in vivo* dialogue, the theatrical hearing that law must apply? (Figure 0.2.)

AUDITE ALTERAM PARTEM

It is not just common law that makes great play upon ear and hearing, justice and the giving of *attent* and time. For Isidore of Seville, in the *Etymologies, auris*, ear, *auditus*, hearing, and *audire*, to hear, all share a root in *haurire*, to draw in, pull together, fetch and in a metaphor drawn from Virgil, the ears drink in the words of others.[5] In all of these instances, the ear is a tie to the world, a chain of potentially heliogabulan strength to the other, to community and authority as what was historically the melodic transmission of law. Recollect first that in the humanist genealogy of law, borrowed from the classics, it is sound, rhythm, verse, and thence poetics that first entrances the subjects into the *amicitia* of relationship. In the not infrequent debates around the priority of the eyes or the ears, it is notable that it is the ears that win: the eyes are of no use in the dark, whereas the ears will warn, and it is hearing, for instance, that in classical Rome saved the capitol. Ears are the weapon of the night watch, their salve and last instance. The auditory is the mode of access and the point of entry, allowing for the maxim that eloquence is greater than force.

The lawyer Alciato in an emblem that has been elegantly discussed by Haldar depicts Hercules wearing a lion skin, with chains leading from his mouth and drawing along his followers by their ears.[6] The eloquence of Hercules pulls even the hardest of hearts towards their proper course, his rhetoric being the force that both directs and binds the fellowship or, in Haldar's depiction he is not simply a rhetor "but a pyschopomp guiding souls away from the underworld and from the collection of barbarous monsters (medieval scholastics, the free flow of imagination, the irrational crowd, etc.) that haunted the humanists."[7] The pierced and so-bridled ear is the feature that here deserves careful attention. The ear has to be penetrated, inducted into the common cause, brought towards the law and the way. A further example from the hieroglyphic images of ears can help expand the point under the Ciceronian title *servitus libera*, or free service.

The singular, rather hirsute—it appears in gaining its individuality to have grown a head of hair—and windblown ear portrayed, rests between two trees. The trees are emblems of *amicitia* and the *putti* on either side of the frame reinforce the connectivity that amity, from *amor*, implies. Why then the ear, and why is it pierced through with an awl? The answer is that the awl is the tool of a cobbler and a carpenter, and so both the mark of a maker, and equally a Christian device. Brought to work on the ear it signifies, according to the hieroglyphic text, the Psalmic request to pierce—to bore—my ears and make them ready: *aures perforasti mihi … in vinculis charitatis …* punch holes in my ears, so as to insert the bonds of charity, as everything leads to the divine—*omnia traham ad meipsum*. It is a heroical symbol and we find it in the 1551 edition of Claude Paradin's devises.[8] In a later edition of Paradin the verse commentary refers to the law of Moses as the source of the image, strict law requiring obedience to the commandments and membership of the commonality. The ear is pierced twice, first by nature and then by the symbolic permutation, the birth into the social (Figure 0.3).

Move then to trace this figure, this shape of the ear into the common law, the *mos britannicus*, in its earliest modern and formative figures and guises. The Inns of Court were built in the medieval era of organic architecture and take the shape of an ear, a space of audition in which jurisdiction is as much the right to hear causes, *querela audita* as the writ would say, as it is the power to do justice, which is a later addition.[9] Here, then, the law is a listening post, a conduit, and conference, as J. H. Baker describes in some detail, wherein a medieval oral law was relayed by those who heard, or heard some of what the Judge had said.[10] This was the *communis opinio* or (learned) common knowledge of common lawyers. The office of the Judge was *oyer*, to hear, and the role of the lawyer, from the itinerant Justice all the way down to the grand little mootman with scarcely a word of Latin, was to lend an ear to the customs and conversations, the ancient practices and antique patterns that would form the common erudition, frequently of the locality—*de cel Countie*—and more often of that audible nature and auricular *humanitas* from which the judges extracted the *commune ley*.[11]

Doderidge, in his remarkable text on method, the closest that any of the early modern Anglican lawyers came to devising explicitly a *modus docendi iuris britannicus*, dictates that "many Grounds and Rules of the Lawes of this Realme are derived from Common use,

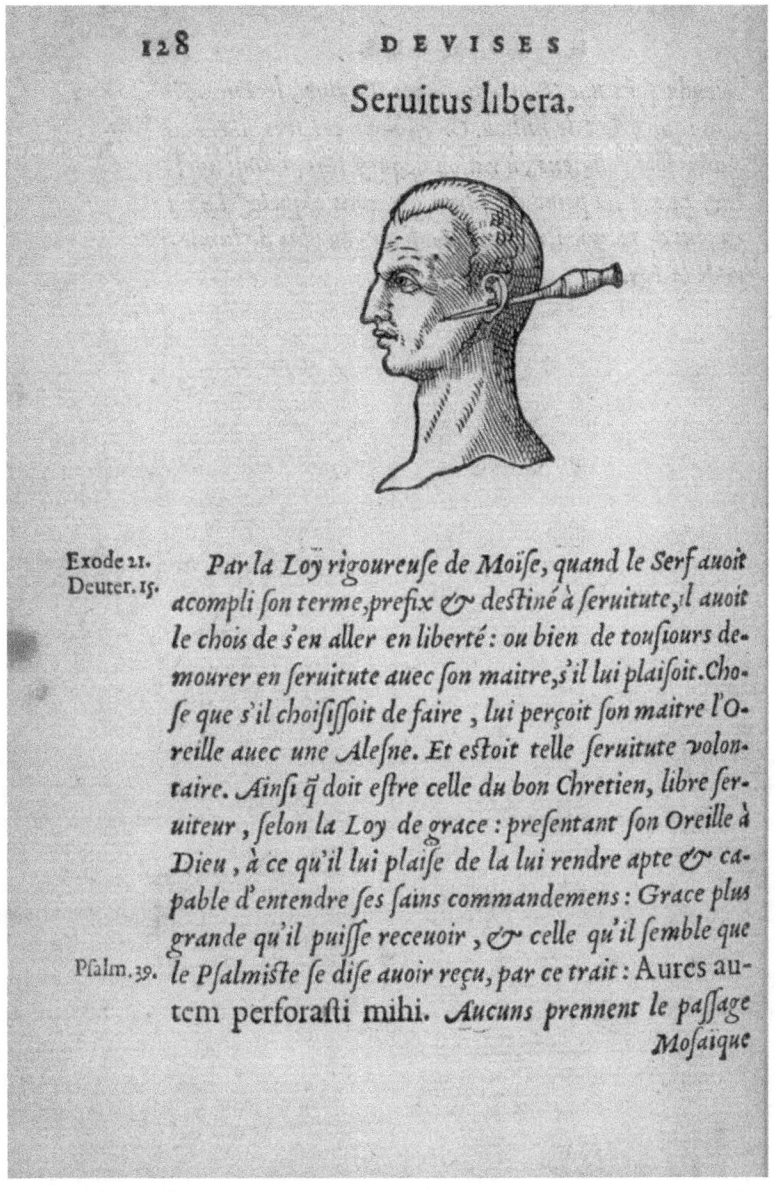

FIGURE 0.3 Servitus libera, Claude Paradin, *Devises heroiques* (1551) at 78. Source: By permission of University of Glasgow Library, Special Collections.

Custome, and Conversation among men, Collected out of the general disposition, nature, and condition of humane kinde." He then proceeds to borrow from the commendable Joachim Hopper's *Tractatus de iuris arte*, the concept of two natures, "one observed out of humane actions, the other out of usuall and ordinarie speech."[12] These derive, Hopper elaborates, by long use and the moral life of the community, and thus are owed not to the reason or spirit of men—*non ex mente hominis aut animo*—but to the diligence of historians, the skills of record keepers, the hands of scribes, who have together gathered, collated, and transmitted the commands of letters—*Literis mandari*. For completion, we should note that Doderidge goes on to discuss what he terms the Proverbiall Grounds of law "drawne from the phrase of speech, and deduced from the ordinary manner of conference by talk among men most usuall in all places, As are the common and ordinarie Proverbs and proverbiall Assertions" which become axioms and principles of law. My favorite among those that he then cites is *Qui ambulat in tenebris, nescit quò vadit*—he who walks in darkness, knows not where he is going.

Doderidge's reference to the dictate of letters, the law of the arts or, in his terminology of a science liberal, is expansive and foundational. The law, in our era, across the Continent, over the Channel, in Britannia as in Europe, is *studia humanitatis*, part of arts and letters, *omnium verbum*, beyond which, recollect, all is darkness, shadow, night. The reference to the arts also invokes the methods of artistic interpretation, the plurality of meanings, the depth of text, of proverbs, parables, cases and other *dicta*. There is first, then, a caution, a cautel, contained in the construction. The lawyer, the legal scholar, *iuris peritus*, must listen over time, attend to the rustles of language, the hints of rumor, the winds of letters so as to track and gather the formation of erudite opinion and common knowledge in conference as well as in court. This is the art and foundation of common law as accretion and pattern over time, as a space of listening, of audience and attention, as a lent ear. A peculiarly pertinent example can be taken from *Boswel's Case* of 1606, though, to borrow from Doderidge again, *ad illustrandum*, and not *ad probandum*.[13]

A brief sketch of the facts of the case can illustrate just what a plurality of voices or pleas the Court of King's Bench had to attend to. Anthony Lowe bought a writ of *quare impedit*, a claim to advowson, the right to present a Benefice, an ecclesiastical living, attached to a Manor that he purchased in the Parish of Wymbish. The writ lay against the Bishop of London, John Lancastre, and Henry Earl of Sussex. John Lancastre had been presented with the living by the Earl of Essex who resigned the living to the Bishop of London, the other defendant, who had devised the Benefice to Lawrence Boswel, now, which is to say, then incumbent. Difficult questions, which led to a lengthy judgment *per totam Curiam*.

The court first reviews the history of advowsons and specifically notes the fact that prior to the Statute of Westminster, at common law, if a clerk (a priest) had been presented to a church that belonged to another, and the clerk was admitted and instituted, then the church was ful, the rightful patron was out of possession, and the usurper had gained the inheritance in perpetuity. To resolve this difficulty, the issue of whether the church was full or not full had then to be tried by the bishop, "because institution is a spiritual act." If not full, then the case went to a jury to determine whether there had been induction "because induction is a thing notorious, and shall not be tried by the bishop."[14] The grounds for this complexity of actions lay not simply in the admixture of jurisdictions but also in the desire that there be *ideona persona* in every parish and that such qualified and instituted individual "should not be subject to actions; and so neglect his duty, in losing his time in suits and troubles in law."[15] As to his role, the epithet *ideona* "includes ability in learning and doctrine, honesty in conversation and diligence in his function, and all that to instruct the people of God in true religion and good conversation and to avoid contention." Thus common law preferred the observance of peace and quiet in the parish, *per ideonam personam*, rather than the right of any other person to the benefice.

The Statute of Westminster intervened to give a cause of action, *quare impedit*, to the lawful patron, where benefice had been passed by another, who, in the words of the Statute, did not have the right to be presented to the living—*jus praesentandi non habens*. Here then, after some further discussion of case law, clerical errors in reporting, the writ of *darrein presentment*, and so discussion of legal reason, citing to the Roman maxims *pari ratione et jure*, and to much the same effect *eadem lex est ubi eadem est ratio* to explain ignoring a precedent case, we arrive at the nub of the decision and the most usual reason for its citation. Boswel, the incumbent clerk, had not been named in the writ, and whether full or not, as it was then put, he had a right to aver and should not be "hurt at common law" without the chance of such averment—the action is "mean," which is to say in modern English suspended: "no incumbent shall be removed ... unless the incumbent be named in the writ, *quia res inter alios acta alteri nocere non debet* although the incumbent be in a defeasible title."[16] I include the last clause to indicate that this was a matter of significant doctrinal principle, namely that you should not be harmed by the act of another without being informed, called, and heard. This point is then legitimated by quotation of a couplet from Seneca's *Medea*: *Quia quicunque aliquid statuerit parte inaudita altera, aequum licet statuerit, haud aequus fuerit*—Who judges, one side unheard, although he judges justly, has not been just at all.[17] As is often the case in law, the normative requirement of a hearing, "a day in court," does not stem from the writ but does require that Boswel be named, notified, and allowed to testify when the case goes to trial before the jury.[18]

Sufficient detail is given to indicate the extraordinary plurality of conversations in which the judges are participating. Their own qualification, *ideonæ personæ*, as being arbiters not only of letters but of several jurisdictions, theological, political, legal, dramatic, and literary are extreme, thoroughly humanistic and commendable. These can be briefly extrapolated. The original conversation is between common law and the Crown, as mediated by the Statute of Westminster. There is then the dialogue between the law spiritual, the *forum conscientiæ*, and the ecclesiastical law represented by the ordinaries—the spiritual judges—and the bishop. Older common law and writs gain detail as well, but there is a further and overarching commerce as to the reason and maxims of law, *sedex communibus moribus vitæ* (seated in communal moral life), part of "humane nature" and so part of the *ius gentium* or law of all nations, shared by humans as such. Starting from ecclesiastical principles and local concerns about parochial life, that the parson not be impeded in his peaceful facilitation of the dialogue between parishioners and divinity, and allowing also for the role of the bishop as having "cure of souls," and being mindful of the answers he must give "at his fearful and final account," the Court has to weave a path between the "presidentes," the Statute, the Crown, and the bishops. As it deliberates and progresses, the judgment gains in generality, moving from authority to legitimacy, from rules to letters, the crescendo of the case being the shift from the intricacies of writs and presentments, advowsons and *darrein*, to conversations of law shared across jurisdictions and between times and peoples, culminating in Seneca and *Medea*.

I have used the plural, *audite*, an insight gained from Hayaert, because there are many discourses, dialogues, conferences, and conversations to be attended to and that plurality opens the law up to the diversity of its interior jurisdictions and reasons. It has biblical resonances which we see in the plurality of auditors in the frontispiece to the *Veredicus Christianus* (Figure 0.4). The pontifical figure is seated on a raised throne, the symbols of faith and of justice on his escutcheon, a skull, a *memento mori* at the base of the Cross, all signal an eternal justice, a divine inscription of law, but one which will here be spoken. The focus of the image is upon the ecclesiastical figure of judgment and what is specifically to be noted is that the raised right hand specifically seeks silence, peace,

FIGURE 0.4 Title page, Jan David, *Veridicus Christianus* (1601). Source: Getty images.

and thus the beginning of the dialogue that is adverted to in the subscript *ventura me*—question me of things to come. The left hand holds the scriptures open and signals the dialogue of authorization of speech by scripture, and of scripture by speech.

The judge in the Christian textual image is both participant and leader, and the maxims and images that surround him, the plurality of the crowd, with men and women, young and old, all suggest *demos* if not democracy, dialogue between these figures, symbols, maxims, and signs. The royal figure standing in the right column even clutches a lyre in his left hand, to signal peace through the harmony of sound. Returning to the judgment in *Boswel's Case* my point has been to emphasize the plurality not only of its sources, its version of *audite me*, but also the plural movement of its reasoning, the easy transition from England to Rome, from temporal to spiritual, from artificial reason to natural law. Take the example of the recourse to reason and the maxims, *pari ratione et jure*, and then slightly later, *eadem lex est ubi eadem est ratio*, the repetition and so emphasis, the redoubling of the point that reason and law are cognate and conjoint, if one is lacking the other too is missing. It is the jointure of law and its multiple maxims and reasons, in sum, that has to provide the legitimation of the invention of a ground for protecting an unnamed and non-present party who might be hurt by the decision on the writ. To legitimate that answer, the court cites to Seneca, to Rome and the theater, and states through the verse that it would be unjust not to hear (*inaudita*) the other side. In the theological discourses from which Seneca draws, *inaudita* and *injustum* are cognate, suggesting strongly that the right to a hearing is at the same time a dialogic injunction, a drawing in through the ear that mandates that none go unheard. *Audite* signifies hear all of the others, and that implies in turn, in potential at least, the other laws, other jurisdictions, other disciplines, and other reasons, or *audite rationem alteram* which might equally be termed, as lawyers sometimes did, *ius quaesitum alteri*, the law of the other.

SUBAUDITIO

The interpretative concept of subaudition, literally to hear a little, to hear beneath, appears first in the *Institutes of Justinian* and suggests a species of synecdoche or, as Puttenham puts it, quick conceit. Thus *Institutes* I.2. says "when we mention 'the poet' without giving the name, we mean (*subauditur*) Homer in Greek and Virgil in Latin." The term thus designates here a hidden reference, a known and so unstated connotation, but also a broader meaning and intimation whereby what is said only states a small part of what is implied. What is transmitted *subauditum* also, however, requires a knowledge of the referent of the implication, an intelligence of the broader meaning and connotations of the indexical word. When these are lost, the term becomes enigmatic.[19] By the Middle Ages *subauditur* was for this reason often used to reference a neglected or forgotten meaning, an enigma in the sense of something half-heard, not quite remembered, audible in the distance, but only faintly and so approaching *inauditum* and *injustum*.

The task of the humanists of our era was precisely to recuperate, to rediscover those missing references, half-heard commentaries, sub-vocal or *sotto voce* meanings. For the Renaissance humanistic lawyers, the concept of historically disinterring, and philologically reconstituting the received tradition, both text and *traditio*, written and oral, revives *subaudire* as a key term of method, the listening below to the murmur of discourse and the attempt to apprehend the non-present reasons, what Derrida termed the said of the unsaid. To recall, to listen in, to patiently give voice to the absent, the hidden, the forgotten sense, the undisclosed discourse, is a key theme and attracts an array of cognate terms, such as *subintellectio, subintelligere, subdeclarare, subinterrogare*, all providing means of access to texts and testimonies not actually present or not literally available on the surface of the text. The brilliance of *Boswel's Case* is not simply its recourse to the *auctoritates poetarum et philosophorum*, the recognition of the place and power of other disciplines within the reason of law, but also the appellation of the absent other, the recognition of the non-present, the apprehension of the importance of including, engaging, remembering, and calling those that are missing. If we expand the concept into a rhetorical, jurisdictional, and disciplinary framework then the dynamic and project of early modern humanist lawyers, their passion for dialogue, their willingness to lend their ears to what now seem obscure and arcane mysteries of history and governance heave into view. Thus the extraordinary range of reference in Doderidge's introduction, but one could reference to even more in numerous of the other antiquaries and philologists of the Inns of Court, as equally across Europe where the humanists spoke to each other across the boundaries of nationalism and the different *mores docendi* of legal traditions, each with their own particular *ius commune*, and *lex terræ*. Thus the importance of a reason of law that exceeded the pragmatic and local and that could piece together the trajectory of the legal traditions both humanistically and nationalistically, locally and generically, ontologically and epistemically.

The humanist sense of interpretative project was expansive and, as Maclean usefully points out, the concept of *subaudire* is a part of such extension, falling explicitly under the category of *interpretatio extensiva* and the purple pen of the jurisconsult's emendation and restoration of the reason of law. The most complete account comes in Caepolla who links extension not only to what is missing but also to legal fictions and the supplementation of the text by the as if, the *scilicet* or to wit of juristic invention: "Interpretative extension is the correct progression from what is expressed to what is not; extension is 'extra tension', which indicates that it has two *termini*, one *from which* (*a quo*) and the other to which (*ad quem*), just as translative or extensive (legal) fiction has."[20] The *casus omissus*, the missing person, the absent intent of the legislator are the points of origin, the tensors, of interpretative trajectory. It is a method of interpretation that derives ultimately from the Pauline conception that the letter kills, but the spirit gives life, which gains juridical expression in the notion that there is a force or power to the law, a spirit and truth that exceeds the mere letter. Selden captures this well in remarking: "*Scrutamini Scripturas*. These two Words have undone the World, because Christ spake it to his Disciples, therefore we must all, Men, Women and Children, read and interpret the Scriptures."[21] Erudition is needed, a knowledge of the Queen of the Sciences, Dame Philology as he puts it in his *Historie of Tithes*, and much more, a sense of law in practice: "If I would study the Cannon-law as it is used in *England*, I must study the Heads here in use, then go to the Practicers in those Courts where that Law is practiced, and know their Customs, so for all the study in the World."[22] And much to that effect.

Selden's dictate of method may seem unremarkable but it references an early modern openness to dialogue within the law that is indicative of a pluralism of scholarly attention and jurisdictional diversity that was lost in the modern era of positivism and scientific closure. Thus if we attend to the subtleties of Selden's remark, the *subaudition* of his comment, its backface, we can discern. The first connotation is obvious enough, we need to listen to the practices and speeches of any specific profession or trade. This means attending to their spaces and customs, argot, and ways. Here, however, the common lawyer is not simply attending to difference, but also engaging with a distinct yet coordinate jurisdiction, that of canon and Roman law. This was but one of sixteen independent legal jurisdictions listed in Coke, and each had different procedures, customs, concepts, and uses. Awareness of that diversity, together with the unwritten undertow of additional humanistic disciplinary knowledges, not least the philological acumen that allows the reconstruction and understanding of the differences that mark each jurisdiction. Remarking on philology as "first philosophie" and as the necessary study of any student of "the Common Laws of England," he continues to observe that such a syllabus is shared by all the common lawyers of Europe—"for every state in Christendom is governed by its own common laws and customs, and hath truly common Lawiers"— and links, in turn, the faculties to the professions.[23] The conversation, for Selden, is one that encompasses the entirety of what the French jurist Budé termed Latinitas, as also dialogue with the entire company of learned professionals from all of the European legal systems with their distinct *mores* but common linguistic and textual roots. Selden's list of colleagues is formidable, the "Chiefest Darlings" of learning, including Budé, Cujas, Brisson, Savaron, along with a swathe of Dutch, German, Spanish, and Italian jurists to support his methodological cause.

On the other side of the great divide, but still in England, the civilian Wiseman in his critique of common law, defending both canon and civil law, opens his apologia with the observation that "the Laws of most of the European Nations (who indeed all of them anciently were subject to the Roman Government) are but copies drawn from that original, borrowing that lustre of goodness they have, from it; and where their particular Lawe fails, thither their Judicatories resort to be supplied."[24] At core, and I am aware of using only readily available and immediately accessible sources, the context of *Boswel's Case* and its resort to Seneca and the authority of classical theatrical and moral reason is a dialogue between jurisdictions and most specifically between the various forms of law that lead or are funneled to reason as such. Wiseman is as correct for the seventeenth century as he would be later for the borrowings of the nineteenth century.[25] More so, in fact, in that the intercourse between the jurisdictions and disciplines was then very much a pan-European and trans-institutional confabulation of discourses that required attention to the subaudition that such transnational and inter-discipline transmitted.

Lacan at a certain point makes an interesting observation as to the subauditory and sub-intellective in the text, the *mi-dire*, as he puts it, of the citation, the half-said.[26] This is the far greater discourse, dialogue, debate, and disquisition that the citation, the name of the author, the reference to the treatise invokes. Despite Derrida's determined efforts to resurrect the subtext, the competing, half disclosed and yet often greater discourse of what we now term the footnoted, the sense of the actual commonality of shared discourse and reference is now vague and rather technical.[27] In the era of *Boswel's Case*, and it is no coincidence that the reference to Seneca, the clarion call of principle, is coded and abbreviated as something known and shared, the manner of debate is both expansive and exegetical in that the common body of received texts, from scripture to the Church Fathers, to classical philosophy and rhetoric, all inhabit the margins of the text, the borders that mark the drift from the tractate to its interlocutors. This space in between is where, in the archetypal debates, the Anglican Church and laws of ecclesiastical and civil polity were established. Text, inter-text and counter-text, interweave as the apologist takes up the citations of the texts they aim to refute, and the margins grow thick with Greek and Latin commentary as also with the specific citations, the *mi-dites*, of their antagonist.

What is specific to the reception, to the humanist engagement with the classical tradition, is an exegetical willingness to base dialogue, debate, "apologie" and "deballacyon," "irenicum" and "confutacyon," upon agreed, which is to say received texts, common margin as it were to the political theology of a corpus and collection. These were the shared scriptures and the writings of the Fathers, the charters, instruments, and rolls that constituted the universal tradition and language which frame the agonistics that debate played out. However much Sir Thomas More, one-time Lord Chancellor, might despise the views of the Chancery lawyer Christopher Saint Germain or indeed those of the

Reformers Tyndale and Barnes, they share their sources and references, their citations and quotations and dispute only the role of tradition, of the unwritten and vernacular in the interpretation and transmission of law.[28] This exegetical model is theological in origin and foundational in purpose and gains an exemplary form in Bishop John Jewel's classic *Apologie of the Church of England*, refuting "the Papistes" and then his *Defence of the Apologie* which refutes and answers Thomas Harding's *Confutation of the Apologie*.[29] There is a settled *corpus* and collect of sources, what the Roman lawyers termed the instruments in which we keep faith, to which the jurisconsult Paulus adds that these *instumenta* or documents include "both oral evidence and witnesses" which persons occupy "the place of instruments."[30]

It is precisely the first witnesses, the corporeal *instrumenta*, the Prophets and Patriarchs whose graphism is enigmatically buried in the texts or, dependent upon theological belief, is interpolated into the text and tradition, that generates the bulk and substance of dispute. The successful tradition, the exegetical theology that succeeds and establishes the early modern Anglican polity and law, is one that subtly intertwines the oral and the written, the instrument and the body of the person and interpreter as joint custodians of an esoteric truth handed down from an origin that precedes the "slaunders and reproches against the truth" of Jewel's contemporaries.[31] The text, for the exegete, is never just the text, but rather a foundation, a scripture, settled authority and instrument of transmission because in its special status, in escaping the margin of the document and passing into a shared space of faith, it exceeds the letter and so, to coin a phrase, it giveth life. *Audi eam, non de novis chartulis, sed de Dei libris*—hear it then, not out of new scribbles, but out of the books of God.[32] That is the point of entry, the portal, the pressing of the ear to the text because, to borrow from Bonaventura, "*gratia est in anima, non in signis visibillis*"—grace is not in the visible signs but in the soul.[33] The bodies of opponents litter the margins of these foundational texts and proffer a species of *mi-non-dit* of half unsaid, the heretical bodies, the false instruments and dead ink—*mortuum atramentum*—of those who cannot hear the tradition and grace that the text carries secretly or the message that the letters sound—*quod sonant*.[34]

It is precisely that faith in the foundational capaciousness of the text, the message that it bears from a time that precedes incursions, interpolations, the *emblemata Triboniani* or false accretions subsequent and inappropriate intrusion have imposed. The fight of the exegete is always for the validity of the source, the return to the origin, the enlacement of the instrument with the scripture, of the body with the text, and of the soul with grace. The text is an apparatus that works on persons, that gives birth or kills, leads or condemns and the task of the exegete is to guide the faithful through the territory of the text and the path of the law. Hooker, the foundational author of the *Lawes of Ecclesiastical Politie*, Master of the Temple, and Preacher thereby to the inaugural sages of the common law, including the institutist Sir Edward Coke proffers a fine if small image of the purport of his work. As the first letter of the Letter to the Reader, penned by the President of Oxford, John Spenser, for the 1617 edition, the printer has inserted a woodcut, an image that paints the picture of entry into the text and equally of exclusion from it, both portal and defense (Figure 0.5). Two muses hold aloft the cross, the crown, and rose of England. The muse on left, sword in hand, offers the defense of justice, while the muse on the right, shield in hand, represents law. So much is fairly standard, the composite image evidencing the justice of sovereignty and the godliness and wisdom of the monarch. To that, however, and less usually we can add the prostrate figure lying defeated on the ground. Wearing the mask of a clown the image is of the vanquished persona, the evil

INTRODUCTION 13

FIGURE 0.5 Woodcut, Richard Hooker, *Of the Lawes of Ecclesiastical Politie* (1617) at 1. Source: Courtesy of P. Goodrich.

FIGURE 0.6 Alciato, *In vitam humanam*, *Emblemata* (1584) at 208. Source: By permission of University of Glasgow Library, Special Collections.

against which law must defend. He has a head of snakes rather than hair, a Gorgon's head that warns against the fate of those engendering civil strife and resistance to law. He has no ears, so is deaf to text and law alike.

If the exegetical text can contain images, cautions, confutations, denunciations, and defenses, then it is in good common law fashion both written and unwritten, both inscribed and inscribed invisibly on the heart, as ethic and behavior, as inner law. The text, as territory, as occupancy, and as belonging, is internally and intrinsically manifold, including and excluding but equally listening, sounding, attending, hearing a multitude of subtextual and subauditory intimations that only the wise, the *iuris peritus*, the jurisprudent can fully apprehend. There are two faces to this hermeneutic process or better two ears that scan for what is not visible, for what sounds, the truth mystical that passes enigmatically and esoterically between the ancients and the moderns, between the text and its instruments, namely the ambulant symbols that legitimate and carry the law.

IN DIALOGUE

It bears note that in law French, debate means to fight and dispute, with further connotations of strife and brawl, while *debatir* means to knock down. *Discusser* means to determine and decide, in effect to judge, while dialogue has an older root in the Latin *dialogus* meaning to converse and, according to Isidore of Seville, its root is in to interweave, *serere*, between two participants. In early modern legal usage, it is the rhetorical figure of *dialogismus* that plays the crucial and irenic role in establishing the legitimacy of the polity and the foundation of law.

Common law begins in dialogue. This is so, in the sense already adverted, both rhetorical and legal, in which the common opinion of the Bar and Bench takes the form of law by *oy dire*—by somesays and hearsays, commonplaces and storehouses—as well as through the hearing of dispute in court. It is also the case, however, that the literary form of dialogue plays a crucial role in the foundation of the principles and pedagogy of the auricular tradition of custom and use in common. From Sir John Fortescue's *Praise of the Laws of England*, a didactic dialogue between the Chancellor and the young Prince, to Saint Germain's *Doctor and Student*, to Thomas Starkey's *Dialogue between Reginald Pole and Thomas Lupset*, in dispute as to the priority of Roman or common law, to Hobbes' *Dialogue of the Common Laws of England*, and variegated exchanges in similar forms on manners and morals, on the civility and justice that precedes and underpins law, the dialogic lies at the root of the juridical.[35] As Fortescue puts it, after a lengthy civil war, the office of the sovereign shifts towards "judging rightfully." Citing the opening to Justinian's *Institutes*, majesty needs both arms and laws.[36]

The tenor of the first six chapters of *De Laudibus* is precisely that of opening the ears of the Prince and connecting in a pedagogic fashion the enthusiasm and physicality of youth to the foundational texts of the legal tradition. These are the Latin sources, the scriptures and commentaries, and the *Corpus iuris civilis* and its glosses. Law is to build a connection between Prince and populace by placing both in the context of common foundation, belief and community. The Prince is being tapped on the shoulder and reminded that he is human, that a theology, totality or third governs us all. There is a greater conversation, dialogue and response, replication, duplication, and reduplication in its juridical form, to which law belongs and in which it participates. The dialogic form is thus emblematic and exemplary. It is the mode of theological and philosophical circumscription and definition of the office of legislator and lawmaker and also the recognition that such a role and responsibility can never be self-defining but must rather be taught, instituted, inculcated through dialogue that engages the legal with an outside, with its neighbors and complementary disciplines. This means both that the lawyer, in this instance the sovereign as lawgiver, is equally himself a subject and by the same token law is scrutinized and reviewed, itself examined and judged, by conscience and the *caritas* that governs theological interpretation.

It is necessary that law not seek a specious autonomy, or engage in senseless monologue, but rather build itself upon a dialogue with the grounds of its establishment, the before of its system and rules. Whitehouse, the redoubtable commentator upon Fortescue, places the dialogic form not only in the classics, in Plato, Trimegustus, Plutarch, Cicero "and hundreds of others" but also makes the point that dialogue is the mode of thought, the interior conversation, *pro et contra*, that is conducted in the court of reason and deliberation. The dialogue spells out "the Rules, which Experience had taught him, the best Conduct and Regulation of life." That Prince is wise "whose ear accepteth counsels."[37] It is thus the polity in the theology, the bond between subject and the sacred, which in Roman law means the community, the many, that is the predicate of grounding law. Saint Germain, and I prefer the phonetics of the older spelling, suggesting as it does a saint who is germane, relevant, speaking still, is to the same effect. The model is again Fortescue and the effort is to introduce a dialogue between theology and common law, to find a ground for the legal outside of its own institution, to base it in theology and the humanities, in the disciplinary traditions that inculcate conscience and truth. The laws of England cannot found themselves and so the Doctor of Divinity seeks to elicit and elucidate the unseen doctrines, the inherited maxims, the holy dogmas that are "the principles or foundations of the laws of England."[38] It is *in forum anime*, in the court of the spirit that conscience, the ground of justice and judgment is formed and developed.

To the great array of murmurs and conversations that law attends, the foundational dialogue mandates a structure and hierarchy of listening, of audition, that distinguishes whose ears are the proper conduit of relay and institution. It is the before the law that the dialogue instantiates, the preparatory and directive moment of inculcation and teaching of foundations, the grounds of conscience, the *regulae vitae et iuris*, in that order, that are brought into contact and intermingled. It is a dialogue of laws and of disciplines which gains reflection in these foundational texts and nowhere more so than in Fortescue's short treatise on the nature of the laws of nature. A king has a brother, and a daughter. The daughter has a son. When the king dies, should the kingdom pass to the daughter, the daughter's son, or the brother? The question is a legal one but it requires attention to "the other sciences ... to deal with this dispute more surely, and with ampler authority, since there are no faculties which are not subsidiary in some direction to other arts."[39] To this is added the full conference of diverse laws, from the divine law to the law of nature, to civil and common, canon and colloquial.

It is not just doubt, or in Fortescue's terms, "filial fear" that prompts the dialogic form of the foundational discourse, but rather the desire to open the opening of law to a genealogy and legitimacy, a conversation with the ancients and with diverse branches of knowledge, the notes of dignity of the various disciplines. It is probably for this reason that the dialogic form of these justificatory and classificatory legal discourses is always one which begins by addressing the beyond or outside of legality, other discourses and disciplines, the questions of ends of law in their dual sense, in *oikonomia* and inhabitation. The question of how to live, proffered in the modes of discussions of love and amity, of manners and dress, fidelity and appearance, happiness and salvation, the question in sum of which law, invariably precedes the entry into the specific and technical details of the instant jurisdiction and its interplay of various orders and rules.

It is Bakhtin, of course, who has done the most in contemporary theory to draw attention to the dialogic and to insist that discourse is always responsive to the other, engaged in a tradition, a chain, a complex of utterances and cultures, contexts and their meanings. It is as utterance, as institutional practice and above all as action that the responsiveness of speech gains its proper attention. Thus, in Bakhtin's words, "the utterance is filled with *dialogic overtones* ... thought itself—philosophical, scientific, artistic—is born and shaped in the process of interaction and struggle with others' thought."[40] The dialogue of legal foundations is replete with the plenitude of thoughts and laws of others to such an extent as to qualify it as an exemplar, an emblem of the complexity and multiplicity of voices, the heteroglossia that make up meaning by reference to the context, the locus and practice that generate the utterance. It is that sense of dialogue, that apprehension of the fullness of the tradition and the imperative of its custody and renewal that the early modern version of the injunction *audite alteram partem* incites and extends.

It is in this sense as well that Bakhtin invokes the immortality or at least the longevity of dialogue and the fact that such a law vested in the other, *ius quaesitum alteri* in one diction, persists: "At any moment in the development of the dialogue there are immense, boundless masses of forgotten textual meanings, but at certain moments in the dialogue's subsequent development along the way they are recalled and invigorated in renewed form (in a new context). Nothing is absolutely dead: every meaning will have its homecoming festival."[41] In that festive spirit, even the old law will return, be rethought, realigned, and renewed. For an image of such return, and for a sense of the depth of the dialogue, an emblem from Alciato, *in vitam humanam*, can provide a suitable finale (Figure 0.6).[42] The depiction is of Heraclitus, the tenebrous and solipsistic philosopher of Ephesus, the thinker of time, sorrow, and death, conversing in an ironically timeless manner with Democritus, the laughing thinker from Thrace. One weeps, the other guffaws. Democritus gesticulates and Heraclitus holds his head in his hands, as if in pain. Those are the options, the two extremes, tears or joy, *hilaritas* in its two forms, depicted here as the beginning and the end of law. Note also, however, the tree, the sign of *amicitia*, that Heraclitus leans against, and additionally that the books are closed, one fallen to the ground, as conversation, dialogue, draws the reluctant Heraclitus from his solitude and his obscure monologue. He is being taught to listen, forced to engage.

These exemplars of exchange, of utterance and response between opposed figures and positions models the office and ethics of attention to the other side. Democritus laughs and points towards the heavens, towards nothing, while Heraclitus closes his books, or in other versions lays them on the ground, discards them, so as to engage, if only negatively, with his "democritick" interlocutor.[43] Their exemplary positions have their festivals, and the early modern era of the juristic emblem book is one such return to the dialogue of these ancient personae, the *serio-ludere* reflecting attention both to gravitas and to lightness, to the serious and to the satirical. It remains only to say that while a good nose is necessary for judgment, it is the ear that grounds the law.

CHAPTER ONE

Justice

VALÉRIE HAYAERT

This chapter[1] aims to discuss the early modern rather diverse concepts and representations of Justice and their relations to practices and processes of trial and punishment. Artworks, paintings, sculptures, broadsheet prints, drawings, and artifacts played an active role in people's experience and the practice of right and wrong. Portrayals of Lady *Justitia, exempla virtutis* and other myths rendered the abstract notions of "law" and "justice" concrete and tangible. City authorities had the greatest painters of their time make prestigious and ambitious scenes of justice to decorate town halls, where justice was administered. Diverse examples derived from antiquity, the Bible or history were exhibited so as to stimulate judges and Aldermen to be fair in the performance of their legal responsibilities.

THE JUDGE'S DAMNATION

It is because of their narrative and didactic nature and their judicial content that pictures of justice are distinct from allegorical and symbolic representations of law and justice: they are often murals, spread out expansively on walls, and are explicitly addressed to judges exercising their office.

Since the end of the fifteenth century, one of the main themes depicted in European courtrooms is the judge's damnation. A strange cohort of the feebleness and failures of justice is represented on the walls of the courthouses: these artworks are all organized around the theme of the responsibility of judges, the dangers and pitfalls of their function and the fragility of human justice. Art is aimed at encouraging the viewer to act justly: it is used as an *exemplum justitiæ* to remind the judge of the duties inherent in the act of judging and the responsibility that the human trial owes towards divine justice. The most common scene adopted by judicial magistrates is the *Last Judgement*. At times, the biblical scene is accompanied by an admonition, addressed to the judges: in 1525, Jan Provoost painted a representation of the *Last Judgment* for the Bruges town magistrate, with this Latin motto: "*Videte quid faciatis non enim hominis exercetis judicium sed Domini*" (2 Chronicles 19.6: Take heed of what you do: for your works are not for the judgment of man, but for that of the Lord). In the *Last Judgment* painted by Frans Sanders in 1526 for the Great Council of Malines, an archangel is holding a phylacter "iudicium time" (fear judgment) and a devil stands in the lower part, threatening the members of the council, who are reflected in a convex mirror, with a lightning bolt. These paintings are explicitly addressed to the presiding judges, to remind them of the gravity of their role.

Aside from this classical, judicial example, other narrative scenes were painted in the courthouses, and some are typical from the early modern period. The *Judgment of Cambyses*,[2] representative of many secular justice scenes, recalls the extraordinary character of the punishments inflicted by the Persian King Cambyses (*c.* 530–522 BC), according to Herodotus (*Historiae*, V, 25):

> Otanes's father Sisammes had been one of the royal judges; Cambyses had cut his throat and flayed all his skin because he had been bribed to give an unjust judgment; and he had then cut leather strips of the skin which had been torn away and covered therewith the seat on which Sisammes had sat to give judgment; which having done, Cambyses appointed the son of this slain and flayed Sisammes to be judge in his place, admonishing him to remember what was the judgement seat whereon he sat.

The story was later popularized by Valerius Maximus (*Facta et dicta memorabilia*, VI, 3). By appointing Otanes, the son of Sisammes, to his father's office, Cambyses admonished him in a particularly gruesome way, to remember on which seat he sat and to judge justly. The version painted by Gerard David (1498), held today by the Bruges Groeningemuseum, is probably the most famous and memorable example of this myth. Gerard David distributed the episodes of this story over two panels: the left panel shows the corrupt judge being arrested, with the bribery scene visible in the background, whereas the right panel is dominated by the scene of his being flayed. The background of the latter panel depicts Otanes administering justice, seated upon the skin stripped from his father. The *exemplum* of the Judgment of Cambyses was then a widespread source to warn as to the proper conduct of Aldermen in their administration of justice. Lawbooks of the time used this *exemplum* extensively.[3] Similar representations of the Judgement of Cambyses turn up in prints in the first half of the sixteenth century as well as in illustrations in legal manuals. The first page of the preface to the German edition of Josse de Damhoudere's *Praxis rerum criminalium* (Frankfurt, 1575) was, for instance, decorated with an image of the new judge Otanes seated beneath his father's skin. Under the print, the table of contents lists all the reasons why punishments must be meted out. Otanes, cruelly warned by his father's fate, is bound to dispense the purest form of justice to succeed in his arduous task. The gruesome throne by itself, without any protagonists, becomes an emblem later in Juan de Horozco's *Emblemas morales*.[4] The iconic judge's seat, with its covering of flayed skin, serves as the purest abstraction of the *exemplum*.

In 1542, Dirck Vellert designed the story of Cambyses for a painted glass roundel (diameter 29.4 centimeters) (Figure 1.1) which shows the slaying of Sisammes in the foreground and the judicial throne of Otanes in the background, where the skin of the corrupted judge has been nailed as in a crucifixion onto the upper part of his son's seat. Cambyses appears twice, pointing at the two cruel scenes with his fingers. The roundel also shows Sisammes being flayed in the foreground under the watchful eye of Cambyses. The explicit depiction of the butchery is significant, as in Gerard David's painting.

Another parallel story used as an *exemplum justitiæ* is the blinding of Zaleucus of Locria. The lawgiver (*nomothete*) Zaleucus had decreed that anyone caught committing adultery would be blinded: when his own son was caught, the father chose to have one of his own eyes gouged out so that he could share the punishment with his son, and he would not be left totally blind. As Zaleucus was famous for his insistence upon equal application of the law, he chose to sacrifice his own sight to uphold the law: he himself had created a law to punish all adulterers by the gouging out of both their eyes. When his own son was caught in the act of adultery, he was faced with the dilemma of either exempting his son from the legal rule or enforcing the law he had created by blinding his own son. By having one eye removed from his son and one of his own eyes removed,

JUSTICE 19

FIGURE 1.1 *The Judgement of Cambyses*, Dirck Vellert, 1542, glass roundel, d. 29.4 cm. Source: Courtesy of Rijksmuseum, Amsterdam.

he found a practical way between the two orders he wanted to preserve: the extreme rigor of the law and his attachment to the bonds of kin. This *exemplum* is given as a model of *epieikeia* (equity), a way of humanizing the extreme rigor of the law. The story of Zaleucus, helped by its memorable gruesomeness, provided a lively topic to reflect on the art of moderating extremes, as conceptualized by Aristotle in the fifth book of the *Nicomachean Ethics*. The stories depicted deal mainly with the moral attributes demanded by legal office; however, these moral *exempla* are often multi-layered and can be interpreted in various ways: Zaleucus' narrative gives way to a reflection about the extreme rigor of law and his choice of substituting one of his own eyes for that of his son is a regular topic for discussion among lawyers. The figure of the clemency of the lawgiver is constituent of a greater conceptual debate about humane law. *Jus civile* is imperfect, changeable, and temporal; it bears the man-made flaws of its counterpart, the divine, natural law. These narratives directly refer to the practical insight required in applying principles to particular situations.

Another similar example is the theme of Plutarch's Theban judges without hands. According to Plutarch,[5] "statues of judges erected at Thebes had no hands; and the chief of them had also his eyes closed up, hereby signifying that among them justice was not to be solicited with either bribery or address." Andrea Alciato gave a visual representation of this motif in his emblem "*In senatum boni Principis*" (The good prince in his council).[6] In Geneva's town hall (chamber of the Conseil d'État, Baudet tower), where the town councilors judged both civil and criminal cases, the same motif has been given a spectacular expression. The fresco, dated 1604, "Les juges aux mains coupées" is attributed to Cesare Giglio, a Vincenzan artist, and was commissioned by the councilors themselves. The image of a maimed justice wished to stress the evil of injustice, embodied here by partiality and bribery. Cesare Giglio did not represent statues without hands, instead, he depicted the judges themselves being maimed: the act of severing hands is depicted on the bodies of the judges and not in abstract sculptures. The motif of the missing hand is a time-honored juristic symbol: the French magistrate Étienne Pasquier (1529–1615) wrote a whole set of poems (nearly 100) about hands during the Grands Jours at Troyes in 1583. The poetic works collected under the title " La Main "start with his own portrait, by Jean de Hoey, who chose not to represent his hands.[7] Pasquier started commenting on this with a first distich "*Nulla hic Paschasio manus est, lex Cincia quippe Caussidicos nullas sanxit habere manus.*" (Pasquier here is without hands, because the Lex Cincia ordered that lawyers should not have any.) According to Roman law, lawyers were forbidden to accept bribes or fees apart from the previously agreed sum. Two epigrams by his friend the lawyer Antoine Loisel relate Pasquier's portrait to the "true effigy of a judge," the one designed for Theban judges and adapted to the French lawyer.[8] In his emblem "*Custodiunt, non carpunt*"[9] (they guard without gathering), Saavedra Fajardo reinterprets the motif of the Theban judges, but the horrific scene of the maimed hands painted by Giglio has been replaced by the innocent figure of garden statues: two terminal figures with a human head, continuing as a rectangular pillar-like form, have replaced the gruesome depiction of the thirteen stumps of arms visible in Geneva's town hall.

Until the seventeenth century, the desire to expose a judge's failures was a regular obsession. The *exempla justitiæ* were shown in town halls so that the judges could explicitly see their own fate were they to err. In the painted decorations of courthouses, in the punishments inflicted on prevaricators, in the "amendes honorables" imposed on the authors of iniquitous judgments, justice has to designate herself as guilty. By exposing its failures and faults, justice shows its essential fragility and its capacity to punish and denounce the judges. Judicial fallibility became a major visual motif in the early modern period.

LADY JUSTICE: THE INVENTIVENESS OF EARLY MODERN ALLEGORIES

Justice iconography has now considerably been reduced to the form of a hefty female figure, holding scales, a sword, and occasionally wearing a blindfold. Early Modern inventions were much more diverse and inventive, and sometimes more provocative than complacent. Theodor de Bry produced an astonishing portrait of *Justitia*: she is in motion, sitting facing backwards on a horse, tumbling off her recalcitrant mount, she flips over and falls, clinging in vain to her sword and disequilibrated scales, head upside down, mouth open and legs flailing[10] (Figure 1.2). The epigram accompanying the engraving stresses that the world is to be compared to an untamed and unbridled horse, hating and tossing off Law and Justice. Switching the usual perspective, this political emblem

IN PEIVS RECIDVNT ET RETRO CVNCTA FERVNTUR

FIGURE 1.2 Johann Theodor de Bry, Dirck Volckertsz Coornhert and Maarten van Hermskerck, *Emblemata sæcularia varietate seculi huius mores ita experimentia*, 1611, engraving, h 94 mmm x w 105 mm. Source: Courtesy of Rijksmuseum, Amsterdam.

depicts justice's languor and reverses completely the conventional hieratic stability of the allegorical body of *Justitia*. Her body is engaged in a fierce struggle: early moden artists had developed a brilliant anatomical rhetoric to express the revelation of the body as an essence in such a conflict.

THE SCALES OF JUSTICE

The concept of equity is one of the paradoxical ideals which is regularly depicted by emblematic images or symbolic creations. Already applied in late antiquity by Latin Church Fathers to describe the Christian ideal of justice, *æquitas* includes not only a measure of equality and proportionality derived from the Aristotelian tradition, but also charity and indulgence in special cases. Equity, as a concept, is the creative element for the development of law. A famous passage from the *Sententiæ* by Isidore of Seville, included later in Gratian's *Decretum* (Dist. 45, c.10), reads: "Everybody judging righteously has to keep a pair of scales in his hand to give the same weight to justice and commiseration: but by justice he pronounces the sentence for transgressions, by mercy he moderates the penalty, so that something is corrected by equity according to the right standard, but something is forborne with commiseration"[11] The title page of Christian Haunold's *Controversiarum de Justitia et Jure* (1671) shows an elaborate symbolic representation of *æquitas* which illustrates well its paradoxical nature[12] (Figure 1.3). Departing from the

FIGURE 1.3 Christoph Haunold, *Controversiarum de Justitia et Jure privatorum universo nova et theorica methodo, tomus primus*, Ingolstadt, Joannes Simon Knab, 1671, frontispiece. Source: Bayerische StaatsBibliothek Digital, Münchener Digitalisierungs Zentrum Digitale Bibliothek.

omnivoyant eye of God, circled with the motto "*Æquitatem vidit vultus ei*" ("His face has beheld righteousness," *Psalm* 10), God holds an even balance, adorned with the motto "*rigorem temperat æquitas*" (equity tempers the rigor of the law). On the left side, *æquitas* wears the crown of the *Regina Coeli* and the mantle of the *Mater misericordiæ*. She puts into the pan of her scales an occulated heart, a symbol of her *misericordia*: she also holds a scepter bearing a radiant triangle where the hebraïc name of God (tetragrammaton) has been written. On the right side, *rigor juris*, wearing a helmet and holding an upright sword placed into her side of the scales an occulated book, which symbolizes the rigorous application of the written word of law. God alone holds the balance: the equity of justice is none other than divine law disseminating *justitia Dei* to humanity. But both the heart and the book, bearing eyes echoing the *occulatissimum oculus* of God, guides earthly justice with heavenly principles. Beneath the monumental entrance of the temple of Justice, symbolized by two columns, the middle panel features the judgment of Solomon. One remarkable interpretation of the judgment of Solomon is the one developed by Jean Carbonnier in his classic work, *Flexible Droit*.[13] The judgment of Solomon recalls first that justice is nothing but the blind observance of the principle of equal division of the objects over which the parties dispute: the verdict "Divide the living child in two" shows the ruthlessness with which justice pursues its own ends. This example of a judgment of equity shows how an individual solution brings an end to litigation, and how compromise and accommodation are the true goals of Justice. The attributes held by *æquitas* and *rigor juris* (a triangulated scepter and an upward sword) are developed by emblematic objects in the stylobats below them: on the left, a triangular plumb-line, with the motto "*hac regula*" [according to this triangular rule] stands in the middle of the caelestial sphere and the earthly word; on the right, the same configuration applies to a downward sword, with the motto "*hoc perpendiculo*" [according to this perpendicular plumb-line].These geometrical lines echo the urban landscape, drawn in perfectly straight lines, depicted in the background: with its Vauban-style fortifications characterized by star-shaped bastions, its prominent churches and vast convents, the city is assumed to be empty, apart from the tiny figures and carts on the road to the city. The star-shaped fortress, composed of many triangular bastions, specifically designed to cover each other, contrasts sharply with the higher elevation of the cathedral. Justice is shown here as a protective power.

Aside from the conventional allegories of Lady Justice, lawyers use their wits and "*mens emblematica*" to elaborate sophisticated emblematic montages. Legal emblems reflect many of the important themes crucial to the practice of humanist lawyers: they bring to the fore moral virtues, ethics, and the ideal of the perfect jurisconsult. The princely ideal, developed in several *Mirrors of Princes*, also aims to show the crucial role of the Prince in imparting justice to his subjects.

One of these is an emblem created by Juan de Solorzano Pereira, called "*Statera regum*" (balance of kings): the *pictura* shows the two scales, balanced, next to both ears of a man's face, which serves as a pivotal point; the scales are held by a crowned head protruding from a cloud.[14] This curious montage is staged in such a way as to frame the spectacle (Figure 1.4). The image is a visual depiction of the principle "*Audi et Alteram partem*" (hear the other side) as judges or anyone exercising a judicial function should hear both sides of every case and each party should have a right to be heard, not only the plaintiff or prosecutor, but also the defendant. This rule is recognized as one of fundamental justice and is part of the notion of "due process." Renaissance lawyers think of it in two ways: it is both a rule of natural justice and a rule of wisdom. Throughout the early modern period, the latin maxim "*Audi(-te) alteram partem*" was regularly inscribed

FIGURE 1.4 Juan de Solorzano Pereira, *Emblemata centum regio politica in centuriam unam redactam*, Madrid Garcia Morràs, 1653, emblema LXII "Statera Regum,". Source: Courtesy of Biblioteca Complutense, Madrid.

in courtrooms and town halls. In the Town Hall of Amsterdam, the phrase was inscribed in gold lettering above the entrance to the magistrates' chamber.

Solorzano starts his commentary with a quote from the jurisconsult Callistratus (D. 1. 18.19): "In the trial of cases, it is not proper for an official to become inflamed against those of whom he thinks ill, or be moved to tears by the supplication of the unfortunate: for it is not the part of a resolute and upright judge to let his countenance disclose the emotions of his mind." The piece is directed against *credulitas* and reference is made to Alciato's emblem about the *manus oculata* (embl. XVI) inspired by a Roman proverb used by Plautus "*oculatæ nostræ sunt manus, credunt quod vident*" (Our hands have eyes: they believe what they see). The emblem is then applied directly to the rules governing accusation and to the risks incurred by calumny. Solorzano describes very precisely his iconic invention: bursting out from a human head, which is the seat of the mind, between two ears, he has figured nature, so that no one believes or weighs out anything before he has examined both alternatives in the scales of his mind. He then quotes a Pythagorean sentence in verse by Ausonius (On the Good Man, *Eclogues*, III), where it is stated that the upright and wise man "weighs himself by the test of a just balance: there must be no hollows, no projections; the angle must be formed of equal lines and the rule not deviate a jot." Among the many authorities cited for the idea that justice requires both sides to be heard, the most commonly quoted is a couplet from the *Medea* of Seneca:

> "Who judges, one side unheard, although he judges justly, has not been at all just" (*Qui statuit aliquid parte inaudita altera / Æquum licet statuerit, haud æquus fuit*).[15]

In *Reason and Rhetoric in the Philosophy of Hobbes*, Quentin Skinner goes further in associating his work on Renaissance humanism with the *audi alteram partem* principle: the practical and dialogical character of moral and political philosophy is a distinct feature of Renaissance culture: one should always listen to the other side because it is always possible to speak on either side of a case:

> The appropriate model will always be that of a dialogue, the appropriate stance one of willingness to negotiate over rival intuitions concerning the applicability of evaluative terms.[16]

MUSICAL METAPHORS: JUSTICE AS A DIVINE HARMONY

The virtue of Justice has musical connotations because the scope of human justice is to realize divine harmony on earth, that is peace and concord. In Justice resides the concord of all virtues: Justice has an overarching role, it contains all other virtues. The musical metaphor also insists on the importance of tempered justice for good governance.

A telling example is the emblem "Regum Tribunal" by Juan Solorzano Pereira ("Court of Kings," emblem LXIII[17]). Instead of the classic "Senate of the Good Prince" (*In senatum boni Principis*), developed by Alciato, Corrozet, and Coustau, where the Prince, deprived of sight, sits before the Theban judges, without hands, so that they may not take gifts or bribes, the King is shown sitting on his throne, presiding over the nine muses. Several musical instruments are scattered on the floor. The senate of the good prince needs to be directed by wisdom (*sophia*) and that's why, says the epigram, kings and muses marry. The emblem's source is Hesiod's *Theogony* (74–93): "All nine muses (especially Calliope) inspire kings They pour honeyed dew on the tongue of any of the Kings cherished by Zeus, whom they, the daughters of great Zeus, honor and look upon favorably at his birth; All the people look up to him as he dispenses justice with fair impartiality." Solorzano uses here a musical emblem to declare the necessary equilibrium between rigorous justice and mercy. In Solorzano's words, the Muses, with the beautiful harmony of their tones and meters, add temperance to the severity of sovereign judgments. The emblem's commentary insists upon the scope of the royal tribunal, which is equity. The ancient formula that jurisprudence was the *vera philosophia* is emphasized by this image of the Tribunal of the muses. The art of legal interpretation is embodied by the ideal type of the *perfectus jurisconsultus*. Lawyers should aim to become jurisconsults, encyclopedic scholars and, therefore, should add eloquence and erudition (*humaniores litteræ*) to the professional training of civil science. This ideal gives way to ambitious projects, such as Honoratus Draco's versification of the basic textbook of civil law, the *Institutes*.[18] Joining Themis with the muses was not only an aesthetic ideal: it also served for mnemonic purposes, giving a poetic, concise form to the words of law. Legal humanists were strong apologists of the poetic nature of Law. They often comment on the mnemonic formulas of the Law of the twelve tables, written with great brevity and linguistic precision. Cicero (*De Leg*. II. 4, 23) mentions that he learned them by heart as a boy: they were a *carmen necessarium*. Poetry was for them much more than a literary *otium*: it was a source of eloquence and a path to achieve elegance and concision (*brevitas*). In Matteo Gribaldi Mofa's words, "what persuades and charms best is precisely what is free from any boredom."[19] He adds that the distinct feature of the lawyers of his age is to seek elegance, as it is clear, he says, that Sabinus, Paulus, Ulpian, and most of the Ancient legislators were familiar with Homer and Virgil. To achieve the status of the ideal lawyer, legal humanists (Étienne Forcadel,[20] Andrea Alciato and many more) extended their skills by writing epigrams, dialogues, or emblems. In his *Cupido Jurisperitus*, Étienne Forcadel use the form of the Lucian dialogue to celebrate Law as a principle of social and cosmic harmony. Accursius, figure of the ideal jurist tries to convince Momus, the god of sarcasm, of the prominent dignity of Law. This witty dialogue reflects the ongoing debate about the status of early modern lawyers: it stages an amusing play between severe law professors such as Accursius and sarcastic defendants of Philologia. Lorenzo Valla is called by the author the "other Momus" (*alter Momus*), but his character, Accursius, turns him into a grubby grammarian ("*grammaticus pediculosus*"[21]). Forcadel follows here the trek opened by Alciato: the grammarians are unable to interpret the subtlety of Roman laws by themselves; they need a sound knowledge of the *mens legis* too, if they want to link successfully the study of laws to *bonæ literæ*.

JUPITER AND THEMIS

The French revolutionary lawyer Mirabeau uses the partnership between Jupiter and Themis as a long-standing example of theocracy:

> La théocratie semble avoir été partout le premier gouvernement. Tous les législateurs ont eu recours à l'intervention céleste pour se rendre plus puissants; et Thémis fut toujours assise à côté de Jupiter.[22]

This image is used in a pamphlet against the arbitrary judicial device of the "Lettres de Cachet" and serves as a token of what he calls sacerdotal despotism. But the early modern reflections about this image tell a very different and rather diverse story. The god and goddess sitting together can serve very different purposes.

The Dutch lawyer Florentius Schoonhovius (Gouda, 1594–1648) authored a book of emblems while he was studying Law at the University of Leiden.[23] The emblem "Juste fiunt quae a Deo" shows Jupiter seated next to Themis on a throne of clouds, above a landscape. The distich below the *pictura* asks: Why is Themis the judicial assessor of Jupiter? ("Cur Jovis adsestrix Themis est?") and the answer given is: Because just things have to be considered as divine and thought by God's will ("Quod justa putandae Quæ Divina Dei mens rata cunque velit"). It is thus because justice or righteousness sits in council with God that in his mind and will she prescribes laws to nature and the whole world. The emblem's commentary starts with verses reflecting Claudian's doubts in his first book against Rufinus (Book 1), (III, 1–3):

> My mind has often wavered between two opinions: have the gods a care for the world or is there no ruler therein and do mortal things drift as dubious chance dictates?

Claudian's famous lapse into doubt reflects a wider issue: Where is divine justice in the world? How can we believe in divine providence, if evil men such as Rufinus are allowed to flourish unpunished?

Hugo Grotius also discusses the association of Jupiter and Themis and gives another interpretation: he refers to Plutarch (*Life of Alexander the Great*) who reports that the philosopher Anaxarchus comforted Alexander the Great who had slain his favorite, Clitus, because he had spoken too sincerely to him, using these flattering words:

> Don't you know what the poets say, that Jupiter has Themis, i.e. Right and Justice sitting by him, which signifies that all that a Prince does is holy, right and just? By which Anaxarchus gives us to understand, that God regulates Justice according to his Will, so a Prince can change, as he pleases, the Rules of Right and Wrong. This is just the language of flatterers, and the principle of Mr Hobbes, who destroys all Justice and yields plainly the will of God to the Humour of Princes, since all that a Prince does being just, because he does it, if he thinks good to do it, God must will it also, and approve of it as just. Plutarch elsewhere relating that story, maintains that Anaxarchus did very ill to speak so to Alexander, because instead of advising him to repent of his Fault, he had laid down a Maxim which would encourage to do the same again. The Truth is (says he) that Jupiter does not have Justice sitting at his side, but is himself perfect Justice, and is more ancient, as well as more perfect than law. This fiction of the Antients tend to make us understand, that without Justice, Jupiter himself could not govern as he ought ... We may see by these words, that this philosopher in establishing the will of God, as the foundation of Right and Wrong, supposes at the same time, that his Will is not purely arbitrary, but that he follows immutably what the Perfection of his Nature requires.[24]

The association of Jupiter and Themis on a throne, one sitting next to the other, is here related to a cynical maxim, invented by a flatterer, to show that whatever is done by supreme power is right. The lawyer and emblematist Pierre Coustau uses the same motif, but he draws a very different warning from it. In his pegma "Ad statuam Jovis et Themidos. Justa a Deo roganda."[25] (On the statue of Jupiter and Themis. Just things should be asked of God), he describes how Themis is placed next to the thunder of Dikè, and how the goddess investigates whether the prayers addressed to her are legitimate. The epigram warns us "Make sure you ask good things of God: divine Themis will cut down the unrighteous prayers with her mattock." Coustau invents this emblem to give a much more ethical interpretation to the association of Jupiter and Themis on a shared throne. Probaby inspired by the motif of Jupiter, consort of Themis, Montaigne devotes an entire essay "Des Prières" (I, 56) to the same issue of illicit prayers, trying to establish the criteria for deciding whether a prayer is legitimate or not.

THE PARADOX OF JUSTITIA'S TRANSPARENT BLINDFOLD

One of the most disputed questions about representing Lady Justice is the one of her blindfold. Sightlessness is problematic: is it a sign of disability or a token of impartiality? One way of adding a contribution to this issue is to show how the blindfold himself is polysemic: its nature is ambivalent: *Justitia* must see, she is *oculatissima*. According to the Renaissance thinker Cælius Rhodiginus, the symbol of Justice is the eye, "*justitiæ servator*," Justice's servant, and Chrysippus, quoted by Aulus Gellius, insisted upon her sight and the keen glance of her eyes. Among the numerous iconic treatment of the eye metaphor, Ripa recommends that *Justitia* should have an acute vision and should wear a necklace around her throat where an eye is portrayed because "Plato said that Justice sees all and that, from ancient times, priests were called seers of all things."[26] By the end of the fifteenth century, justice's blindfold started out as a negative attribute: the earliest known representation of blindfolded justice is a satirical woodcut for Sebastian Brandt *Das Narrenschiff* (*The Ship of Fools*, 1494), attributed to Albrecht Dürer, in which the author criticized the abuse of trials and the foolishness of court arguments. Despite the scathing criticism expressed by Sebastian Brandt, the image of blindfolded justice will develop a positive connotation at the beginning of the sixteeth century: it then came to denote the impartiality of an ideal justice.

Several painters have produced inventive blindfolds suggesting that the bandage is not simply a blinding device. When the blindfold is diaphanous, clearly showing eyes wide open, it becomes a sign that a bandage's function is not a way of removing sight. It acts more like a filter or a stigmata, indicating that *Justitia* is a gifted seer: sometimes the blindfold is nothing but a piece of transparent gauze: it lets us see her meditative gaze. This type of translucent veil has a glorious antecedent in painting: Fra Angelico has painted an analogous blindfold in his depiction of the mocking of Christ with the Virgin and Saint Dominic (1439–1443) fresco, cell 7, at the Convent of San Marco, Florence. The blindfold is transparent and Christ's peaceful and compassionate gaze is visible, through the veil, which is left unable to cover Christ's eyesight.[27] The bandage seems to serve as a visual index: it shows that its bearer has overcome its obstacle to reverse its meaning. The bandaged eyes seem to indicate that even if Lady Justice claims to be no respecter of persons, her blindfolded eyes, symbolizing her lack of preferential favor for any individual, are not closed by the bandage affixed on her eyes: her sight goes beyond this obstruction.

A vivid example of a paradoxical blindfold applied to *Justitia* appears in a roundel engraved by Jacob de Gheyn (II) circa 1593 (Figure 1.5): the bandage covers only half of her sight and her revolving eyes and half-open mouth makes her look as she had fallen into deep ecstacy. Crowned with laurels, her ecstatic mind expands her interior sight and spiritual awareness: she stands as the exact opposite of strict justice, the kind that seeks to make an adequate compensation. This ecstatic justice goes beyond the mere norms of human justice: her excess shows the enthusiasm of pure love as she embodies the superior sight of divine justice.

Crispijn de Passe (I) in an allegorical frontispiece of 1627, shows a type of thin gauze blindfold, through which Justitia is looking. (Figure 1.6). In an anonymous print showing Oliver Cromwell as Lord Protector in 1653, Justitia's melancholic eyes are also perfectly apparent on her blindfold (Figure 1.7). Lastly, the allegorical portrait of Ferdinand III, "defensor Justitiæ," engraved by Michel Natalis in 1645, shows, through another transparent blindfold, the expressive gaze of Justitia: looking up towards the sovereign, her hands lifted up, she has left her sword in equilibrium on her left knee. Through her

FIGURE 1.5 *Justitia*, part of a series of the seven virtues, workshop of Jacob de Gheyn (II), 1591–1595, engraving, d 148 mm. Source: Courtesy of Rijksmuseum, Amsterdam.

FIGURE 1.6 Crispijn van de Passe (II), Frontispiece for the edition of the *Corpus Juris Civilis*, by Denis Godefroy, Paris, Antoine Vitré, 1627, engraving, h 347 mm x w 212 mm. Source: Courtesy of Rijksmuseum, Amsterdam.

FIGURE 1.7 Workshop of Claes Jansz Visscher (II), Satire on Oliver Cromwell and the Protectorate suggesting that he aimed to become king, published by Rombout van den Hoeye, 1653–1654, engraving, h 402 mm x w 458 mm. Source: Courtesy of Rijksmuseum, Amsterdam.

wide open eyes, charitable justice is modulated by mercy; it affords a degree of leniency where the rigor of Law would be expected and deserved. Charitable justice allows her compassionate eyes to pop out from the blindfold; she reshapes what is "just" in light of what she sees, between the imperatives of war and peace. These examples of translucent blindfolds show the variable polysemy of the bandage: the blindfold is a visual index for an ambivalence as to Justitia's sight.

EARLY MODERN JUDICIAL PRACTICES: THE "AMENDE HONORABLE" AND THE ROLE OF PENANCE EFFIGIES OF *JUSTITIA*

The ritual of early modern courts, especially, though not exclusively, in cases of criminal trials, operates within particular settings, creating a spectacle that builds on cultural symbols as part of a rite. Reflecting on the various threads linking early modern judicial rituals and their connection to the apparent legal principles underlying them enables us to understand their symbolic significance. In the context of the Reformation, seditious persons often expressed "blasphemous remarks" publicly or in defamatory writings. Despite the many differences between these crimes, all these verbal offenses or blasphemies were linked to the concept of honor. Blasphemy or insults uttered by a single person could dishonor an entire family. In France, the Edict of Nantes explicitly forbade Huguenots and Catholics from insulting each other or using any speech that might lead to a rebellious action. In all these cases, the offender was sentenced to perform an "amende honorable," a criminal penalty that implied a ritual apology, a public humiliation and a process of dishonor. The offender was forced to appear bareheaded and barefoot, dressed in a simple shirt, without any outward mark of wealth or status, with a rope around the neck, carrying a large lit torch. The criminal then had to kneel, acknowledge aloud his misdeed and beg for God's pardon. The "amende honorable" had to be performed in a public space, under an extensive purview. The local judge would specify the location of the process: the steps of a church, a law court's public session, an open square on the day of public market. The "amende honorable" was often performed as a ritual inversion of an offense and it contained a moment of humiliation and a moment of reconciliation. In his *Praxis rerum criminalium* (Anvers, 1557), Josse Damhoudere has provided a representation of an "amende honorable" before the tribunal.[28] The penitent is shown kneeling in front of the court under the purview of the public, symbolized by two open windows crammed with spectators on both sides of the scene, in the background.

In the particular case of judicial errors, the humiliating practice of "amende honorable" could also be imposed on the failing judge himself. A magistrate who had wrongly sentenced someone to death had to perform the "amende honorable" in a particular way: dressed as a penitent, in a simple shirt without belt, holding a lit torch, he was forced to walk again the itinerary followed by the procession of the wrongly convicted and to pause at the courthouse and at the place of execution to beg for pardon. More importantly, as Robert Jacob has pointed out, the memory of the judicial error had to be preserved and the judge had to have executed at his own expense an artistic representation of his "amende honorable" which was to be kept in the local church to recall his fault.[29] Some of these effigies of penitent magistrates have been preserved: the French bailiff Jean de Bove, who had sentenced an innocent to jail, had the sculptor Guillaume Danolle execute a statue of him, kneeling in front of an effigy of *Justitia*. The Musée of Cambrai still has a wooden model of this statue "Jehan de Bove, bailli de Marcoing, demande grâce à la Justice,"[30] a model for the bronze version of this sculpture, which was placed on the façade of the courthouse of Cambrai to perpetuate the memory of his punishment. The example of the practice of the "amende honorable" is thus directly linked to the creation of particular effigies of *Justitia*, designed to show to the public sphere the penitence of the failing judge.

TRIVIAL IMAGES: JUSTICE'S BROOM

Aside from *exempla justitiæ* and refined allegories, the concept of justice can also be conveyed by a more trivial imagery, composed by simplified and formulaic forms, in order to make abstract concepts tangible through the use of familiar, straightforward, recognizable objects. This popular visual language operates at a fairly basic level of signification, but it shows the diversity of legal symbols. The remarkable variety of broadside prints throughout the early modern period shows that most images displayed in chapbooks or pamphlets elicit a multiplicity of reading styles and cater for various degrees of visual and textual literacy.

In his *Géométrie Praticque* (1542 edn, extended from 1511), the French philosopher Charles de Bovelles used a rather peculiar image to represent the three orders of Justice: a broom.

Les trois justices de l'homme sont joyeusement et visiblement comprises sur les trois parties d'un balay. Chacun sçait que c'est, et à quoy il sert en la maison.³¹

The metaphor of Justice's broom is a joyful symbol, all the more persuasive because everyone knows what it is and what purpose it serves. Each order of Justice (low, intermediate and high) is compared to a part of the broom and corresponds to an age of punishment: low justice is situated on its inferior part and punishes young children with the birch; intermediate justice is located on the broom's handle, chastizing young men and servants with the rod, on their back; high justice is located in the rope that holds the brushes of the broom tightly together: it is reserved to those who are not willing to be amended and who are punished by the gallows. In Charles de Bovelles practical manual of geometry, two images of the broom are accompanied by an allegorical poem: the broom is first shown in its entirety; secondly, each part of it is associated with a type of justice.

FIGURE 1.8 Peeter van der Borcht, *The Broom of Justice*, Antwerp, 1578, published by Adriaen Huybrechts (I), engraving, h 298 mm x w 220 mm. Source: Courtesy of Rijksmuseum, Amsterdam.

This mnemonic tool is expanded figuratively by Peter Van den Borcht in large broadsheet published by Adriaen Huybrechts in 1578 (Figure 1.8). The broom is a visual symbol of the three levels of justice. This is a good example of a print combining popular culture with more recondite influences. In his interpretation of Bovelles' Justice's broom, he has added three lively depictions of punishment to the tableau and a representation of Moses with the Law tables and a rod, along with three versions of the explanatory poem, one in Latin, one in French and one in Dutch. Each punishment scene is crowned with an isolated piece of the broom: the first scene, under the emblematic motive of birch twigs, shows a schoolmaster spanking disobedient and bare-bottom children with a cat o'nine tails. The second picture, under the motive of an emblematic rod, represents the same schoolmaster hitting a young, half-naked, man fiercely, this time with a rod. The last scene, located under the motive of a tied rope, shows the interior of a church, where blasphemers have stolen a chalice and other holy objects. The important scene here is in the background, where several criminals have been hanged on scaffolds. This hierarchy of the three orders of justice shows vividly the rise in violence of corporal penalties: this tiny, somehow trivial, theater of punishment is set up to shape an obedient subject and prevent future lawbreaking. This representation of a constant coercion, gradually set in accordance with the age of man, takes place in the enclosed and protected space of a school. The triple tableau identifies the scale of coercion as an incremental series. The disciplinary method figured here reveals a linear evolution over time: in accordance with a man's motive, it shows that disciplinary punishment has to be corrective according to the age of the miscreant, while generally favoring gentle punishments, because they are considered as training exercises.[32]

THE SYMBOLIC GEOMETRY OF JUSTICE

Many early modern emblems of justice express a fundamental connection between law and geometry. Aristotle in *Nicomachean Ethics* (V, iii, 12) had already offered geometric proportionality as an appropriate model for distributive justice: this form of justice is meant to apportion goods according to the respective merits of the receivers. Distributive justice is thus the identification of rewards with merit, by geometric proportions imagined as a series of ratios. In his *Six livres de la République* (1576), Jean Bodin argued that monarchy should be restrained by rules of mathematical proportion. Distributive justice was meant to set up proportional relations between unequals. According to Aristotle, the determination of distributive justice requires the establishment of a "geometrical" rather than "arithmetical" equivalence, in which greater service receives proportionally greater reward. In an emblem book authored by Heinrich Oræus, a Lutheran pastor, one emblem is dedicated to the notion of *Justitia distributiva* and develops this geometrical metaphor[33] (Figure 1.9). The figure of an equilateral triangle is associated with a strange accumulation of objects: God's hand shows an index pointing downwards, holding a *caduceum* (for *Prudentia*) towards a regular triangle bearing three faces: in the middle of the triangle a rectilineal plumb-line holds a balance, whose scales are in equilibrium. The complex combination of objects reaches a perfect state of harmony. The emblem commentary gives several scriptural sources for a definition of distributive justice, one of them being expressed in Romans 13.17: "Render to all their dues; tribute to whom tribute, custom to whom custom, fear to whom fear, honor to whom honor, is due." The image of the plumb-line is drawn from Isaiah 28.17: "I will use justice as a plumb-line and righteousness as a plummet."

FIGURE 1.9 Heinrich Oræus, *Viridarium hieroglyphico-morale: in quo virtutes et vitia ... illustrantur*, Francfort, Jacques de Zetter, 1619, pp. 52–53. Source: Courtesy of archive.org.

CIVIC JUSTICE AND FORMS OF GOVERNMENT

Bartholomeo Del Bene (1515–1595) published in 1609 a volume entitled *Civitas Veri sive Morum* (*The City of Truth or Ethics*) with a commentary by the humanist scholar Théodore Marcile (1548–1617). The work, illustrated by a dozen engravings, was an allegorical poem reorchestrating Aristotle's *Nichomachean Ethics*, on the pattern of an initiation through travel, performed by Marguerite, Duchess of Savoy, his patroness. Del Bene's City of Truth is an utopia, fashioned on the model of Thomas More's idealized microcosm. Two contrasted engravings describe the antagonism between Injustice and Justice and their relationship to forms of government. The statue of Injustice (Figure 1.10) sits in the middle of a decayed palace, on the top of an ill-built pyramid, she is tearing apart the books of civil law, she's surrounded by Avarice, Ambition, and Intemperance, sitting between Bacchus and Venus who accompany her. The pyramid on which she is sitting is occupied by Tyranny, Oligarchy and Ochlocracy (which means the

FIGURE 1.10 Bartolomeo Del Bene, "Domus Injustitiæ" (Temple of Injustice) in *Civitas veri sive morum, Aristotelis de moribus doctrinam carmine et picturis complexa, et illustrata commentariis Th. Marcilii*, Paris, Ambroise et Jérôme Drouart, 1609, p. 165. Source: Courtesy of archive.org.

false domination of the people, a degeneration of democracy, perverted by populism and mob-rule). By contrast, the *domus Justitiae* is a marble palace, adorned with columns and porticoes (Figure 1.11) In the middle, the statue of legitimate Justice holds the book of Laws, she rules over the three positive forms of government: Monarchy, Aristocracy

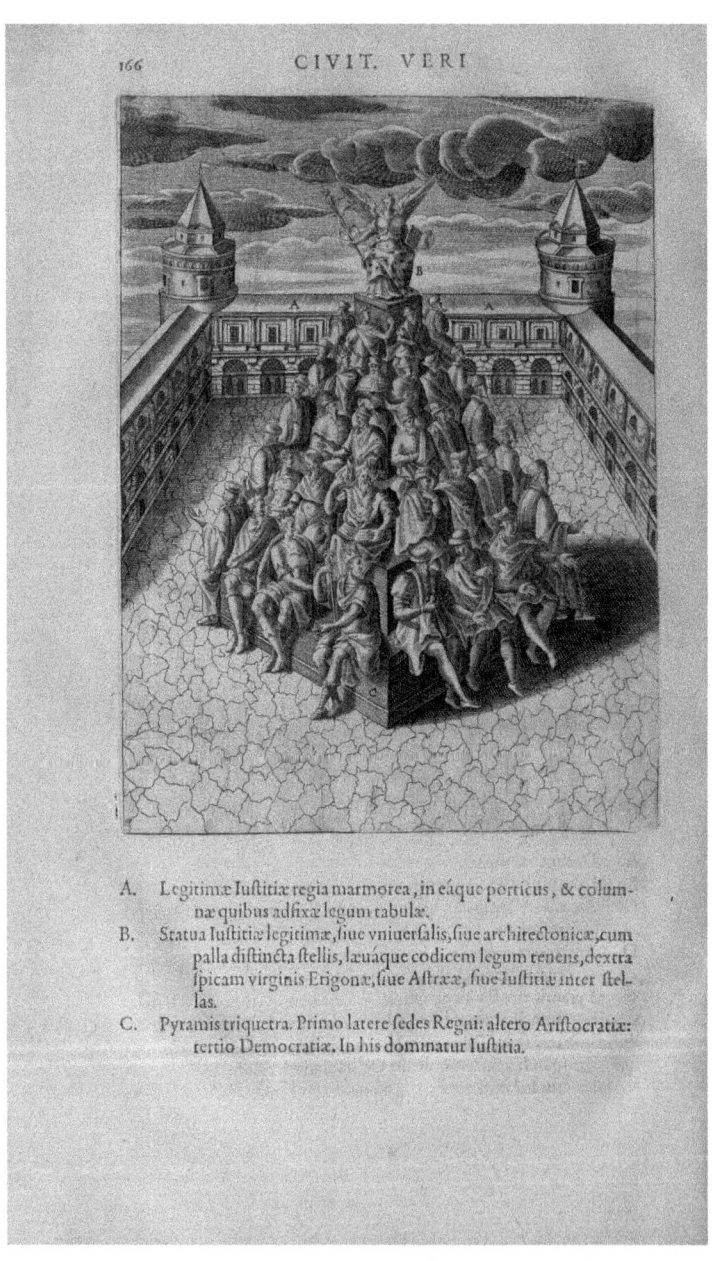

FIGURE 1.11 Bartolomeo Del Bene, "Domus Justitiæ" (Temple of Justice) in *Civitas veri sive morum, Aristotelis de moribus doctrinam carmine et picturis complexa, et illustrata commentariis Th. Marcilii*, Paris, Ambroise et Jérôme Drouart, 1609, p. 166. Source: Courtesy of archive.org.

and Democracy. This important idea of a classification of polities by governmental form was first elaborated by Aristotle (*Politics*, VI) and then by Polybius (*Histories*, 6. 5–18). Constitutional forms, together with their corruptions, succeeded to each other inevitably: monarchy degenerates into tyranny, aristocracy is transformed into oligarchy and democracy, ultimately, is displaced by ochlocracy.

This double and paradoxical effigy of justice versus injustice leads to a lengthy analysis of stability and instability in the cities and to a rephrasing of the theory of polity which is then very influential in Renaissance minds. The image of a civic Justitia opposed to its contrary is designed to reflect on the three traditional types of government in their good and bad forms, tracing their cyclical alternations. Justice throning over the three good forms of government suggests that the only way to stabilize a state and to prevent it from corruption is to combine all good forms of government, where each form controls the other to obtain equilibrium. Polybius called the Roman constitution "the best political order yet realized among men" because it combined monarchichal, aristocratic and democratic elements configured so that the virtues of each preserved them from their vices: their systems being counteracting, to achieve political equilibrium. Each individual source of power was constrained by the others, but two powers could not combine to overthrow the remaining third.

This brief survey of Early Modern images of justice has shown its extraordinary vitality and ubiquity. Painted on the walls of courthouses, exposed on their façades, displayed in public spaces such as fountains or marketplaces, effigies of Lady Justice were abundant. Allegorical images of justice were commonly elaborated for ambitious title pages of law books. During early modern times, more complex allegorical scenes are part of an important tradition: the *exempla justitiæ*, where the damnation of the erring judges is depicted with great acuity. These allegorical programs are meant to be deontological; they serve as a visual memorandum of judicial duties. The power of these legal images was then theological and political; their status gradually waned in later ages. The allegory of Justice was to endure a greater reign than the *exempla justitiae* presented here. From the beginning of the late seventeenth century, the flayed judge, the king who had one one of his own eyes and one of his son's gouged out, the maimed hands of the Theban judges, all these horrific scenes were to be replaced by less violent and more complacent topics. The age of the judge's damnation was at an end. The seventeenth and eighteenth centuries would soon adopt classical themes and hefty allegories which would not offend the new sense of decorum.

CHAPTER TWO

Constitutions

SUSAN BYRNE

Constitutional scholars identify two main aspects of formal constitutions: the establishment and coordination of structures of governance, and the protection of individual human rights under those institutions.[1] In the broader sense in which the term was read in the early modern period, however, constitutions are simply the laws one lives by. Late fifteenth- to early seventeenth-century definitions for the word "constitution" include the one word "a statute"[2] and the three-part "Constitutions, statutes, decrees."[3] Constitutions generally develop out of usage, custom, and court rulings: in 1616, Pierre Ayrault asked: "For what is a constitution but something taken from many judgments and opinions?"[4] The U.S. Constitution is similarly described as "an historically discontinuous composition ... the product, over time, of a series of not altogether coherent compromises ... a set of sometimes reinforcing and sometimes conflicting ideals and notions."[5] Those opinions, ideals, and notions are codified in legal writings, but comprised in brief in creative texts, which offer a wealth of informative detail on actual conditions and attitudes. Speaking of Tudor constitutional documents, Tanner makes the case for study through full historical contextualization: "The dry bones of Star Chamber history clothe themselves with flesh and blood in the records of actual cases in which human beings are concerned; and arid legal propositions about the Law of Treason take on a new character in the story of things that really happened in a treason trial."[6] Even more broadly for Hardin: "Constitutionalism without social science is an arid intellectual pastime."[7] Statutory, customary, and revolutionary concerns are addressed in a number of early modern Spanish texts and, in what follows, I will combine creative and serious letters to draw attention to the expression of evolving constitutional principles in the early modern era. Legal and historical documentation provides background, while creative works serve as first-hand witnesses to that early modern mix.

Spain might seem an odd choice for early modern constitutional study, given that it would not have a formally ratified constitution until late in the twentieth century.[8] Nonetheless, its legal models influenced multiple modern constitutional principles:

Some of the research for this article was carried out with the help of two grants, one from the Griswold Research Fund of the Whitney Humanities Center, and another, a Faculty Research Grant from the MacMillan Center for International and Area Studies, both at Yale. My thanks to those committees and their sponsors, as well as to three colleagues with whom conversations regarding some of the material herein were particularly helpful: Adrienne Martín, Kevin Poole, and Fernando Rodríguez-Mansilla.

Spain was the first European nation to publish a code of commerce; she possessed and exercised a writ of *habeas corpus (manifestación)* in Aragon before America was discovered; and Gothic democratic principles were there developed and exercised more liberal than those recognized in any monarchy of today, and, being evolved with time, formed the basis of the Republic of Ireland, the Magna Charta of England, and the American Declaration of Independence. (Walton 2002, v)[9]

The Visigoths ruled the Iberian Peninsula from 415 to 711 CE and their democratic principles, expressed in the seventh-century *Forum visigothorum*, would later also be codified into the various *fueros* [founding charters, constitutions, usage and custom law collections][10] granted to cities, towns, and reigns as Christian forces reconquered them from ruling caliphates during the period 718 through 1492. The process of centralization that would result in the peninsula's absolute monarchy of the seventeenth century began in the fifteenth, with the consolidation of the peninsula's two most powerful reigns under Ferdinand and Isabel. That marriage joined one central monarchy to a union of constitutional monarchies, each of which maintained the rights to its own *fueros*.[11] Over the course of the following century, debates on central versus periphery governance, the rights of specific individuals and groups, and questions of liberty and equity were rife on the Iberian peninsula. Battles to retain individual and collective constitutional rights figured prominently, and creative authors capitalized on that subject matter. By the beginning of the seventeenth century, many of those political battles would be lost under the absolute monarchy brought into place by Phillip II and his successors. Nonetheless, the topics remained contentious enough to provide a wealth of popular thematic material for creative writers.

On the Iberian Peninsula, the word "constitution" was used for founding charters as early as the year 1020 (León, *Cortes*, 1020; Coyanza, *Cortes*, 1050).[12] It was also the term applied to the rules of religious orders, the personal mandates of last wills and testaments, and university regulations: the 1568 *Recopilación de leyes* demands that university constitutions be enforced (*Recopilación* 1.7.22).[13] There are references to apostolic constitutions, to the arrest of a lawbreaker in the year 1504 according to "the laws and constitutions" of Navarre,[14] and a circa-1529 debate on the comparative worth of constitutions regarding two different prohibitions, "fornication which is prohibited *jure divino*" versus the human constitution that bans eating meat: "I will admit that you are right, on one condition: that you tell me why you do not consider it more serious to sin against the human constitutions than against divine law."[15] A precise distinction among constitutions as codified in the thirteenth century *Siete Partidas* is reviewed by Hugo de Celso in his 1540 *Repertorio universal de todas las leyes de estos reinos de Castilla*:

> Constitutions: some are general, for example those made by the Pope or General [Ecumenical] Council, and these must be obeyed by the whole world (Partida I, Title 5, law 5). Others are particular, such as those made by the patriarchs, archbishops and bishops in their patriarchies, provinces and obispates, and must only be obeyed in those places (Ibid. law 13).
>
> In similar fashion, kings and princes make constitutions and laws in their reigns, adding to or abrogating old ones as times and customs change (Partida II, Title 26, law 3).
>
> Secular persons who make constitutions or statutes against the clerecy, prelates, churches, or against the liberties of those [persons or places], are excommunicated with high excommunication (Partida I, title 9, laws 2 and 19). (Celso 1540, f. 84r)[16]

The first and last provisions highlight the problem of church–state tensions and demonstrate the power of the clergy in the thirteenth century, able to demand not only that "all the world" obey their constitutions, but also royal assurance that no local ruler might promulgate laws unfavorable to them. By the time Celso wrote in the mid-sixteenth century, the state had been battling church interference in civil court cases for two centuries, and it would continue to do so with ever-increasing efficacy.[17] Miguel de Cervantes famously illustrates this schism in an episode of *Don Quijote*, when his protagonist grants an appeal to galley slaves while highlighting a very specific legal procedure for such appeals, the "way of force" (*vía de fuerza*) by which the crown reasserted control over an appeal unjustly denied by the ecclesiastical courts.[18] In the creative text, an appeal is granted, but the intent of the knight-turned-judge is foiled, as he proves unable to prevent the ensuing mutinous escape of all prisoners.

Not found in common dictionaries, even today, are the individual protections clauses that constitutional scholars include *de rigueur* in their definitions: for Bryce in 1901, a constitution was "a frame of government designed to prescribe the form which the administration of a state takes, to define its powers over the citizen, and the rights of the citizen against it.[19] In 2013, Galligan and Versteeg emphasize those protections clauses with the word "limits": "A constitution establishes a system of government, defines the powers and functions of its institutions, provides substantive limits on its operation, and regulates relations between institutions and the people."[20] Alphonse X's *Siete Partidas* themselves are a prime example of a failed contractual constitutional model due to their having infringed on such customary rights, and they were roundly rejected by the nobility for that contravention of statutory privilege. Local rulers who promulgate laws are liable to local inhabitants and customs, but when Emperor Justinian's legal codes were recovered in the eleventh to twelfth centuries, jurists were understandably intrigued, and contemporary Bolognese legal experts would advocate the incorporation of those classical codes into existing customary juridical practice. Alphonse X's principal jurist Jacobo de Junta (AKA Jacobo de las Leyes), known to be an expert in Roman law, followed the same *mos italicus* model in the *Partidas*,[21] mixing medieval usage and custom with laws from Justinian's sixth-century Digest, Code, and Institutions.[22] Rejected when first published, the *Partidas* would not be formally promulgated until the reign of the Catholic monarchs Ferdinand and Isabel and even then, they would never become the primary ruling legal standard. A later Spanish juridical voice, commenting on a collection of early *fueros*, advocates a more moderate approach:

> Although these legal constitutions of prior centuries might seem an unorganized assemblage, they offer useful knowledge and acquaintance with past times and ways. I do not mean to say that these constitutions in the common Spanish language, taken as a whole, offer an understanding of the presiding legal codes of any given moment, but the reader will find much here to admire. (Gaspar de Baeza)[23]

Writing in the middle of the sixteenth century, Baeza finds early constitutions informative but warns that they should not be taken as fully prescriptive. Spanish jurists from the School of Salamanca, among them Baeza, were seeking a middle-ground approach to contemporary *mos italicus* versus *mos gallicus* debates regarding the incorporation of ancient Roman law into contemporary usage and custom collections. Their hopeful, yet non-actualized, juridical *mos hispanicus* would be ironically realized in a fictional setting in Miguel de Cervantes' *Don Quijote*, as the novel's protagonist endorses ideals of justice and truth while simultaneously wreaking havoc on his world.[24] The haphazard mixing of old codes and modern mores, Cervantes suggests, can have disastrous results. Along with the sixteenth century's literal sorting out of legal codes, the constitutional parameters of the governments of today's European states would be framed through a similar process of old, yet newly recovered models mixing with existing regimes and ideologies. Early modern humanists debated the rise and fall of republics with reference to Christian virtue and the Holy Roman Empire (Botella-Ordinas),[25] but they also discussed ancient and classical thought regarding systems of governance, particularly following Italian philosopher Marsilio Ficino's translations of and commentaries on Plato's dialogues. Two in particular, the *Republic* and the *Laws*, would inspire consistent debate on the optimum form and functioning of a state up to and throughout the seventeenth century.[26]

Much of the early modern social dynamic and debate behind what would evolve into the concept of a constitution as a social construct among members of a society, and on the basis of which those members have and exercise individual rights, is found in texts that address juridical and political issues through an innovative lens. Some of those writings are decidedly legal: the 1215 Magna Carta codifies the rights of free men while settling a dispute between powerful warring parties, as it assures the "customs and liberties" of all men (number 60).[27] Others are not: the earliest extant full-length Spanish epic poem, the 1207 *Cantar de mío Cid*, ends with the king's decision to right an injustice by certain noblemen of the high aristocracy. Instead of physically confronting the evildoers, two *infantes* who had ravaged and left his daughters (also their wives) for dead in the wilderness, the epic hero Cid takes his case to court. He is an evolving hero who wields both sword and lawsuit, the Magna Carta's "free man" brought to life in verse. Both the legal document and the epic poem narrate a negotiation between powerful parties who leverage what they have to get what they want (i.e., a contract). Unlike the barons who challenged England's King John, however, the Cid was not of the high noble class, and his story is complex: banished on the basis of unfounded slander, he continued to prosper in battle and never failed to send the required tribute back to the king. His later demand for the rights of a loyal subject wronged by some of the state's partners is a type of "elite bargain"[28] although not a truly privileged stance as he, powerful but of lower, rather than higher, noble rank, directly challenges the elite status quo between king and high nobility, the two existing powers that conformed the ruling classes and in whose favor matters of state were typically determined. The king's decision in his favor upsets contemporary constitutional expectations.

The main human rights goal of a constitution—justice—is, in modern terms, predominantly a legal matter.[29] A modern constitution's frame of government is meant to assure justice for all, although it is well known that "all" has not always been read literally. What that administrative frame will be, how the parties will bargain, contract or coordinate among themselves to live within it, and which rights and responsibilities they treasure (ergo defend) the most, are the substantive concerns. Punishments for those who break with a constitution can be extreme. King Alphonse V of León's founding charter for his kingdom ends with decree number 48:

> Whosoever shall attempt or determine to break this our Constitution, whether they be our descendants or foreigners, shall have their hands broken, and their cervix and eyes removed, and they shall be disemboweled with their insides scattered over the land, to be cursed and excommunicated and to suffer the pains of hell in perpetual damnation, with the devil and all his [evil] angels for ever and ever. Amen. (León, 1020, *Cortes* law 48, p. 21)[30]

Later constitutions tend to be less explicit; within thirty years, the punishment for breaking with the dictates of Coyanza's Constitution omitted the physical penalties while retaining the spiritual condemnation (*Cortes*, law 13, p. 29). In the early modern period, Spain's playwrights and creative prose writers brought this same thematic material (laws, justice, liberty, government, abuse of power, role of the people, the rulers, and the church) to the stage in theatrical representations and into the pages of a new genre in the making: the modern novel.

As Jacob Grimm famously said, law and poetry "were rocked in the same cradle" (27).[31] Poetry is one of the earliest representations of divine law: the poet is a medium, a celestial messenger capable of understanding the will of the divinity and transmitting those exalted messages regarding pre- and proscriptive behavior to a community. In 1904, Eduardo de Hinojosa traced the relationship between priest, legislator, judge and poet in a number of ancient cultures, and highlighted alliteration and rhythm as two shared expressive elements in both types of writing (7–8).[32] Even more telling, the language of law includes both specification and blurring of temporal concerns: has been, is, will be—past, present, and future are collapsed into an atemporal object lesson, as what has happened becomes the basis for a present decision as well as the prescription for, or proscription against, future behavior. That is also the modern novel, a verisimilar imitation of real-life events for which we suspend disbelief [33] and simultaneously participate in multiple perspectives[34] as we accept a timeless fictional reality of semi-invented truths.[35] During the sixteenth century, Aristotle's division of writing into history (what happened) or poetry (what might have happened) gave way to a split understanding of the latter as formal, metered, poetry or poetry in prose. This last medium for creative expression allowed for dual realities: imagined events could be expressed in realist novelistic prose, yet that verisimilar reality mirrored was not the real world. Writers were scribes of real and invented truths, and readers were asked to be judges. Theater, like a reiterated court case, presents timeless reality acted out over and over: situation, complication, resolution. Early modern Spanish novelists and playwrights appropriated multiple points of juridical and political detail into their creative texts. For example, the first picaresque novel, the 1554 *Lazarillo de Tormes*, is structured as a legal deposition and is directly related to previous court findings.[36] The 1499 *Celestina*, read today as a bawdy, groundbreaking novel, was glossed in the middle of the sixteenth century with multiple references to specific points made by its characters as "principles of law" (*Celestina comentada*).[37] Creative works reflect and refract developing constitutional debate and practices as regards (1) persons and privileges, (2) systems of governance, (3) elections, and (4) liberty. Those categories will serve as the structure in what follows.

PERSONS AND PRIVILEGES—INDIVIDUAL PROTECTIONS

Far from the later U.S. Declaration of Independence with its claim that all men are created equal, early modern laws on the Iberian Peninsula defined persons by their "status and condition," a phrase that incorporated a number of points: social, legal, economic, and governmental (status), as well as position, rank, and circumstance (condition). The seventh-century *Fuero Juzgo* distinguished only free from slave and noble from not, but by the end of the sixteenth century a non-exhaustive list of legally classifiable groups of "the people" would include: royalty, nobility [higher and lower ranks], clergy, court officials, council members, deeded landowners, knights, scholars, royal pages, local government officials, artisans, craftsmen, shepherds, laborers, and the poor.[38] Those categories determined rights and responsibilities, including noteworthy benefits such as exemption from taxes, as well as expectations for keeping arms at the ready at all times. Over the course of the sixteenth century, the same rankings began to determine mandated forms of address identified as "treatments and courtesies" (*tratamientos y cortesías*) that would for a time, supposedly if ineffectively, be regulated by law. Perceived slights in social greetings were easy fodder for creative commentary. In the 1554 *Lazarillo*, one lower-ranking noble (*escudero*) explains two insults that convinced him to abandon his hometown. Repeatedly meeting a colleague of equal rank on the street, each recognized and conformed to the need to tip their hat to the other but the *escudero*, peeved that he was always the one to do so first, began to avoid the other man by ducking into stores or altering his route. The greater insult came when a man of lesser rank greeted him in what he deemed an insufficiently respectful manner, with the phrase "May God protect your grace" instead of "I kiss your grace's hand."[39] The novel's author puts in servant Lazarillo's voice the overriding moral of the story, in an aside overtly directed to, but not heard by the *escudero*: "Well, damn ... so this is why you are so careless about taking care of yourself: you won't even allow someone else to ask God to protect you."[40] The *escudero* is penniless and hungry, but keeps up the pretense of honor by donning his cloak and sword every day before leaving the abode that he will skip out on paying the rent for by the end of the month. Lazarillo comments this particular societal fault with a biting "that black shadow called honor,"[41] as his anonymous author satirizes the customs of his society. Merely court custom when *Lazarillo* was written,[42] half a century later the requirements for allowable terms of address would be codified into law, repeatedly ignored, and constantly repromulgated to little effect. In 1615, Miguel de Cervantes has Sancho Panza's wife question the use of "don" by *Don Quijote*'s protagonist as a presumptious overreach, and Sancho himself will plan his daughter's marriage into an upper class that merits the address "señoría" (Cervantes II, 5).[43] The jockeying for position obvious in these creative texts reflects conscious manueverings in inherited and economic status. As the peninsula's monarchs became stronger and their state bureacracies more centralized, the nobility lost power and honor. A patina of required forms of address allowed those nobles to save face for a while, but they were fighting a losing battle.

Concerns with social status and opinion were repeatedly problematized in juridical, political, moralizing, and creative texts. In a 1571 treatise on mercantile contracts titled *Suma de tratos y contratos*, Fray Thomas de Mercado considers the need for legal restitution of unjustly deprived honor second only to the recompense owed for crimes against life and health.[44] Defining fame as "opinion, credit and reputation," he notes that some consider reputation even more important than "natural life and being itself" (f. 158r). Mercado references the "divine Boethius" on the transitory and questionable nature of worldly fame, but he also underscores that the more a quality such as rich, wise, or illustrious is necessary to a man in accordance with his status and condition, the more it is a crime [sin] to defame him on that basis (f. 158v). He offers as an example the harm in calling a man an idiot when letters are his profession (f. 161r). For defamation, explained as "to impute to a person, whether in his presence or absence, transgressions or defects that would cause him to lose existing good credit, or to gain ill opinion," Mercado offers a full list of such insults, from heretic and liar to lustful and lascivious, noting that Spaniards are particularly sensitive to questions of lineage (ff.158v–159r). Fame is intellectual virtue and inspiration, an "invisible good" that resides in "understanding" and is the principle motivating force for a human being (f. 159r), whereas honor is the deference accorded to those who embody it: "the reverence and courtesy" that leads one man to tip his hat to another in passing (f. 159v), to accord special seat placement at community gatherings, or to offer honorific epithets (f. 160r). Mercado laments the days when honor was granted more for virtue than "status and worldly pomp" although he simultaneously assures his reader that honor is due to a man on the basis of social rank, as well as for virtuous comportment (f.160r). Concerns with maintaining honor are a consistent theme in Spanish theater of the early modern period, comprising a category known as the "honor plays," and playwright Lope de Vega is specifically known for his "democratization of honor"[45] in plays dealing with class conflict. That very aspect of Lope's works, however, makes honor less hereditary, thereby weakening exclusive claims to it by the aristocratic class alone. Mercado's lament for the good old days is actualized in Lope's plays, with honor represented as a virtue commonly found in peasants and laborers but sorely lacking in mid-level nobles who, on the contrary in these plays, are more prone to vice than virtue. Specifically, Lope stages sexually aggressive knight commanders ruling towns while abusing the populace at large, with dramatic closure and social calm realized only through the intervention of beneficent, virtuous monarchs. Honor is a virtue of kings and peasants, and the latter rely on the former to exemplify good conduct while also protecting the constitutional rights of all subjects.

Restoration of honor following sexual transgressions is a particular concern in early modern Spanish theater. In *El alcalde de Zalamea*, Pedro Calderón de la Barca dramatizes the dilemma of a father whose daughter has been raped but who, as the recently elected mayor of the village, is now honor-bound to uphold law and order. Ignoring his lack of actual jurisdiction over the offender, the father puts him on trial, finds him guilty, and executes him. One honor code (civil) is played against another (personal). A well-known serial trangressor in questions of honor is Don Juan, the protagonist of Tirso de Molina's *El burlador de Sevilla y el convidado de piedra*. Having sexual relations with woman after woman by promising his hand in marriage, Don Juan repeatedly fails to abide by his word, contrary to Mercado's stipulation that "*omne promissum est debitum*" (f.193v). In Don Juan's case, the restoration of honor to each woman is physically impossible, as he cannot be forced to wed them all. The transgressor meets his fate only through the intervention of the afterworld, when the murdered father of one attempted conquest returns to "invite" Don Juan to dine with him in his sepulcher, leading to a final scene of conflagration, shouts of repentance, and apparent divine castigation of the malefactor. A series of three conjugally themed honor plays by Calderón (*A secreto agravio, secreta venganza; El médico de su honra; El pintor de su deshonra*), in each of which a husband murders his wife on suspicion of adultery, are widely read for their character motivation and questionably Christian moral judgments in the seeking of revenge. Abascal Monedero notes the prevalence of non-castigated cases of adultery in the era as another possible motivating factor for these plays, referencing a complaint filed with Phillip IV in 1658 regarding 143 married women in the court known for their "licentious ways" (107–108).[46] That complaint register includes the reaction of one of those women to the man charged with investigating: "she cursed him, then tried to hit him with her clogs (darle muchos chapinazos) and to pull his beard."[47]

Looked at strictly in terms of juridical norms, however, uxoricide was a state-sanctioned practice: the *Fuero Juzgo* specifies that should a husband find another man with his wife, he may kill them both if he so chooses (3.4.4); finding a man with his daughter, the father may kill just the man (3.4.5).[48] In both instances, he who executes the honor killing is free of all charges. The same legal collection also states that a woman who has sexual relations with another woman's husband is to be placed in the hands of that wife, who is free to avenge herself as she sees fit (3.4.9). The 1568 *Recopilación de leyes* does not include this last of the *Fuero Juzgo*'s laws, nor is it found in creative texts, despite its promising possibilites for thematic development. The *Recopilación* does, however, offer further specificity on the other two legally condoned revenge killings: the husband who finds another man with his wife is free to do with them both what he will, but should he choose the ultimate vengeance, he must kill them both (8.20.1). The dramatic works, thus, are the escenification of the assertion of a constitutionally codified right that was seen as morally questionable.[49] Calderón, particularly, holds those legally sanctioned honor killings up to the light, as the jealous husbands in his three plays kill, in total, three wives and two lovers that the audience knows are innocent. The only lover left alive is a noble of greater social rank than the putatively wronged husband, and therefore is not slain due to prohibitions on violence against one of higher social rank. Not staged by Calderón in these plays is the other viable contemporary legal option for the male who felt wronged: he could have issued a "Pardon for Cuckolding" to forgive and forget whether for love, religious scruples, or benefit to be paid.[50] One template collection for legal scribes includes the requisite *Perdón de cuernos* to be prepared in such a situation (Díaz de Valdepeñas, f. 42r).[51] Another contemporary writer, Francisco de Quevedo, writes biting satire to criticize this particular social norm: "And another thing, seeing that this matter of cuckolds is becoming so honorable and profitable ... we propose that it be made a profession, and that no one be allowed to practice it without a full examination and approval."[52] The constitutional question at issue in these matters is personal sexual freedom, a legal right that, in Spanish legislation, would only be recognized fully in 1978.[53]

Social concerns with specific privileges and transgression of the outward signs of status and condition were the focus of laws that would repeatedly prove unenforceable, yet become more and more common under Phillip II in the last third of the sixteenth century.[54] Sumptuary laws disallowed brocade, textiles woven with gold or silver thread, adornments of various types, and all clothing woven with pearls, amber or precious stones (*Recop.* 7.12.1). There were precise details on what could be worn by whom: brocade was only for the royal family or over armaments by those going to war (7.12.1, para.2), metallic threads were *verboten* to all (7.12.1, para.3) yet a little bit of silk adornment was fine (7.12.1, para.4). Women who earned a living with their bodies were singled out for restrictions on clothing both outside and inside their homes (7.12.1, para.13), and theatrical troupes were limited on stage just as all others were on the street (7.12.1, para.12). After six months in the country, foreigners were to be bound by the same sumptuary laws as natives (7.12.1, para.17). One hundred and twenty strict regulations governed the preparation, weave, dye, and sale of fabrics (7.13.1–120), with further declarations on how those laws were to be interpreted (7.14–16). These proscriptions were routinely ignored by the populace at large and by Spain's creative authors, who describe servant girls "dressed all in gold, with strands of pearls, diamonds, rubies, and brocades of the richest sort,"[55] or the father of a family wearing "a purple tunic threaded with gold and a suit of red brocade."[56] The duchess in the Second Part of the *Quijote* rides on a "silver saddle"[57] prohibited by law (*Recop.* 7.12.2, para. 3), although the "tawny velvet overcoat" (II, 16, 561)[58] worn by the same novel's Caballero del Verde Gabán is fine for a "man of letters" (*Recop.* 7.12.1, para. 6). In 1602, court chronicler Luis Cabrera de Córdoba described a royal event to celebrate a wedding, noting that although the monarchs and the happy couple dressed in conformance with the sumptuary laws, the rest of guests were in clear violation (1857, January 5, 1602).[59] In fictional venues, both textual and theatrical, Spanish authors consistently portrayed social resistance to such regulation of personal behaviors. Within two weeks of passing his own reforms and reinforcement of the sumptuary laws on March 1, 1623, Phillip IV had to declare them null and void for a period of two weeks to allow the necessary pomp and circumstance during a court visit by the Prince of Wales.[60] By 1869, the author of a dictionary of administrative terms called the sumptuary legislation "unfortunate," alleging that as it attempted to control displays of luxury, it did much to decimate agricultural and industrial production on Spanish soil.[61]

Other early modern Spanish laws mandated allowable behavior at, and spending on funerals, including permissible mourning clothes: "no black-hooded gowns, whether worn open or closed" (*Recop.* 5.5.2). First promulgated in 1565, this stipulation was also ignored, then reissued in 1593 (*Recop.* 8.26.21). Apparently mourners had begun to appropriate the dress of scholars and the religious, for whom such gowns were the sign of their status and condition. There were also repeated prohibitions on women covering themselves (*las tapadas*) so as to be unrecognizable on the street. Calderón's protagonist in *La dama duende* escapes her brother's keen eye by doing just that, as do a whole raft of women in plays and novels. Other laws were equally restrictive of personal behaviors. In 1565, those who could afford servants were ordered to limit the number: "We hereby order that no Grandee, nor Knight, nor any other person of any status, condition, and preeminence whatsoever, whether it be man or woman, may be accompanied by more than two lackeys or footmen, and anyone who is so accompanied will pay 20,000 maravedís for each infraction" (*Recop.* 6.20.1). Also routinely ignored, and reissued in 1593 (*Recop.* 8.26.21), this law is flouted by Cervantes in *Don Quijote*, as he describes the "six maidens" who serve his protagonist as pages in the castle of the Duke and Duchess (2005, II, 31, 668),[62] or the "four maidens" who come to shave him in the next chapter (II, 32, 676).[63] Subsequent monarchs would increase the allowable number of servants but also complain about evasion of the law through the invention of new titles for those servants, specifically the addition of diminutive endings to insist, for example, that a *lacayuelo* (footman-uelo) was not a *lacayo* (footman) (*Recop.* 6.20.6). The *Quijote*'s Duke and Duchess themselves go hunting with "as many hunters and huntsmen as might be allowed a king" (II, 34, 690).[64] Who may hunt, and how, was another constant concern throughout the sixteenth century. The excesses of the hunting party of Cervantes' Duke and Duchess have been noted, but apparently they are not in violation of a law that might have existed, had it not been rejected by Phillip II in 1563, when Court attorneys asked that the number of dogs allowed to a party of hunters be limited to four because canine excesses were "destroying the hunt" (*Cortes de Madrid*, 1563, chapter 124).[65] Phillip rejected the petition and thus the Duke's hunting party, with its "great noise, shouting and yelling, such that one could not hear the other, as much for the barking of the dogs as for the sound of the trumpets" (II, 34, 690),[66] is in full compliance with all extant law.

The same monarch's jurists singled out one group, "women who earn a living with their bodies," as a particular focus for control of perceived excess. In 1575, such women were forbidden to have lady's pages to serve them, denied any female servants under the age of forty, prohibited from bringing cushions to sit on in church, and barred from wearing religious scapularies or habits (*Recop.* 8.19.7). Earlier collections had expressed more immediate concerns with religious persons having secular sexual relationships with such women: the seventh-century *Fuero Juzgo* prohibited clergy from having women (3.4.18),[67] and the *Siete Partidas* mandated that should those women exist, they were to wear a sign in the form of a three-finger wide scarlet cloth outside their outermost garment (1.3.21, 22).[68] Variations in laws regarding clergy and women dating from 1487 through 1502 demonstrate consistent, if frustrated, attempts to prevent those unions (*Recop.* 8.19.1, 96, 97). By the end of the sixteenth century, apparently, the concern had become a simple problem of "women who earn a living with their bodies" having lady's pages and bringing cushions to sit on in church. These prohibitions were also routinely flouted and the law, repromulgated to little effect (8.26.21).

In short, attempts by Phillip II to control personal behaviors that would seem immaterial or at least peripheral to governance repeatedly failed. The people ignored lifestyle proscriptions issued by the Court, and creative authors openly mocked them. The same public and its writers would, however, side with the monarchs in regard to an actual governance matter, by helping them reduce the power of the nobility, thus paradoxically strengthening the same central power that was attempting to erode their own personal protections under the law.

SYSTEMS OF GOVERNANCE AND ABUSE OF POWER—COLLECTIVE PROTECTIONS

An early seventeenth-century play frequently read as a clarion call for justice and delivery from tyranny by an oppressed town offers a clear perspective on this reconstitution of social roles and its relationship to systems of governance.[69] Lope de Vega's *Fuenteovejuna* is a dramatic rewrite of an historical event that took place in 1476: a *comendador* from one of Spain's Military Orders so abused the townspeople over whom he ruled that they rebelled and murdered him. Whereas the U.S. Constitution prescribes an orderly means of impeaching a renegade government representative, the checks and balances method of the citizens of Fuenteovejuna was the somewhat more violent approach of riot followed by defenestration. Following the act, the town's inhabitants take a collective stance to insist that they all committed the crime, and each individually withstands torture to maintain that posture: "Who killed the *comendador*? / Fuenteovejuna did it!" (vv. 2280–2281). The investigating judge informs the monarchs that he has tortured 300 of the town's inhabitants in an attempt to ascertain the truth but that "Even ten-year old children / subjected to the rack" (vv. 2375–2377) resisted his methods. As a result, the ruling monarchs are unable to blame, ergo punish, any one person. Composed at some point between 1604 and 1618, the play for the most part follows the chronicled events of 1476, although it does differ on certain salient points, notably omitting the townspeople's appropriation of the symbols of juridical power after their overthrow of the tyrant. As María Marín points out, the playwright was a monarchist in favor of the strong central government of his day.[70] Not only did he delete any indication that sovereignty resides in the people, he also asserted that monarchs rule by divine right, an aspect directly at odds with traditional peninsular thought, as reflected in the *Fuero Juzgo*'s specifications for the election of monarchs. Lope's democratization of honor weakened exclusive claims to it by the nobility, much as had the case of the Cid, who accused the *infantes* of "being worthless" (*menos valer*).

The reshuffling of social roles and governmental positions over the course of the preceding centuries is made evident in *Fuenteovejuna*, which ends with the king pardoning the town and asserting his, rather than the military order's, right to control it. The final word is given to one townsperson who praises the monarch's decision, then informs the "senate" or audience that the play has ended. Although the apostrophe to a "senate" is derived from Latin comedic tradition and is not in any sense unique to this play, it is here charged with multiple meanings. The audience judges the townspeople's actions, the king's determination, the playwright's representation, and the social contract of obedience and fealty: the town vows its allegiance to the king while he reasserts his right to eliminate the comendador, or middle man. With this bargain, two parties to the social contract squeeze out a third, who had previously held a powerful hand in matters of social arbitration. Perhaps not a contract in either constitutional sense that one might be read today (i.e., as overt agreement or tacit acquiescence) it is an early modern version of negotiated governance. As Lope presents it, the least powerful of the ruled insisted on change, and the most powerful of the ruling class acceded due to the disciplined persistence of the former. The people spoke and they were heard[71] but their request also, and not insignificantly, allowed the king to assert a writ of *praecipe in capite* (i.e., to take jurisdiction and deforce the *comendador* and the Military Order of their title to the land holding) interestingly an Act specifically prohibited by the 1215 Magna Carta, and by prior legislation on the Iberian peninsula (*Fuero Juzgo* 2.1.5).

The rights of the ruled to not be abused by their rulers had been stated in the peninsula's laws as early as the year 1050, when a court session of the Concilio de Coyanza issued the following as part of its founding charter:

> We order that all earls and royal district judges who rule in towns justly held by the king are not to oppress the poor without regard for justice and their rights, and they are not to take testimony except from one who was eye- or ear-witness [to an act]. And should any false testimony be found, it is to be punished as prescribed in the book of false testimonies. (*Cortes*, Coyanza, law 7, p. 28)

Despite the early date, this is a democratic proclamation: the least powerful (the poor) are not to be forced to give testimony to an act they have neither seen nor heard. The king's response highlights the problem of perjury for the valid operation of the courts, and the mere existence of the law would indicate that such pressure had been applied and a complaint levied. Laws to protect the legal rights of the poor were still being written in the early sixteenth century: in 1525, royal council presidents and judges were ordered to sit on Saturdays to hear legal cases brought by the indigent (*Recop.* 2.5.26), with specific sorting of those cases to allow those already jailed to be heard first (*Recop.* 2.5.27). A 1528 Court petition declares that the encarcerated must be informed of their rights (*Quaderno*, 1528, f. 41r).[72] A sonnet penned in a manuscript titled "Treatise on judgments" advises a tribunal to be even-handed with all, whether "shepherd or courtesan, rich man or beggar" (Figure 2.1).[73]

These laws [and poem] demonstrate concern for the basic constitutional principle of the rights of all citizens: whether charged with a crime or bringing charges against another, Spanish law accorded the people, even poor people, basic rights.

The voices of the powerful, of course, were also heard, if not always heeded. Laws dating from 1367 mandate that the king will sit two days a week to "hear petitions and complaints" from all who come to Court to voice their concerns: on Monday to hear Court officials and on Friday, the encarcerated (*Recop.* 2.2.1). Court registers show

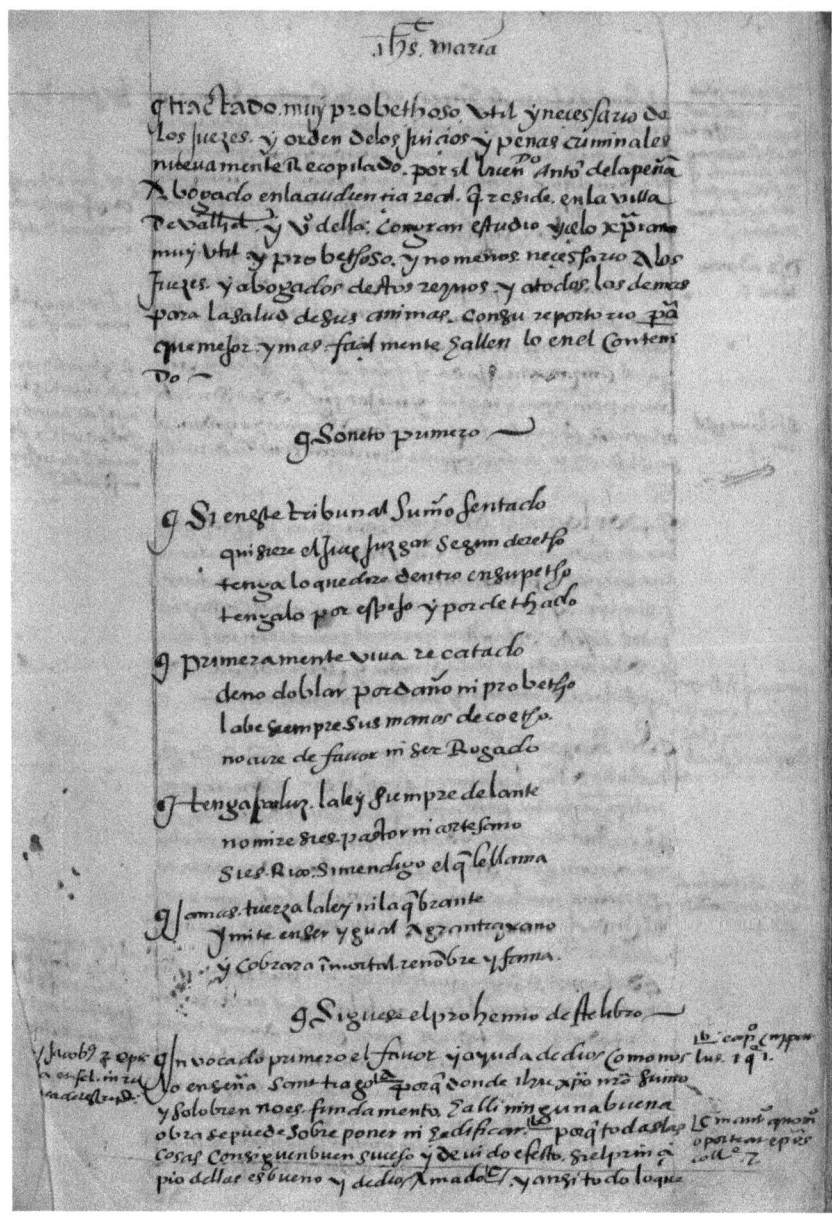

FIGURE 2.1 "First sonnet." In *Tratado de los juicios* by Antonio Peña. BNE, MSS/6379. Source: Courtesy of the Biblioteca Nacional Española.

consistent strategizing on the part of attorneys for the Peninsula's various reigns in these court petitions: during the 1563 Cortes, a request was made that the king's attorneys not attend judiciary council sessions concerning votes on cases in which the monarch was a party, as the practice provided an unacceptable advantage for appeals. Phillip II rejected the request, saying that it was "not convenient to introduce change" (*no conviene que haga novedad*) (*Cortes de Madrid*, 1563, f. 24r). Twenty years later, the same petition is again put forward, and Phillip again responds in the negative (*Cortes de Madrid*, 1583, f. 37r). A different petition first brought to Charles V in 1527, regarding the perceived benefits in de-tenuring university professors, led to an identical court conclusion: it was still being rejected with the same no conviene que haga novedad by his successor Phillip II in 1573 (*Cortes de Madrid*, 1573, ff. 362v–363r). The people spoke and the monarchs listened, but the latter did not always grant the former's petitions. The monarchical constitution held strong against democratic pressure unless, as seen above in *Fuenteovejuna*, it was convenient for the monarch to concede.

As to the general juridical–constitutional status of "we the people" in early modern Spain, the 1568 *Recopilación* clearly ratifies the underlying principle that the law is for everyone, and should be equally manifest to and fair with all:

> The law loves and teaches things that are from God; it is the origen of enlightenment, the instructor of rights and justice, the ordering of good customs, and a guide for the people and their lives. Its purpose is to order, prohibit, punish and castigate. The law is common for men as well as women, of any age and status. It is for the wise as well as the simple, for both inhabited and uninhabited places, and it is the keeper of the king and the people. The law should be manifest, so that every man might understand it and none be deceived by it; it should be appropriate to the land as well as the times, and it should be honest, forthright and beneficial. (*Recop.* 2.1.1)[74]

That pre-Enlightenment ratification of the law's scope and regard for all men has quite a populist tone to it. Perhaps not as drastic a declaration as that penned by Thomas Jefferson in 1776: "that all men are created equal, that they are endowed by their Creator with certain inalienable Rights, that among these are Life, Liberty and the pursuit of Happiness," it nonetheless asserts the constitutional privilege of all citizens to the most basic tenet of equality under the law. An attendant juridical liberty had been confirmed in 1348, in "free will" *fueros* that guaranteed self-rule to the nobility (Salón de Pace f. 69a).[75] Celaya Ibarra stresses that the old laws on the peninsula were laws of freedom and liberty (355).[76] Frequent in theater pieces from the late-sixteenth and early-seventeenth centuries is propaganda in support of the erosion of those formerly guaranteed constitutional protections, by playwrights closely linked to the monarchs and writing for popular entertainment. The play referenced above, Calderón's *El alcalde de Zalamea*, ends with the monarch granting life tenure in his position to the mayor who breached jurisdictional oversight to execute the wrongdoer. As seen earlier in *Fuenteovejuna*, the power equation is again reduced to king and people versus noble class, and the latter always lose.

A second dramatic example of the *vox populi* clamoring for and getting the ruler they want is found in another well-known theater piece, Calderón's *La vida es sueño*. More recognized for the monologues of the protagonist, whose existential doubts stem from his father's having secretly banished him to a hidden dungeon at birth on the basis of astrological predictions of disaster in his future reign,[77] there is a moment in the play when the townspeople first learn that they have a hereditary prince. The people insist that he, rather than the outsider chosen by his father, rule the kingdom. The play's denouement turns on that moment, and the people's choice is proven to be the best ruler. Rather than rid themselves of a middleman who does not govern well, the townspeople in this case insist on a native rather than foreign ruler, despite the king's trepidation about his son's predicted penchant for abuse. Although set in Poland, the message regarding foreign rule also resonates with contemporary concerns about a land closer to home for its peninsular public.⁷⁸ Complaints regarding legitimate rule and foreign rulers had been levied for decades regarding the central state's appointment of rulers in Aragon. A sketch for a non-extant theater piece based on historical events includes a proposed piece of dialogue in which fifteenth-century King Juan II of Aragon cedes land and title to a grandson, "in conformance with the customs and constitutions of Catalonia"⁷⁹ as all details of the ceremonial rite, including a notary to be present and hand over the document, are outlined for presentation on stage. With historical references to the constitutions of particular places common and much debated, theatrical enactments of such socio-political problematics are rich with nuance.

COORDINATION OF KINGDOMS—PERIPHERY VERSUS CENTRAL STATE

Questions of oversight and authority in the peninsula's various reigns were prominent in the sixteenth century. By its end, the concentration of power into the centralized, absolute monarchy had been realized, but there was still much resistance. In 1600, a newly glossed edition of the Visigoth *Fuero Juzgo* was published in Toledo and, in his "Necessary Foreword" to this seventh-century collection of laws, glosser Alfonso de Villadiego notes that some of its mandates were published to be eternally honored, thus "they maintain their first force and effect, and must be observed, especially because the lack of observance was accidental, and not formal" (4–5). One of the democratic principles expressed in this legal code is the election of kings by the people, with a specific note that princely sons do not inherit their fathers' thrones: this is stated in the Prologue: "Princes should be elected," and reinforced in the first law: "In carrying out justice, a King may have the name of King. The ancients have a proverb: King you will be if you carry out justice, and if you do not, you will not be King" (Prologue, law 1). While this might neatly presage Blackstone's later remark that "judges [rather than justice as above] are the mirror by which the king's image is reflected" (270), the following law of the same collection contradicts that jurist's thoughts on princely inheritance rights (?49) ⁸⁰ The *Fuero Juzgo*'s second law affirms that on the death of the king, "another will be elected in Toledo" and the sons of the former will specifically not inherit his throne. Villadiego notes that this process was superseded by the mandates of the *Siete Partidas*, yet his explanatory three-page gloss to the word "elected" includes all arguments in favor of elections. The date of this re-issuance of the *Fuero Juzgo* is telling. The legitimacy of the conquest of Navarre in 1512 was still debated at the end of that century, and remains a strong point of contention today.⁸¹ Within a decade of Celso's recap of the various uses of the term "constitution" in the *Partidas*, Jerónimo Zurita would employ it in a thoroughly comprehensive sense, pairing "constitutions" with privileges, statutes, acts, customs, laws, liberties, and rights. Writing in 1562, Zurita chronicles the annals of events of the Crown of Aragon, distinguishing between the "written laws of the land" and the "general constitutions" of Catalonia, to stress that in 1343, the king of Mallorca was subject to both (III, 538).⁸² In 1588, Phillip II's appointment of a non-Aragonese native to the position of viceroy engendered a lawsuit brought by the Crown of Aragon against the monarch.⁸³ It was answered by Phillip's Attorney General, who identifies himself in the filings as "attorney Valencia, famous lawyer of the Valladolid Chancillery" (Figure 2.2).

Valencia begins with three principle arguments to justify the king's right to appoint whomever he chooses:

First, that as to this action all laws, natural and civil, including the fueros of Aragon, support its legitimacy.

Second, given that no privilege, law, nor custom of Aragon exists that in specie prohibits or is an obstruction to the king's viceroy being of foreign extraction, nor is it stipulated that one must be a native as well as resident of and in the Kingdom of Aragon, since such law does not, nor has been proven to exist, a response will be given

FIGURE 2.2 "Famous attorney" Valencia. Allegation of rights of the king to appoint a non-native viceroy in Aragon, 1590. BNE, R/8525. Source: Courtesy of the Biblioteca Nacional Española.

> to the privilege and laws on which the Kingdom [of Aragon] bases its case and alleges to support its claim.
>
> Third, it will be shown that his Majesty founds his claim on the solid foundations of all laws, and that there is no privilege, law, custom, nor act of the Tribunal of Aragon to the contrary, although the foregoing alone would suffice to support his Majesty's cause. In further support it will be shown that by the same laws of Aragon his Majesty may, and is permitted to put in this Kingdom his own Deputy General, even if he might be a foreigner: and that, the foregoing being true, this has been done and has been the practice in this Kingdom on many occasions. And here a response will be given to that alleged by the kingdom against this existing practice.[84]

With support from multiple authorities, Valencia argues each point at length. Given that Aragon has brought the case and alleges laws in support, he insists, it is incumbent that said acting party produce such laws,

> because it is a legal principal, and also conforms to reason, that he who declares and affirms, be he complaining party or prisoner, that a thing is prohibited, or must not be done, or that someone is incapable of a certain position, must show and place on the record a law, statute, or constitution on which said prohibition might be based. (p. 5)

Valencia supports with specific reference to a full gamut of legal authorities, both civil and canonical, with sources that range from classical Roman to fifteenth-century peninsular. He relies on the negative proposition, "if the law does not specify" (*quod lex non dicit*), to argue against the Aragonese proposition regarding non-appointment of a foreigner to the post (p. 6), quoting the *Digest* to insist that the king is the law (*Princeps legibus [solutus est]*) (p. 22)[85] but not directly alleging the same source's much debated *regula iuris* regarding the force of law as resting in the king's pleasure: "*Quod principi placuit, legis habet vigorem*" (Ulpiano, Digest 1.4.1).[86] Nonetheless, Valencia's conclusion is exactly that: the monarch is free to determine the law in matters of such appointments.

One year later, the defense published its response. Valencia's central idea is identified, and Balduin's commentaries on Justinian's Institutes are directly referenced to refute Valencia's unstated but obvious reliance on the *Quod principi placuit* argument (66).[87] Aragonese attorney Pedro Luis Martínez begins with a review of the roles of kings and people governed: "first, according to natural reason and to the law of gratitude that is born of it, kings are obliged to govern with love and kindness, to benefit their subjects with largesse and liberalness, and to conserve the laws, customs and liberties of their reigns" (f. 2r).[88] With an overabundance of deference and allegiance to the crown yet not giving an inch on the arguments, Martínez echoes the *Fuero Juzgo* to comment directly on how kings get to be kings "through free election" by their subjects (f. 2v). He recognizes the difficulty in bringing a case against the monarch: "because the light of the greatness of his glory must trouble the spirits and tongues of the attorneys of the reign," much as Demosthenes and Theophrastus found themselves incapable on "inferior occasions" (2). He warns that such grandeur has also been know to corrupt judges: "the power of princes has very often corrupted the understanding of great jurisconsults and judges, so that they responded to his [the prince's] wishes, while forgetting the rectitude and indifference that judicature obliges them to guard" (3).[89] With this last, Martínez references Bartolus in the Digest regarding the donation of the Emperor Constantine, along with a host of other authorities, to conclude that the problem is resolved by remembering that "reigns were not instituted for kings, but rather kings for reigns" (4), a proposition for which his sources include Aristotle, Plato, and Cicero. Martínez buttresses his claim against foreign viceroys in Aragon with an assertion made in 1520 by Phillip II's father, Emperor Charles V, that contradicts the king's attorneys on such an appointment (7), and points out that this "imperial confession" was in conformance with a court counsel dictum of October 16, 1482, which stated: "the laws of this kingdom plainly prohibit that a foreign viceroy might rule it" (8). Martínez disputes the sufficiency of the proofs adduced by Phillip II's attorneys (10), references Catholic monarch Ferdinand of Aragon's dying words in support of his part (10–11),[90] and reviews the full history of the founding and rule of the Crown of Aragon, highlighting that laws to live by were made by the Aragonese before they ever "elected" a king (12). Martínez's 426-page response to the king and his attorneys, published in Zaragoza in 1591, is followed by a full index to its arguments (Figure 2.3).

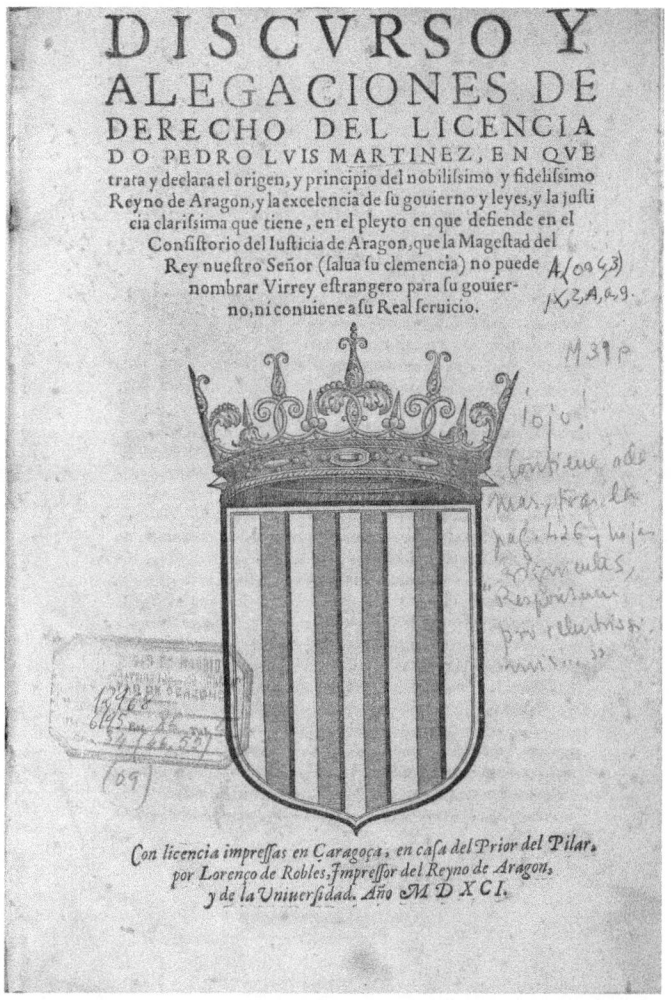

FIGURE 2.3 Pedro Luis Martínez. Response to king's defense, 1591. BH DER 20324 (1). Source: Courtesy of the Biblioteca Histórica Marqués de Valdecilla, Universidad Complutense de Madrid.

The case outlined above demonstrates the continual jousting for power as the peninsula's reigns were "coordinated" into a central state, and the absolute resistance that grew in the face of the developing absolute monarchy. The contentions ranged from matters of rule to processual particulars: in March of 1602, an ambassador from Barcelona complained to the Court of Phillip III that five specific constitutions promulgated by the monarch during the latest court sessions "had not been given in the prescribed form" (Cabrera de Córdoba 141).[91] The monarch charged the Earl of Miranda and the Vice-Chancellor of Aragon with the task of resolving this bureaucratic snafu. Tensions between the central state and Aragon persisted and in 1640, there would be a full revolt against Phillip IV (Elliott; Corteguera 2002).[92] One important point that has not been made is that these juridical debates were easily available to the populace at large. Far from being restricted to the venues in which they were heard, or to the cities and towns in which they took place, legal filings and proceedings of formal court sessions were printed and circulated. The cover of a 1523 printing of Court sessions in Valladolid includes the propagandistic note that "no jurist, nor administrator of justice, should be without this book" (Figure 2.4).

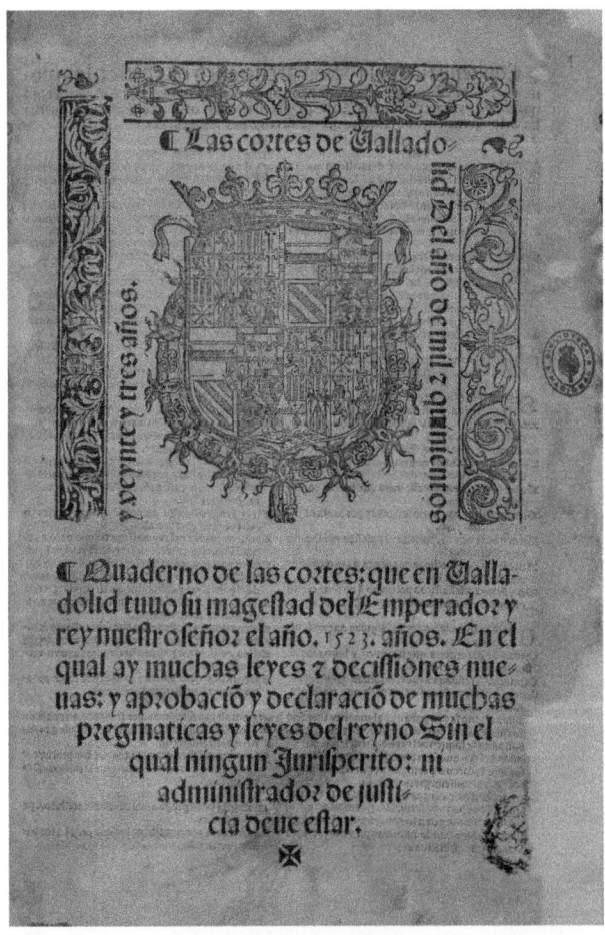

FIGURE 2.4 Cover page. *Quaderno de Cortes, Valladolid.* 1523. BNE R/14090 (1). Source: Courtesy of the Biblioteca Nacional Española.

A 179-folio filing for a different case regarding civil versus ecclesiastical jurisdiction can be found today in more than two dozen libraries worldwide and its subject matter resonates in Miguel de Cervantes *Don Quixote*.[93] Even more importantly, and quite logically given their nature and purpose, these filings were the only printed materials never subjected to censorship. The 1558 law mandating prior approval for publications includes the following exceptions: "the information and filings for legal cases may be freely printed," along with missals, church breviaries, songbooks, hourlies, grammar books, and vocabularies already in print. Eleven years later, an updated 1569 law mandated pre-printing review for all those other texts, while maintaining the exception for filings in lawsuits. The same freedom to print legal writings is preserved in the censorship laws of 1598 and 1610. Witness statements were published and the populace at large was given six days to denounce any perceived false testimony (*Recop.* 4.8.1).[94] Lawsuits and legal arguments were the only freely-circulating reading material at the end of the sixteenth century, people were attuned to their nuance, and creative writers took full advantage of that situation.

Phillip II's changed political direction, from "his father's Christian Imperialism to the pursuit of a more aggressive Universal Monarchy"[95] fed multiple dissenting voices that were heard in court circles and also resonated widely outside of them. Richard Kagan has detailed the intersection of one young woman's unease with Phillip's policies, as learned through court gossip in her native Madrid: a series of related predictive dreams were followed by her imprisonment and questioning by the Inquisition. Concerns for the shape that governance was taking were also frequently expressed on the late sixteenth-century stage, and referenced in novels. The former allowed for speedy airing of concerns, whereas the latter took longer to get to print.[96] Although Watson saw this as a disadvantage to the novel as a means of political expression, authors who wrote in both genres could and did expose the concerns quickly in theater pieces, but also avoid censorship by sprinkling veiled references to them in prose works.

Miguel de Cervantes took full advantage of legal–political topical concerns in both generic forms. His full-length play "La Numancia" has been studied as a critique of Phillip II's expansionist policies.[97] His most celebrated novel, *Don Quijote*, is replete with *sub rosa* legal commentary.[98] In that text, Cervantes implicitly comments the periphery states' political question when his protagonist and squire encounter a Catalan bandit named for an actual historical figure who, in the novel, is praised for his "courtesy and generosity."[99] The same legal privileges that permitted a challenge to the appointment of a foreign viceroy also led, in the eyes of contemporaries, to perceptions of a general sense of lawlessness and proliferation of crime in those regions with their own *fueros*, but in Cervantes' text the Catalan bandit is found to be more like "Alexander the Great than a known crook."[100] When Don Quijote and Sancho Panza leave his company after three days, the narrator sympathetically remarks on the difficulty of such a life with its constant worrying, spying and fear of arrest.[101] In general, in Cervantes' writings, the Catalan question takes on the feel of a wild-west endeavor, and the *bandoleros* of Barcelona are free-spirited lawbreakers of a finer sort.[102] In *La cueva de Salamanca*, one character remarks that he was robbed in Catalonia but that if the bandits' leader had been present, such an attack would have been prevented because that head *bandolero* is "courteous and polite, and besides, he gives to charity."[103] In the *Persiles*, Cervantes describes all Catalans in general as "courteous people" who are at once "angry, terrible, and pacific, calm; people who will easily give up life for honor, but to defend both will go up against even themselves."[104] A more advisory position is offered by a character in Tirso de Molina's novel *Cigarrales de Toledo*: he arrives in Barcelona only to be accosted by two masked men. After slaying one, the other clamors for the authorities as the victim- turned-vigilante runs off, fearing the "Catalan justice" for which the "republic" of Barcelona is well known (314–315).[105] As we saw above, in popular theater the monarch had an ally in his stance against divided power. In prose, however, the messages were more subtle, and mixed. Perhaps not fully demonstrative of Bryce's claim that "Constitutions are the expression of national character, as they in their turn mould the character of those who use them" (4),[106] these creative texts do illustrate the views that contemporaries had of the Catalan character or, better said, characters. Those perceptions directly related to the peripheral governments' insistence on their rights to their own *fueros* and constitutions. Court attorneys for those regions repeatedly requested restoration of those rights but, already by 1579, Phillip II's response is a simple statement that "exigent and pressing" needs have forced his hand regarding changes (*Cortes de Madrid*, 1579, n. 4, f. 3v).[107]

OFFICIALS: ELECTED AND APPOINTED

In addition to references about the constitutions and laws of specific places, more general questions of liberty and equity are common topics in early modern Spanish texts, as they were in contemporary historical and political writings.[108] While such concerns and debates predate to a certain extent the late fifteenth-century translations of Plato's dialogues by Marsilio Ficino, those translations along with the Italian philosopher's commentaries on the texts spurred renewed interest.[109] Of particular concern by the end of the sixteenth century was the question of equity, by that date read as everything from a communal state prohibitive of private property to judicial freedom in granting special favors.[110] Spain's creative writers criticized lawgivers who abused their power, and pointed out that reason of state could be a perversion of justice in particular cases as well as an overriding heavy-handedness in governmental operations.[111] The political–creative representations of republics and their constitutions include specific commentary on the fitness of "the people" to elect, appoint, or function as rulers. In a brief theater interlude, *La elección de los alcaldes de Daganzo*, Miguel de Cervantes stages a farcical situation that had its parallel in an actual court case. The legal challenge in *Daganzo* involved a feudal lord or regent (*señor de vasallos*), the Earl of Coruña, who exceeded his authority by appointing a magistrate of ordinary jurisdiction (*alcalde mayor*) for the town. The earl was condemned for the act in a 1589 ruling (upheld on appeal in 1592) by the Valladolid Chancillery, the first time any such ruling lord had been so rebuked (Castillo de Bobadilla 2.16.74).[112] Castillo de Bobadilla offers two arguments in support of the decision: "first, most of the towns in this kingdom have the right, granted by privilege or custom, to elect their own magistrates for the district courts" (2.16.72)[113] but second and somewhat contradictorily, "only the king has the right to send judges to act at a district court level with the magistrates, even if this might be contrary to the will of the people" (2.16.74).[114] Castillo de Bobadilla adds that neither dukes, earls, marquises nor prelates can interfere with this structure, and that in Daganzo, the error was compounded by the appointed magistrate not having sufficient title or experience for the post.

In the theatrical interlude, Cervantes portrays a perverse example of just such an election of a magistrate by a specific group of people. Four leading citizens of the town examine four candidates for the position, insisting that since there are similar exams for the posts of barber, blacksmith, tailor, and surgeon, there should be a procedure for magistrates as well (vv. 104–12).[115] The candidates are buffoons, their qualities suspect at best, and he who stands out for his logic is the aptly titled Peter of the Frog (*Pedro de la Rana*), who promises to govern with a staff (*vara*) strong enough to resist the weight of coins offered in bribes, and vows to refrain from gratuitously insulting those brought before him to be judged (vv. 189–213). There are comical references to jurists: "I could loan some laws to Lycurgus / and clean myself up with Bartolus" (vv. 181–81), and the interlude ends with a prelate (*sacristán*) who tries to interfere in the election tossed about in a blanket. This farcical commentary on the ineptness of "the people," as represented by the town's juridical best (two Aldermen, one attorney and a scribe), to carry out a democratic procedure might sound tongue-in-cheek to today's reader, but it did have a solid basis in contemporary concerns regarding rulers, the ruled, and elections. Changes in election procedures are notoriously difficult to realize: witness the U.S. Constitution's Electoral College, still in force despite its obsolete nature and obvious failure to uphold the voice of the people in quite recent memory. The unprecedented decision in the Daganzo case shows how a law on the books, ignored for a few centuries as feudal regents were allowed to have their way but suddenly politically valuable for a monarch who wished to undermine those fragile yet customary shared governance systems, could be reasserted and enforced. Possibly not a true critique of competence for self-governance, Cervantes' commentary does highlight, nonetheless, the inadequacies of the juridical elite who might conduct such elections and the suspect qualities of candidates for positions.

The same 1595 manual for magistrates that includes mention of the Daganzo case also offers a detailed list of the qualities and skills of an ideal governor. Castillo de Bobadilla speaks of the optimum age for a magistrate: mature yet also vigorous and strong of body, two characteristics that, as he notes, are not easily found in one man as the first demands experience and the second, youth (1.7.2). The ideal magistrate must be able to withstand the business dealings, pestering, and impertinence of envoys and negotiations, he must have the necessary drive to carefully study the legal cases brought before him, and he must demonstrate "the energy to respond to questions, put down upheavals, look for crooks, patrol at night, always be alert and walk, as it is said, a constant tightrope" (1.7.11). Castillo de Bobadilla laments, but accepts, that the governing official or judge might be illiterate. He states a clear preference for a learned man but also admits that "men without letters tend to be more astute and wiser than those with them," to conclude that since a ruler must deal with all types of men, the best choice just might be the unlettered but astute and naturally wise governor, who can simply hire someone to help him with the written law (2.9.2). The finest representation of just such a governor is found in Miguel de Cervantes' *Don Quijote*, a novel that also includes multiple tongue-in-cheek commentaries on various and sundry political matters.[116] In the 1615 Second Part of the *Quijote*, the illiterate Sancho Panza is given an *ínsula* to govern.[117]

Sancho's lack of letters had previously been put forth as an objection to his possible rule: "those who govern must at least have grammar"[118] says Sansón Carrasco, and Don Quijote warns that "it is unseemly for governors to be unable to read and write,"[119] although the latter, like Castillo de Bobadilla, also recognizes the pragmatic realities of his day: "we know from vast experience that in order for one to govern, it is not necessary that they have much ability, nor many letters, and one can find a hundred [governors] who barely know how to read yet govern in grand style; what matters is that they are well-intentioned."[120] Sancho Panza proves to be so astute in his deliberations and legal judgments that the citizens of his *ínsula* call him "a new Salomon."[121] His reasoning and his "resolute yet discrete determination"[122] greatly impress them, and after complying with all the required acts listed by Castillo de Bobadilla in his manual (negotiations, sitting as judge, patrolling at night, looking for crooks), Sancho leaves the citizens of his *ínsula* with a set of Constitutions (*Las constituciones del gran gobernador Sancho Panza*) that remain, the reader is told, in effect today.[123] Sancho's constitutions prohibit inflationary pricing through re-sale of goods, permit all imports of wine with the caveat that place of origin be clearly labeled to allow proper pricing, threaten the death penalty to anyone who waters down or re-labels said wine, place limits on the exorbitant price of footwear and on the salaries of servants, and mandate certain restrictions on free speech: neither lascivious songs nor unfounded miracles may be sung. Further, Sancho orders a special mayor for the poor, specifying that this is not to persecute those persons but rather to determine if they are truly poor, ergo eligible to beg for alms. Hardly constitutional in the sense the we read the word today, and in all likelihood stated with a strong dose of ironic intent, Sancho's constitutions are nonetheless informative regarding pressing pocketbook-level economic and social concerns of the period. They are all, not incidentally, related to actual Spanish laws of the day: the crown prohibited imported wine but Sancho finds a wiser way to regulate it; certain excessive footwear was banned by pragmatics and a servant could not demand higher wages by negotiating with a neighboring house, but Sancho simply regulates the prices and wages. His constitutions are quite modern in their coordination of economic needs and demands with reasonable controls.

I will conclude this review of expressions of constitutional concerns by early modern Spanish writers with a look at the resonance of that same novel, Cervantes' *Don Quijote*, in the lives and thoughts of the framers of the U.S. Constitution. In 1612, an English translation of the 1605 First Part of the novel was published in London. By 1620, the same year in which the *Mayflower* set sail for North America, a translation of both parts of the novel (1605 and 1615) was available for English-language readers. The *Mayflower*'s pilot, John Clarke, had previously been held captive for five years by the Spanish following a 1611 raid on Jamestown; he was released in a 1616 prisoner exchange for Diego de Miranda. Whether or not Clarke, or any of the *Mayflower*'s passengers had already read or brought the novel along with them is unknown. There are indications, however, that they had some familiarity with it. The *Mayflower*'s captain, Miles Standish, so outraged one early modern British attorney who immigrated to the colonies that the latter penned a satire on the puritans at Plymouth Plantation, comparing Standish to Don Quijote: "the nine worthies comming before the Denne of this supposed Monster, (this seaven headed hydra, as they termed him,) and began, like Don Quixote against the Windmill, to beate a parly, and to offer quarter, if mine Host would yeald" (Morton 1990 [1637], 186).[124]

It would be a surprise if Morton's references were not immediately grasped by contemporary readers. Quixotic imagery was rife in early modern England,[125] and we know that John Locke, who wrote constitutions for Carolina in 1669,[126] was an admirer of Cervantes' novel.[127] The *Quijote* was held in quite a few colonial libraries: Winans finds it one of the most frequently listed novels in American catalogs of books from 1750–1800 (178).[128] Cotton Mather (1663–1728), "the author of the first book written in Spanish in the northern colonies,"[129] references *Don Quijote*[130] and uses the adjective quixotism.[131] Harvard medical student George Alcock, who died in 1676, had the novel in his library,[132] as did Colonel Ralph Wormely when he passed away in 1701 (Libraries in Colonial Virginia 174).[133] Davis lists a number of later library inventories with copies of the novel: merchant Daniel Crawford of Charleston, who died in 1760 (II, 573–574),[134] the Reverend John Green, who passed away in 1767 (II, 575), Dr. John Jackson of Queen Anne's County, deceased in 1768 (II, 533), and "Robert Morris [(1734–1806)], founder of the great financial family" (II, 537). The last is known as the financier of the American Revolution. Davis also lists references to specific details from the novel made by other colonial intellectuals (III, 1380, 1388), and Williams notes that in the late eighteenth century, "Copies of Don Quixote in Spanish, French, or English were to be had in the following libraries, public or private: Redwood, Burlington, Loganian, Harvard [three copies by 1790], Yale [one copy by 1743], Williamsburg" (I, 329, n. 67 to chapter 2).[135] The Library of Congress holds a broadsheet catalog of books to be sold in the Post Office of Williamsburg, Virginia prior to 1760, and Smollett's English translation of the Quijote is among those listed.[136]

Contemporary references by the writers of the U.S. Constitution are even more striking. By the second half of the eighteenth century, English satirists had repeatedly portrayed Cervantes' protagonist spearheading one rebellion after another (Figures 2.5, 2.6, 2.7).

FIGURE 2.5 *The Politician*, 1771, with picture of Don Quixote battling a windmill in the background. Source: Courtesy of The Lewis Walpole Library, Yale University.

FIGURE 2.6 *Captain Bun Quixote attacking the oven*, 1778. Source: Courtesy of The Lewis Walpole Library, Yale University.

FIGURE 2.7 Isaac Cruikshank. *Aristocratic crusade*, 1791, with Edmund Burke as Don Quixote. Source: Courtesy of The Lewis Walpole Library, Yale University.

One of Don Quijote's proclamations in Cervantes' novel has particular resonance for those seeking asylum from tyranny: "Liberty, Sancho, is one of the most precious gifts that the heavens have granted to man; no treasures found on this earth nor hidden in its seas can be equalled to her; for liberty, just as for honor, one should and must risk his life."[137] The echo in Patrick Henry's 1775 cry to the Second Virginia Convention is clear: "give me liberty or give me death!"[138]

Thomas Jefferson's fondness for the *Quijote* is well known:[139] this founding father recommended that his children learn Spanish, and his idea on how best to do so was to read Cervantes' novel. In epistolary exchanges with his daughter, he questioned her progress in the novel: "How many pages a-day [do] you read in Don Quixote? How far are you advanced in him?" (Jefferson to Mary Jefferson, April 11, 1790); "I read in don quixote every day to my aunt and say my grammar in spanish" (Mary Jefferson to Jefferson, May 23, 1791).[140] As for George Washington, he "bought his first copy of Don Quixote on September 17, 1787, the very afternoon on which delegates at the Constitutional convention signed the U.S. Constitution."[141] Washington had two copies of the work, one in English and the other in Spanish, this last a present from Spanish ambassador Diego de Gardoqui in 1787: "I cou'd have wish'd it was in English for your particular entertainment, but it being reckoned the very best Edition of that celebrated work & one in which every thing has been manufacture[d] in Spain induces me to request your acceptance" (Gardoqui to George Washington, November 9, 1787).[142] Benjamin Franklin praised the high quality of the four-volume Ibarra edition published in Madrid in 1780, apparently on the basis of his copy of the novel.[143]

In the years following the U.S. Revolution, the American founding fathers also made good use of quixotic imagery: "I never can think of a Wind-mill, but what Don Quixote, comes into my mind. He used to fight Wind-mills, and if his Head, had not run so much upon fighting, perhaps he might have built them. There is no great difference, between the two projects" (Adams).[144] Jefferson conceived the project of the United States in similar terms, in a letter regarding common law and the Sedition Act: "but good heavens! Who could have conceived in 1789 that within ten years we should have to combat such windmills."[145] Sancho Panza's *ínsula* and *constituciones* also figured in these discussions, albeit in a more pragmatic sense. Nathaniel Irwin wrote to congratulate James Madison on his new post as Secretary of State and added: "On this occasion I would remind you, that 'you were once my friend.' Do not be alarmed. I am not going to ask your influence with the President, that I may be promoted to an embassy or the government of an Island, like Sancho."[146] Notwithstanding that assurance, Irwin goes on to do just that, asking Madison for a job for Irwin's son. James Monroe described to Jefferson his own response to the offer of a political post: "As I had not expected such a proposal, I was somewhat surprised at it, and rather embarrassed how to answer it. The answer given by the King of Prussia to Count Saxe, when he offer'd him the Island of Barbadoes, occurr'd to me, that he must find another Sancho for his Baritaria."[147] In a letter to his wife, John Quincy Adams describes the beginning of the theater season in Ghent, criticizing a company for its bad actors with one exception: a talented singer who sadly, he writes, had the physical aspects of Sancho Panza.[148] The only positive commentary about Sancho found in these various epistolaries deals directly with his constitutions. In 1781, William Jackson writes to John Adams about the return of Adams' son Charles to North America. Noting that Charles is reading the *Quijote* in French, Jackson adds: "if Sancho's principles of government equalled the Constitution of Massachusetts, Charles might soon emulate his Sire as a Law giver."[149] It was Adams, of course, who counseled that all local governments have constitutions and who wrote that of Massachusetts, the oldest still in force today, and the model for the U.S. Constitution. It is clear that the first modern novel shaped the thinking of the designers of the first modern constitution. Using Andersen's phrasings, the "reading coalitions" (79) of the Thirteen Colonies modelled their own "popular linguistic nationalism" (109) on the most quixotic of ideals: battling a windmill of one's own imagination, and successfully governing an *ínsula* despite all the odds. The penchant of intellectuals in the United States for the *Quijote* would continue unabated.[150] Scholars of the cultural aspects of constitutions speak of them as "expressions of national character"[151] or "national values" and "identity."[152] If one accepts the idea of a national character, this would lead to the conclusion that the U.S. Constitution, inculcated with the quixotism of its designers, has created a nation of Quijotes, tilting at windmills and insisting on the uncompromising validity of an individualist perspective. Frankly, this does not seem too much of a stretch.

In sum, the absolute monarchy forged in Spain in the early modern period led to a loss of constitutionally guaranteed individual and collective rights that had been respected and protected for centuries. Most of the serious and creative texts referenced above offer reactions to that loss of constitutional privileges and priorities in the voices of individuals who resist and rebel, or who aid and abet in that process. Nonetheless, as the Spanish government was establishing restrictive structures of governance that limited constitutional and individual rights, one Spanish author penned a text that called in no uncertain terms for the guarantee of just those human rights, protections, liberties, and freedoms, and that novel would become a clarion call for those crafting incipient democratic constitutional models. The most poignantly modern of early modern thought on constitutions is beautifully illustrated in the enduring principles of justice and liberty called for by, and personified in, the protagonist of Cervantes' *Don Quijote*.

CHAPTER THREE

Codes

Redressing London—Sumptuary Laws and the Control of Clothing in the Early Modern City

SOPHIE PITMAN

On January 24, 1565, Richard Walweyn was apprehended in the City of London. He was immediately brought before the Court of Aldermen, his case the first order of the day. While Walweyn awaited punishment, the court scribe jotted down details of the crime in the official repertories: wearing "a very monsterous & outraygyous great payre of hose."[1]

While precise details of the offending leg garments escape the historical record, Walweyn had transgressed the 1562 clothing proclamation which attempted to curb the fashion for the stuffed and decorated stockings that had "crept alate into the realm to the great slander thereof."[2] This edict was one of many attempts made in the Elizabethan era to restrict the consumption and wearing of dress. As a servant, Walweyn was prohibited from wearing velvet, taffeta, or satin hose, or overstuffed legwear (Figure 3.1). Whether Walweyn's "outraygyous" hose were too sumptuous, too voluminous, or both, the Court of Aldermen went to some pains to punish him. First, they stripped Walweyn of his hose, which were to be held up "in some open place," where any passer-by would see his "example of extreme folye." Walweyn was detained until he could purchase a new pair of "decent & lawfyll facyon & sort accordynge to the form of the quenes highness proclamacyon." His presumptuousness in wearing hose above his status was a lesson to the people of London. Walweyn escaped long-term incarceration or a fine, but he had been redressed by the city.

This chapter will explore how Londoners were *redressed* in accordance with the law during the Elizabethan period. It will challenge notions that sumptuary law was no more than an historic peculiarity and will argue that the cultural importance of dress and its repeated entry into the law is important for an understanding of the cultural history of Europe. It will investigate the forms that sumptuary legislation took in England, tracing its roots in medieval law and plotting the Elizabethan use of proclamations before a final repeal of legislation in 1604. Furthermore it will argue that the control—or rather, the attempted control—of clothing did not end with the repeal. Most importantly, this chapter, focusing on London, will challenge recent claims that sumptuary legislation was not enforced. Early modern English dress code was established and developed through a combination of laws, moral and social pressures, and markets that sometimes promoted but often limited innovative fashions; masters and ministers controlled clothing, as well as magistrates.

FIGURE 3.1 Mor's Gentleman was clearly of noble enough status to proudly wear such stuffed hose in his portrait. Their style, size, and shape might have been similar to those worn and removed from the servant Richard Walweyn. Antonis Mor, Netherlandish, (1519–1576), *Portrait of a Gentleman*, 1569, oil on canvas, 119.7 x 88.3 cm. Source: Courtesy National Gallery of Art, Washington, DC, Andrew W. Mellon Collection, 1937.1.52.

Sumptuary code focused on tangible, multisensory things, so this chapter will refer to extant garments demonstrating that clothing's allure—and its danger—lay in its materiality.

LONDON AND URBAN GROWTH

With better technology, the arrival of the printing press, and advancing methods of trade and transport, an ever-increasing variety of goods were being produced and consumed across early modern Europe. As trade expanded, urban centers grew—few more so than

London. As London's population grew sevenfold, from approximately 50,000 in 1550 to 350,000 by 1650, the city spilled out from its ancient walls, placing increasing pressure on city services.[3] London waxed richer thanks, in part, to her role in the international clothing trade. The river Thames bustled with fabric-laden vessels carrying finished textiles and raw materials for manufacture—including silks, threads, dyes, and calicoes—which comprised over half of all exports into the city. London paid for these luxurious textile imports from her lucrative export of woolen goods, which accounted for approximately 90 percent of export trade throughout the period.[4] The clothing industry incorporated Londoners of all social groups. Over a fifth of the population was involved in clothing manufacture, not counting the Londoners involved in leather manufacture and trade, or clothing merchants and shopkeepers.[5] Migrants flocked to the city to gain employment, which transformed it into a wealthier, more diverse center of trade and exchange. New shopping spaces such as the Royal Exchange were built, and as inhabitants grew richer and were exposed to an ever-increasing range of goods, new fashions developed and circulated.

In London, textiles were particularly important in economic and social terms. The cloth trade enriched London's growing merchant class; some of the very Aldermen who punished Walweyn for his illegal hose were lining their own pockets from the profits of clothing exports and imports. Elizabethan London, previously a peripheral locus of the textile trade, was becoming a prominent player in the global market. Clothing laws, anxieties, and tensions must be understood in relation to this seminal shift. Clothes were of personal economic importance to their owners. Not simply textiles to keep the wind, rain, sun, or snow off the backs of their wearers, clothes were a material store of value and a way of communicating identity.

LIVERY

When Walweyn entered court, he came face-to-face with London's leading men. Throughout Elizabeth's reign, the Court of Aldermen was made up of twenty-six men, one from each of the city's wards, who had risen through the ranks of the trade guilds and paid substantial sums of money to acquire the position.[6] The Aldermen had a visible presence on the city streets, wearing fine red or violet gowns, which marked out their office in processions and official ceremonies. In 1622, John Earle praised a London Alderman, "He is Venerable in his gowne ... wherewith he setts not forth so much his owne, as the face of a City ... His Scarlet gowne is a Monument, and lasts from generation to generation."[7]

This praise helps to explain why clothing was subject to regulation in early modern London. Earle's Alderman loses individual identity when he wears his gown and becomes the city personified. His gown is understood as a civic "monument," which will outlive the Alderman himself. Here, a garment is not just a powerful sign of office; it *is* the office.[8]

This power is explicit in the meaning of the term "livery." From the late twelfth century, livery referred to the payment of dependents in food, lodging, and clothing.[9] Early modern London was a livery economy, with many members of society such as apprentices and servants being paid in some combination of cash, housing, food and apparel. The word "livery" increasingly referred to the clothing itself, not only as payment, but also as uniform or a badge of office. London's trade guilds were known as "livery companies" and were so closely allied with their ceremonial garb that it was synonymous with the membership; when a Londoner became a member or freeman of the city, he was said "to be clothed."[10]

Under the authority of the Lord Mayor and in conjunction with the 212 members of the Common Council, the Aldermen controlled London. Court business often focused on London's services and the pressure of the expanding city: the need for cleaner streets, avoiding the plague, and controlling migrant workers. But the Alderman were also beneficiaries of London's growth. By custom, they had to be members of one of the twelve great livery companies; in practice, the majority also belonged to the cloth-exporting Merchant Adventurers. As key members of the livery companies, they benefited from economic, legal, and political privileges in regulating and controlling the craft trades.[11]

The Court of Aldermen policed the correct use of livery. John Aldriche was imprisoned for wearing the livery of the Lord President of Wales "being not his servant."[12] In 1562, a minstrel by the name of Sherman was apprehended in Bishopsgate ward for "wearing velvet in his dagger shethe contrary too the forme of the Statute." Sherman claimed to be a servant of Lord Windsor but when examined by the Court "did plenly confesse that he had neither mete drink wage or livery of hym."[13] Sherman then stated that Lord Windsor had allowed him to wear livery if he paid for the clothing himself, suggesting it was not a negative marker of servitude. An individual might aspire to wearing the sumptuous livery of a superior, even paying for its purchase himself.

DANGEROUS STUFFE

While livery culture connected nobles, Aldermen, and servants alike to a medieval hierarchical culture, the early modern period witnessed a great shift in access and attitudes to clothing. Walweyn was not the only man to have his hose scrutinized at court. In his *Anthropometamorphosis* (1653), John Bulwer relates the story of

> a Prisoner ... who being to go before the Judge for a certaine cause he was accused of, it being at that time when the Law was in force against wearing Bayes stuffed in their Breeches, and he then having stuffed his breeches very full, the Judges told him that he did weare his breeches contrary to the Law: who began to excuse himselfe of the offence, and endeavouring by little and little to discharge himselfe of that which he did weare within them, he drew out of his breeches a paire of Sheets, two Table Cloaths, ten Napkings, foure Shirts, a Brush, a Glasse, and a Combe, Night-caps, and other things of use, saying (all the Hall being strewed with furniture) your Highnesse may understand, that because I have no safer a store-house, these pockets do serve me for a room to lay up my goods in.[14]

This comic tale of a man pulling his belongings from between his legs at an ever-quickening pace mocks the fashion for overstuffed breeches while showing the widespread delight in "stuffe." The increasing availability of "wordly goods" has been studied by historians, many of whom find a proto-consumer society in Renaissance Europe.[15] The prisoner's stuffing fulfilled the dual purpose of padding out his breeches into the fashionable shape and safekeeping his belongings. His attachment to these possessions was so "accepted and well laughed at" that the court decided not to prosecute.

For all the joy that these new "things"—from humble combs and linens to delicious spices, bright silks, decorated ceramics, and stimulating coffee—brought to consumers, governments and rulers were anxious about their economic, social, religious, and cultural impact. Objects filled courtrooms, as governing bodies issued "sumptuary laws" in an attempt to control the purchasing and use of certain goods. Such laws were passed in virtually every type of political system across medieval and early modern Europe, in centralized states as well as cities and communes and in both Catholic and Protestant societies. These laws took many forms, from limiting the number of guests at a Paduan feast, to demanding that Nuremberg men should not part their hair in the center of their heads.[16] What we now understand as "sumptuary legislation" (from the Latin word *sumptus*, meaning expense) encompasses a diverse range of laws that controlled food, ceremonies, appearance, and dress, and each law and location deserves its own historical inquiry. For, as we shall see with the English laws, legislation and policing took on a local character that had as much to do with regional trades, economic fluctuations, and the relationship between lawmakers and law enforcers, as it did with larger questions of social status, hierarchy, and the moral status of luxury. Cultural attitudes and local circumstances shaped the laws and their implementation. Not all sumptuary legislation was concerned with clothing, and not all legislation about clothing was concerned solely with expenditure. This chapter will investigate laws about clothing, many of which could be defined as "sumptuary" laws, but some of which were economic and protectionist, and others local in focus.

THE LAWS IN ENGLAND

Controlling dress through law was not a new phenomenon in Elizabethan England. The first English statute of apparel, issued in 1337, prohibited fur and foreign cloth for all but the most elite. Subsequent acts appeared in 1363, 1463, 1483, 1510, 1515 (twice), 1533 and 1554, each specifying textiles prohibited to those lower down the social order. Elizabeth herself did not pass any statutes; her authority rested upon the 1533 and 1554 Acts, to which she repeatedly referred. Elizabeth's legal involvement in sumptuary legislation was more urgent and insistent than any other English monarch. She passed twelve proclamations relating to the statutes of apparel during her reign, more than any other ruler before or since, the first of which was announced less than a year after her coronation.[17] In addition, Elizabeth issued six proclamations regarding the making of caps, following the successful passage of the 1571 Cappers Act.[18]

Elizabethan proclamations often extended earlier statutes by adding new regulations and amendments to include new fashions such as ruffs and large hose or to introduce allowances or prohibitions to new sections of society. Women, for example, had been exempted from sumptuary legislation in 1514, but in 1574 Elizabeth imposed restrictions upon them, in line with their familial status.[19] Although she purported in the 1574 proclamation to refer to the 1533 Act, limitations on women had no precedent there.[20] Elizabeth's sumptuary proclamations were based, therefore, on the authority of statutes passed during the reigns of Henry VIII and Philip and Mary, and upon the royal prerogative.

Few members of the English population would have had the opportunity to hear their monarch speak, but through the proclamations, English subjects could access the thoughts and voice of the Queen herself. For this reason, proclamations held a certain power and aura. Their announcement was accompanied by a great deal of ceremony, often including local dignitaries processing on horseback. In London, proclamations were read aloud to reach the illiterate population in various busy locations (many of which were important areas of clothing retail) such as the great cross on Cheapside, St. Magnus in Fish Street, Leadenhall, the conduit in Fleet Street, and Lombard Street. For

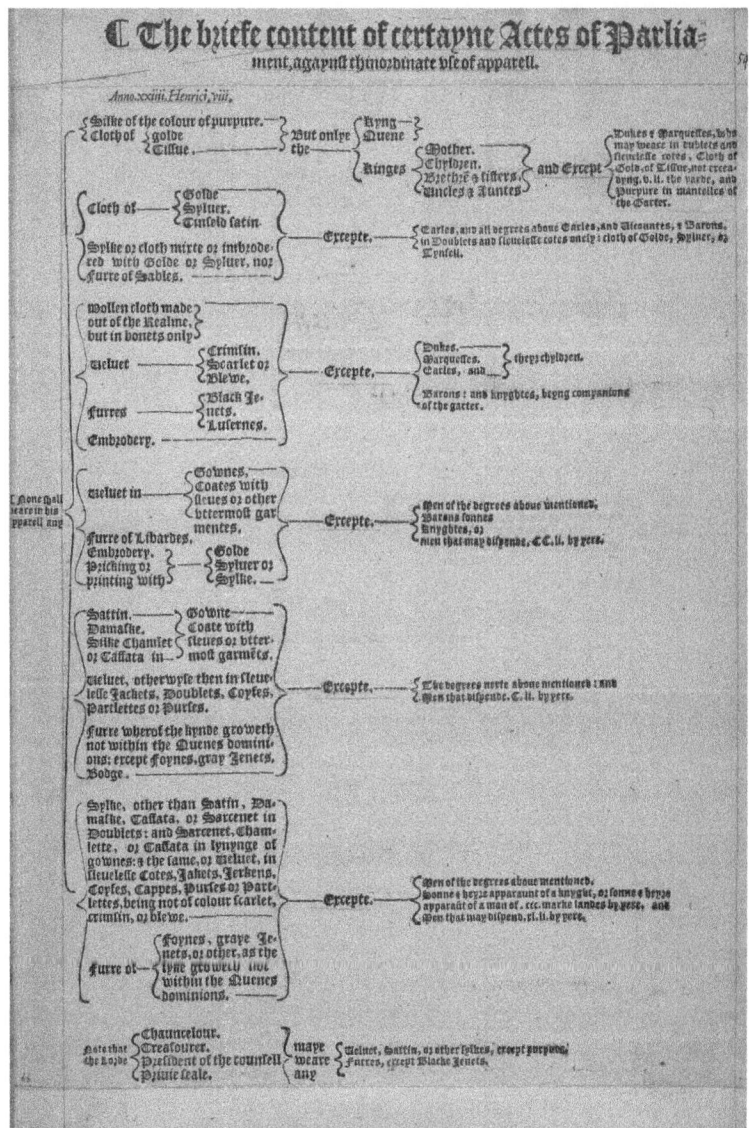

FIGURE 3.2 Even for the illiterate population, these tables showed clearly that clothing and social status were hierarchical. "The brief content of certayne Actes of Parliament" from 16 February 1577 Proclamation Enforcing Statutes of Apparel (London: R. Jugge, 1577). Source: G.6463.(205), page 54. ©The British Library.

those who could read, the proclamations were printed on parchment by the Queen's printer, and then mounted on posts throughout the city to remind Londoners of their obligations (Figure 3.2).[21]

Rule by proclamation was a tactical and practical approach. Despite at least five attempts to introduce new bills during Elizabeth's reign, efforts to issue new statutes of apparel were unsuccessful in both the Houses of Commons and Lords.[22] One case reveals why the Commons put up significant resistance to Elizabeth's attempt to push a bill through Parliament in March 1575. While the Commons agreed "disorder of apparrell is very greate in this tyme," they posed five objections. Some regarded the proposed punishments as too harsh, or worried that subjects would not be given enough time to reform their wardrobes, but the most critical question focused on the legislative power that the Crown would gain from passing the bill. One member summed up: "Th' effect of the bill was that the Quene's Majestie from tyme to tyme might by her proclamacion appoynt what kynde of apparrell every degree of persons within the realme should weare." This might, it was feared, "prove a dangerous precedent in tyme to come."[23] When James I took the throne, he repeated this attempt to rule by proclamation, and started by wiping the legislative slate clean, repealing all former apparel laws. In 1604 his bill was sent from the Lords to the Commons, but failed on first reading. Only one clause passed: the repeal of former apparel acts. Sumptuary acts ended in England not because of the failure to police the laws, or because the ruler recognized them as ineffective. Rather, they ended because they became bound up with questions about royal authority.[24]

Dress was not only controlled by statute and royal proclamation. In London, the Courts of Aldermen and Common Council, with the authority of the Lord Mayor, tackled civic issues by taking matters into their own hands. For example, seven years after sumptuary laws had been finally repealed, a Common Council Act prohibited all apprentices from wearing "strange fashion of Apparrell" such as ruffs of over three yards in length "before it be gathered & sett into the stocke nor two inches in depth" or hats broader than three inches, lined, faced, or tufted with velvet, silk or taffeta, or that cost above five shillings. The 1611 Act limited the fabrics of apprentices' doublets, hose, cloaks, coats and jerkins, and stated that gloves had to be plain and not worth above twelve pence a pair. Silk or ribbon garnishing, girdles, points, garters, and shoestrings—any "suchlike toyes at all"—were prohibited. Spanish leather shoes or those "with Polonia heels" were likewise forbidden. Rather, apprentices were charged to be "contented with suche decent Apparrell as is fittinge & their Masters well able to afford to them."[25] A clause was later inserted stipulating that hair must be "cut short in decent and comelie" with no fashionable "tuft or lock."[26] The master would "admonish & rebuke his apprentice" for a first offense. A second offense was dealt with more harshly, and both master and apprentice suffered. The apprentice would be taken to "Little Ease"—a prison in the Guildhall too small to stand upright in—for at least eighteen hours, while the master would be fined the hefty sum of three shillings and fourpence for each day that the apprentice had dressed inappropriately.[27] The fine was split between the parish and the informant.[28] Londoners were expected to take care of their own clothing issues.

SUMPTUARY STUDIES

As Ulinka Rublack has noticed, sumptuary legislation across the early modern world has been "chronically understudied." For Rublack, the lack of scholarly investigation is explained by the breadth of sources the sumptuary historian must explore; "this involves more than looking at ordinances. It implies the much more laborious task of reconstructing the implementation of these laws through council minutes and court records in different cities and territories, and also of finding out what garments, fabrics and accessories exactly were referred to."[29] Scholars who have explored sumptuary laws often dismiss them as ineffective, odd, and a barrier to modernity. G. R. Elton deemed them "peculiar" and "extraordinary" and, for Lawrence Stone, debates on apparel in the Commons were "absurd."[30] Even while pioneering the study of clothing for social and economic historians, Daniel Roche allied sumptuary laws with a "sartorial *ancien regime*" marked by "inertia and immobility" and "conformity to custom."[31]

In contrast to Roche, Alan Hunt's unparalleled survey of sumptuary legislation connected the laws to the emergence of a proto-modern urban society in line with Foucault.[32] Sumptuary law, Hunt claimed, "was a response to at least three of the most distinctive features of modernity ... urbanization, the emergence of class as the pervasive form of social relations and the construction of gender relations."[33] A few regional studies have successfully charted the laws and their impress, particularly in the Italian states.[34] The English laws have received several focused studies,[35] although none which attempt to connect them to extant items of clothing.[36] Maria Hayward studied portraits and clothing bequests in wills and found widespread compliance with the laws during the reign of Henry VIII. Hilary Doda, in her study of the laws until 1533, also argued for compliance.

This chapter challenges Roche's claim by arguing that sumptuary legislation did not impose a sartorial "regime" in early modern England, and builds on the work of Hayward and Doda by exploring infractions as well as motivations to comply with the law. Sumptuary laws must be studied alongside other social and economic pressures that prompted Londoners to dress in a particular manner. In letters, reports, and court records, it seems that few ignored or flouted the laws outright. Rather, the law left scope for ingenuity and innovation, and infractions could be the result of individuals exploiting legal ambiguities.

MOTIVATIONS I: SOCIAL DIFFERENTIATION—BREECHES

Sumptuary law in England encoded a widespread belief neatly summarized by the poet Barnabe Barnes in 1606 that, "all garments should be neat fit for the body, and agreeable to the sex which should wear them: in worth and fashion correspondent to the state, substance, age, place, time, birth, and honest custome of those persons which use them."[37] But while a livery culture expected that each individual should express his social status and affiliations through dress, new fashions enabled men and women to stand out from the crowd. And nowhere in England was more crowded, or fashionable, than London.

Over the course of the sixteenth century, the English textile trade had been transformed through the development of "new draperies"—lighter mixed fabrics, often bright, colorful, and highly finished. Tailors developed new techniques to fashion clothing that altered and reshaped the human form.[38] Clothes were no longer just draped and sewn, but stiffenings—often made of non-textile materials such as bombast, card, horsehair, and whalebone—were used to create new sculptural shapes.

The Grimsthorpe and Drummond Castle Trust own one of the few pairs of English breeches or hose to survive from the sixteenth- and seventeenth centuries.[39] Too fragile for display, and undergoing extensive conservation, the hose are no longer mounted with their matching doublet and canions (extensions to hose that taper to the leg). Thanks to costume historian Janet Arnold's close observation and pattern taking, we have a great deal of information about this rare survival of a once popular fashion, offering a sense both of the allure and legal issues of such a style (Figure 3.3). The uncut brown velvet and voided satin were probably once bright mulberry with a detailed design of leaf sprays and curving stems, which have all but worn away. The hose are lined with layers of springy

FIGURE 3.3 Doublet and Trunk Hose with Canions, uncut silk velvet on a voided satin ground, English, *c.* 1604, Grimsthorpe and Drummond Castle Trust. Source: Pencil drawings by Janet Arnold, © The School of Historical Dress, London.

white wool, white fustian, and coarse linen or hemp. Large fustian pockets hang between these two linings, which could be stuffed to further inflate the size of the hose.

When worn, these mulberry hose would have created a striking large round silhouette (Figure 3.1). As Elizabeth had reminded her subjects in the 1562 proclamation, no man under the degree of a baron was allowed to wear velvet or satin, so these hose were only appropriate for nobility. Such ornate velvet was an expensive Italian import. But the London authorities did not only scrutinize the outer visible layer of these hose. The law dictated that only one fabric lining, in addition to linen cloth, be used "next to the leg … as in ancient time was accustomed" and that this lining could not lie loose. There are two layers—fustian and wool—in addition to the linen lining of the mulberry hose, but the tailor worked the velvet outerlining and woolen interlining together. This clever technique forced the breeches to stand away from the leg in the fashionable shape, but whether this would have been allowed within the terms of Elizabeth's proclamation is unclear.[40]

Contemporaries also had trouble making sense of the proclamations. Richard Onslow, the Recorder of London, wrote to Sir William Cecil from his house in Blackfriars in February 1565 in order to ask about this very issue—could "a lynyng of Cotton stytched to the Sloppe, over & besides the lynnen lyning" be permitted within the terms of the proclamation? Onslow reported that the question was on the minds of many hosiers who had asked him for advice. He had answered them that "upon consyderacion of the words of the proclamacion" this was not allowed. But the hosiers returned, reporting that their customers had moved their business to hosiers "dwelling without Temple Barr" who were prepared to include additional lining.[41] Onslow felt it his duty to report to Cecil for clarification so that the London citizens for whom he was responsible may not "be sore hindered & impoverished by losse of ther customers" to "foryners."[42]

The ingenious tailoring in these mulberry hose might have placed their fustian lining (just) within the compass of the law, or perhaps they were made by a hosier from outside Temple Bar, but in cultural terms fustian had something of a negative reputation. In the late sixteenth century "fustian" referred to a cloth made of both cotton and linen threads to resemble velvet, one of the "new draperies" introduced into English manufacture by Walloon and Dutch immigrants. Later it became a reference term for a twilled thick cotton cloth. While the term warped from one kind of cloth to another, by the 1590s it had also acquired the derogatory meaning of inflated turgid language, as did "bombast," another kind of padding for trunk hose and stuffed peascod bellies.[43] In John Marston's *Jacke Drum's Entertainment* (1601), the satiric commentator Planet claims to "hate these bumbaste wits, That are puft up with arrogant conceit of their owne worth," while a barber in Robert Greene's satirical pamphlet was accused of using "fustian eloquence" to flatter his clients.[44] These materials, which enabled the shaping and stuffing of breeches, rapidly became allied with claims of exaggeration, dishonesty, and social pretense.

Clothing had multisensory allure. The prohibited shapes and fine textiles reserved for elites had significant visual and aural impact. When Philip Stubbes described men and women in their finery, he highlighted the sound effects of the fine textiles reserved for nobility in the Statutes of Apparel: "some ... ruffle now in silks, Velvets, Satens, Damasks, Gold, silver and what not else." Stubbes noticed that "it is impossible for a man to weare precious apparrell and gorgeous attire and not to be proud therof." Overstuffed hose physically inflated their wearer, making noise as they moved, allowing them to feel socially superior and make their presence known. As Stubbes put it, "by wearyng of Apparel more gorgeous, sumptuous and precious than our state, callyng or condition of lyfe requireth, whereby, we are puffed up into Pride, and inforced to think of our selves, more than we ought."[45]

In the later sixteenth century fashionable men began to wear pear-shaped breeches known as "Venetians." As fashions changed, accusations of monstrousness shifted from rounded trunk hose to this new style. In the pamphlet, *A Quip for an Upstart Courtier* (1592), a "costly paire" of breeches are not just deemed monstrous, they are mistaken for a "monster." Despite "wanting a body," the breeches are anthropomorphized as an "artificial braggart ... passing pompous in their gestures," their arrogance bolstered by "best Spanish satine." These breeches are likened to a "Florentine" flaunting "up and down the streetes before his mistresse." Their monstrousness lies in their foreignness, visual allure, and social pretension; they are "exceeding sumptuous to the eie" and "pompous."[46] It is important to note that although the frontispiece to *Quip* depicts two men wearing breeches, the pamphlet is about breeches that walk and talk without a body. Clothing is so powerful that it can speak for itself, threaten hierarchies, and challenge identities without even being worn by a person.

These breeches are a metaphor for the city dweller, and they are dismissed by the protagonist in favor of "a plaine paire of Cloth breeches," which remind him of the time of his "great Grandfathers," when "neighbourhood and hospitality had banished pride out of England."[47] As *Quip* suggests, clothing was a scapegoat for London troubles. Londoners were succumbing to "pride," which, in turn, destroyed all social obligations in the form of "hospitality" and community. Sumptuous clothing here embodies anxieties common to London: shifting social status, immorality, and foreignness. This moral must have had some currency in early modern England, for *Quip* went through six editions in its first year of publishing alone.[48]

Clothing was supposed to enable social differentiation. Cloth breeches were for humble countryman, whereas sumptuous velvets were the mark of a courtier. Sumptuary legislation made this belief explicit, creating a hierarchy of fabrics and colors. In a printed copy of the statutes issued with the proclamation in February 1577, this hierarchy is made visible, with a complicated table full of brackets, lists, and exceptions, structured "None shall weare ... except ..."(Figure 3.2). At the very top, purple silk and cloth of gold or tissue are reserved for the king, queen, and their immediate family and—as a final bracket neatly packed just inside the far margin, "Dukes & Marquesses, who may weare in dublets and slevelesse cotes, Cloth of Gold, of Tissue." The table descends through the ranks of the nobility past earls, viscounts, and barons (who may only wear cloth of gold, silver, or tinsel in their doublets or sleeveless coats), past dukes, marquesses, earls and their children, barons, and Knights of the Garter (who may wear crimson, scarlet, or blue velvet, bonnets of woolen cloth made outside of the realm, certain furs, and embroidery) and down to the lesser nobility and men who spend £40 per year (allowed silk other than satin, damask, taffeta, or sarcenet in doublets, and velvet in sleeveless coats, jackets, jerkins, coifs, caps, purses or partlets "being not of colour scarlet, crimson, or blewe.")[49] The vast majority of the population is not included in this table, but they were expected to listen to the proclamations, view the tables in public (where even the illiterate could recognize the tabulated visual hierarchy), and avoid the listed textiles and colors. In preambles to the proclamations, the non-elite were targeted for their transgressions, with the accusation "no sort of people have so much exceeded, or do daily more exceed in the excess of apparel, contrary to the said statutes, than such as be of the meaner sort."[50] As Stubbes protested, "there is such a confuse mingle mangle of apparell in Aligna [England], and such horrible excesse thereof, as euerie one is permitted to flaunt it out, in what apparell he listeth himself, or can get by any meanes. So that it is very hard to knowe, who is noble, who is worshipfull, who is a Gentleman, who is not." This, Stubbes decried, led to "generall disorder in a Christian common wealth."[51]

This visual hierarchy, encoded in law and repeated in literature, was also preached from pulpits across the realm and supported with reference to the Bible. As the "Homily Against Excess of Apparel," (1563) ordered to be sermonized to congregations across England, claimed, "all may not look to wear like apparel, but every one, according to his degree, as God hath placed him."[52]

MOTIVATIONS II: MORAL—RUFFS

Clothing matters infused religious, as well as legal, discussions throughout the early modern world. As Peter Goodrich has argued, as religious leaders across Europe questioned the importance of images and symbols, it is unsurprising that the governance of appearance was closely allied with religious ideology.[53] In Elizabeth's early reign, clothing was at the heart of religious debates and was a significant factor in the emergence of Puritanism as a distinct movement.[54] The "vestiarian controversy," as it has come to be known, erupted over disagreements about the appropriate rites, ceremonies and apparel for clergy; in short, how English Protestant ministers should dress.[55] Debates centered on whether the ecclesiastical garments established in the Roman Catholic medieval church were appropriate for a post-reformation Church of England. Many English ministers, particularly those returning from Marian exile who had seen Continental Protestant clergyman in plain black gowns, associated their old caps, chasubles, and surplices with popery. In 1565, in response to "open and manifest disorder," Elizabeth commanded Archbishop Parker to restore "uniformity of order" in church dress. Parker responded with a "book of articles" and the *Advertisements* (1566), which demanded that outdoor apparel remain as caps and gowns, and the white alb, chasuble, stole, and cope be worn in Cathedrals and Collegiate Churches, but be reduced to a white linen surplice in parish churches.[56] For many, this was not reform enough. In London, thirty-seven preachers refused to sign their conformity to the *Advertisements*, believing that the garments had the symbolic power to damage the reputation of the church and the confidence of their congregations. As Robert Crowley argued in *A Briefe Discourse Against the Outwarde Apparell of the Popishe Church* (1566), while the material garments "of themselves, they be things indifferent ... when the vse of them will destroy, or not edifie, then ceasse they to be so indifferent."[57] Furthermore, they had a signifying purpose. For just as ecclesiastical garments were intended to distinguish the clergy from the laity, so they should distinguish Protestants from Catholics: "as we wolde haue a diuers shewe of aparel to be knowe[n] from the comon people, so is yt necessary in aparell, to haue a shew, howe a protestante is to be knowen from a papiste."[58] It has been argued that the vestiarian controversy was predominantly an urban issue, only taken up in London, the university cities, and the diocese of Durham.[59] In any case, Elizabethan Londoners witnessed their religious ministers debating in material form the terms of their reformed church and the symbolic power of a physical garment.

Worn next to the skin by all men and women across the social spectrum, linen was the foundation of dress. Easily washable, linens were considered healthy, pure, and clean. But this fabric was not impermeable to controversy. While some shunned the flowing white gowns of the clergy, others were more concerned with the increasingly elaborate linen neckwear in vogue at court and among the urban populace. In the sixteenth century it became fashionable to gather excess volumes of linen at the neck and wrists of the undershirt so that they protruded from beneath the overgarments. Innovative seamstresses added lace or decorative embroidery to these visible edges, and sometimes added another layer of linen to increase the volume of the edge ruffles. By 1562, Elizabeth noticed "the outrageous double ruffs which now of late are crept in" and added them to the list of controlled garments in her proclamation, which declared that "ruffs shall not be worn otherwise than single, and the singleness to be used in a due and mean sort, as was orderly and comely used before."[60]

Ruffs and cuffs quickly became associated with sin. On April 11, 1562, Henry Machyn recorded in his chronicle that "a pyde calf" had been brought to London "with a grett ruffe [about] ys neke." Machyn was not recording some instance of a cow in costume, but rather the birth of a deformed calf with excess skin at the neck, which he regarded as a symbol, or in his words, "a token of grett ruff that bowth men and women [wear]." On May 8, one day after the Queen's proclamation had been announced, it reached Machyn who summarized it in an entry that read simply, "a proclamation of the aht [act] of a-ray, and grett ruffes and grett breechys, and that no man to have butt a yerd and a half of kersey."[61] Not only does this entry show how rapidly news of each proclamation reached the metropolitan population, and that it could be quickly condensed and summarized, it also demonstrates that Machyn regarded these two events significant enough to be included in his chronicle of religious events and local news. The proximity of these two entries in the chronicle almost certainly struck Machyn, a deeply religious parish clerk in Holy Trinity-the-Less, as a religious sign.[62]

A number of children and animals born with "ruffs" featured in popular broadside publications and histories which presented these deformities as evidence of God's displeasure with pride in fashions.[63] John Hayward made this explicit when he described a child born in Chichester with "a collar of fleshe and skinne, pleighted and foulded like a double ruffe, and rising up unto the eares, as if nature would upbraide our pride in artificiall braverie, by producing monsters in the same attires."[64] These monstrous births and the proclamations did little to halt the fashion for large elaborate ruffs, for in the proclamation enforcing statutes of apparel dated February 12, 1580, Elizabeth announced that "no person shall ... use or wear such great and excessive ruffs in or about the uppermost part of their necks as had not been used before two years past; but that all persons should in modest and comely sort leave off such fond disguised and monstrous manner of attiring themselves."[65] Stubbes went a step further when he declared that ruffs had been invented by the devil. Ruffs had become so "great and monsterous," standing "a full quarter of a yarde (and more) from their necks" that, according to Stubbes' character Philoponus, they could not stand up by themselves. The Devil "underpropped" his "kingdom of Pride" with the very supports that held up large ruffs—wire and cardboard underproppers, supportasses, and also a "certaine kind of liquid matter, which they call Starch, wherin the Deuil hath learned them to wash and dive their ruffes wel, which being dry, wil then stand stiffe inflexible about their neckes."[66] In pamphlets, diaries, broadsides, and proclamations, the great size of ruffs particularly attracted attention from ruff critics.

Only a few English ruffs are known to have survived. An extant example now held in the collections of the Rijksmuseum shows the visual effect, scale, and allure of vast amounts of pleated linen (Figure 3.4). Portraits may illustrate how ruffs were worn as part of an outfit, and how they might be pleated, but the sheer materiality of the Rijksmuseum ruff demonstrates that these tactile, soft accessories could be transformed to stiff sculptural neckwear by careful washing, starching, and setting. It is appropriate to use a Dutch example, as both the materials and techniques of maintenance for ruffs were imported to England from the Netherlands. The finest ruffs were made of "holland" linen from Holland, "lawn" from Laon in France, and "cambric" from Cambray in Flanders. According to John Stow, Queen Elizabeth's first starcher was the wife of her Dutch coachman Guillan. In 1564, an enterprising Protestant immigrant from Flanders, "Mistris Dinghen," set up a London-based starching business and taught women to starch and seeth for a fee.[67] That female immigrants, rather than the Devil, introduced ruffs to

FIGURE 3.4 This large ruff is marked with the initials 'CY' in small red silk stitch, probably to ensure its safe return from the laundry. Ruff, c. 1615–1635, linen, h3cm x c38cm, l1950cm x w13cm, Rijksmuseum, on loan from H. G. Rahusen, 1923, BK-NM-13112. Source: Courtesy Rijksmuseum, Amsterdam.

London, indicates something about xenophobia in this period. That the ruff's size was policed tells us much about the motivations for this act of legislation.

Ruffs could be set in numerous different arrangements—one band could be styled in regular figures of eight on one day and irregular soft folds the next, enabling a great degree of experimentation. Starches were sometimes colored blue or yellow to enhance the look of their wearer's complexion, although efforts were made by Elizabeth, James, pamphleteers, and clergy to taint colored starch by associating it with the Scots, the Irish, and treachery.[68] Starch, made from wheat, was a valuable commodity, particularly during times of hunger. Although other materials could be used for cleaning and stiffening linens and other textiles—including milk, gum arabic, glue, and stew made from parchment cuttings—starch was preferred, and was used in vast quantities by domestic staff and professional laundresses alike.[69] Between 1594 and 1601, 600 quarters were sold in London every week.[70] Such rapid consumption provided employment for large numbers of craftspeople, but put strain on grain supplies.

In 1585, William Cecil, Elizabeth's Lord High Treasurer, raged that starch was used "to the setting forth of vanity and pride which would staunch the hunger of many that starve in the streets for want of bread." In response, Cecil issued a monopoly to patentees in 1588 and later prohibited production. Starch-making became illicit and was pursued by an inestimable number of illegal English traders.[71] A ruff of the Rijksmuseum's size—containing 1,950 centimeters of linen—would have absorbed large quantities of starch each time it was washed and reset. It would have needed restarching regularly—after exposure to water (a common problem in rainy London), whenever it became soiled with sweat, cosmetics, or food, or after repeated use. Economic and moral concerns converged in this one garment. The ruff was the target of sumptuary legislation (it being one of the garments added by Elizabeth, not in the original Acts of Apparel), indirect legislation on starch, and attacks from the church and pamphleteers. Yet ruffs and linen falling bands only became more fashionable, and were worn by male and female Londoners from the elite down to young aspiring apprentices, throughout the late sixteenth and early seventeenth centuries.

MOTIVATIONS III: ECONOMIC—CAPS

Many items of clothing besides ruffs were attacked for misdirecting national resources and impoverishing the nation. In his *A Discourse of the Common Weal of this Realm of England* (1549), Sir Thomas Smith blamed imported luxuries for the decline of local economies. As Cecil put it, any law that enabled an increase in the consumption of foreign goods such as "the excess of silks ... wyne and spyce" was "consent to the robbery of the realm."[72] This belief still circulated a century later when John Evelyn lamented that the English taste for French fashions damaged English national morale as well as the economy.[73] Correspondingly, sumptuary legislation often controlled what it called "the superfluity of unnecessary foreign wares" and prohibited foreign textiles such as woolen cloth "made out of this realm," fur "whereof the kind growth not within the Queen's dominions," and fine silks, damasks, and taffetas.[74]

While other legislation sought to limit the purchasing and display of sumptuous attire and foreign textiles, one Act alone prompted the purchase and wearing of apparel. The "Cappers Act" of 1571 obliged all non-gentry men (excluding office holders in cities and towns and those belonging to a London company) to wear a knitted woolen cap, made in England, on Sundays and holy days. The motivations behind this Act were clear. Woolen caps, which "of late days ... men have ... left the using and wearing of," were no longer in vogue, and a 1566 Act banning felt and cloth caps had clearly not prompted enough sales of the woolen style.[75] The Act stated that the trade employed 8,000 Londoners, and was suffering because of shifts in fashion.[76] Until its repeal in 1597, the Act was repeated six times by proclamation,[77] each time lambasting those who for "disobedience and wanton disorder of evil-disposed and light persons more regarding private fancy and vanity than public commodity" refused to support the trade and so sent "multitudes" of cappers into "idleness and misery."[78]

This flat split-brim knitted cap, now muddy brown, was a familiar sight on sixteenth-century London streets (Figure 3.5). In their survey of eighty-six caps in the Museum of London's collection, Jane Malcolm-Davies and Hilary Davidson found that the split-brim style was most common, with thirty-three of the caps made with two overlapping brims with rounded ends.[79] Other caps, some brimless, others with single brims, earflaps, or neck flaps, show a diversity of styles and functions. This example, now in the stores of the The Metropolitan Museum of Art, was probably discovered during building work and excavations in early twentieth-century London. Unfortunately, the precise provenance of most surviving caps, their location in the ground, and the context of their discoveries is now lost. The relatively large numbers of surviving examples indicate their ubiquity.[80]

Many examples show evidence of personalization with ribbons, slashed brims, colorful dyed linings, and room for feather accessories, demonstrating that even those London men with limited income and social status were keen to dress individually and exuberantly,

FIGURE 3.5 Knitted cap, sixteenth century, English, wool, 23.5 cm wide. Source: The Metropolitan Museum of Art, Bashford Dean Memorial Collection Funds from Various Donors, 1929, 29.158–485. Courtesy www.metmuseum.org.

in spite of this law which seemed to force a uniformity of dress on the majority of the male populace. Other men resisted the law rather than decorating their "statute cap," the most famous case being William Shakespeare's uncle Henry, who showed up to church without his woolen cap and then failed to appear in court to pay his fine. The Stratford Court Leet records list his fine of ten pence in total (eight for the cap, two for his failure to attend court). Other men also disobeyed, as church records report collections of 10s. 8d., 14s., 7s. 5d., and 3s. 7d. "for the Statute of Caps."[81]

ENFORCEMENT: LEGAL

One central question regarding sumptuary law is whether it was substantially enforced. Most historians have assumed that no concerted efforts were made in England, and that this was one of the reasons for its early repeal, in comparison to other European countries and city-states.[82] Both Frances Baldwin and N. B. Harte, in their extensive research, concluded that "it seems unlikely ... that many people were actually brought before the law courts for wearing fabrics or garments made illegal by the Acts of Apparel or the subsequent Proclamations."[83] Hunt, too, could not find evidence "writ in official black ink" and stated that even other sources "throw up scarcely the faintest whiff of enforcement of these laws."[84] Certainly, the preambles to many of the proclamations complain of a lack of enforcement.[85] But as we have seen, many parties were responsible for policing apparel and, in the case of London, efforts were made by the authorities establish controls. Individuals were brought to court there, as we have seen with the cases of Walweyn, Aldriche, and Sherman above. Additional examples of both court records and other sources will demonstrate how London apparel was subject to legal, religious, and familial enforcement.

The 1562 proclamation ordered each London ward to appoint "4 substanciall & well meanyne men" to examine offenders, and similar measures were demanded of the Inns of Court and Chancery, Westminster, and London's suburbs, and other cities and towns throughout England.[86] Officers were given "abbreviats" of the statutes (lists summarizing banned apparel), which were issued from 1561 and appended to later proclamations.[87] But such measures were insufficient. Instead of four men for each ward, by February 1565/6 two men were appointed to watch in each parish.[88] The livery companies were ordered to appoint four men to guard the entrance gates to the city from seven until eleven in the morning, and from one in the afternoon until six at night.[89]

The Lord Mayor's courts prompted surges of enforcement in the city. Walweyn's appearance before the Aldermen initiated a period of concerted effort to crack down on hose in the city. Immediately after his hearing, the court charged all those in attendance to "dylygently" search their whole wards "this afternoon." They were told to focus on drapers and tailors, and any other makers of hose "contrary to the some of the proclamacion lately sett oute" in order to "remove & take" any great hose "from there shopps and stalls & not to putte them ... to sale." The next day, the wardens of the livery companies were to attend court to organize a watch.[90] The searches worked, as on the next day William Pole appeared in court for both great hose and "sylk & other apparell of the bodye."[91] Thomas Weaver, a master of fence, also appeared with his two servants and agreed to reform his hose "without delaye."[92] On January 30, just six days after Walweyn's case, the Aldermen placed a £20 bond on Robert Worsey to ensure that he would "leave of & putte awaye aswell his great & monsterous hoase as also all other his apparell of sylke" as "the wearynge whereof he ys not able to justyfye by the lawe." As a gentleman, Worsey was treated with more respect than Walweyn, and so was charged to "personally appeare" before the Lord Mayor in "comelye & decent apparell as the lawes do permytte him to use & wear."[93] On February 23, the court filled with offenders seized by constables from the parish of St. Magnus and on London Bridge: Edmund Dancye, Master of Fence, for his silk doublet and girdle, Martyn Baskyn for a velvet cap, a silk girdle, and a pair of hose trimmed with silk, John Mortymer for hose lined with silk, Edmund Foster in a pair of hose with silk and with a velvet covered dagger sheath, John Gyllon wearing a pair of hose lined with silk, John Haywood in hose lined with silk and a double ruff on his shirt, and an apprentice named Henry whose sartorial transgressions were not noted.[94]

This wave of enforcement, which focused primarily on hose, and later surges targeting apprentices, seem to have been prompted by particular pressure placed on the Lord Mayor by the Queen and the Star Chamber. On May 21, 1592, the Lord Mayor reported to his Common Council that he had been in the Queen's presence at court and "by her owne mouth geve [him] expresse chardge and commandment to see the abuses of Apparell reformed" in London.[95] This prompt spurred the Mayor to action, and he ordered all freemen to ensure that their apprentices were dressing according to the proclamation. The Mayor reminded his court again on May 30 to police the dress of their freemen "and their wives." Those who refused were to answer "att your uttermost perille."[96]

London sometimes resisted this legal enforcement. In 1571 the Lord Mayor William Allyn wrote to Lord Burghley to explain that the £40 bonds imposed on each tailor and hosier were too costly. Bonds were a clever way of attempting to limit troublesome hose; if demand could not be stifled, supply might be curtailed. But as Allyn explained in his letter, most tailors and hosiers were "verie poore men" and the "extremitie of these bonds" would leave them "utterlie undone."[97] The Lord Mayor also had trouble prosecuting certain offenders. In 1579 he wrote to the Lord Treasurer stating that when members of the Companies of Haberdashers and Leathersellers had been watching Aldersgate on March 8, they had stopped Lord William Howard for wearing ruffles "much out of order." One of his men was also carrying a sword of forbidden length with the point upwards. The citizens "in respect of his quality" did not apprehend Howard, brother of the Earl of Surrey, but simply "reminded" him that he and his servant were in violation of the law, and requested that the servant cut his sword shorter. In response, the servant offered to strike the citizens and Howard called them "odious names of culines, rascals, and such like." This was the third time Howard had been in contempt of the law, and so the Mayor felt compelled to write to the Treasurer so "that the citizens might not be discouraged in their duty."[98] Again, on May 15 1580, the Lord Mayor wrote to the Treasurer for support when Mr Hewson, son-in-law to the Lord Chief Baron, wore "excess of Ruffs, in the open street." Hewson had taken "great offence" to being "friendly admonished" by the Mayor. Sumptuary policing could be risky business when those on watch were of inferior social status to the offenders.[99]

In addition to active watch, offenders who appeared in court for other reasons could also find themselves punished for dressing against the law. On January 11, 1591, a "presumptuous" attorney was dismissed from his office when he appeared before the Privy Council "in apparrell unfitt for his calling, with a guilt rapier, extreame greate ruffes and lyke unseemelie apparrell."[100] Active and passive watch by the courts were both effective, albeit irregular, means of policing apparel in Elizabethan London.

ENFORCEMENT: HOUSEHOLDS

Although it was politically difficult to police the elites, top-down enforcement was key. As Burghley put it, "I doubt much that the length of all these commandments and provisions will hardly be executed abroad until there be some good example in the Court and the city."[101] Even in the Jacobean period, when the reinstatement of sumptuary law was being discussed, a committee on trade suggested the nobility and gentry wear English cloth in winter "by example rather than by comaund."[102]

Within households, the authorities emphasized that it was important to set a good example. Masters were expected to police their servants and apprentices. Thomas Foxdayle, for example, brought his apprentice Phillip Wood to the Tailors Hall "to be punished" by the wardens of the Merchant Tailor for wearing "grete hosen."[103] Wives were ordered to dress according to their husband's status.

The enforcement and anxieties surrounding sumptuary control suggest significant generational conflict. This was a particular problem in London, a youthful city dominated by single men—apprentices, law students, and the sons of noblemen—on the make.[104] In his tract on youth, Francis Lenton depicted a young student wearing "Embroidered suits such as his father never knew" and spending the money which "His parents him supply to buy books" on "alluring hooks."[105] Describing sumptuous dress as an "infection" which had "spread amongst the youth," the 1588 clothing proclamation singled out young people as most problematic. The proclamation was drafted after a meeting between the Lord Chancellor and the heads, ancients, and principals of the houses of Court and Chancery, the Inns of Court, and Cambridge and Oxford, and referred to the Lord Mayor's discussions with the Queen. These authorities were in regular contact with the students, apprentices, and young noblemen who had the time, inclination, and often the money to dress extravagantly.

ENFORCEMENT: RELIGIOUS

Legal measures and controls from the heads of households and institutions were reinforced by religious invective. Preachers often criticized their congregations for lusting after new and sumptuous fashions. Henry Smith, preacher at St. Clement Danes, deemed covetousness "the Londoner's sin."[106] Nathaneall Cannon asked those who attended his sermon at St. Paul's Cross, "Of what nation and country doth not your City borrow pride? And for your fashions as they are many, so they are monstrous."[107] Whether or not Londoners took to heart this message is questionable. Sir John Harrington's epigram seems to suggest that the message fell on deaf ears: "Our zealous preachers that would pride repress, Complain against Apparells great excess, / For though the laws against yt are express, / Each lady like a Queen herself doth dress."[108]

After sumptuary legislation had been repealed, James I continued to order the London clergy to preach against immoral dress, in 1620 targeting women who dressed in masculine fashions such as broad brimmed hats, pointed doublets, stilletoes (short daggers), and short hair.[109] The Dean of Westminster, Robert Townson, even prevented women wearing yellow ruffs from taking a seat in one of his pews.[110]

The "Homily Against Excess of Apparel" (1563), sermonized to congregations across England by royal order, restated sumptuary law and allied it with God's will. In addition to targeting young men who spent their father's money on inappropriate fripperies and chastizing women for unnecessary and dissembling ornamentation, the sermon focused on national pride. The sermon told the tale of a painter who found it impossible to depict a clothed Englishman, for he changed his clothing so regularly that the artist could not keep up with the fashions.[111] The painter instead depicted the Englishman with a bolt of cloth under his arm, so that he could "make it himself as he thought best." The sermon allied this fickleness with a loss of national identity, and claimed that it made the English "laughing stocks to other nations."[112] It critiqued this constant search for novelty, "new toys, and inventing new fashions."[113]

IMPACT: INNOVATIONS

While proclamations, sermons, and pamphlets critiqued shifting fashion, the clothing laws did not prevent many innovative new fabrics, colors, and shapes. Far from imposing a "sartorial regime" in Roche's terms, legal confines spurred fashionable men and women to find clever alternatives, mimetic substitutions, and new styles not covered by proclamations. Many Elizabethan fashions were not reliant on expensive imported and prohibited textiles. The fantastical shapes—rounded peascod bellies for men or flat elongated torsos and hooped underskirts for women—were made with paddings of horse- and pig-hair, reeds, pasteboard, wires, as well as costly whalebone. Stockings made of English wools—dyed bright colors, and knitted in patterns or stripes—replaced more expensive imported silk hose.[114] Simple pasteboard "vizard" masks covered with fabric were wildly popular, despite their quick construction and relatively cheap materials.[115] The simple woolen cap, staple of the wardrobe of many young male non-elite Londoners, could be personalized quickly and cheaply (Figure 3.5). Bridewell apprentices dyed their hats black, much to the infuriation of their governors, and as we have seen, extant caps show traces of bright colored dyes, slashes, and ribbons.[116] The wide variety of clothing accessories—pins, hooks, laces, points, colored silk threads—found in the sole surviving Royal Exchange inventory from this period, attests to the range of possibilities available to the London consumer. No wonder young students might spend their book money on "alluring hooks."[117] Leather shoes, jerkins and purses were punched through with decorative shapes for the cost of a penny or two at the tailors, or slashed with a knife by their owner.

While they did not curtail the invention of and appetite for new fashions, the proclamations did impact the price and circulation of goods. One letter offers a rare glimpse into the short-term economic impact of a proclamation on the substitution goods to which Londoners turned when fine fabrics were being actively policed. On July 6, 1574, John Knyveton wrote to the Earl of Shrewsbury from Cold Harbour in London, to tell him that he was sending fringes by messenger, but was unable to purchase other goods the Earl had demanded. Knyveton explained, "all kyndes of tufted mockadoes be so deare because of the proclamation for apparel, that now paye xd in every yarde more than before and therefore I staye to bye any till the price be better."[118] Mockado was a fabric designed to resemble velvet, usually made with wool rather than silk to provide a cheap simulation of a luxurious imported textile (Figure 3.6).[119] Surviving fragments of wool velvet show that their detailed patterns mimicked the more expensive silk velvets and provided a fairly convincing substitute. Knyveton's letter was sent less than a month

FIGURE 3.6 Piece of woolen velvet, sixteenth century, Flemish, 27.9 x 30.5 cm. The Metropolitan Museum of Art, Rogers Fund, 1909, 09.50.1075. Courtesy www.metmuseum.org.

after the June 15, 1574 proclamation, and it seems that the law spurred Londoners to buy and sell textiles that mimicked the velvet restricted to the likes of Dukes and Marquesses. As an Earl, Shrewsbury would have been legally allowed to buy silk velvet, but his choice to purchase mockado suggest that this fabric was desirable even to those who were at liberty to acquire the real thing. While the proclamation had a significant impact, pushing prices up by ten pence per yard, Knyveton's note also suggests that this would only be a temporary increase.

Even after the repeal of sumptuary law, the clothing trade was still influenced by rumors of new legislation. In November 1616, Nathaniel Brent explained, "every houre we expect a proclamation about wearing of clothe, which because it hath bin long talked of hath made a great number of people forbear to buy stuffes and silks, and hath caused a deadnesse of merchandise in Cheapside."[120]

IMPACT: THE LEGACY OF SUMPTUARY LEGISLATION

Brent's comment came in 1616, suggesting that contemporaries still anticipated a return to sumptuary control over a decade after their 1604 repeal. That the laws were not revived was not for lack of trying; bills were read, debated, and rejected by the House of Commons, the House of Lords, and the monarch in 1604, 1610, 1614, 1621, 1626, and 1629.[121] The London authorities continued to police the dress of certain communities. From 1610 to 1611, the Court of Common Council put in place new rules governing the clothing and hairstyles of apprentices and maidservants.[122] These regulations, which were even more specific than many of the Elizabethan proclamations, targeted some new fashions, and prohibited fine linens, stomachers decorated with silks, and farthingales, bodies, and sleeves shaped with whalebone or any other form of stiffening except canvas or buckram.[123]

Sumptuary laws were discussed and debated for decades after their repeal, which suggests that some believed this kind of control was both necessary and effective. For instance, in 1616 Francis Bacon wrote to James I urging him to issue a proclamation for the wearing of cloth in order to support this declining local trade. A proclamation was drawn up but never published.[124] Even in 1668, members of the House of Lords—a generation who had grown up without sumptuary laws—considered the reinstatement of "Sumptuary Laws, and the Fashions of Apparel" and "the Distinction of Degrees of Persons by Habits."[125] Elements of clothing control remained in place. Protectionist economic measures limiting exports and controlling foreign imports and luxury goods continued throughout the early modern period.[126] Even deceased Londoners were dressed in accordance with the law. From 1666 until 1814, the Burying in Woolens Act required that the dead be buried in English woolen shirts, shifts, or sheets in order to limit the importation of foreign linens.[127]

Critics were vocal about the social and economic effects of sumptuary law, even a century after its repeal. In *The Fable of the Bees; or, Private Vices, Publick Benefits* (1714), Bernard Mandeville argued that the conspicuous consumption of luxuries increased national wealth and international trade. Adam Smith declared in his *Wealth of Nations* (1776) it was "the highest impertinence and presumption ... in kings and ministers, to pretend to watch over the economy of private people and to restrain their expense, either by sumptuary laws or by prohibiting the importation of foreign luxuries."[128]

Sumptuary legislation remained in the cultural and legislative memory throughout the early modern era, however most commentators looked for alternative measures to control clothing. John Evelyn noted on October 18, 1666 that he had presented his pamphlet, "Tyrannus or the Mode: in a Discourse of Sumptuary Lawes" to Charles II, urging him to "fix a Standard [of dress] at Court" in order to halt the "slavish defference of ours to other Nations." If a "constant" form of dress was set, Evelyn argued, "there will need no Sumptuary lawes to represse and reform the Lux."[129] Just ten days before, Samuel Pepys recorded in his diary that the king had declared "his resolution of setting a fashion for clothes, which he will never alter. It will be a vest, I know not well how. But it is to teach the nobility thrift, and will do good."[130] This vest did "alter" however, when it fell from fashion in the 1670s.[131]

Any effort to control dress, particularly in the vibrant, growing, and fashionable city of London, was a temporary fix. Londoners craved innovation, new shapes, colors, and textures in their dress, and laws or economic measures designed to prohibit one style merely encouraged traders, tailors, and consumers to look elsewhere for mimetic or novel substitutions. While London authorities—the courts, the church, and the crown—might try to redress London upstarts, the very people who were transgressing the laws—merchants, artisans, craftswomen, and servants—were largely responsible for the economic and cultural success of the city. Like them, the city was constantly reinventing itself.

The case of Thomas Bradshaw, a Merchant Tailor arrested in 1570, demonstrates the contradictions of clothing in the early modern city. On November 24, Bradshaw was caught strolling through London, "contrary to good order," in a "payre of monstrous great hose."[132] As a member of the largest guild in the city, the guild partly responsible for the increasing rapidity of fashion, the making of much clothing, and trade of foreign cloth, Bradshaw embodied a positive and negative "mingle-mangle" of London's changing identity in the period. He not only represented all that was driving London's growth in size and wealth, but also embodied the anxieties of foreign influence and social climbing. As a young member of the urban nouveau riche, he could evidently afford to dress above his social status. The Court of Aldermen, keen to put Bradshaw in his place, ordered "that all the stuffinge & lyninges of one of his said hose shalbe cutt and pulled out presently" and he was to be led home through the streets to his Master's house, literally deflated.

Each time an apprentice lined his hose with silks or "new draperies" and filled his pockets with stuffing, he lined the pockets of London merchants, shopkeepers, and traders. London authorities might temporarily redress stylish Londoners, but despite fines, protectionist policies, and the watchful eyes of the church and the law, very little could stop Bradshaw from lining and restuffing his hose in an even more fashionable manner the following day. Nothing and no one could stop the increasingly inflating fashion industry and city of London itself.

CHAPTER FOUR

Agreements

LAURENT DE SUTTER

It was a commonplace of early modern thought to regard the particular case as a microcosm of a universal, macrocosmic generality. So it was that legal agreements were considered to be much more than the meeting of two persons but something like the re-enactment of God's covenant to be present in human relations. From that early modern perspective, there was no agreement without the mark of God engraved at its core and every particular agreement was to be considered an imitation of a greater compact, actualizing for a specific situation what was the rule of all situations.

With this in mind, 1689 might be considered the most important date in the history of modern civil law—the year where all the features defining civil law finally fell into place, taking the form of a single oeuvre. The oeuvre in question was the first volume of Jean Domat's masterpiece, *Les lois civiles dans leur ordre naturel*, that was printed, in Paris, by Auboüin, Emery and Clozier, and whose publication covered the last years of the lawyer's life.[1] With *Les lois civiles*, Domat introduced into what was still a chaotic ensemble, a new set of principles that was to govern law during the next centuries, up to the present day, especially the rules concerning obligations. These principles were simple: on the one hand, they concerned the justification of law through nature; on the other hand, the ordering of law according to this very principle of justification. If to claim that "nature" would be the model to be followed in the grouping and classification of rules (or, at least, of the rules respecting "nature") was not new, but Domat gave it an unexpected, and yet decisive, twist. The explanation for this twist was not too distant: as a Jansenist and a close friend of Pascal, he believed in a version of Christianity that would be more authentic, and more moral, than the one expressed by the church.[2] In Clermont-Ferrand, at the centre of France, where he was exercising his duties as a King's advocate and *échevin* (magistrate) he even took an active part in the fight opposing the Jansenists to the Jesuits. For Domat, the Jesuits were the incarnation of numerous flaws, which were also manifestly shared by the magistrates of his time. They forgot that there was no justice outside of divine justice, and no law outside of divine Law. The presence of God, according to Domat, should not only be perceived as a gaze embracing law with its almighty benevolence, but as an actual presence in actual legal institutions—such as in compacts. When Domat stated what to this day remains the fundamental belief of the law of contracts, it was with this idea in mind: "once a convention is formed, all that has been agreed upon takes the place of the law for those who consented to it."[3]

The introduction of God into the interior of a legal institution such as a contract was not an idiosyncrasy of Domat's; it was a belief shared by his fellow Jansenists—including, besides Pascal, Jean Racine himself.[4] In *Les plaideurs*, his only comedy, which premiered at the Hotel de Bourgogne, in Paris, in November 1668, Racine decided to put on stage magistrates similar to those against whom Domat fought during his office in Clermont.[5] The story of the play is that of a crazy judge, named Dandin who is perpetually trying to find a new case to decide, and who is fooled by the young Léandre, who wants to marry Isabelle, the daughter of the bourgeois Chicanneau. As indicated by his name (*chicane*, in French, means a judicial quibble), Chicanneau never ceases to quarrel—and mostly with the Countess of Pimbesche (*pimbêche* designating an irritatingly annoying lady). Léandre takes advantage of the quarrel between Chicanneau and the countess to force the former to sign a document that, he claims, will solve the case presented to Dandin, and much to his advantage. But once the document is presented to the judge, he recognizes a contract of marriage between Isabelle and Léandre that he immediately validates, forgetting all about the original case at hand. Even though Racine was not as strongly attached to the Abbey of Port-Royal (the home of Jansenism) as Pascal, or even Domat, his education at the Abbey had nevertheless left a trace. *Les plaideurs* was a comedy that tried to ridicule the way the madness of judges could lead to delirious interpretations that identified contracts with the law—an identification that was oblivious of its divine nature. The *ordre naturel* that Domat tried to defend in his classification of the rules composing the ensemble of civil law was turned into a farcical parody where nothing was ordered or natural anymore. What the spectators at the Hotel de Bourgogne witnessed was nothing other than the perfect exemplification of what happens when order is replaced by individual arbitrariness, and nature by the mundane games of culture. *An agreement is a serious matter*: this was the maxim that was evidenced by Racine in *Les plaideurs*—so serious a matter that only the most outrageous comedy could give a correct approximation to its denial. And the fact that the agreement in question in his play concerned the sacrament of marriage was only another way of providing evidence of the fact that to turn it into a comedy was actually a way of inverting the natural order, and turning the sanctity of covenants upside down.

THE MARRIAGE CONTRACT AND ITS SUBVERSION

The importance of the contract of marriage, as the supreme form of agreement, at the end of the seventeenth century, was not only proven by its staging in comedy, but also by its representation in painting. Actually, of all the possible types of agreements mentioned by Domat in his *Lois civiles*, the contract of marriage was the *only* one that seemed to deserve some sort of depiction. Marriage itself, of course, never was the result of a contract—yet, on the other hand, the conditions pertaining to the acceptance of marriage (such as dowry) were very carefully discussed and drafted. One of the most famous examples of a painting representing this discussion and drafting is *Le contrat de mariage*, painted in 1712 and ascribed to Antoine Watteau, the year he was elected to the French Academy in Rome.[6] As in other paintings of the same subject, the scene depicted by Watteau is the opposite of an intimate moment—or even of a moment that would take place inside the study of an *avoué* (an attorney) or the living room of a bourgeois household. The signing of the contract is taking place in the middle of the countryside, witnessed by a large group of persons dressed as if for a garden party, and being only moderately interested in the signature itself. While some are dancing, and others chatting, the two fiancés are sitting behind a stone table, on which someone in the costume of an attorney or a notary is about to sign an apparently very thick document. The moment seems at the same time both very solemn and very mundane—a mixture of the importance of the stakes involved, and of the context of a society for which to have fun remains more important than the signing of any legal affairs. Of course, there are less light-hearted examples of paintings related to the topic of the dowry and its execution—such as *L'accordée de village*, exhibited in 1761 at the Paris Salon by Jean-Baptiste Greuze (Figure 4.1).[7] Instead of an aristocratic picnic, the moment when the father of the bride is to pay the dowry to his new son-in-law, presents something of a pathetic, almost painful scene, as was observed by Denis Diderot.[8] Contrarily to *Le contrat de mariage*, the scene is set inside of a peasant's house, where the whole family of the bride is gathered, as well as the groom, and the *tabellion* (notary) looking at the marriage contract on the table. As for the attorney in Watteau's painting, the latter seems the only one depicted character deprived of any form of emotion, as if it was necessary to confirm Racine's intuition in his *Plaideurs* (Figure 4.3).

Yet, the importance and seriousness of an agreement such as a contract of marriage, as well as its eventual link with some transcendental instance, was also what allowed for its transformation into an unexpectedly subversive device. It is not by chance that eccentric forms of agreements appear in the works of Choderlos de Laclos, Giacomo Casanova, or Donatien de Sade—the three most important figures of eighteenth-century French erotic literature. While French law was slowly heading towards the elaboration of the Code Civil, which follows the ordering suggested by Domat, Laclos, Casanova and Sade immediately imagined its dark side.[9] With *Les liaisons dangereuses*, in 1782, Laclos told the story of the perverse agreement between the Vicomte de Valmont and the Comtesse de Merteuil: if Valmont succeeds in conquering the virtuous Présidente de Tourvel, then the Comtesse would be his, too.[10] In *Histoire de ma vie*, written in French between 1789 and 1798, Casanova enumerates the various pacts and contracts that he makes with friends or lovers, such as the arrangement made with the Marquise d'Urfé.[11] And Sade never ceases to invent new forms of contracts tying together the members of the different criminal communities that he stages in his novels—as for instance, in the *120 journées de Sodome*, in 1785.[12] At the very moment when Jean-Jacques de Cambacérès was trying to impose upon the revolutionary assemblies his proposals for a Civil Code, Laclos, Casanova or Sade were writing the anti-Civil Code. They were using the most important apparatus created by the law to try to actually ruin it—or, at least, to ruin its pretense at benefiting from a moral justification, especially if this justification was God. If contracts are indeed a serious matter, this seriousness is so far reaching that they turn into ridicule the very instance aimed at providing this seriousness with an external, superior ground. As was pointed out by Gilles Deleuze, the "classical image of law" as a form finding in itself its own moral justification (embodying God, as Domat would say), Sade (but also Laclos or Casanova) juxtaposed a pact perverting it.[13] The pretense at grounding law on some sort of superior Good was transformed, overturned, perverted by this libertine pact which enacted the reality of its un-grounding in an absolute Evil, which contaminated every aspect of it. Rather than being the incarnation of the perfection of law, the agreement became the incarnation of its imperfection—the moment when it revealed its fundamental and irreducible flaw.

From the Jansenists to the novelists of the dark side of the contract, the history of legal agreements from early modernity into the modern era was the history of the simultaneous consolidation and "critique" of the presence of God in an institution. The theology of legal positivism, as opposed to the theology of natural law, developed its ambiguous roots in the law of contract, as much as did the critical attempts at ruining its proponents' presuppositions. From a certain perspective, the development of the modern understanding of the notion of contract, and its abstraction from customary practices concerning agreements, is the key to all the legal novelties of the time. Besides private law, the figure of the contract became, during the seventeenth and eighteenth centuries, a central feature of political theory—the very feature that would eventually redefine the meaning of sovereignty and the state. If, with Hugo Grotius, Thomas Hobbes introduced the topic of the contract in the world of politics, through the concept of "covenant" developed in 1651 in his *Leviathan*, Jean-Jacques Rousseau gave it its final face.[14] With *Du Contrat social*, in 1762, the shift from a vision of sovereignty as some sort of a dialogue of the sovereign with the divine towards one where the divinity was displaced *inside* the relationship between the sovereign and its subjects was finalized. Just as Domat integrated the figure of God into the practical legal institution of the contract, the divinity of the state was also, through the idea of a covenant or a pact of delegation of sovereignty to a given body, integrated into its very functioning.[15] Obviously, this required the *technicization* of the categories of political theory—and the progressive invention of some sort of a positive public law that could put these categories into practice. This didn't happen before the nineteenth century, and the progressive emergence of public law as an academic discipline in France and in Germany; yet this emergence was prepared by the shift operated between Hobbes and Rousseau.[16] In the former's work just as in the latter's, the category of "the people," and its abstraction from the actual reality of the subjects, was designed as some sort of a necessary condition for the "social contract" to be efficacious. Its theoretical design had no other purpose than to try and introduce into legal vocabulary a version of the contract that could benefit from the prestige attached to the law in general—namely, precisely, its generality and abstraction.

DOMAT'S RELATION TO LATER THOUGHT

The "classical image of law" of which Deleuze wrote was an image which including both its private and its public dimensions—as was made obvious in the work of the one who incarnated, for Deleuze, this image: Immanuel Kant.[17] In his 1785 treatise on the *Grundlegung zur Metaphysik der Sitten*, where he tried to justify the prevalence of the universal laws of reason in morals, Kant didn't distinguish between individual and collective reason. Under the rules of reason, what mattered the most was obedience to the formal nature of these rules—the recognition of the value of the fact that there were rules *because of their form as rules*.[18] The formality of moral rules, of which legal rules were only derived products, was the key element in the understanding of their general character, that is, of the fact that they would know no boundary of topic or subject. Whereas political theorists in the sixteenth century attempted to define external limits to the authority of the sovereign, Kant formulated internal limits to this very authority, through an unlimited extension of legality through morality. Kant's formalism was the laic version of Domat's theory of law; it was the progressive integration into the nature of rules of the formerly external power that offered them their force, or their efficacy. If, for Domat, God was the guarantor of every legal institution, for Kant such a guarantor could vanish, and be replaced by some inner feature of the institution itself—a feature that he qualified "moral." This is the reason why it was possible to imagine a "public" version of what Domat only offered in a "private" version: the form of the contract was all that was needed to reach a higher level of moralization in politics. If things were still ambiguous in the case of Hobbes, they had become absolutely evident by the time of Rousseau—as it is proven by the absence of any decisive reference to God in *The Social Contract*. The possibility that an instance resembling a legal agreement could become the foundational stone of a given political society required the preliminary recognition of the inner power of such an agreement. Despite the fact that Rousseau didn't explicitly made the case for the inner power of contract, Kant's philosophy could be considered as providing the key explanation why, at the end of the eighteenth century, this could have gone without saying. The "classical image of law," both public and private, was the image of the generalization of the figure of the contract, as embodying the revolution of the inner power of law, as a moral form.

The importance of the role, played by Domat, as a precursor of the Code Civil in general, and of the dispositions concerning contracts in particular, shouldn't lead one to overlook the role played by other legal scholars. Among them, the most crucial was Robert-Joseph Pothier, whose *Traité des obligations*, published in 1761, constitutes the first generalization and ordering of the ensemble of rules applying to the topic in France at the time.[19] Pothier was very close to Henri-François d'Aguesseau, the chancellor appointed by King Louis XV to further pursue the codification of customs work started under Louis XIV, with whom he corresponded throughout his life.[20] He was also somehow close to the Jansenist circles, even though they were continuously persecuted by the authorities—or, at least, he behaved in a way that was respectful of Jansenist values and ideas. This might explain why Pothier was very keen to further explore the systematization and rationalization of the law of obligations, but also why he considered that positive law should be submitted to moral law. There was an austerity in Pothier that presented traits comparable with those of Kant's, so providing further evidence for Harold Berman's famous claim of the growing influence of Protestantism on the history of modern law.[21] Even though Pothier was by no means a Protestant, his refusal of what constituted the central feature of Jesuit thought, namely casuistry, was the same as that formulated by Kant in the *Groundwork*. The insistence on the formal dimension of law, as the very place of manifestation of its moral dimension, also implied the critique of casuistry, since case-by-case adjudication always needs ad hoc justification. If, since Louis XIV, the French authorities wanted to codify law, it was precisely to avoid what were perceived as the inconsistencies and lability of casuistry, as well as the freedom left to the one actually deciding cases. The fact that between the Ancien Régime and the French Revolution the general orientation remained the same revealed well enough how the fight against casuistry, in the field of obligations and contracts as in any other field, was the true goal of the transformation of the conception of law. Pothier's systematization of the law of obligation obeyed this very logic, considering casuistry as the most *immoral* form of law—a form of law that, as a matter of fact, was anything but a form: the very name of the informal.

PASCAL AND THE PRIMACY OF PRINCIPLE

Declaring casuistry immoral was an unexpected twist of history, since it was long the most sophisticated legal technique available—a technique that, ironically, was brought to its highest level by the virtuosity of the canonists. When Pascal attacked the Jesuits in his *Provinciales*, in 1656, what he critiqued was the liberal attitude towards morality that was implied by casuistry—the fact that casuistry might allow for morally doubtful solutions.[22] Putting the principles *after* the cases to be solved was, for Pascal, something utterly scandalous, since it made the principles dependent on the cases, and not the other way round. It meant that principles could be changed if the set of cases demanding them were different, so negating the eternal validity of God's commands, and potentially leading to heresy. If, then, the Jansenists insisted on the primacy of principles over cases, it was to get rid of the legal pragmatism that was the rule in Jesuit circles, and in particular with Jesuit specialists in canon law. In this context, it was no big surprise if the country that most resisted the abandonment of casuistry in the domain of law was the one where the Jesuits were the most powerful, and where the resistance towards Protestantism reached its peak—namely Spain. The Spanish Golden Age, which lasted until the symptom that was the death of Pedro Calderón de la Barca, in 1681, marked the last moment of triumph of Catholicism in Europe, and hence of casuistry. The very incarnation of this triumph was none other than Francisco Suárez, the Jesuit theologian who gave to legal scholasticism its masterpiece, the *Tractatus de legibus ac deo legislatore*, in 1612.[23] In this treatise, Suárez defended the supremacy of the figure of God in the foundation of political society and of its the legal order—God being the one who created the former as well as the latter. Contrary to what will later be defended by Jansenists, Suárez was not interested in looking at the inner morality of legal agencies, since it was the general architecture of law that was morally guaranteed by God. Once this was accepted, any method could be followed in the human practice of law, as was the case in the notoriously disordered state of law and jurisprudence of the Spain of the time. And the exception represented by some satirical discussions of contracts in Miguel de Cervantès' *Don Quixote* (regarding the status of Sancho Panza as employee and servant of Don Quixote's) could be considered as that: an exception.[24]

BONDS IN SHAKESPEARE AND MARLOWE

If Berman has consistently shown the importance of the consequences of the Protestant revolution throughout Europe, he has forgotten to describe the cultural context that allowed it to spread. Contrary to what one might think, this context was absolutely unified: the criticism directed towards casuistry, the promotion of a more moral conception of law, and the resulting defense of codification was not idiosyncratic of civil law. In the common law world, too, novelists and playwrights staged the conflict between the true, authentic law, and its counterfeit version, as used by judges and attorneys in their everyday life. William Shakespeare's *The Merchant of Venice* is, of course, the perfect incarnation of the simultaneous criticism of law, through the institution of the contract, and of the aspiration towards a higher legal morality.[25] In Shakespeare's play, the mean attachment of the usurer Shylock to the letter of the contract was presented as the vilest possible understanding of law—an understanding that would be purely legal. For law to have a legitimate existence, it should be redeemed by something else, what Shakespeare called "justice," and Kant, one century-and-a-half later, would call "form," as the embodiment of morality. In itself, the letter of the contract was what disgusted the man of higher consideration, the moral soul, the one capable of perceiving in law the supplement that would make it more than a worthless quibble. Obviously, the fact that, in *The Merchant*, the one who claims his attachment to the letter of the law is a Jew in a Protestant context only adds insult to injury, as has been often observed by commentators. To the Jewish religion, assimilated to the religion of the letter, Protestant legal ethics can always oppose the privilege of the spirit—provided that this spirit encompasses the totality of law. In Shakespeare's comedy, when the Doge (called "the Duke") explains to Shylock that his contract is invalid because it breaches several other rules of the Republic of Venice, his reasoning is based on the same kind of logic as Domat's or Pothier's. The spirit of the law is what infuses the very legality of the legal apparatus; it is not simply an overarching principle towards which one can turn to find the right answer to a problem. Again, it is inside of the law of Venice that the Doge can discover the rationale according to which the usurer's contract is not valid—as if it was the very structure of the legal system that was the incarnation of justice.

Of course, Shakespeare was not alone in thinking that way; his assumptions were shared by many of his contemporaries as well as followers, as if contempt for law, in the name of its spirit, was the rule for the elevated mind. At the other end of the early modern period, Samuel Johnson, for instance, expressed views that seem completely consistent with Shakespeare's in two articles on debt and debtors published in 1759, and signed "The Idler."[26] In these articles, Johnson manifested his "horror," one resulting from his hearing "a rueful cry, which summoned (him) to remember the 'poor debtors' " put in prison for being unable to pay back what they owed to others.[27] According to him, an agreement placing someone's liberty at the mercy of what he called "the passions of another," and eventually driving the weaker person to jail, was something of which the admirers of English law should be ashamed.[28] There was something lacking in the harshness of law, and its willingness to accompany an agreement until its very, and most unpleasant, conclusion—a conclusion contrary to the true purpose of law in general. If law had any meaning, it would be that of protection: the law is there to protect those who need comfort—and the various rules implementing this principle should follow the same direction, rather than contradicting it.[29] This meant that, for Johnson, there were two kinds of legality: the positive legality of the rules and the superior legality of the principle incarnated by the very idea of law—a principle of justice leading to the protection of liberty. As was equally the case for Shakespeare, and most of the cultivated men of the time, Johnson believed that the former kind of legality was unbearable, and could only be redeemed by recourse to justice. Yet, the criticism that opposes the actual functioning of the law of contracts (when debts were involved) was a criticism directed towards this functioning itself—rather than towards the idea of rules on debt. Johnson's view was that to imprison failing debtors was simply a waste of manpower at a time when such manpower was needed, and that this waste was due to the importance given to the creditor in the decision concerning his debtor.[30] What Johnson asked for was a *reform* of the laws on debt—taking for granted their very existence, and the fact that something could be done to improve them, within the framework of principles defending liberty.

This reformism can also be observed in a series of six satirical paintings produced by William Hogarth between 1743 and 1745, known as *Marriage-à-la-Mode* (Figure 4.2). They depict the laborious maneuvers of two fathers wanting to settle a contract of marriage for their children.[31] As usual with Hogarth, the series provides a most bitter morality— namely, that marriages concluded for reasons that are primarily pecuniary are doomed to fail in the most pathetic and dramatic way. It starts with the two fathers (a bankrupt Earl and a rich City merchant) negotiating the terms of the contract that will unite the son of the former to the daughter of the latter, although none of them seems in the least interested in the other. This first scene, called *The Marriage Settlement*, shows the two old men sitting at a table and looking at the usual pile of paper, while a lawyer discusses matters with the bride, as if he was trying to seduce her (which, eventually, he would). From these doubtful preliminaries, the failure of the marriage is only a matter of time—as is evidenced by the following paintings, starting from *The Tête-à-Tête*, the second in the series, where evidence of an adulterous affair is found in the husband's pocket. It then goes from bad to worse, with the husband catching syphilis from a prostitute, the bride cheating on the husband with the lawyer (as expected), the latter killing the former when discovered *in flagrante*, up to the suicide of the bride—while her newborn son bears the marks of his father's disease. Even though the series was somewhat of a commercial failure, it well illustrates the type of ideas that a man of elevated views could nurture while considering the subject of agreements, such as marriage contracts. Once again, the moral dimension is what requires and dictates that there is something wrong with the way legal agreements could be settled individually in important moments of life—and the power inherent in that to destroy what is inherent to them. What is needed is some sort of a moral correction of an otherwise immoral institution—or, at least, an institution that is powerless when faced with the immorality of those who make use of it. But this correction, in the case of Hogarth, originates in some sort of dark humor—in a bitter satire, that shows how the most accepted of practices is the absolute contrary of what it claims to be. As was the case with Racine's *Plaideurs*, or Shakespeare's *Merchant*, the denunciation of the failures of legal agreements mainly came as a form of comedy—a comedy of mistakes.

It might be possible that the most radical statement on the devilish nature of agreements, when not redeemed by moral virtues leading to social justice, could be that of Christopher Marlowe. In his treatment of the German legend of Dr. Faust, of which the first printed version was a booklet titled *Historia von D. Johann Fausten*, published in Frankfurt in 1587, and somewhat later adapted into English in 1592, Marlowe clearly focuses on the question of the morality of the agreement signed by Faust and Lucifer. *The Tragical History of the Life and Death of Doctor Faustus*, a tragedy with comic interludes first published in 1604 (arguably ten years after the première of the play), is indeed a tragedy of moral mistakes, akin to the above-mentioned comedies.[32] As is well known, Faust is a brilliant scholar, who feels frustrated by the lack of recognition of his achievements, especially concerning love and money, that is, from a certain point of view, life itself. In signing the pact that Lucifer offers to him, he suddenly agrees to resign his soul in exchange for twenty-four years on earth dedicated to the actual realization of whatever he wants. Of course, at the end of the twenty-four years, he does not appear to have benefited from the pact, having been incapable of using his power to any effect—and so is forever damned for nothing. What is capital in Marlowe's interpretation of the story (two centuries before Goethe's famous reinvention) is the double insistence on this moral failure—and the fact that it took a comical form in the framework of a tragedy. The pact between Faust and Lucifer was a pact of renunciation of everything that made Faust human, starting from his very soul, the living core of his moral life; yet, this pact was finally enforced, as if it was valid. The possibility that a contract could become the law for those who agree it, as Domat would say almost a century later, was the possibility of the complete negation of what made a person a moral subject capable of agreement. A little bit like Johnson's distinction between two types of legalities, there are two types of subjects that are involved in a pact: the legal subject, bound by its decisions; and the moral subject, who can be taken hostage by the legal subject. The story of Faust is the story of the surrendering of the moral subject to the legal subject—a subject always making bad decisions, since its reign is eventually based on the foreclosure of what the moral subject wants.

The place of the legal subject in an agreement has been explored under different guises during the seventeenth and eighteenth century and the supremacy given to the moral subject somewhat criticized, along the way. The impossibility of a moral subject governing the legal subject was one of the key themes of Laurence Sterne's *Tristram Shandy*, the first two first volumes of which were published in 1759.[33] Paying his dues to John Locke's 1689 *Essay Concerning Human Understanding*, Sterne portrayed in his novel the figure of a father who thinks that everything can be learned from experience—and that there is no innate knowledge. This leads to multiple pedagogical experiences to which the father submits his son, the ill-fated (because, according to the said father, ill-named) Tristram Shandy himself, narrator of the book. At the end of the *Essay*, Locke attempted to formulate moral consequences attached to the general thesis of the empirical dimension of human knowledge—and then the empirical dimension of subjectivity.[34] Morality, just as any other "secondary quality" singularizing an individual, is not something innate; it is something to be learned from the confrontation with, and examination of the current status of morals and politics. This implies that the moral structuration of the subject has nothing to do with the redemption of any form of reality, however legal; on the contrary, it has to do with some sort of coherence with it. The legal subject is not more inherently moral than the moral subject itself—or, at least, it doesn't owe anything to the figure of the moral subject, starting with the necessity of its redemption. In his novel, Sterne played around with this tricky topic, with his customary wit and sense of un-traceability, by describing subjects whose decisions always seemed at the same time a little bit absurd, and too excessively grounded. The best example of this might very well be the marriage settlement by which Walter Shandy, the father of the narrator, concealed from his wife the right to give birth in London, rather than in their home town.[35] It is a masterpiece of legal gibberish, whose only conclusion would be that those who discussed, and those who wrote it were complete maniacs, incapable of discerning the important from the accessary. Yet, for Sterne, if this was laughable, it was not because of the gibberish itself; it was because of the "reality effect" (to quote Roland Barthes[36]) produced by the document—its strange adequacy with the absurdity of life.

There was some kind of a relationship between the legal delirium manifested in *Tristram Shandy*, and the promotion of casuistry by early scholasticism: a relationship based on the suspicion shown towards general principles.[37] It was the same kind of suspicion that pushed Laclos, Casanova, or Sade to invent the extraordinary case records that their works were—looking for all possible variations on a given theme (sex, in their case). The agreements, in Laclos, Casanova, or Sade, were meant to question the very attempt at grounding them in the moral form of any legal apparatus—or, rather than question it, to dissolve it into multiplicity. Indeed, it was not by chance that in his small study on *Sade, Fourier, Loyola*, in 1971, Barthes analyzed side-by-side the writings of the founder of the Society of Jesus, and those of the inventor of the Society of the Friends of Crime.[38] The casuistry defended by Saint Ignatius of Loyola, as well as the spiritual exercises that made him famous, were not foreign to the casuistry of perversions developed by Sade—or those of pleasures invented by Charles Fourier. To put it this way: there was something *empirical* about casuistry, and the endless exploration of the world of variations that each case incarnates, be it theological, moral, legal, or sexual. This empiricism took the form of a renewed version of contractarianism that, rather than being opposed to the constraints of reality, consisted in its very assumption. Whereas theoreticians of the "social contract" developed versions of contractarianism that were opposed to the reality of a given society (whatever that means), those who resisted it where also conventionalist insofar as they assumed that social reality is what proffers what can be agreed upon. *Anything can be agreed upon*; there is no principle that would limit the power of agreements, and subject it to more or less moral, more or less grounded principles—even, as Johnson put it, the limit of an agreement denying the capacity to agree. Every scenario can be envisaged, provided that it is envisaged for itself, and not as the illustration of a general framework devising which scenario belongs to the logic of agreement, and which not. So that, contrarily to what one might think, the seventeenth and eighteenth centuries were actually restaging an old quarrel: the quarrel between natural and real law. But, whereas scholasticism had long been on the side of natural law, the new logic seemed to point towards a possible new alliance between it and empiricism.

As far as agreements are concerned, the general tendency of the seventeenth and eighteenth century was a tendency towards generalization and abstraction, that is, a tendency towards the triumph of the law, understood as an overarching principle. This general tendency was accompanied by a corollary tendency towards the legal internalization of morality, from then on considered as immanent to the legal apparatuses, and no longer transcendent. But this double tendency was immediately undermined by a counter-tendency: the tendency towards the ruining of the pretense of the law to constitute the horizon of law in general, and of the pretense to consider this horizon as a moral one. It was possible to observe these different moves not only at the level of private agreements (marriage settlements, contracts of employment, debts, and so on), but also at the level of public agreements (social contract). The very well-documented tradition of political contractarianism from Grotius to Rousseau, and passing by Hobbes, Locke, Kant, but also including later figures such as Fichte or Hegel, was, of course, a perfect incarnation of this double tendency.[39] But the triumph of this tradition, as well as the triumph of the defenders of codification, should not lead us to overlook that it did not take the form of a unanimous success-story—quite the contrary. Besides the tenants of another well-documented tradition (the counter-revolutionary, from Edmund Burke to

FIGURE 4.1 *The village bride* or *The village agreement*, 1761, by Jean-Baptiste Greuze (1725–1805), oil on canvas, 92x117 cm. Source: De Agostini/Getty Images.

FIGURE 4.2 *Mariage à la mode—The settlement*. Source: Imagno/Getty Images.

FIGURE 4.3 Watteau, *Marriage contract*. Source: ART Collection / Alamy Stock Photo.

Joseph de Maistre[40]), a secret tradition of writers and intellectuals defending another view on agreements has indeed existed. Yet, this tradition does not belong to the official realm of legal or political thought; it is rather the lateral consequence of narratives or depictions from which we are put in the position to read or see something different. In the present chapter, this tradition was represented by a small handful of writers, either scandalous or humorous (or both), but they indeed were more numerous than a superficial impression might lead one to think. To some extent, it might lead to the idea that the opposition presented here was close to that dividing the common law from the civil law—but nothing could be further from the truth. As historians have consistently shown, and as this chapter should have hinted at, both the common law and the civil law, in the seventeenth and eighteenth centuries, were haunted by the same desire towards the law—and agreements that would satisfy its demands.

CHAPTER FIVE

Arguments

The Visual Mediation of Arguments in the Renaissance

PIYEL HALDAR

INTRODUCTION

No account of the theory of early modern legal argumentation (with which this chapter deals) can ignore either the influence of classical rhetoric and logic (Plato, Aristotle, Cicero, or Quintilian) or the Christian tradition of rhetoric (Boethius, Saint Anselm or Saint Augustine). The principles of rhetoric drawn from these sources are signaled throughout various manuals and learning exercises that instructed lawyers in the art of pleading. For many, the purposes of both lawyer and orator were correlative. Both sought, according to the English judge John Doderidge, "to defend the causes and controversies of friends, to succour the oppressed, to relieve the grieved, to raise the afflicted."[1] This being the case, the influence of the humanist reception cannot be underestimated. Even in cases where new methods of argumentation were proposed, the legacy of these traditions quite obviously exerted a strong influence over legal argumentation.[2] Nevertheless, limiting our attention to the variety of past philosophical or theological stimuli runs the risk of ignoring contemporary influences that shaped the formulation and conduct of arguments. It further runs the risk of underestimating the particular contribution made by Renaissance humanism to the development of a visual rhetoric and a deeper understanding of the visual nature of argumentation.

In large part the influences that shaped the development of Renaissance arguments were technical and account needs to be taken of the medium through which arguments were made. Classical and medieval *actiones* of argument were conceived in cultures of oral transmission and aural reception. Renaissance culture tilted towards visual forms. Print media, in particular, shaped and manipulated the manner in which arguments could be presented. It set the contours according to which arguments were spatially (that is to say visually) set. The more general effect of the print revolution across the *studia humanitatis* has been well noted by, among others, Elizabeth Eisenstein and Walter Ong. For Eisenstein, the shift from scribal to print culture was of such a radical nature that she proposes replacing the term "renaissance" with that of "communication revolution."[3] However, the point might be given more emphasis. Humanism depended upon the materiality of print media for more than the purposes of communication. Print shaped the very structure and content of the intellectual aspects of the Renaissance humanism. Further, it shaped the ability of the reader to receive and respond to those aspects. What, in an oral context, required the temporal unfolding of a narrative was, after the print revolution, presented in greater proximity to the reader. Print allowed for things to be read and so to be perceived immediately on sight. This latter point is taken up in more specific terms by Walter Ong who gives greater accent to the relationship between formulating an argument and presenting the argument in the spatial terms made possible by print. In *Ramus, Method and the Decay of Dialogue*, Ong provides a detailed account of the work of the Huguenot philosopher and martyr Petrus Ramus.[4] Ramist rhetoric utilized the visual dimensions of the page to rearrange logic in spatial terms and present that argument to the eye of the reader. Knowledge, which of course was always divisible into subject areas, could be schematized and tabulated. These tables were presented on the page running from left to right enabling subjects to be indexed and then further divided into dichotomies. Dichotomies could then be subdivided into further categories. The process of division and subdivision was limited only by the width of the page and the size of the print. Print regulated the form and the substance of the argument to be presented; it enabled arguments to be displayed and inspected rather than spoken and heard. In terms more specific to legal practice, print made available a greater range of material (statutes, writs, forms of action, pleas, legal commentaries, *consilia*, treatises, common place books, and eventually precedent decisions). Spatial arrangements such as sequential volumes, chapters, pages, paragraphs, and lines had an obvious impact on the manner in which lawyers were able to discover, inspect, use and cite (with an increasing technical set of protocol) arguments. Textual features such as headings and subheadings, grammatical features such as colons and semicolons, visually organized and mediated material in ways that classical argumentation theory could not have considered.

Admittedly, there is little to be found in the numerous textbooks on lawyer's logic and rhetoric which accounts for this shift in the nature, conduct, and ultimate reception of arguments. Seismic though the shift undoubtedly was, early modern lawyers and jurists were largely silent as to the effects of this visual mediation of arguments. It may be that, for many lawyers, logic remained in thrall to technical systems that were developed from the conventions of oral tradition and from the assumption that orality was non-performative. Moreover, if early modern law was linked to the emergence and crafting of the state, then legal argumentation was linked to the narrower province of administration. A new and restricted ethos was forged according to which the task of lawyering came to be determined by the procedural administration of legality.[5] Legal arguments were directed towards concrete and individual cases without need to express the broader universal values that had characterized the spiritual jurisdiction of medieval canon law.

It would be a mistake, however, to assume that these curricula manuals provided the only source for constructing a theory of argumentation. A limited yet still influential range of visual treatises existed prior to the Renaissance. They treated the Roman law of images, the legal art of devices, the genealogical function of heraldry, and the use of symbols. The medieval jurist Bartolus de Saxoferrato, for example, had already published his tract on the legal governance of signs, flags, heraldry, and trademarks.[6] Gerard Legh, Abraham Fraunce and, somewhat later Henri Estienne all treated and theorized the various incarnations of the image through juridical lenses.[7] The most notable exception to the oral tradition is provided by the invention of emblems. The emblem tradition drew on these disparate legal ideas of the image and cohered the production of arguments in a strikingly visual format. It is from within the emblem tradition that lawyers were able to articulate, indeed visualize, what was at stake in the visual mediation of arguments. It is here that they were able to take advantage of moveable typefaces, printed woodcuts, and paper formats to present arguments. By shifting attention away from oral performance, emblems provided jurists (as opposed to the practical or pettifogging lawyer) an opportunity to develop an alternative model of argumentation unrestricted by the limitations of orality or procedure. Emblems provided an alternative paradigm, a model of conduct which sought to shape the construction, authorship, and reception of arguments within a visual economy. In doing so they sought to link universal principles (broadly conceived of as *logoi*) to both the ethos of office and the pathos of reception.

The argument below pieces together the structure of emblematic arguments displayed throughout the emblem tradition. After providing some background information on the emblem tradition and its links to the protocols of legal argumentation, this chapter addresses the emblematic argument according to the classical trinity of logos, ethos, and pathos. The section on logos ventures the argument, that emblematic argument was determined by the status of axioms and maxims within the visual frame of the image. The finding (*inventio*), arrangement (*dispositio*) and the development of the argument, however, cannot be reduced to any sense of what is posited within the frame. As Peter Goodrich has argued, emblems played on the theme of the *absconditus*; the absent and invisible source of law.[8] The emblematic argument concealed as much as it revealed and it dissembled as much as it postulated. It will be ventured that, far from being deductive or inductive, the emblem as an alternative paradigm of legal argumentation was mediated between the material and the immaterial worlds, between the obscure and the clear or between universal values and concrete hypotheses. One might argue that it had more in common with what Foucault (following Heidegger) terms "world disclosing arguments."[9]

In order to present the emblematic argument as both concealment and revelation, the emblematist had to conform to certain protocols. A section on ethos and character seeks to establish the emblematist as exemplary model of how the orator must seek the topics of argument. The emblematist was an ideal persona conditioned by the protocols of office to act as *honestas*. The emblematist was neither antagonistic nor did he (or she in the single case of the French Calvinist emblematist, Georgette de Montenay 1540–1581) wish to identify an ideal audience of subjects who were bound to agree. His role, conceived of in terms of ethos and decorum, was simply to be faithful to the forms of nature, to present the emblematic argument and to invite inspection rather than agreement. The ethos of the emblematist meant granting their readership the opportunity to uncover and resolve for themselves what was presented through perplexity, periphrasis, and *aenigmata*. It ought to be stressed that the term "emblematist" does not simply refer to the named author of the emblemata, or to the penmanship of the accompanying adages or poems. To be sure, the author held the esoteric knowledge and the classical training required to constitute the subject matter of the argument. But the construction of the emblematic argument was a joint enterprise between author, printer, woodcutter, publisher and where appropriate, translator. The author, it could be argued, was simply the visible figure, the fabricated image, that hid a much larger endeavor than the term "emblematist" indicates.

Finally, it follows that once the visual mediation of arguments is taken into account then the very idea of an audience changes. The section on pathos maintains that the act of inspection has to be differentiated from the act of listening. Where the latter relied on a supine audience, the former relied on more active forms of participation. The task of finding a meaning behind the terms of an argument was something left to the ideal citizen. They were the ones who had to see and so also to judge. The visual mediation of arguments did not aim to produce a passive and ideal audience, or a community of shared values. The reader was left to decide the merits and demerits of each case. This pathos of emblematic argumentation was also conceived as a question of decorum. Whether visualizing dialogue or individual arguments, the place of the reader as judge is not left unappreciated. The emblem did not simply present an argument to passive inspection. It required from the person inspecting it an active mode of participation. It required a method of deciphering and figuring out the wider argument at stake in an individual emblem.

EMBLEMATIC ARGUMENTS

The impact of the emblem tradition on the theory of argument was more relevant to the early modern lawyer than to members of any other branch of the *studia humanitatis*. And it is through this tradition that early modern lawyers sought to develop the relationship between law and rhetoric. It might be argued, however, that the presentation of emblems is but one aspect of an overall print culture and that in and of themselves emblems had, and continue to have, little to do with the logic and/rhetoric of legal arguments. Indeed, in its classical context, the emblem was no more than an insertion of a moral adage, a commonplace or illustration into an argument. The emblem could not be taken, *pro pars toto*, for the whole argument. The French humanist scholar of emblems Claude Mignault (1536–1606), reminded his readership that for the classical orator emblems simply provided speech with color and charm: "How charming are *ses dits* put together artfully like all the little stone dice of mosaic in a paved floor or in an inlay of wriggly pattern."[10] The emblem itself was inessential. If ornaments could be grafted onto speech they also could be detached. An argument could well survive without the sentiments and affectations provided by these emblematic *ses dits*. Quintilian, Mignault reminds us, advocated caution; maxims ought to be inserted discretely and judiciously and only as a means of summarizing an argument.[11] Used excessively, ornamental adjuncts, maxims, insertions, or whatever euphemism might be used to describe the emblem, might over encumber and threaten to destroy an argument. This was the most obvious danger of the supplement. There was always the possibility of "gilding refined gold," "perfuming the violet," "over-gilding the lily" or adding yet another "hue to the rainbow" to make a point particularly if that point were basic.[12]

For the classical orator, the emblem exceeded the point of the argument. For the humanist, the emblem took on more essential and demonstrative qualities. Humanism shifted the emblem's status to centre of the (printed) page. Much of this shift occurred due to the extraordinary popularity of emblem books during the Renaissance. The emblem book, as a collection of individual emblems, was invented, and first published by the Italian humanist jurist Andreas Alciato in 1531. Running into numerous editions and translations, Alciato's *Emblematum Liber* consisted of a number of individual emblems (eventually 200).[13] Each emblem consisted of a woodcut image accompanied by a Latin or vernacular subscription which articulated a commonplace maxim or motto (sometimes known as the subscription or *lemma*). Such maxims were theological, moral or legal and more often located in classical or biblical sources. Additionally, the third part of the emblem (alongside the image and subscription) was an explanation in verse of the image and subscription. Often the meaning of motto, image, and verse complemented each other. Given the cryptic and often hermetic nature of the enterprise, the parts of individual emblems would also on occasion deliberately contradict each other.

That Alciato was a jurist is telling. Indeed many of the emblematists who followed in his wake were also lawyers (Guillaume de la Perrière, Pierre Cousteau, Gabriel Rollenhagen and Barthélemy Aneau) who adopted the use of emblems to illustrate the five volumes of the Senneton edition of the *Corpus Iuris Civilis* (1548–1550).[14] Among the common lawyers, we might note in particular Gerard Legh, Geoffrey Whitney, George Wither, Thomas Blount, and Henry Peacham (whose illustrations for a manuscript edition of the *Basilikon Doron* provide an important gloss to King James I's theory of kingship).[15] The interest shown by the civilian and common lawyers betrays a deeper-rooted understanding of the visual in law.

The shift in the status of the emblem, from being a mere feature of an argument to being centre page allows us to discern what is at stake in the visual turn in Renaissance approaches to argument and argumentation. No longer detachable, ornamental, and supplementary, the emblem became paradigmatic, not just of the diffusion of legal norms that were directed towards the social and individual subject (per Goodrich), but of a mental habit that emerged from this visual turn. An example can be taken from an esoteric, admittedly non-legal text by the German Franciscan satirist and baiter of Lutheranism Thomas Murner (1475–1537). In his *Logica Memorativa*, Murner illustrated the logical parts of argumentation. Logical terms such as "predicament," "syllogism," "fallacy," "dialectic," "exception" and so on were individually emblematized by a variety of memorable signs and figures (fish, crowns, stars, moon, etc.). Each of these would then be printed on individual playing cards. The aim was to use these cards in a manner similar to today's (post-nineteenth century) "flash cards." As a pedagogic tool, they assisted in the memory of terminology and as a tool to drill in the study of logic.[16]

In terms of Renaissance argumentation, the emblem provided much more than an illustration of the tenets of logic. Each emblem existed as an argument in its own right. Robert Burton, for example, gave exactly this purpose to the emblem used as a frontispiece to the second (and subsequent) editions of *Anatomy of Melancholy* (Figure 5.1).[17] The image, engraved by Christian Le Blon, is given the title "argument of the frontispiece," and is divided into ten scenes, or in his words; "Ten distinct squares seen apart / ... joined together by cutter's art." Along with accompanying twelve stanzas, the emblem economically conveys the logical form and content of the book. Burton's frontispiece might be described as a species of paratext (the term Genette uses to describe those parts of a book—subtitles, prefaces, indices, dedications, colophons—seemingly incidental to its main business).[18] From the outset, this particular image strategically controls the reception of the main contents of the book. If the manner in which the main text is to be read is determined by the emblematic argument then the image is epideictic. It does not simply condense the argument contained in the book (there are other species of paratext such as the synopsis and the lengthy subtitle that manage this). It displays the very argument, unfurls it for closer scrutiny. On one, albeit obvious level, the squares depicting the various conditions of melancholia, as well as those depicting the author (Robert Burton/Democritus Junior) and Democritus Abderites depict their subject matter in a melancholic manner. Everything takes place beneath dark skies, in front of dead trees or under the signs of Saturn. The figures of Democritus senior and Hypochondria are listless, that of Inamorato is suitably wretched. There are carcasses, graveyard owls, bats, and other assorted auguries. For a treatise on the causes of conscious feeling and on the aberrations of rational thought, the life and language of images cannot be ignored. On another level, the image does more than display the argument of the book. It performs it. The image introducing us to a book that professes to anatomize its subject matter itself dissects melancholia into its different symptoms. It anatomizes the books thematic contents into individual compartments. Burton's emphasis of the "woodcutter's art" is made clear. The art of Le Blon is analogous to that of a surgeon. It exposes the hidden science of an organized body in order to reveal its inner workings. Moreover, this visual anatomization, performs what text cannot. The accompanying poem and the rest of the book arranges the argument into a sequence of sections and sub-sections. The woodcutter, however, is able to present all simultaneously so that the reader can directly and readily compare symptoms. As Burton himself makes clear, this recognition of the symptoms of melancholia does not even require further explanation. The symbols of jealousy (top left) which to us might appear the most obscure are for Burton (and for his contemporary readership) self-explanatory. A landscape of kingfishers, swans, fighting cocks, and roaring bulls were already well-established tropes in emblemata, hieroglyphica, and bestiaries. No research would have been required to decipher melancholic jealousy reflected in nature. The image speaks for itself. All Burton adds in the appropriate stanza for jealousy in the accompanying poem is this; "symbols are these, I say no more."[19] He is more emphatic in his description of inamorato. If any reader should fail to recognize this forlorn, wretched and abandoned lover then he needs to "take his selfe by the nose."[20] In brief, the anatomized image suffices to depict, display, and perform the main argument unaided. No more need be said. The rest of the book proceeds not by way of coherent argument but by scrutiny, anecdote, philosophy, satire, and wonder. All the while, the frontispiece continues to control the reading of the main text long after the page has been turned.

Burton's frontispiece is a singular image that took advantage of the general vocabulary of emblemata in order to visualize its argument. The more general emblem books themselves compiled a range of individual arguments. Some of these were arranged round similar themes. Others tackled a single subject, or a limited range of subjects, but from different perspectives, and often contain contradictory arguments. Thomas Palmer's "*Two Hundred Poosees*" (1566, arguably the first English emblem book) can be taken as a useful example. Here emblems of opposing morals were paired next to each other; the shortcomings of poverty, for example, might face the corruptions of wealth. As John Manning points out, the arrangement of opposing emblems imitated the protocols of academic debates and dialogues (such as those contained in works by Plato, Thomas More or Christopher St. Germain, etc.).[21] Both sides of an argument could be presented in visual terms, both sides of an argument could face each other, verso and recto, in a visual stand-off. For Palmer, as for a number of humanists (most notably Montaigne), such *in utramque partem* arguments were also a technique of avoiding strict adherence to a single truth. Emblems allowed the alternative to be argued. They enabled to return moral life to other perspectives, to other opinions, or, according to Montaigne's own maxim supposedly inscribed on one of the beams in his library, to *iudicio alternante*.

Whatever the subject matter, whether political, legal, religious, or moral, emblems emerged from a specifically legal mentality. For one thing, they were composed either by lawyers, or by those schooled in forensic argumentation, and like all good lawyers they enjoyed a certain state of lawlessness. They sought and found a way out of the strict application of the supposedly immutable. They sought and found loopholes and lacunae, arrowslits and *balistraria* within long held convictions. They tested moral principles in strategic situations and varied their applicability. As if *advocati diaboli*, they visualized the normative scenes from different perspectives, uncovering within them faults and falsifications. The technique of arguing in *utramque partem*, for example, was to be understood as specifically legal, part of a legacy inherited from Cicero's account of his defense of Sextus Roscius in which the Orator assumes the ability to argue both sides of a case.[22] They behaved as if in court, as if at trial,

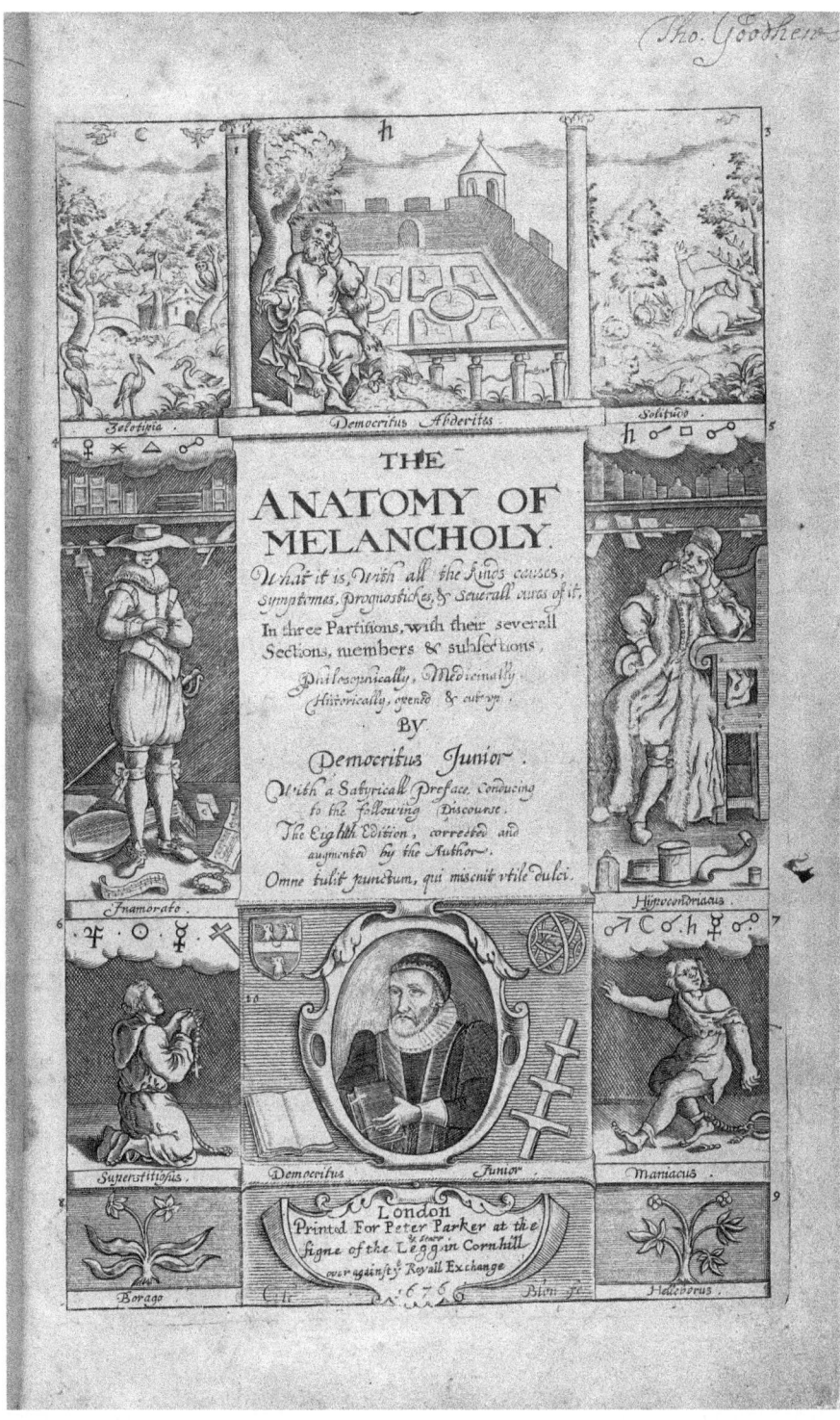

FIGURE 5.1 *Anatomy of Melancholy*, Frontispiece. Source: Robert Burton, Wellcome Collection.

but with the aid of the woodcutter were able to redraft the field of vision. Above all, they employed the classical trinity of argumentation—logos, ethos, and pathos—that had long been associated with legal rhetoric.

LOGOS—FRAMING THE ARGUMENT

What is instructive about Palmer's emblem book is that no conclusions were necessarily offered between competing emblems and this is the case with all emblems. Judgments were unstated and held in suspension. The emblematist simply offered the argument by hiding the final resolution. Emblems were emphatically ambiguous, enigmatic, and often hermetically coded. The mode of reasoning was neither inductive nor deductive. This did not mean that emblems escaped the protocols of *logos* prescribed by classical theory. To propose an alternative to the normative order, the emblematist had first to understand that normative order. He had first to uncover the parameters of *logos*.

In its classical context, the term *logos* refers to a number of issues relating to speech and discourse. It refers to the technical ordering of arguments (*dispositio*), to the process of reasoning, as well as to the provision of supporting evidence (*inventio*). Its application in the field of rhetoric was not unrelated to theodicy which wrought from the concept of logos a generative and animating principle; the universe generated from logos (*logos spermatikos*). Similarly, for the classical orator, the axiomatic position of logos allowed a reasoned argument to flow. The status of the axiom was central to logos since arguments were made possible by, and could only unfold from, an axiomatic position. Axioms ordered the argument and determined the inclusion of evidence, proofs, or illustrations. Moreover, they were regarded as self-evident and free from doubt. The point might be familiar to students of analytic philosophy. Wittgenstein notes more generally of logic; "if God creates a world in which certain propositions are true, then by that very act he also creates a world in which all propositions that follow from them come true."[23] Only the establishment of these normative framing devices could allow an argument to take shape, which means that arguments could only proceed within circumscribed closures. Speech depended on norms that could not be subjected to any logical method or process of reasoning. The well-reasoned argument depended upon a premise that existed beyond reason. In which case, we might surmise, if axioms affirmed an argument, then that argument itself provided proof of the irrational axiom, normative principle, or assumption that framed it.

For both the classic orator and early modern humanist, what framed a particular argument might be described as being pre-determined and pre-reflexive but the examples of such axioms were numerous. The most obvious instance from Christian rhetoric might be the irreducible and manifest status of God. Anselm's famous and controversial argument that "God is something than which a greater cannot be thought" (the *unum argumentum*) provided the premise from which all other arguments followed. Equally, the axiomatic frame might have been institutional authority or some other form of sovereignty. To argue that a particular man was of virtuous character might have been drawn from the dogma that the church was the foundation of man. To argue that the same man might be guilty of a crime might have proceeded from an exception to the fundamental proposition that God is first cause of all things. To argue over questions of jurisdiction might have proceeded from postulating a normative text (such as the Bible or the *corpus iuris civilis*). Each argument was circumscribed by, or within, a proposition, text, or institution. Each argument, therefore, also reified that proposition, text or institution. Each argument, as well as having a frame, simultaneously built and rebuilt that very frame. Norm preceded *logos* and *logos* proved the norm. The theoretical status of these framing devices was subject to the numerous commentaries by the early modernists who addressed the work of the sixth-century Roman philosopher and Consul Boethius. The influence of the Boethian systematization of dialectics, across the humanities cannot go unmentioned. His main claim in *Topicis Differentiis*, repeats the relationship between axioms and argument in slightly different terms. Arguments unfold from "maximal propositions." Maximal propositions were self-evident, universal, and accepted truths; things that were so well known that no proofs could come before it (e.g., every number is either odd or even). Only after the maximal proposition was declared could invention and discovery then be applied to the argument allowing the orator to uncover and seek out further arguments from the world of things (or *topoi*). Since the maximal proposition was an unassailable truth, it could be used to prove other propositions. Only once a frame, a maximal proposition, a precondition, or a normative ethic, had been established could arguments be allowed to develop.

Such approaches were not anathema to lawyers. The whole of the first section of Justinian's *Digest* stipulates that legal methodology operated only under the ambit of maximal propositions: "Jurisprudence is the knowledge of things divine and human."[24] To which is added more emphatically: "The maxims of law are these: to live honestly, to hurt no one, to give everyone his due."[25] Only once understood, can argumentation proceed and the exposition of the law commence "with utmost care and exactness."[26] It might well be profitable to examine the relationship between Boethian philosophy and Tribonian legal methodology. The two systems of thought were roughly contemporaneous with each other. But, for the purposes of this argument the relationship between the two matters little. Both exerted a strong influence on early modern argumentation.

Whether philosophical or legal or not, the fundamental point for the analysis of emblematic arguments was that of the frame. We could replace terms such as axiom, maximal proposition, or norm with that most marginalizsed of modern terms: the "frame." It is this capacity of the self-evident and heuristic "frame" that indicates the manner in which argumentation took a visual turn during the Renaissance. The *logos* of the frame is given its most emblematic expression where it is most visible, self-evident and therefore least obvious. It is given expression where it is both least and most expected. It is given expression in the very depiction of the frame that surrounds the pictorial elements of the emblem and divides the image from the text. The frame was more than what we would now assume to be a simple decorative border since the term "decorative" (as well as derived formations such as *decorum*) has been rendered hopelessly plain and redundant by modern use. It was more than a means of glorifying the emblem, giving it a frock coat or a fancy ruff collar, so to speak. It was for this reason that the French lawyer (non-practicing) and emblematist Guillaume de la Perrière placed the image of a blank frame at the end of the preface to his *Theatre de Bon Engins*. The frame, in other words, was the device that made possible the presentation of all the emblematic arguments that followed (see Figure 5.2). Pierre Le Moyne's De L'Art Device, while strictly speaking not an emblem book but rather a collection of moral devices, also includes a depiction of the frame in its frontispiece (Figure 5.3). This time the frame opens out onto the world. It discloses all that might be hidden were it not for the heroic labors of particular individuals who point the way. The frame, like any other window in a darkened room is what allows the antisepsis of daylight to be glimpsed. It is what allows for a vision of whatever high celestial entertainments the author has in store elsewhere in the book.

FIGURE 5.2 Guillaume de la Perrière, *Theatre bon engines*. Source: By kind permission of Peter Goodrich, private collection.

FIGURE 5.3 Pierre Le Moyne, *De L'Art Des Devices*. Source: Pierre Le Moyne, *De L'Art Des Devices*. (Paris: Sebastien Cramoisy and Sebastien Mabre Cramoisy 1666). Source: By kind permission of Peter Goodrich, private collection.

It is instructive that the term "frame" was sometimes translated as *aedificare* or *configurator* since the frame built and configured the emblem. There is an architectural form to the frame that arranges and fixes the image to the page, as if to the surface of the earth, and simultaneously situates within it all that is proper to the construction of the argument. The frame is what prevents the constituent parts of an argument from falling apart. It configures and gives coherence to an otherwise random collection of fragments.

By visually rendering and configuring an argument, it is what gives that argument a sense of rational coherence it would not otherwise have. The *dispositio*, or the organizational scheme of the image is thematized, and continues a discourse initiated by the axiomatic proposition. The frame visually replicated the logical framing of an argument giving the logos a visible diagrammatic form.[27] In the case of emblems collected by the Dutch emblematist Gabriel Rollenhagen and his English counterpart George Wither, the axiom was inscribed on the circular frame itself.[28]

Indeed the very status of the frame as an axiomatic device is given expression by George Whitney in his emblem *sine iustitia, confusio* (emblem 122).[29] For Whitney, the very act of creation is an act of framing from which all other things follow. He takes as his subject the myth of Themis translating it into a Christian account. His verse describes the chaos which preceded the age of justice, where elements and seasons bore no coherent relationship to each other, and where truth was given no proper shape. Only through His act of framing heaven and earth does God allow for justice and then coherence:

> But god that of the former heape:
> The heaven and earthe did frame,
> And all things plac'd therein,
> His glorye to declare

It is in this sense that the frames of individual emblems can be taken seriously as a visible mode of framing an argument. Just as His act of framing reveals "the heaven and earthe," the emblem's frame reveals the argument contained within, making it visible to inspection. Just as the axiom allows an argument to flow, so the frame gives birth to the argument. Strikingly, in a visual representation of lips both enunciating and giving birth to an argument, the more baroque frames are labial designs. These marginal folds, seemingly illogical in form, are what give passage to the argument. They represent the feminine obscene that gives life to the argument, visually depicting the transcendent irrationality of all axiomatic propositions that enable rational argumentation. Another, equally striking version of the nativity of arguments is provided by Georg Stengel in his curious collection of *Ova Paschalia*. Each emblematic image hatches from a frame that is deliberately constructed in the shape of an egg.[30] If giving birth implies parenting it also implies the act of making apparent. The frame was *procreo apparens* and established the emblematic argument as a form of what Peter Goodrich has termed the *argumentum ad apparentiam*. That is, what was framed was simply the outward appearance and manifest form of things. There was always something concealed by the argument, something beyond the frame, something that came before the egg. The image, in other words, was not simply an entity without prior cause. It was a cipher to the spiritual principles that informed religious thought, civic organization, social justice, or normative ethics.

The frame alluded to the status of the axiom as a generative moment prior to the argument. For the emblematist the image and therefore the argument was a visible reminder of an invisible source.[31] As that which was beyond doubt or dispute, the axiom properly referred to an ulterior provenance beyond mortal logic and did not conform to any principle by which meaning is determined only by what is stated. The emblematic argument exposed its own unsaid and unseen sources (or, in a much repeated vein throughout the emblematic tradition, it exposed the vanity of attempting to understand God's nature through language alone). The normative axiomatic order remained outside the field of vision and transcended the materiality of the page. The frame constituted both inside and outside. It both announced the gestation of the visible argument and woke a spiritual and therefore invisible site of conception. This is not to suggest that all emblems required contemplation of the Christian divinity. That might have been the case for the theologically minded emblematist. The frame might refer to the spiritual government of civic organization, it might refer to the spirit of monarchical rule (as it does in Henry Peacham's *Basilikon Doros*), or it might refer to the absconded spirit of the law. The use of the grotesque in some of the frames suggests riddles derived from Ovidian tales. A border consisting of palm trees might either suggest antique biblical lands or the hermeticism of Egyptian sources. A baroque frame of harvested fruit might indicate an emblematic argument to the framing logic found in the Ciceronian basket of nature. Such allusions and suggestive indications were open to decryption. But they were what distinguished emblematic arguments from oral forms of rhetorical delivery. The frame not only spatialized the inset image. By pointing to an absent source, they created a sense of distance that enabled the reader to perceive the relationship between the manifest and the invisible. They projected the rectilinear page onto a different plane. The frame not only allowed the reader to see the image portrayed, but to reflect on things missing and on a spiritual source that had left humanity adrift. In doing so, the framed emblem made apparent what was normally hidden in oral delivery. Moreover, the emblematic argument might be more emphatically contrasted to classical argumentation. In their classical context, axioms circumscribed and closed off an argument. The emblem opened the axiom up. It allowed space for a reflection on the provenance of arguments.

What is decisive is that while these allusions to distant and encrypted sources determined and corrected the rectitude of the emblematic argument they did not necessarily guarantee the *truth* of the argument. On the contrary, the emblematic argument only attempted to expose an invisible source and subject that source to summary and hypothesis. The term "hypothesis," it ought to be remembered, applied to plot summaries in Greek drama.[32] Its function was to propose, and only propose, an explanation of the drama. While clearly related to its classical Greek heritage, the use of the emblem as hypothesis might bear stronger connections to the modern use of the term. That is to say, the emblem sought to do no more than provide an opportunity for the reader to reflect upon a possible truth from the distance spatialized by the emblem. Put differently, the emblem sought to test the axiomatic parameters of the frame. It did not marshal its content as evidence in order to validate its conclusions. Truth was only ever a proposition. Emblems were, in a deep sense, trials, visual essays, that allowed for critical responses to axiomatic principles that were supposedly beyond doubt. They gave to the reader the opportunity to conclude upon and judge for themselves disputed questions (what the schoolmen called *quaestiones disputatae*) of established authority, false religion, human wisdom, evangelical militancy, and so forth.

ETHOS—THE DECORUM OF EMBLEMATIC ADVOCACY

Presenting arguments, whether in court or on the page, was a matter of *ethos*. The *ethos* of composition, for example, was not simply a matter of constructing an individual image/argument. The orator must choose what, and what not, to show. Criteria of relevance and admissibility determined the overall construction of the emblem. The general difficulty of choice was an often repeated theme among emblematists. The emblem *La Finis Coronat Opus* by the French poet Jean-Jacques Boissard, for example, displays a Y-shaped tree referring both to the Pythagorean *upsilon* and to the parable of the two paths in Matthew 7.13 (Figure 5.4).

In both cases, the choice between the two paths is a matter for the soul. Choice is not only difficult; the correct path to take is also a difficult path. That is the one entwined with thorns. But it is also the path crowned with beauty. The broader path, the path of easy access, is the path of easy virtue (*voluptas*), which ends with the cross of ignominy. Boissard's emblem and his accompanying verse, however, adds a different gloss to the usual business of electing between a life of virtue or of vice. The figure seated on the right hand side is portrayed in the act of writing upon tablets. Everything in nature has been counted, every feature recorded. God can distinguish even the individual "hairs on your head." In order to choose the right path, in life or in art, one needs to imitate Divine knowledge. One needs to see in order to distinguish and what one needs to see one needs to see in detail. Illumination (as distinct from the soul's enlightenment) is what is at stake and this means that the art of composition is a matter of choice. It is a matter of deliberating what to write, what to portray and what to leave out and erase (*litura*).

As well as deciding on the form, the emblematist had to distinguish the details of nature in order to cull and gather the elements that constituted the image. Emblems were, to borrow the pun from the previously mentioned Thomas Palmers' *Two Hundred Poosees*, both part of the Renaissance tradition of poesie and *poosees* in their own right; they were bouquets, the flowers of rhetoric, offered to a readership.

But there was more to the *ethos* of the emblematist than the art of composition. In Aristotelian terms, *ethos* refers to the character of the speaker including his credibility, integrity, or expertise. It might also include the tone of the message of speaker, his role in the proper construction of speech. For Cicero, the propriety of speech is as much a question of ethics as it is one of logic and properly falls under a discussion of *decorum*.[33] More emphatically than Aristotle, Cicero stresses the orator as *honestas* (a good virtuous man) obeying both the laws of nature and the spiritual legacy of ancestry. Decorum was copied from nature and required the *honestas* to look among the living forms of nature. The mind was a hunter of forms (*venator formarum*) looking for "beauty, loveliness and the congruence of parts of the things that sight perceives."[34] Once found, the orator transferred decorum found in nature to his own deeds and the construction of speech. Similarly, the orator must look to the wisdom of the past, to the *mos maiorum*. Only by doing so was the *persona* of the orator able to shine brightly (with *enargiue*), to cause the audience to love him (ii.32) and to win their faith (ii.33).

The political and legal thought of the Renaissance held the concept of decorum as central, applying it across a range of relevant areas.[35] Erasmus, for example connects decorum to the private cultivation of manners and etiquette.[36] But he also fuses it to the conditions of service and ceremony within which eloquence and the perorations of dignitaries and other officials were able to take place. Puttenham, to provide another example, connects the term to the image of the speaker.[37] Indeed, by the time of the Renaissance, the term had come to replace the medieval concept of dignity so well covered by Ernst Kantorowicz as the continuing form of life that exceeded the life of any mortal incumbent of office.[38] It is this connection to, and derivation from the political theology of dignity that allowed the humanist to assimilate the category of decorum into their own understanding of office and consequently to the construction of arguments. Nevertheless, decorum, though related, had a specific set of functions distinguishable from those of dignity. For Alciato, decorum was strictly a legal feature. The standards of decorum as he emphasizes in his "*Praetermissa*" were better suited to lawyers.[39] When divorced from law and justice, when applied merely for its own sake or for the sake of vanity, decorum ran the risk of causing disaster in the commonwealth.[40] Lawyers, he claims, were best equipped to seek order, determine propriety and maintain the rectitude of social order. Decorum, moreover, as an aspect of *ethos* required the ability to be vigilant. Vigilance, for Alciato, was a singular, if perhaps idealized, trait of both lawyers and orators and it is why, for the emblematist Junius Hadrianus, the lawyer, the orator and the emblematist all study by night: "It is about the watch that Demosthenes, the Lord and chief of orators kept."[41]

The point to emphasize here is that decorum, unlike dignity, was a matter of seeing and distinguishing. In claiming that the hunter of forms copied the forms of nature, Cicero gave heavy emphasis to the capacity of sight. It was vision that allowed the orator to perceive the congruence of forms in nature and transform decorum found in nature into the deeds of his office. This capacity to see the ideal forms of nature, perhaps quite obviously, applied to the role of the emblematist in the construction of emblems. The faithful compositor copied and glorified nature without excessive elaboration.[42] He gave nature a form in concordance with established decorum. This feature alone distinguished the ethos of the emblematist from that of the Renaissance poet and the Renaissance artist. It put him in close connection with a much older ideal of the *officium poetae* whose function, according to Petrarch, was to disclose and glorify the truth of things woven into the decorous cloud of fiction (*veritatem rerum decora velut figmentorum nube contextam*). Unlike the Renaissance version of the poet laureate or the poet in the mold of Dante, the emblematist did not pass judgment on mankind (which is a role that Ernst Kantorowicz ascribes to the cult of the poet).[43] Neither was the emblematist marked by any sense of divine genius (or by a type of sovereignty analogous to that of political sovereignty) ascribed to the Renaissance artist.[44] The composition of emblems was distinguishable from the idea of a work of art, which was created out of nothing. Emblems were created out of something. The peculiar *ingenium* or wit of the emblematist lay in his ability to discover, retrieve, and rehabilitate that which already existed. He was a conduit and a mediator between universal often cosmic principles and the concrete world in which he lived. This role was not without its antecedents. In this, the emblematist was heir to a tradition that was heavily determined by the protocols of legal intelligentsia. The Aristotelian image of the judge as an intermediary between natural law and positive law, between inanimate *potentia* and its actualization, would have been well accepted. The emblematist was a jurisprudent who, to advert again to the very first section of Justinian's *Digest*, sought knowledge of things both divine and human. What was decisive was that the emblematist did not merely submit to the law of nature; he had also to visualize it. He did not merely direct universal principles to concrete situations; he had also to visualize those situations and test them out within the frame of an image.

The argument, in other words, did not rest on the opinions of the individual orator. He simply transmitted what he saw; namely the incorporeal, the axiomatic, or the laws of nature. To put it in Ciceronian terms: "Time erases the comments of opinion and confirms the judgment of nature" (*opinionum commenta delet dies; natura indicia confirma*).[45] Emblematists had to hold back to let nature speak. Montaigne's own personal medal, for example, which was engraved with the phrases "*epokhe*" (I hold back) on one side, and "Que Sais-Je" on the other, can be taken as emblematic. For Montaigne, the task in presenting an argument, an essay, or an image, was one involving abstention. Since human intellect was powerless to discover truth it had no option but to suspend judgment. Montaigne might be the most famous exemplar of this position but he does not stand alone. Alciato, to provide another example, crucially refused to use his emblems to confirm his own religious beliefs. Unlike Erasmus, he did not wish to engage in doctrinal debate. What mattered to him was scholarship and that required self-discipline and self-sacrifice.[46] Again, the roots of this particular feature might well be found in the Ciceronian ethics of legal advocacy. In linking arguments not to logic but to ethics, Cicero allowed counsel to defend clients who they knew to be guilty. As a matter of decorum and custom, the role of counsel was not to discover or state truth since that was the role of judge/jury.[47]

This figure of the emblematist as an ideal practitioner of oratory can also be given sharper focus by contrasting him to the lawyer who might suffer from a singular lack of decorum. If the ideal form of argument hid as much as it revealed, the indecorous argument was one which revealed too much. The figure which came to be identified with indecorum and which provided a foil to the ethical *honestas* was the *rabulas*, the pettifogging and garrulous lawyer. The lawyer was a figure much lampooned by the emblematists for sharp practices, for turning law into mere trade without honor. Little wonder that, as Chaim Perelman notes, Renaissance utopian literature never left room for lawyers.[48] At stake was a rhetorical style. Pierre Coustau's emblem *In Rabulis et Operarios Lingua Ce Lexi* takes as its subject such masters of litigation (Figure 5.5).

FIGURE 5.4 Jean-Jacques Boissard, *Finis Coronat Opus*. Source: Jean-Jacques Boissard, *Emblematum Liber*. Metz: Jean Aubery and Abraham Faber, 1588 at p. 23. Source: By permission of University of Glasgow Library, Special Collections.

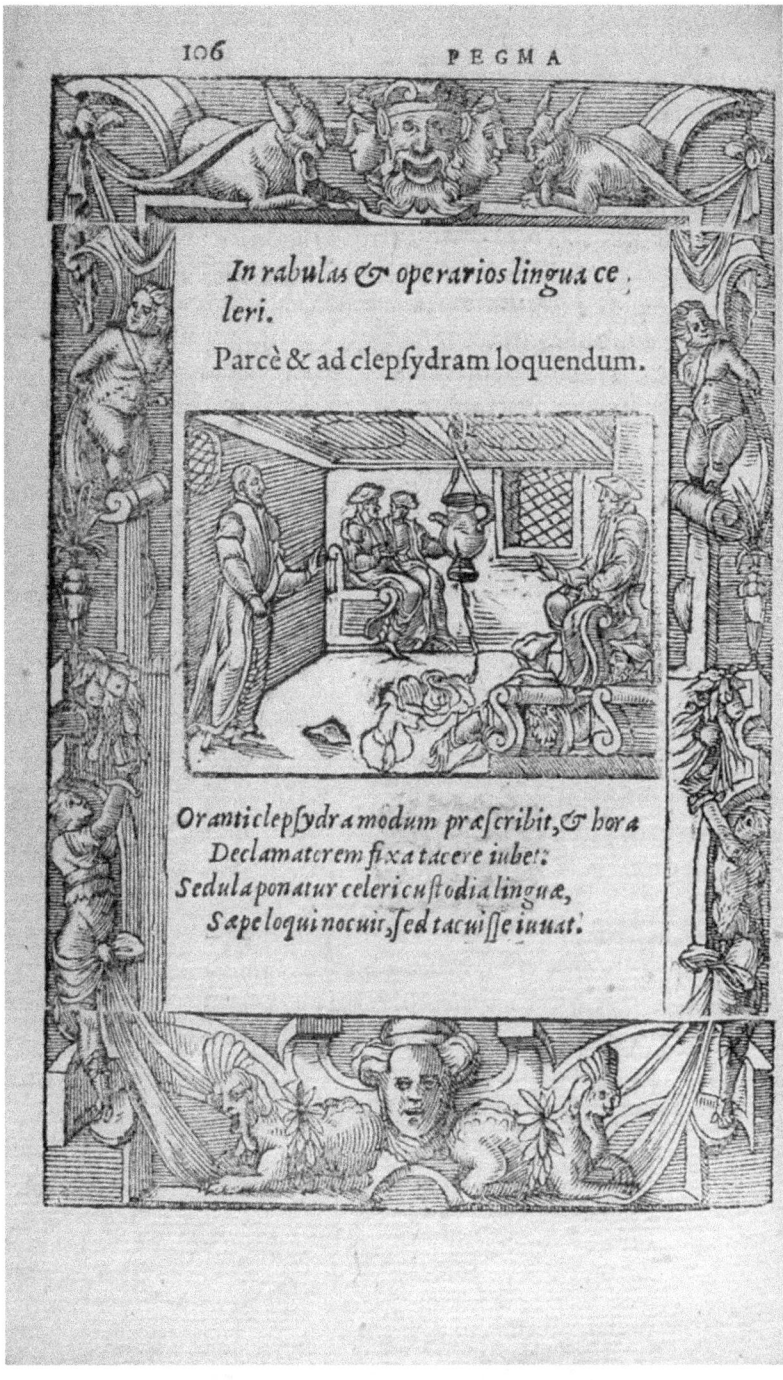

FIGURE 5.5 Pierre Cousteau *In Rabulis et Operarios Lingua Ce Lexi.* Source: Pierre Coustau, *Pegma.* Lyon: Bonhomme, 1555 p. 106. The subscription reads: "*Oranti clepsydra modum praescribit et hora / declamatorem fixa tacere iubet. / Sedula ponatur celeri custodia linguae, / Saepe loqui nocuit, sed tacuisse iuvat.*" Source: By permission of University of Glasgow Library, Special Collections.

The woodcut depicts the scene of a tribunal. On the left, a pompous lawyer in the middle of his perorations addresses himself to a patient judge who raises his hand as if to say "enough." In the middle of the room hangs a water clock which, we are told, "sets the speaker his limit, and orders that the orator cease talking at a fixed time." Nature in the guise of time places a "conscientious watch … on the gabbing tongue." Legal argumentation, for it to conform to decorum, had to be distinguished from the *ethos* and style associated with the pettifogger who, by over-talking, revealed too much and said too little. It is better to speak little and by the clock (*parce et ad clepsydram loquendum*).

While there is a satirical purpose to the emblem it is important to stress that the emblematist still holds off from passing judgment. Satirical edge derives from portraying those who depart from the decorous forms of nature. It is nature that judges and that is what the audience must negotiate. Although less immediately obvious and more ambiguous, this feature of satire is given more pronounced reflection by Alciato in his use of the image of the pelican in his emblem *garrulum et gulosum* (against a noisy and gluttonous fellow) to portray the manner in which lawyers might depart from natural decorum (Figure 5.6). Frequently used as a symbol of Christ's justice, late medieval and

FIGURE 5.6 Alciato, *Garrulum et Gulosum*. Source: Alciato, *Emblematum Liber*, n. 13 (Emblem xcvi). Source: By permission of University of Glasgow Library, Special Collections.

early Renaissance literature usually portrayed the bird piercing her breast in order to feed her own blood to her offspring. During the Elizabethan period, it would come to symbolize the maternal care of the Virgin Queen. Alciato, unencumbered by mystical dogma and willing to play with its traditional associations, transforms the pelican into a more ambiguous symbol of justice. Here the bird, while retaining its connections to justice, is also a distorted ranter, a *rabula*, who is so enslaved by his own appetites. It is a thick set and gluttonous creature "addicted to its own belly and gut." By extension, the over-loquacious and over-fed lawyer (or legal academic) is one who fails to exercise any form of self-governance and who fails to consider what, in the name of decorum, is required of his audience. So much so, that even in talking and exposing so much, he fails to make sense. What is required is not a heavy torrent of words, even (or, rather especially) if such words are made in the name of justice. What decorum required was eloquence and that required veils, concealment, abstinence and a recognition that the task of lifting the veil to reveal the judgment of nature is a task for to the audience.

PATHOS—ACTS OF RECEPTION

Even if the *logoi* of emblems hid the full resolution of meaning and if emblematists, as a matter of *ethos* and decorum, abstained from judgment, it cannot be assumed that readers were left in the dark. Starved of light, it was left to the "glorious lustre" and spiritual efficacy of the image (or what Puttenham respectively terms the *enargia* and *energia* of rhetorical ornaments) to illuminate the dark recesses of the inquiring mind to access what was hidden. Through sight, the emblem invaded and modulated the interior space of cognition, judgment, and memory. In Puttenham's terms, sight "inwardly worke[d] a stirre to the mynde."[49] Yet it was obvious that the task of image reception was not a passive one. In the pre-humanist scheme of the world, the word of God (conceived of as spoken) rendered blind obedience of faith to the concealed judgment and hidden counsel of God. The appropriate response was "to adore rather than scrutinize" what "the Lord has left hidden in secret."[50] This passive and relaxed mind set (*animum sedatum*) characterized the culture of orality, and fastened audiences to apparatuses of power and the founding function of the sovereign. It was to be distinguished from the exercise of active reasoning proposed by the humanists and necessitated by the inspection of images.

Images and vision required a set of more radical sensibilities than speech and hearing in order to pierce the veil of meaning. They required, according to Henry Peacham, an appropriate intellect that "changes silver into gold" in order to "better rather than abate the view."[51] What was needed, according to Puttenham, was "the parties own assoile."[52] The term "assoile" is instructive. Not only does it imply effort, but, in its religious context, what was at stake was a journey towards absolution and redemption. Take, as an example, a short tract published in 1564 entitled *A Dialogue against Fever Pestilence* by the English puritan divine William Bullein.[53] The epidemic of plagues to which the title refers is taken as a symptom both of social decay and of the spiritual malaise of the protagonist Cives. Before achieving redemption Cives embarks on a journey away from London. He proves himself to be a worthy citizen only after he has chanced upon a number of emblems hanging on the walls of a village inn. These emblems, which crystallize a set of laws, as well as religious doctrine, provide the visual cue for Cives' redemption. By interpreting these emblems, Cives connects his knowledge of law both to the social and to the supra-social metaphysical realm. He proves his worth. He finds, through the visual, a channel to the divine guarantor of social conduct. Only by understanding what was concealed through his spiritual redundancy is Cives able to die a citizen both of the kingdom of eternal glorie and of England.

Cives' journey begins from a point of ignorance and this concealment of knowledge was conceived of as a starting point from which the journey towards absolution could proceed. Since ignorance was the condition of post-lapsarian existence, darkness, and obscurity were posed as necessary difficulties to understanding. As the Elizabethan judge Thomas Wilson put it:

> Manne, by nature hath a sparke of knowledge, and by the secrete working of God, judgeth after a sorte, and discerneth good from evill. Before the fall of Adam, this knowledge was perfeicte, but through offence, darkenesse folowed, and the bright light was taken awaie. Wisemen therefore, considerynge the weakenesse of mann's witte, and the blindeness also, invented this arte [of reason], to helpe us to findeth the trueth.[54]

The roots of these arguments are Augustinian whose influence was not undiminished by the humanist turn away from medievalism. For Augustine, the "reign of love" involved careful, patient reflection from within darkness in order to pierce the veil of ignorance. Obscurity was a necessary difficulty since "no one denies that things sought with a certain difficulty are found with much greater pleasure *(facile investiga plerumque vilescunt)*."[55] That "certain difficulty" on the path to pleasure was no more than the exercise of spiritual reason. If ignorance was darkness, if God represented the maximum learning of ignorance, the image provided at least a "sparke" to ignite the process of "reason" (or what Nicholas de Cusa termed *docta ignorantia*).[56]

It is through this process of a journey proceeding from darkness that mental habits were structured to receive the visible world of arguments. What emerged, as a matter of the pathos of argumentation, was a recognition that the reader might possess a suitable mental forum since "the seed of God's word doth fructify according to the quality of the ground."[57] This mental forum cannot be explained simply by the term vision (or correlates such as inspection or sight). Since the image was only the visible and material presence of the invisible and immaterial, vision was only part of the process of participation. The practices of visual reception conformed to a range of practices instituted by the early modernists, humanists, and Protestant reformers, but it was only a condition for the process of reasoning itself.

Such mental habits were not restricted to theological matters or religious practice; indeed, they were more fastidiously developed by early modern lawyers. It is possible to trace similar processes in manuals of logic and rhetoric. To borrow the subtitle of the earliest logic manual in English (Ralph Lever's *Art of reason, rightly termed Witcraft*) the decorum of reception was given expression as a form of "witcraft"; a fashioning and crafting of the interior dimensions of wit.[58] No less consistently than with other forms of the civilizing process, the mind had to conform to the standards of civic manners. It conformed to a model that regulated thought not as the opposite of action, but as a form of action itself. For the logicians, this meant that witcraft was conceived as "internal mocion."[59] Once the eye perceived the image it had to stage its own theater, its own performance. Thought became the microcosm of drama and opened up an interior dialogue according to which the "eie directs wit" and imagination guides reason.[60] For Thomas Wright visual perception ignited a whole inner experience wherein "spirits flocke from the brayne, by certain secret channels to the heart, where they pitch at the dore."[61]

This microcosmic drama which proceeds from vision stands in contrast to what is often claimed by modern scholars of rhetoric. As Chaim Perelman and Lucie Obrechts-Tytreca have influentially claimed, the orator, lawyer or jurist, prepares their speech for an ideal universal audience.[62] Appealing to their shared values, rhetoric must aim to produce agreement. Arguments are, as they were in the classical scheme, forms of persuasion imbued with values shared in communion with audience. At this level, arguments are supposed to be audible speech performances and the *sensus communis* of the civis is no more than a community of passive listeners.

Once conceived in the terms described, visual argumentation placed the inspecting subject under duty to act upon and within the argument. Being confronted by an image or, for that matter, by the spectacle of the trial, required participation. The exercise of reason meant being inserted into the image or spectacle, of inhabiting the law as living materiality in order to be part of the law. As Pierre Legendre argues, seeing meant inscribing oneself in the visual backdrop, inhabiting the *mise en scène* to dwell in the world.[63] The appropriate behavior was neither hushed solemnity nor passive obedience. It was thought as action.

CONCLUSION

All legal arguments, in so far as they are performative, take place within a field of vision. Whether oral, textual, or reliant on digital media, today's legal arguments are subject to a regime of display, transmission and inspection that ought potentially to correspond to classical standards of *logos, ethos,* and *pathos*. It might seem that the possibilities of pitching law against its administrative ethos and directing it towards normative values that better reflect concerns of spirit might be discerned at the level of argument. Nevertheless, today's forms of argument stand in sharp contrast to the forms of argumentation that emerge from the juridical tradition of emblems. The frames within which modern legal arguments typically occur are set by the case itself. Winning becomes everything. So that the content of the argument, the appeals to reason or emotion are determined by the outcome hoped for. Arguments are determined not by any higher universal principles, or *logoi*, but by a posterior outcome. In this sense modern argument might be described as *argumentum ex culo*; shapeless, clueless, bottom up.

The problem lies in forgetting the visual nature of argumentative performances and a reluctance to take seriously the conceptual framework and theoretical repercussions of these routines.[64] For this reason, a turn towards a study of rhetoric (understood according to its oral–aural assumptions) is insufficient in attempting to return law to its relationship to its civic offices and values. It is only a more robust historical appreciation of visual argumentation through the framing, composition and inspection of emblems that allows for a return to values that might correct the administrative application of law.

Turning attention to the visual framing of an argument does not determine argumentation under the heavy weight of universal precepts. First, it helps to remind us that arguments carry an unexpressed normative ethic within them and that there are pre-conceptual frameworks, beyond reason, that condition and determine what the lawyer does. What lawyers say, and how lawyers mediate what they say, expresses something beyond the immediate horizon of their arguments. If emblems allowed for inspection to transfer from the particulars of the image to what lay unexpressed beyond the frame, then such a visual model helps to pan from the material particulars an argument to a wider picture. It enables us to see things at a distance. So that, second, the somewhat understated aim of this chapter has been to claim that arguments conceived of visually, take place within an institutional structure. They afford a view of what lies beyond the immediate horizon of concrete terms. Paradoxically, only by being performed in recognition of these parenting and apparent institutional structures are things able to be perceived at a distance. It is at this level that we might better be placed to challenge the letter of the law. This distance is what enabled the humanists both to negotiate normative, universal values and to inscribe new forms of predicates.

It might be added, that the visual form of argumentation that emerged from the medium of emblematics was an alternative model to those administrative forms practiced simply by lawyers. In this sense, visual argumentation held a much broader appeal. Its functions applied to jurists and poets, philosophers and theologians, legal scholars and humanist theorists. Visual argumentation, in other words, affords those of us not involved in legal practice certain pedagogic value. Legal theory today, particularly critical legal theory, might well draw lessons from the visual composition and transmission of arguments. Much of legal theory tends to fall into the trap of false mysticism. This is more prevalent in those forms of argument that are heavily determined by a sense of political purpose. My objection is not to political purposes themselves, but the danger of turning those purposes into dogmatic formula that attempt to seek affirmation and obedience from an audience. Part of the problem tends to be a heavy overstatement of targets and objectives. Speaking truth to power may or may not shake the foundations of power. But such speech in the name of truth forgets that truths need to be subjected to the decorum of understatement, or even suspension, for them to be negotiated and subjected to re-invention. Whatever the case, there is a further danger that the audience is directed away from the mechanics of institutional life and towards a state of de-institutionalized and illusory supremacy. The irony is that such arguments tend increasingly to claim a politics of resistance. Yet nothing about these arguments enables an audience to participate in any form of resistance. Rather, arguments become discrete units that mimic institutions in themselves while forgetting the institutional structure that enables them in the first place. They become closed and internally coherent formulas. Legal theoretical arguments that forget their provenance also forget a duty owed to the audience as a collection of legal subjects. Consequently, any potential idea that law might owe an ethic of care to its audience (or that it might need to replenish that ethic) tends to be buried. The administrative ethos undergoes further processes of calcification. Conceiving arguments as visual performances at least helps prevent theory from falling into the trap of closure.

CHAPTER SIX

Property and Possession

THANOS ZARTALOUDIS AND RICHARD BRAUDE

To possess is not merely to relate to a part of the world in the sense of taking power over it as a matter of right, nor property the inherent character of an unchanging self. To possess, however, is to enter into a culture of such juridical embracing, and to define, through the act of taking and taking over, a property-owning entity, a legal subject, as well as to delimit and reproduce its object. The formation of a property system in the sixteenth and seventeenth centuries was a significant, while terrifying, achievement, going hand in hand with the forcible, if not predictable, creation of a proletariat, divorced from the land. This particular aspect of English culture, of Englishness, aided the circumscription of legal subjects and modes of possession far beyond the cliffs and shores of the British Isles. The workforce of slaves, indentured laborers, domestic servants, waged artisans, manufacturing workers, and farm hands, the limitation of whose rights were interwoven with the limitation, almost often to nil, of the rights of women and slaves, was formed through the expropriation and reappropriation of land, and the institution in law of the depoliticized justification for this neutralization and expulsion.

At the same time, these people—their lives, struggles, creations, and deaths—worked up from below into this thought. They were not only delimited by, but formative of, these cultures, deliberately or otherwise. The concepts inherited from this period, which continue to circumscribe the plural, changeable, resistible meanings of "to have," owe much of their dreams to the nuances and details of daily life and death in early modern England, even while those same concepts have been reworked and refashioned into different cultures and forms, at times almost beyond recognition. Our concern here is how, in the wider extension of a culture of property in later medieval England and eventually a global sphere, the complexity, contradictions, and fissures of this legal-cultural rationalization expressed themselves in the realm of cultural production. Let us note from the outset that such expression can never be a pure relation—indeed it is only the very culture we are examining which would claim the power of such an equivalence, Bacon's *scientia universalis*.[1]

The finite, entirely specific, history of English property, much as it might deserve to be a side issue in the chronicles of the world, has instead become a fulcrum of international analysis and debate, from at least as early as Marx's documentation of the sixteenth-century clearances (which he saw repeated in the highlands in his own time) and further analysis by Marxist historians.[2] Indeed, the concepts of enclosure and of the commons have come to be central to our understandings of the privatized "world," a moment of early modern legal understanding, both plebeian and elite, which provides a rhetorical springboard for identities as diverse as graduate students, peasant guerrillas, surrogate mothers, and computer programmers.[3] Yet it is worth revisiting, for the specificities of the period, some moments of break and fissure, of "shifting" which its laws of property and possession engendered and perhaps permitted. These move beyond the opposition of commons and enclosure, and into contradictions within technologies of property as they were conceived in the early moments of the great capitalist experiment played out on the English fields and their colonial gardens.

We trace this through three fragments. The first focuses on two characters in Shakespeare's *The Tempest* of 1610, Gonzalo and Caliban. Gonzalo, advisor to the King of Naples, stumbles across the paradox of sovereignty within utopianism facing all who attempted to provide advice to and advocacy for their monarchs and emperors. The dreaming counselor wants to be a sovereign to renounce his sovereignty itself. One tempestuous figure is met by another, Caliban, who we show to be a figure formed by the division and different attitudes between Roman law and common law, defined as both a legitimate human inheritor (so that he can be officially dispossessed), as well as an inhuman object (so that he can be legally owned).

The second moment engages with the way women were objectified culturally and legally under the doctrine of "coverture" and the fissures that allowed potential shifts within, and reversals of, such enclosure—both in court as well as in literary depictions. Parallels will be drawn with the theological roots of the matter, as well as with its colonial metaphorization, showing the symbolic valencies of the legal status of womanhood within cultural production.

Finally, we turn to problems in the language of property within the common law at the moment of the Civil War, focusing on the jurisprudential combinations of two pamphleteers with opposing political allegiances: the cloth merchant and egalitarian militant Gerrard Winstanley, and the lawyer, landholder, and printer Richard Atkyns. Thus, this chapter moves from the pairing of the figures of sovereign and slave (the all-powerful and those devoid of power), through to the legal position of women as owners, objects and objectors to their ownership, and finally to the rich and fluid legal language manifested in the moment of the dissolution of English absolutism.

CALIBAN AND A WOULD-BE-KING

The characters of Shakespeare's *The Tempest* (1611), born from a meeting of humanist literature and real-life shipwrecks, have consistently provided effective spokespersons for provocateurs and upstarts.[4] Here we focus on the opposition of a would-be-king and a quasi-slave, Gonzalo and Caliban, which represents some fundamental problems in the conflict of civil and common law conceptions of property within England's expanding, colonizing world. Early on in the play, the King's advisor Gonzalo, shipwrecked on the island, muses that if he were sovereign over the island, he would construct, or maintain it as a utopia:

> Had I plantation of this isle, my lord ...
> And were the king on't, what would I do? ...
> I' the commonwealth I would by contraries
> Execute all things; for no kind of traffic
> Would I admit; no name of magistrate;
> Letters should not be known; riches, poverty,
> And use of service, none; contract, succession,
> Bourn, bound of land, tilth, vineyard, none;

No use of metal, corn, or wine, or oil;
No occupation; all men idle, all;
And women too, but innocent and pure;
No sovereignty;

His discourse is, however, interrupted by the two shipwrecked sailors:

Sebastian	Yet he would be king on't.
Antonio	The latter end of his commonwealth forgets the beginning.[5]

The sailor Sebastian, a proletarian wayfarer, supplies an important criticism of Gonzalo's utopian dream, which is that to speak of a land of which one is a king implies sovereignty, entering immediately into a paradox: Gonzalo would be sovereign in a land without sovereigns. Antonio's subsequent quip—that Gonzalo, in his senility, has forgotten that he named himself king, by the time he has described the island as being without sovereignty—inadvertently implies that a commonwealth is a construction of speech or a fiction, and vice versa, utopia's legal–rhetorical locus is laid open for the audience to hear, as much as the secret joke shared between friends. Shakespeare then leaves the following description of the wonders of "common nature" either open to mockery, or itself mocks Antonio's cynicism.

Gonzalo	All things in common nature should produce
	Without sweat or endeavour: treason, felony,
	Sword, pike, knife, gun, or need of any engine,
	Would I not have; but nature should bring forth,
	Of its own kind, all poison, all abundance,
	To feed my innocent people.[6]

The utopian and his critic are thus juxtaposed.[7]

As has been well noted, the speech seems to take inspiration from Montaigne's essay on cannibals, written in the last quarter of the sixteenth century and translated into English in 1603.[8] For Montaigne, the cannibals lived with "no respect of kindred, but common; no apparel but natural; no manuring of lands, no use of wine, corn, or metal. The very words that import lying, falsehood, treason, dissimulation, covetousness, envy, detraction, and pardon, were never heard of amongst them."[9] There is an important shift, however, between Montaigne's and Gonzalo's speeches: whereas Montaigne describes a people as they are, a people characterized by their innocence and commonality, Gonzalo describes the conditions necessary *for the protection of his* "innocent people." He acts as a protector and guardian, pitting nature—which provides abundance—against contract and inheritance. The sovereignty which he conveniently forgets derives from this very contradiction, that to maintain the innocence of those on the island, he must first rule them, but in ruling them he introduces the very principle of sovereignty he wishes to preclude.

This double bind—the desire to own in order to govern the property-less—was not unique to England, but a central part of early modern thought about slavery in the New World. It was a paradox contemplated by the legal theorists of the School of Salamanca in the sixteenth century.[10] Palacios Rubios and Francisco de Vitoria argued that Amerindians were rightful owners of their property and that their own hierarchies exercised justifiable jurisdiction. In defending their right to property, Vitoria also defended their status as human beings, with all the natural rights which humans held. Like Grotius after him, the Spanish jurist argued that theft was against natural (and not just human) law, and thus that it would be against God to rob the Amerindians of their property.

We see a very different formulation of the relation between subjects and property in the fantastic humanist work of Thomas More, a real-life advisor to the king (although again, as with *The Tempest*, Erasmus hovers nearby).[11] *Utopia*, written almost a century before Gonzalo's dream, features a people who have *abolished* property (i.e., it once existed but has been done away with). Unlike both Gonzalo's and Montaigne's new worlds, More's prototypical utopia is a tour of a land where a legal choice had been made, rather than the maintenance of a primordial paradise. The Utopians are not irrational, but experimental. Nonetheless, they meet with the narrator's criticism, who comments that "Life cannot be satisfactory where all things are common."[12] Money too is abolished, but the Utopians have not abolished contract: free contracts between people are held to be Utopian, but monetary exchanges are not, and are done away with along with property. As Winstanley would rephrase the distinction, it "was the project of Tyrant-flesh (which Land-lords are branches of) to set his Image upon Money."[13]

This is reminiscent of the tradition of the *De contractibus* treatises which propagated the correct use of commerce and exchange, consistently noting the problems which money, rather than contract in itself, brought to the Christian merchant.[14] We thus see a decadence of options: in More the Utopians willfully accept contract but not money or property (to the narrator's dismay); in Montaigne the cannibals live in a state of nature, potentially about to be corrupted, while Gonzalo describes a new world which he promises to protect and maintain. The move is from the institution of a property regime collectively, accidentally, and protectively. Sovereignty moves mythically from the collective, to nature, to the Prince who must—as Gonzalo discovers—reconcile the paradox of popular and natural sovereignty. Gonzalo's paradox was exactly that which the English Civil War would reconcile, through the decapitation of the sovereign, precisely so that "the process of the primitive accumulation of the category of modern politics" could be concluded.[15]

The would-be king is matched in this process by his double, the quasi-slave. Gonzalo's speech, his dream of an island without sovereignty but protected by a sovereign, becomes all the more poignant given the virtual war waged between the inhabitants of the island through the play, first and foremost, that between the magician Prospero and his indigenous servant, Caliban. Caliban is the native islander, full of fictions and violence, whose illiteracy, contrasted with that of the sage Prospero, does not inculcate his innocence but his primordial culpability. We see Caliban as being pulled between two different legal systems: Roman Law and common law. On the one hand, Caliban is the rightful owner of his island, gifted it through inheritance from his mother Sycorax, a witch. His property claim is denied him by Prospero, who takes control of both him and the island, it is implied, because of his illiteracy, his lack of reason. Indeed, the recognition of the property claim itself is in keeping with Spanish court practice, as in Quito (Ecuador) the pre-Columbian legal titles had to be defended in Spanish courts, thus transforming them gradually, via the courts own paperwork, into Spanish titles.[16] If as a civilian Caliban is an inheritor, however, as a commoner (i.e., a subject under common law, in which the play was more directly embedded) Caliban is a form of slave, owned by his master Prospero. Caliban is not the only slave: Prospero also controls the fairy Ariel, and in a different way also his own daughter, Miranda. The fairy and the cannibal are controlled seemingly by Prospero's words and spells. Indeed, the importance of

Prospero's powers of rhetoric and learning invite comparison with Shakespeare himself, always performing spells through the acts of others, like a playwright working through their actors. Yet another interpretation is that Prospero really does own these servants, in a manner which remains somewhat enigmatic throughout the play. They fear his magic, but he never performs it—his power over them is more like that of an abstract legal title, with the implication of violence but never its manifestation (although it is significant that his threat to Ariel is one of imprisonment).

The common law held no particular place for slaves.[17] There was a law for the enslavement of vagrants from 1547, but this only encompassed a slavery of two years.[18] This does not mean, however, that there was no slavery in the early English colonies, far from it: even if slavery of Amerindians was rejected early on, there are plenty of references to black servants in the early seventeenth century.[19] It is often claimed that the English did not make claims to slaves, not only because there was no legal position for slaves within the common law, but also by reference to texts such as *The Golden Trade* (1623), in which Jobson wrote in his diary that on being offered slaves in Guinea, he answered "We [i.e. the English] were a people, who did not deale in any such commodities, neither did wee buy or sell one another, or any that had our owne shapes; [the slaver] seemed to marvell much at it, and told us, it was the only marchandize."[20] Jobson's further response is rarely included however: "We answered, They were another kinde of people different from us, but for our part, if they had no other commodities, we would returne againe."[21] This celebrated proto-abolitionist did not take a great deal of persuading to drop his principles of human commerce. Furthermore, the London-based Guinea Company, set up in 1618, maintained a state-backed monopoly on slaves, gold, and ivory from West Africa until the monopoly was broken by the interlopers in 1638.[22] It is suggestive that the company was established only a few years after *The Tempest* was written.

If Caliban were not legally a slave, however, what would his position within the jurisprudential framework of the play have been? By the 1640s there are notices of black people in America being sold along with furniture, which aids our understanding of the reason that there was no English common law of slavery: there already was ample legal provision for property *in general*. Slaves, and especially black slaves, were treated as chattels.[23] In English colonies, slavery was rare until the end of the seventeenth century, turning from indentured servants to black slaves. Even in 1654, in the earliest relevant Virginia Statute, the provision was made for Amerindians to become indentured servants, not slaves. It was not until after Bacon's Rebellion (1676) that a law was made allowing the enslaving of Indians taken in war.[24] But in most of the period, when slaves did exist socially, they were simply owned. Prospero's enigmatic control of Caliban is thus perhaps not so strange after all: it is the relation of an owner to their inanimate property.

Ariel, on the other hand, is a thief or vagrant, condemned to a temporary imprisonment—or more intriguingly still, an indentured servant, representing that almost typical racial division of labor between the white indentured slaves and the black "true" slaves which developed in the seventeenth century.[25] Indeed, the idea of slavery had become part of English discourse strongly enough by the period of the Civil War that it was used as a description of the situation under tyranny. Even while he was also advocating a global English empire, the Civil War preacher Peters "could wish all markes of slavery might be taken off, and since God hath invested us with our almost lost liberty, let it be our care that after ages may not say we conquered our selves into a new slavery."[26]

In Richard Ligon's history of Barbados, he describes "The Iland [as] divided into three sorts of men, viz. Masters, Servants, and slaves. The slaves and their posterity, being subject to their Masters for ever, are kept and preserv'd with greater care then the servants, who are theirs but for five yeers, according to the law of the Iland."[27] These are represented by Prospero, Ariel, and Caliban, the owner, the indentured servant, and the slave as chattel. Ligon's observation of the slave's commodity-nature resulting in their better treatment than the servants, finds succour in the ending of Shakespeare's play: as Prospero leaves and Ariel is freed, Caliban's fate remains uncertain—he leaves in silence, perhaps to remain a slave to the sorcerer, or perhaps to reclaim the island which is his by inheritance. Ligon's *History* provides another clue to Caliban's fate, however. Published in 1657, after he had lost his fortune in the Civil War, and failed to establish a plantation in Barbados, the royalist chronicler recounted a time when he asked to allow a slave, Sambo, to attend church. Sambo's owner responded that:

> we could not make a Christian a Slave. I told him, my request was far different from that, for I desired him to make a Slave a Christian. His answer was, that it was true, there was a great difference in that: But, being once a Christian, he could no more account him a Slave, and so lose the hold they had of them as Slaves, by making them Christian.[28]

Sambo is kept in both spiritual and bodily imprisonment to maintain a fiction whose paradox is openly admitted. Like Gonzalo, Caliban's paradox is not only an error within the law, a conflict in jurisprudential thought, but a contradiction by means of which it functions.

SHIFTING, MUZZLING

From the representation of the slave and sovereign at the turn of the seventeenth century, we move to fragmentary aspects of the juridical position of women in the period, particularized by the common law of "coverture," by which a woman, on marriage, rescinded her capacity and personality to her husband as her sole proprietor.[29]

As such women were both deterritorialized in that their property rights were removed, and thus they became "free," property-less entities; but also reterritorialized in that they themselves became a very particular kind of property. This enclosure of women was thus not concurrent with that of the land, but certainly predated it, since historiography no longer conventionally opposes the Saxon period (as one of some substantial control by women over their own "property," even within marriage, as well as having the power to make donations), to that of the Norman favoring of primogeniture and patriarchy via the common law of coverture.[30] While the objectification[31] of women is evidenced by some hundreds of cases of wife-selling transacted from 1553 and to the eighteenth and nineteenth centuries,[32] and while the concept of coverture mostly eclipsed the subjectivity of a married woman, there were nevertheless some possibilities of subversion, direct or indirect, legally as well as culturally.

As with Prospero's relating to Caliban simply as an owner to a commodity, that men were seen to relate to women in a similar fashion is well depicted, as De Grazia notes, in *King Lear*, where "locking persons into things" in an attempt "to withstand flux or fluidity" results in an ideology of identification with things of a particular kind in Renaissance culture.[33] The poet Elizabeth Cary in 1613 summed up the totalizing nature of this doctrine thus, in which the very thoughts of a wife belong to her husband:

When to their husbands they themselves do bind,
Do they not wholly give themselves away?
Or give they but their body, not their mind,
Reserving that, though best, for others' prey?
No sure, their thoughts no more can be their own,
And therefore should to none but one be known.[34]

The theological–cultural roots of this form of the categorization of women's bodies and minds as objects resultant from the scission of genders, are evident in the explanation of coverture that one finds in the early legal treatise *The Lawes Resolutions of Women's Rights* (printed in 1632 but dating from the end of the sixteenth century),[35] as grounded in Genesis where the common law "shaketh hand with Divinitie."[36] The husband in his dominion over all external things takes absolutely, every divested property of the wife under his affective governorship, the legal subjectivity of the woman being renounced so that a single legal subject can be formed, yet without diminishing the husband's own position.

In Rachel Speght's defiant invective of 1617, *A Mouzell for Melastomus*, she defends the rights of women by nonetheless referring to the custodial, rather than pillaging, role implied in this juridical unity: "For a King doth not trample his Crowne vnder his feete, but highly esteemes of it, gently handles it, and carefully laies it vp, as the euidence of his Kingdome ... So husbands should not account their wiues as their vassals, but as those that are heires together of the grace of life."[37] The private and public bodies of the sovereign—the king himself and his sovereign crown—are compared with the position of the two bodies of the married couple. Speght plays on a biblical line from 1 Peter 3.7, undermining the description of wives as "vessals" and emphasizing the mutuality of their access to eternal life. For Speght, as with Sambo the slave, the entrance into the world of Christianity guarantees her freedom from bondage. *The Lawes Resolutions* also exposes some fissures through which a woman might, in practice, assert more control and authority over property than legal theory alone would lead one to assume. After explaining how husband and wife are by "fiction of Law, one person," the text also asserts, "yet in nature & in some other cases by the Law of God and man, they remain divers" (1:4). Cracks in the system may enable women to reverse or subvert the effect of coverture. Indeed, the author asserts, "I know no remedy [to subjugation] though some women can shift it well enough" (1:6).

Some of this shifting took place in the courts of equity and the ecclesiastical courts. For instance, while the common law concept of coverture restricted married women's property rights in the extreme, it was also eventually the case that "[t]he ecclesiastical courts ... assumed a marital economic relationship by consistently allocating a widow well over the legal portion of one third of her intestate husband's estate."[38] The use of settlements, wills and trusts did eventually provide further minimizing effects on coverture's grasp, while women were indeed active in litigation over property contrary to earlier perception.[39] Another primary reason for such potential deterritorializing fissures were the persistent traces of conflicting legal traditions from the earlier co-existence of three legal cultures for a significant part of our period (Celtic law in Wales, Ireland, and Scotland, which was itself a multi-faceted system;[40] Germanic law—from the eleventh century to be found in England, Wales, and Scotland—and Roman civil law in Scotland; canon law in England, Wales, and Ireland).

The main site of such fissures could be seen in operation in particular with regard to inheritance where the right to dower could be excluded by a marriage contract. A jointure, however, an increasingly popular contractual device, made provision for the potential widowhood of the wife by providing her with life interest upon the purchase of land. As a result, contrary to a usually restrictive practice, in the right circumstances, this device could provide her with more than she would be otherwise, by law, entitled to. In the celebrated diaries of the aristocrat Anne Clifford, who negotiated her jointure to secure a larger inheritance, one can note an (albeit privileged) experimental agency in how such inheritances were perceived.[41] As Chan and Wright have written, Clifford can be said to have experienced a rather unconventional relation between herself and the properties represented by her inheritance and her dower: "she differentiated her inheritance as an attribute essential to her self-constitution," whereas she perceived her "dower lands ... as objects separate from herself." In this sense, they add, she resists convention since she refused the idea "that her relation to her legal right of inheritance is that of a subject to an external object;" instead, her writings suggest that her self-perception was grounded in possession of her inheritance. Her privileged derivation of the claim to the property out of earlier feudal rights notwithstanding, Clifford would claim her inheritance and base upon it her identification as a woman of full civic personhood.[42] The earliest expression of her right is evidenced in her writings from 1649 to 1652 as follows:

> The Title of the Lady Anne Clifford sole daughter and heire generall to the late right honorable George Earl of Cumberland Lord Clifford Westmerland & Vescy to ye stile and title of the said other baronies ... The said lady tendreth and ... groundeth the same upon the ancient [laws and customs] of this Realme of Eng-land ... with the customs and usage of other Realmes and Dominions adjoining thereunto wheare Women are capable of Foedalls [i.e., feudal rights and obligations] ... [43]

Salzman, along similar lines, has observed that Clifford's writings are "all part of her attempt, not just to assert her own rights over her inheritance but to influence those who came after her both within and outside of her family."[44] Inheritance becomes a tactical weapon of civic critique. While in 1523 Anthony Fitzherbert employed the term inheritance to describe property rights in the sense of legal possession ("Their title and interest grew by inheritance"[45]), female authors would employ the otherwise economic disadvantage of a lack of inheritance as an impetus to critique. For instance, Aemilia Lanyer's "The Description of Cookeham" (1611), on the eponymous estate leased by Lanyer's patron, the countess of Cumberland, becomes at first a symbol of loss to Lanyer "because the Countess and her extended female community had to leave the estate in an apparent property dispute with the Countess's estranged husband."[46] The estate, however, also becomes the subject of critique as to the disenfranchisement of women. As Ingram analyzes, Lanyer's "estate" poem indicates "the contingent nature of the women's relationship to the estate" to critique the implications of "ownership and stewardship, rather than being focused on a family 'house'."[47]

The objectification of women, furthermore, could be further "shifted," in a sense, when by the seventeenth century it would be objects that became the most valuable element of estates in the form of moveable property (goods, money, debts, livestock, etc.).[48] In fact, "during the late sixteenth and early seventeenth centuries, relations between subjects within the home became increasingly centered around and mediated by objects."[49] Crucially, Natasha Korda writes, "women's *de facto* and *de jure* control over household property became important sites of struggle and resistance to England's patrilineal property regime."[50] While in *King Lear* France declares that the disinherited Cordelia "is herself a dowry," and in *The Taming of the Shrew*, Petruccio notoriously claims ownership of the newly married Katherine,[51] the anxious struggle as to property becomes more multi-faceted. As Korda illustrates,

> In *The Taming of the Shrew, The Merry Wives*, and *Othello*, this anxiety attaches itself to the figure of the housewife, who, through her excessive consumption, insufficient vigilance, extravagant curiosity, or disposal of paraphernalia, threatens to undermine patrilineality from within the familial household. In *Measure for Measure*, it attaches to the even more threatening figure of the single woman whose refusal to assume the role of 'keeper' threatens to foreclose patrilineality entirely, from without.[52]

The figure of the rebellious wife, no longer merely an object under control but a being out of control, was considered threatening enough to pass over from simply murderous to treachery against the realm itself.[53] As Dolan notes: "Both legal theory and popular representation participated in the paradoxical process of constituting married women as subjects; they also informed but did not reflect legal practice. For instance, in her assessment of assize indictments that describe defendants as married spinsters, Wiener argues that the married spinster was 'a useful legal fiction' invented by judges in response to the contradictions of married women's legal status."[54] While the numbers and actual threat posed by the "murderous wife" were relatively low in comparison with women as the victims of spousal murders, the cultural anxiety of the inverse was matched by the reaction of the law in constructing them as actors of petty treason (rather than murder).[55] The home of their proprietary and subjective subordination was also the place of marking the cultural as well as legal representation of a space of uncertain order and potential struggle, if not female bloody triumph.[56]

As Silvia Federici has noted, the cultural intersection between women as property and the ideology of improvement, progress or advancement for the taming of "wild nature" (whether of nature as such or vulgar peasantry and native land) underlies the assumed values of literal enclosure.[57] Burgundy's speech in *Henry V* illustrates the rather peculiar English metaphor further, in describing the fate of France:

> ... all her husbandry doth lie on heaps,
> Corrupting in it own fertility.
> Her vine, the merry cheerer of the heart,
> Unpruned dies; her hedges even-plashed,
> Like prisoners wildly overgrown with hair,
> Put forth disorder'd twigs; her fallow leas
> The darnel, hemlock, and rank fumitory
> Doth root upon, while that the coulter rusts
> That should deracinate such savagery.[58]

Siemon notes in his analysis of "garden scenes" in Shakespeare, the wildness of this nature is to be managed according to time and utility against its idleness and disorder, in the emergent sphere of a nascent capitalism, evoked in the unusual imagery (beyond that only of the *hortus conclusus*) of enclosing "hedges."[59] The equation of the common with waste and the ills of untamed possession articulates an ideological pursuit of enclosure as a feudal–capitalist–cultural inter-articulation.

But it could also do the opposite as it was the case earlier than in our period of concern, such as when in a class-conscious manner John Ball, the English priest who had a prominent part in the Peasants' Revolt of 1381, addressed the rebels at Blackheath as "good husbands" who must transform the savaged "garden of England." The Song of

Songs may be a key root for the theological tradition of the garden as the *topos* of the well of life and the magical structure of marriage. In it we find a direct depiction of a bride's body "transformed into a paradise regained" by Solomon as his:[60] "My sister my spouse is as a garden inclosed, as a spring shut vp, and a fountaine sealed vp."[61] Similarly to the way that virginity as such is characterized, in literary practice, as before competing attempts of enclosure whether by the dignity of virginity or the superior power of marriage over it as the *hortus conclusus*.[62]

Order needed to be restored by the ruling class against the threat of the "mowers," the "True" Levellers and the Digger-villagers who attempt, treacherously, to seize the garden, as in Marvell's poem "Upon Appleton House." Here, however, it is "mother" nature which levells the earth, rather than the commoners:

> But Nature here hath been so free
> As if she said leave this to me.
> Art would more neatly have defac'd
> What she had laid so sweetly wast.[63]

Marvell (eulogizing Lord Fairfax's lands after the Civil War) would rather a feminine force of nature leveled and laid waste to the land than "The Villagers in common chase / Their Cattle, which it closer rase." Here, landed property is destroyed by a woman freed from masculine power, in preference to the open treason of the wartime levellers.

The cultural prevalence of the metaphor of the garden becomes ever more evident when observed further in the ceremonial practices employed for the initiation of colonial rule over the New World (often depicted as the "garden of nature") which stemmed from gardening rhetoric and agricultural fertility rituals.[64] The English colonists, following well-established English cultural custom as well as law, would settle and establish legal possession by making a choice for their "plantation" and by building a house, drawing boundaries (by a fence or a hedge; the so-called improvements) and planting gardens.[65] Seed notes well that the colonial practices of using a fence or a hedge to draw a boundary anew were the very same practices that were used in the enclosure process in the sixteenth century.[66] In this manner, a plantation signified the taking of legal possession which was facilitated by "bestowing culture," which, in turn, meant husbandry (planting a garden or raising animals, etc.) and it implied replenishing, subduing "new" or "unused" land.[67] Paradise was, in this manner, to be regained, and utopia thus built on the foundations of the very same system which was enclosing (territorializing) land and freeing (in the sense of deterritorializing) labor.

UNBINDING, INCLOSING

As we have shown in relation to juridical subjectivity, systems of property met with moments of shifting from within the very language they employed, as well as their claims to liberty also being mired within this same enclosure. In this final section, we move to the archetypical expropriation of the land and the installation of property regimes, frequently dubbed the "enclosure of the commons," whether of the conquistadors in Brazil or royal agents guarding Norfolk hedges, and their systematization within a majoritarian legal language. More recently, the resistance to this process has been termed "commoning," with important implications from the early modern period for contemporary understandings of property regimes and their challenges.[68] The reinvention and refashioning of such a term works backwards onto its early modern source, as much as the historical context inspires or molds the present usage.

However, the historical concept of the commons is often treated as a one-sided, traditional activity of the poor for the maintenance of their self-sufficiency, and against the individualist enclosing methods of the rich. In this section, we again attempt to show the complex ways in which cultures of possession maintained themselves through juridical rhetoric and systems which nonetheless opened up fissures exploited across political class bases. We focus on two contemporary figures: the revolutionary leader Gerrard Winstanley and the book printer and polemicist Richard Atkyns.

The place of common custom and its wider role in plebeian political culture in England in the period in question is a significant factor to note.[69] While common custom entailed multiple understandings through time, it was relatively institutionalized by the sixteenth century as custom (the "principal magistrate of man's life," according to Bacon) that it "held its greatest force within plebeian political culture."[70] But this was not just a matter of the way the elite institutions gradually affirmed or restricted customary rights, but also of how the plebeian culture saw itself as law-abiding to its own customary commons. And, further, on how both elite and plebeian perceptions and identities were forged during, in part, on the basis of the particularly English differentiation of, for instance, freehold and customary tenure among English peasants and the commoner status of English manorial lords, both of which derived from the English form of feudal class society, all the way to the unique enclosure movement by which England ceased to be a peasant society and the customary law of the manors was dissolved in favor of separate individual ownership.[71] In its legal form, custom applied to manors, parishes and boroughs and, in its essential nature, it was pragmatically driven by local, in a sense, communal, use rather than property right, developing thus, aside the common law, as subsidiary law.[72] While custom would be indifferent to tenure as understood by the common law this was not to say that peasants could have no security of tenure under customary rights; by extension, this renders illegitimate the claim that the expropriation of such customary tenure, in it being not of the strictly speaking legal sense of right (a real estate) would be a justified "progression."[73]

While the materiality of custom was to be criticized by someone like Bacon as severely restricting human agency, at the same time, it was, for him, in custom that both dead images of time immemorial prevailed as much as "engines moved."[74] It should not be forgotten that this expanded across political cultures in that, for example, while plebeian culture would rely on the rhetoric of "custom" to defend its local rights,[75] elite culture would eventually rely on the political force of custom to appeal to the past and recover, or uncover, the inalienability of certain liberties and rights.[76]

Nonetheless, despite the loss of a particular sense of community and self, arguably lost along with the denial of custom, it can be noted that custom was no utopian plateau since it was itself, for instance, gendered; and often customary rights were defined to the exclusion of women, since custom (the "memory of old men") often misplaced them. Having said that, this should not be taken as a wholesale exclusion from memory since, as Wood reminds us, "where gleaning rights were threatened, it was usually crowds of women who rallied to their defence."[77] And the consequences of enclosure and the consolidation of large estates would show that when male farmers lost access to land, their wives also lost the means to common "women's work" that supported both the family and the market.[78] Opposition to enclosure and attempts at reversals, in addition, did take place within the equity courts and in particular in the *Camera Stellata* at Westminster.[79] As McDonagh has analyzed such action was possible "because for most of the sixteenth century the act of forcibly depopulating settlements was illegal, although by no means unknown."[80] In fact, a combination of direct action and litigation was often seeking reversals by continuing occupation of land and litigants claiming that they were dispossessed as a key strategy to force the court to decide title.[81]

The class struggle between commoners and enclosing landowners was reflected and refracted through a discourse of trade, in the opposition of privileged and free market commerce. Thus in 1623 the Virginia Assembly petitioned that: "We the poor planters of this colony have a long time groaned under the cruel dealings of unconscionable merchants," merchants to whom they were vastly indebted for all the commodities which were necessarily imported while the colonies were establishing themselves.[82] But the interlopers' sentiments for free trade, against the granting of royal privileges, are best expressed in the proposal they made to the revolutionary government in 1651, concluding that: "trade, being the basis and well-being of a commonwealth, the way to obtain it is to make it free trade and *not to bind up ingenious spirits by exemptory privileges* which are granted to some particular company and men that will not adventure and take pains as ingenious as other laborious spirits will do."[83] What is noteworthy is that here privileges are opposed to free trade and enterprise; it is the enclosing of market opportunities from one section of the bourgeoisie which was "binding up" the spirits of another. The enclosure of the commons was, conversely, often defended as the necessity of not only freeing enterprise but also of controlling the "tragedy of the commons," through which unlimited access to the land by commoners was inherently inefficient. In the interlopers' argument, however, it is exactly the equivalent enclosure, the granting of privileges, which ties up "ingenious spirits" (their own colonizing, adventuring commercialism).

When the interloping merchants essentially came to power in the Commonwealth, along with the Puritan radicals of the city of London, their preference was to put aside the model of granting trading privileges for companies and instead to build a colonial empire.[84] The radical preacher Hugh Peters stated that "I wish this Army might be sent to encounter them, and teach Peasants to understand liberty."[85] Opposed to this, Winstanley's argument in the Levellers' famous *Declaration* is that the earth was made "a common Livelihood to all, without respect of persons" and that the "buying and selling of Land, and the Fruits of it" was a "cursed thing."[86] The argument here, while seemingly anti-propertarian, is specific: Winstanley is careful to include the "fruits" of land (i.e., usufruct) as well as the land itself, and he does not blame only property as such but *commerce*, the buying and selling, as the problem. Indeed, later on he was to write that "we must neither buy nor sell: Money must not any longer ... be the great god, that hedges in some, and hedges out others; for Money is but part of the Earth." The language of commons enclosure is again invoked, as in Shakespeare's *Henry V*, through the metaphor of hedging. More emphatically, however, Winstanley employs the argument that money is part of the earth and thus itself also common to all. This act of property is described as one of *theft*: "for buying and selling is the great cheat, that robs and steals the Earth one from another ... and makes great Murderers and Theeves to be imprisoners." For Winstanley, thieves become the enemy and theft the inimical activity; he might be a commoner and anti-propertarian, but he nonetheless instrumentalizes the figure of the thief as a fulcrum for his rhetoric.

Winstanley does, nonetheless, follow this by claiming that "the power of inclosing Land, and owning Propriety, was brought into the Creation by your Ancestors by the Sword; which first did murther their fellow Creatures, Men, and after plunder or steal away their Land, and left this Land successively to you, their Children." Addressing himself here to the monarchy, Winstanley argues that property itself is established through violence, but importantly, however, this is not a current but a past violence: "And therefore, though you did not kill or theeve, yet you hold that cursed thing in your hand, by the power of the Sword." Winstanley, in the process, employs a conservative legal argument, which is the tracing of lineage to justify property claims. Here he does not only say that land *ought* to be held common, but that it originally *was*. Similarly, he does not oppose the current use of force, but the historic use of violence.

Winstanley's defense of the commons becomes still more conservative as his tract develops, making a rhetorical move between the declaration that all the earth is held in common, and the idea of specific commons. For although claiming at the start that the Earth "was made to be a common Livelihood to all," he later declares his intention to "lay hold upon, and as we stand in need, to cut and fell, and make the best advantage we can of the Woods and Trees, that grow upon the Commons." Far from abolishing all commerce, Winstanley declares that "we intend, that not one, two, or a few men of us shall sell or exchange the said woods, but it shall be known publikly in Print or writing to all, how much every such, and such parcell of wood is sold for." And indeed, they return to the request for no less than their *"priviledge*, to be quietly given us, out of the hands of Tyrant-Government, as our bargain and contract with them." This is the most functional point of the text, after which Winstanley builds to a final attack on "the cursed thing, called Particular Propriety, which is the cause of all wars, bloud-shed, theft, and enslaving Laws, that hold the people under miserie." Nonetheless, we can see a peculiar combination of the interloping merchants' defense of free trade, and the resort to the Merchant Adventurers' language of privilege. Winstanley's argument may have been an attack on private property, but it employed a variety of jurisprudential combinations and exploited a number of fissures in order to find support.

We now turn to the final document in our study, Richard Atkyns' searing defense of the King's ownership of the craft of printing. In his post-bellum *The Original and Growth of Printing, collected out of History and the Records of this Kingdom* (1664),[87] Atkyns outlined his argument for the total control of the press by the king through the abolition of the stationers' register and the granting of privileges by the king as the only means to print anything. Atkyn's argument politically relied on the accusation that it was the free press which had caused the Civil War. Print culture had been too free: "If the Tongue, that is but a little Member, can set the Course of Nature on Fire" he observed, "how much more the Quill, which is of a flying Nature in itself?" He then, in a reversal of the Huguenot's form of argument, claimed that as the king owns the entire art, he can invest his subjects with delegations, as officers: "Men use to trust, when they cannot avoid it; but that there may be a Derivative and Ministerial Power in them, with Appeal to Your Majesty, I do with all Humility admit and propose." Thus, privileges were to be defended in the name of the ability to govern.

As with Winstanley, Atkyns relied on the conservative argument of lineage in order to plead his case, providing a narrative of a kind of genetics of the craft of printing, claiming that:

> Thomas Bourchier, Arch-Bishop of Canterbury, moved the then King (Hen. the 6th) to use all possible means for procuring a Printing-Mold ... They having received the said Sum of One Thousand Marks, went first to Amsterdam, then to Leyden, not daring to enter Harlem itself; for the Town was very jealous, having imprisoned and apprehended divers Persons, who came from other Parts for the same purpose ... a Bargain (as he said) being struck betwixt him and two Hollanders, for bringing off one

of the Work-men, who should sufficiently discover and teach this New Art: At last, with much ado, they got off one of the Under-Workmen, whose Name was Frederick Corsells (or rather Corsellis) who late one Night stole from his Fellows in Disguise, into a Vessel prepared before for that purpose; and so the Wind (favouring the Design) brought him safe to London ... the Printers having the Honour to be sworn the King's Servants, and the Favour to Lodge in the very Bosome of the Church; as in Westminster, St. Albans, Oxon, &c. By this meanes the ART grew so famous ... by being Concorporated, that they turn'd this famous ART into a Mechanick Trade for a Livelyhood.[88]

We can observe several kinds of property claim moving through Atkyn's argument. The first is that the king desires to "procure" a printing press. Second, his men steal away to Holland, which is represented not dissimilarly from a colonial expedition, wherein the foreigners have been imprisoned for wanting to expropriate the discovery. Third, a bargain is struck in Holland, suggesting mutual agreement. Fourth, it is the person himself, *and his knowledge*, who is brought to London, not the press anymore. Once in London, the printers swear their allegiance to the king. Finally, the argument against the stationer's register is given through the recourse of the conflict between property and commerce: the art is turned into a mechanical trade. Here the opposition of ownership and trade is represented through the old Latinate distinction of the liberal and mechanical arts, in which mechanical is brute commerce, and property—the well attested lineage of the art to the King's title—is, by association, elevated.

Atkyns makes an extraordinary parallel of printing piracy with the poaching of deer. It was only in 1540 that a statute was introduced to make the poaching of the King's deer a felony as theft, but it was still argued that hunting was not theft in common law, as a wild animal could not be stolen (a caged one could).[89] Nonetheless, by 1664, Atkyns could comfortably make the following analogy:

I shall give you one Similitude of the like Nature; The King, as belonging to the Honor of Windsor, hath a great Quantity of Ground of which he makes little or no benefit, because it lyes in Common; And the Neighbours thereabouts, do not onely eat the Herbage, but steal the Kings Deer, and destroy his Woods, without giving any Accompt or Satisfaction whatsoever.

The solution to the problem was obvious as well, as Atkyns continues:

To prevent which Mischief, the King Incloseth several Parks, and gives the keeping of them to several Persons by Patent, reserving what he pleaseth out of them, the rest he gives the Patentees. What wrong doth He to His Neighbours, by Inclosing His own Lands, whiFitzch He denyes to none of His Subjects? Yet His Neighbours are troubled, because they cannot wrong Him as before; and upon every Distemper of the Commonwealth, destroy the Fences, and make it Common again.[90]

It is through this analogy that Atkyns in "the interest of the pattentees, to defend the Kings Right" suggests "Inclosing Printing." His argument relies on a very strict parallel between the king's right to the enclosure of his parks for the protection of his deer, and the necessity of privileges granted like delegates of the sovereign. He relies on a host of jurisprudential terms to cobble together an argument, drawing on the rhetoric of an agricultural counter-revolution for the defense of the legal technology of the Merchant Adventurers.

Both Gerrard Winstanley and Richard Atkyns, in their very different pleas, a republican's venom against a sovereign and a sycophant's desperation for his own financial protection through recourse to the monarchy, made their arguments by drawing on odd combinations of terms within early modern property discourse. This gives the lie to any simple distinction between a plebeian culture of commoning *vs* a ruling class one of enclosure: not least, as Robert Brenner has shown, the different sides of the English Civil War were divided between free marketeers and privileged adventurers, rather than a more traditional class divide. And yet mingling contradictory juridical manners and fields, in their very contradictions, allowed for moments of "shifting" and, to an extent, resistance, whether within and against the common law of coverture, the overlapping jurisdictions of ecclesiastical and monarchical courts, or the recourse to historical lineages of popular ownership. Furthermore, these contradictions were not merely problems and accidents within the law, but constituted their own operative moments of legal shift. Gonzalo's forgotten promise to his innocent and sovereignless people, his neglected crown, was the legal fissure by which the juridical culture of very real, militarized utopias was reterritorialized in England's colonies; while the figures such as the otherwise anonymous, half-forgotten Sambo the slave, would be locked out of those same promised lands.

CHAPTER SEVEN

Wrongs

CHLOË KENNEDY AND LINDSAY FARMER

INTRODUCTION

A number of the contemporary distinctions we use to categorize different species of wrongs, such as the boundaries between criminal and civil wrongs and between breaches of law and breaches of morality, were significantly less pronounced in early modern Britain. Ideas of sin and crime were closely aligned and tackling ungodliness was seen as vital not only to addressing and preventing social disorder but also to building God's kingdom on earth. In the absence of clear distinctions between different kinds of wrongs, it was believed that minor sins or moral lapses would lead to more serious transgressions and that it was therefore necessary to discipline vices of every kind.[1] This connection between moral and social discipline is evident in early modern ballads, broadsides, and penny chapbooks, which often featured moral aphorisms,[2] and reports of last dying speeches, which charted the reprobate's descent into sinfulness and criminality and were intended as cautionary tales.[3] Images depicting a godly and moral life served a similar, if less baleful, didactic purpose, as did the biblical verses and moralizing proverbs that were commonly painted on the walls of homes.[4] Such images served to bolster each individual's battle against vice, a battle rendered in intricate detail in the seventeenth century broadsheet "The Spiritual Warfare" (see Figure 7.1). The scene depicted is that of a sole Christian warrior, surrounded by twelve graces and seven battalions (including Hope, Faith, God's word and Strength), enclosed in a castle that is besieged by the devil and his armies of vice. At the top of the page, an exhortation encourages the reader to keep "a fortified guard" against the "hellish powers" which might otherwise overwhelm him.[5] These ungodly vices, if kept unchecked, were a threat not only to the immortal soul of the sinner but also to the polity of which they were part.

The blurred distinction between sin, moral failings, and legal wrongs was reflected in enforcement practices. Both ecclesiastical and secular authorities were active in this regard, though often in pursuit of different ends. From the start of the early modern period until their collapse halfway through the seventeenth century, the English church courts handled a fluctuating array of wrongs, which mainly consisted of offenses against religion or community harmony and contraventions of sexual mores. In the years following the Reformation, legislation brought a number of offenses, including blasphemy, buggery, perjury, and witchcraft, within the realm of the royal, or common law, courts, thereby removing them from the jurisdiction of the church courts. In conjunction with several other factors, such as resentment among the laity, these changes contributed to the deterioration of the authority of the ecclesiastical courts which, by the 1640s, had effectively perished.[6] While these courts regained some of their jurisdiction with the

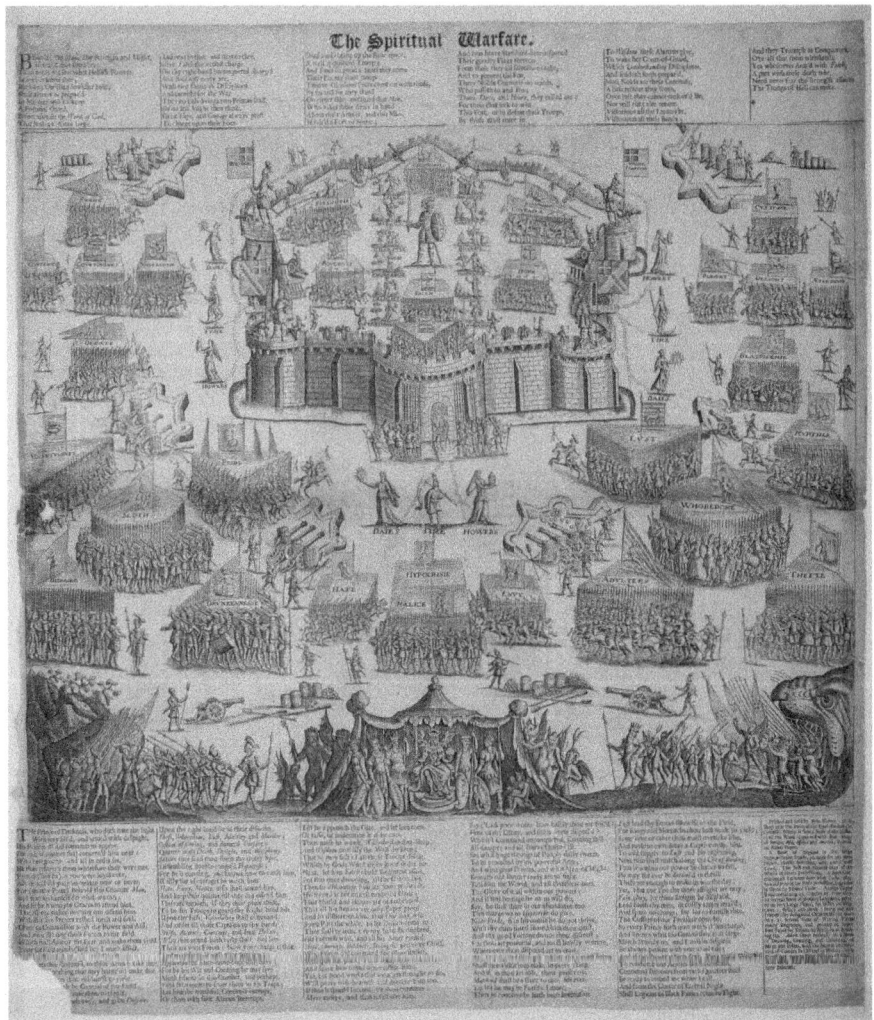

FIGURE 7.1 The spiritual warfare. Source: Courtesy of the Bruce Peel Special Collections & Archives, University of Alberta.

revival of episcopacy in 1660, in the years that followed their core remit would be the prosecution of religious offenses.[7] In Scotland, ecclesiastical discipline was more robust and the network of church courts established after the Reformation continued, supported by the secular courts, to impose censure for sexual misconduct and miscellaneous morals offenses until the eighteenth century.[8]

As for temporal wrongs, those justiciable as crimes ranged in gravity from treason and other felonies to a large number of petty offenses related to vagrancy or forms of disorderly conduct. In Scotland, a range of courts could take cognizance of criminal matters and, due to the largely de-centralized administration of justice, the degree of authority granted to each local court as well as the gravity of the offense would determine where a case was heard.[9] In England, too, a complex hierarchy of courts had jurisdiction over these crimes and the gravity of the offense would often determine the court in which it was prosecuted.[10] The seriousness of crimes was broadly measured in terms of the threat posed to the King's Peace. At the core of the criminal law were the Pleas of the Crown: crimes that were justiciable at the instance of the sovereign and in the royal courts. Originally, these had included only crimes which were understood as direct and manifest threats to social order and royal authority, comprising the felonies of treason, homicide, mayhem, wounding, false imprisonment, arson, rape, robbery, burglary and larceny.[11] However, with the restriction of the jurisdiction of the ecclesiastical courts noted above these were, over time, supplemented by a number of other statutory felonies and serious misdemeanours which could be prosecuted either in the common law courts or in the Court of Star Chamber. What was distinctive about many of these crimes—from sodomy to perjury, forgery, fraud, extortion, conspiracy, and sedition—was that they were crimes of "cunning," as opposed to traditional common law felonies, which were based on conspicuous disruptions of the peace by force and arms.[12] The criminalization of this conduct recognized that wrongdoing was becoming more sophisticated, or could be committed in ways that did not necessarily involve the direct use of force, and that these kinds of conduct could pose an equal or greater threat to the King's Peace. With the abolition of the Star Chamber, these offenses were largely absorbed within the jurisdiction of the common law courts as common law misdemeanours.[13]

This tension between the demands of sovereign and divine authority was reflected in the major treatises of the period. In an age of theocratic royal government any wrongdoing was theoretically an offense against both divine and kingly rule.[14] The treatises accordingly deemed especially reprehensible those crimes which were explicitly directed either against religious orthodoxy, the king and commonwealth, or both. Thus, in descending order of odiousness, the crimes listed first by Sir Edward Coke in his *Institutes of the Laws of England* were treason in its various forms, felony by compassing or conspiring to kill the king or any lord or other of the king's council, heresy and then witchcraft. Similarly, the first chapters of Sir Matthew Hale's *Pleas of the Crown* deal with offenses "immediately against the divine majesty," namely heresy and witchcraft, and the subsequent chapters cover high and petty (or petit) treason. The most significant Scottish work on criminal law from this period, Sir George Mackenzie's *Matters Criminal*, gives greater prominence to religious offenses by considering blasphemy, heresy, simony, and barratry before treason and sedition, perhaps reflecting the greater dominance of Calvinist beliefs in Scottish culture.[15]

Just as there was no clear demarcation between spiritual and temporal wrongs, there was no sharp distinction between crimes and civil wrongs either.[16] It is therefore difficult to point to a unified body of torts or delicts. Nevertheless, it appears that in English law deceit and conversion were emerging bases for civil liability, and trespass and actions on the case, both of which would form the modern law of negligence, covered other forms of intentional and unintentional wrongdoing.[17] In Scotland, by the end of the early modern period several nominate civil wrongs existed: assythment, an action for recompense for bodily injury or the killing of a relative; spuilzie, the wrongful dispossession of a person of moveable property; intrusion, molestation, and ejection, all wrongs against possession; defamation; fraud; extortion; and a number of delicts against keeping the peace and intervening in the course of justice.[18] There was some suggestion of a more general principle of reparation, extending beyond the nominate delicts, but the basis, limits, and application of this claim are unclear.[19]

A good example to illustrate the way that wrongs could span the distinction between civil and criminal liability and secular and ecclesiastical authority is defamation. In England, slanderous words imputing sin could be heard by the ecclesiastical courts and, from the start of the sixteenth century, words imputing a temporal offense were actionable in the secular courts. Matters were complicated by the fact that the church could not order any financial compensation. This meant that accusations of spiritual transgression might be actionable within the secular courts if there had been some temporal loss. From the end of the fifteenth century, before the common law courts had begun hearing actions for words, the Star Chamber would hear actions for defamatory words, the majority of which were written with the chief aim of punishing the speaker for his seditious or disruptive behavior. With the abolition of the Star Chamber in 1641, and the absorption of its jurisdiction by the common law, the libels it had dealt with continued to be treated as a punishable offenses but they also came to be treated as civil wrongs, actionable when a crime was alleged or damage had been caused.[20] Defamation straddled civil and criminal liability and the ecclesiastical and temporal jurisdictions in Scotland too. Though the exact position is unclear, it is possible that the church courts had exclusive jurisdiction over *injuria* during the early sixteenth century. From at least the middle of the seventeenth century, however, the lower secular courts appeared to deal with such cases by way of a mixed civil and criminal process and, in 1671, the Court of Justiciary, Scotland's superior criminal court, asserted its jurisdiction over written or printed defamatory words.[21]

From the mélange of boundary-transcending wrongs that were acknowledged during the early modern period, we have elected to focus on three classes that capture the relation between sin and crime and how this changed over time. The first, witchcraft, was one of the most serious crimes and clearly demonstrates how religious and secular understandings of wrongdoing intertwined in the defense of the godly society. In addition, by the end of the seventeenth century, the crime was practically obsolete—a shift that gestures towards a transition in metaphysical beliefs and expectations about social order that fits loosely with the phenomenon of secularization. In contrast to witchcraft, sexual wrongs spanned a broader range of conduct, from lesser vices to serious crimes. They nevertheless raised a similar set of concerns about the relationship between religious and temporal misconduct and the impact of individual conduct on the wider social order. By looking in particular at the crimes of rape and sodomy we can see how these concerns were articulated in different, but cohesive, ways. Finally, the related offenses of blasphemy and obscenity provide a further illustration of the interrelationship between heavenly and earthly discipline and how, from the late seventeenth century onwards, wrongdoing began to be understood in more emphatically secular terms.

WITCHCRAFT

Witch-craft be the greatest of Crimes, since it includes in it the grossest of Heresies, and Blasphemies and Treasons against God, in preferring to the Almighty his rebel and enemy, and in thinking the Devil worthier of being served and reverenced, and is accompanied with Murder, Poysoning, Bestiality, and other horrid Crimes. (Mackenzie 1678: 85)

This description captures several of the traits of witchcraft, as it was understood during the early modern period: its perceived heinousness, its deep irreligiosity and subversiveness, and its association with various other forms of wrongdoing. As with a number of wrongs from this time, witchcraft was both a sin, commonly considered to be a violation of the First Commandment "Thou shalt have no other gods before me" (Exodus 20.3),[22] and a secular crime. In addition to comprising a discrete wrong, witchcraft was often bound up with other forms of misconduct, both figuratively and literally. Perhaps the most striking examples of this are the depictions of witches' sabbaths that appeared throughout Europe. These paintings portrayed large gatherings at which participants would engage in a multitude of transgressive behaviors, including orgies, shapeshifting, cannibalism, diabolic baptisms, and other perversions of the holy sacraments.[23] Though the sabbath was less prevalent in British representations of witchcraft, the connection between witchcraft and other iniquities was nevertheless strong.

For example, in his *The Discoverie of Witchcraft* the English skeptic Reginald Scot identified no fewer than fifteen crimes that had been attributed to witches.[24] As well as being accused of *maleficia*, alleged witches drew suspicion of other anti-social activities and would sometimes be charged with witchcraft when alternative offenses were suspected but could not be proved.[25] In essence, witchcraft was "a composite crime that allowed lay and ecclesiastical, local and central judicial authorities to prosecute individuals for engaging in those activities which represented the greatest perceived threat to religious orthodoxy, political stability, or the social order."[26] This association between witchcraft and religious and political order is evident in the way that the offense was conceptualized and defined within early modern Britain and in the way its prosecution was undertaken and justified.

The first English legislation designating witchcraft a felony and thus a secular crime was passed in 1542 and prescribed death for conjuring spirits and for attempting to find treasure, provoke love or cause harm to persons or goods through the use of witchcraft, enchantments, or sorcery. Following the repeal of this Act in 1547, a further Act against witchcraft was passed in January 1563. This Act appears to have been drawn up by the Privy Council in response to attempts by a group of Essex Catholics to use sorcery against Queen Elizabeth and was supported by the bishops, who recognized the inadequacy of their powers in the face of such a grave offense.[27] The provisions of the 1563 Act were less severe, with execution being reserved for those whose acts caused death to another. Later that year, the Scottish Parliament passed legislation stipulating that both practicing witchcraft and consulting witches were capital offenses. The ecclesiastical impetus for this Act was more pronounced than its English counterpart; it was likely drafted by a member of the new Protestant church, possibly John Knox, in furtherance of its vision of a godly society.[28] When this Act was later strengthened by an Act of 1649 the incentive again came from members of the national church, intent on demonstrating their godliness.[29]

In 1604, another English Act appeared, which fixed harsher penalties for the infractions prohibited under the 1563 Act and introduced new offenses of invoking, conjuring, feeding, rewarding, employing, entertaining, or covenanting with any evil or wicked spirit. Some scholars have suggested a possible connection between these new measures and the arrival of King James I in London. Although James was unlikely to have requested the Act, the year he left for England marked a surge of interest in witchcraft, as demonstrated by the publication of a second edition of the king's treatise *Daemonologie* and a number of other works on witchcraft.[30] Furthermore, James's earlier involvement in the trial of a group of alleged witches, who eventually admitted to plotting harm against him, had been documented in the pamphlet "Newes from Scotland," which was published in London in 1591. One of the accused confessed to having met with a group of fellow witches at the church of North Berwick, where the devil had addressed them from the pulpit and they had vowed themselves unto him. These practices, depicted in Figure 7.2, were a clear inversion of the Scottish covenanting tradition, so the focus on covenanting with the devil in the 1604 Act was perhaps unsurprising.[31]

The legislation rendering witchcraft a secular crime therefore appears to have reflected the religious and political conditions in which it was wrought. The same can also be said for the way the offense was defined more broadly in ideological and rhetorical terms and, to some extent, in the way it was prosecuted and its punishment justified.

FIGURE 7.2 Newes from Scotland, declaring the damnable life of Doctor Fian [i.e. John Cunningham], a notable sorcerer, who was burned at Edenbrough in Ianuarie last, 1591 [for practising sorcery against King James I. A reprint of the ed. printed in London probably in 1591. Edited by Sir George H. Freeling]. Source: Reproduced by permission of the National Library of Scotland.

Of course, a number of peculiarly legal factors were important in determining the volume and pattern of witchcraft prosecutions in early modern Britain. In Scotland, where several periods of intense witch-hunting resulted in the execution of thousands of witches, local authorities with little or no legal training conducted the majority of prosecutions. In England, which experienced fewer and less acute witch-hunts, witch trials took place at assizes and were presided over by judges from the central criminal courts. These procedural differences, coupled with the use of torture by Scottish authorities and its prohibition under English common law, meant that when witch-hunts occurred in Scotland they were more difficult to restrain and were more likely to result in conviction.[32] As Mackenzie noted, "scarce ever any who were accused before a Countrey Assize of Neighbours, did escape that trial."[33]

Yet patterns in the prosecution of witchcraft, and the justifications that were offered for its punishment, also mirrored the way it was conceived of as a wrong against religious and political order. As a matter of practice, the church courts, which had dealt with individuals suspected of divination, charming, sorcery, and cursing from the start of the early modern period,[34] continued to be involved in the prosecution of witchcraft after it became a secular crime. By virtue of their jurisdiction over moral offenses, any act committed by an alleged witch that fell within the church courts' disciplinary remit might be prosecuted by the clergy. In Scotland, church officials would also refer cases that fell outside their jurisdiction to the secular authorities, after interrogating the suspect and recording his or her testimony.[35] Beyond these interventions in individual cases, religious factors had a bearing on the prosecution of witchcraft on a larger scale. This is clear from the spikes in witchcraft prosecutions that occurred in revolutionary Britain when, during a period of political instability and increased Protestant fervor, accusations and convictions reached intense levels.[36] In England, the lead up to the Civil War was characterized by small numbers of witchcraft prosecutions and, to the frustration of radical Puritans, by the 1630s trials for witchcraft had all but ceased.[37] According to Brooks, this trend can be discerned in dramatic renditions of witches and witchcraft from the time. Whereas plays written in the wake of the 1604 Act portrayed witches as dangerous practitioners of the kind of conduct prohibited by the new legislation, the witches depicted in *The Witch of Edmonton* and *The Witches of Lancaster*, dating from around 1621 and 1634 respectively, are objects of pity and the overall tone of the works is incredulous.[38]

In contrast to the relative indifference towards witchcraft that distinguished the pre-revolutionary era, the 1640s saw an upsurge in prosecutions, including England's only serious witch-panic, the East Anglia witch-hunt of 1645–1647. A combination of religious zeal and political upheaval contributed to this development and, although there were differences in the number and distribution of prosecutions and in the details of political and religious disagreement, similar circumstances help account for the episodes of witch-hunting in revolutionary Scotland as well. During these tumultuous times, the nexus between witchcraft and religious and political disorder took on an ideological dimension. Royalist preachers called upon the text of 1 Samuel 15. 23, "For rebellion is as the sin of witchcraft," in an effort to denounce their adversaries as allies of the devil and enemies of the church and state.[39] This extract derived from the story of King Saul the Israelite, which played an important part in contemporary understandings of witchcraft more generally. For example, the frontispiece of Joseph Glanvill's 1681 *Saducismus Triumphatus: Or, Full and Plain Evidence Concerning Witches and Apparitions* featured a tableau from this biblical narrative: the witch of Endor summoning the spirit of the prophet Samuel, at Saul's request (Figure 7.3). This disobedience led God ultimately to abandon Saul, who

FIGURE 7.3 Joseph Glanvill *Saducismus Triumphatus: Or, Full and Plain Evidence Concerning Witches and Apparitions* (1681). Source: Rare Book Collection, Kislak Center for Special Collections, Rare Books and Manuscripts, University of Pennsylvania.

had already flouted His instructions to destroy the Amalekites in an act of insubordination which Samuel condemned as akin to witchcraft (1 Samuel 28.3-25).

Of course, the link between witchcraft and political disorder existed at a purely literal level too. Practitioners of magic had been known in the Middle Ages to use their powers to attempt to harm authoritative political and ecclesiastical individuals.[40] Likewise, as mentioned above, both King James and Queen Elizabeth had endured threats to their persons at the hands of alleged witches during the sixteenth century. Even prior to the North Berwick witch trials, James's political standing was obliquely related to witchcraft by way of allegations made against the Bishop Patrick Adamson, an adversary of the reformers who was supported by episcopalian sympathizers. A scathing satire of Adamson's putative dealings with healing witches emerged some time around 1584 and influenced anti-episcopal polemic for decades to come.[41] In a similar way, during the revolutionary period, partisan rhetoric invoked the long-standing comparison between divine and civil treason for political ends. As the Protestant theologian William Perkins had written the century before:

> For this cause Samuel told Saul, that rebellion was as the sin of witchcraft; that is, a most heinous and detestable sin in the sight of God … The traitour … betraies his Soveraigne, and consequently can not bee a friend unto the common-wealth. In like manner … the Witch … hath renounced God His King and governour, and hath bound himself by other lawes to the enemy of God …[42]

Royalist propaganda drawing on the tale of Saul extended beyond sermons to include musical performances. Recitals of the dialogue song "In guilty night," which recounted an exchange between Saul, the witch of Endor and the ghost of Samuel, were undertaken in anti-Puritan spirits during the 1650s, though by the 1670s the song had been repurposed to serve anti-Catholic sentiments.[43] Even after the Restoration, the association between political rebellion and witchcraft retained currency. At a royalist pageant held at Linlithgow in 1661, an arch depicting the policies of the Wars and Interregnum bearing the slogan "Rebellion is the Mother of Witchcraft" was burned in a symbolically charged denunciation of the Covenanters.[44]

The account of Saul and the witch of Endor, which was prominent in political and religious discourse, also appeared in juristic writings. Coke speaks of the "reprobation and death of King Saul"[45] in explaining how the capital punishment of witchcraft was justified under the early law and Mackenzie describes the trepidation shown by the witch of Endor when asked to use her sorcery, which was attributable to the laws imposing death on witches, wizards and those with familiars that were "in such observation amongst the Jews."[46] As Charles Zika has noted, images of the encounter between Saul and the witch of Endor appeared with increasing frequency across Europe over the course of the early modern period, testifying to the long history of the offense and providing clear authorization of legal and political endeavors to combat its threat.[47] By citing this instance of prohibited necromancy and its divine retribution, Mackenzie and Coke thereby reinforced the judicial approbation the sin attracted, and had previously attracted, in each jurisdiction. Both authors made additional biblical references to similar effect. Coke called upon the books of Exodus, Deuteronomy, and Numbers to explain the punishment of witches by death in the years preceding the witchcraft statutes, concluding that "it would have been a great defect in government, if so great an abomination had passed with impunity"[48] and Mackenzie relied on Scripture to justify the capital punishment of all acts of witchcraft, irrespective of the harm caused. Citing Exodus 22.18, "thou shalt not suffer a Witch to live," he wrote that it was clear witches should be executed "not only when they Poyson or murder, but even for Enchanting and Deluding the world."[49] This was, of course, the way the offense was treated under the Scottish Witchcraft Act. Although prosecutions were commonly based on maleficence, the Act did not distinguish between "good" and "bad" uses of magic and punished by death all practitioners of witchcraft, who misled their clients into believing they might benefit from their magical expertise.[50]

In spite of Mackenzie's insistence that witches deserved to be punished with the "most ignominious of deaths," he was cautious about the crime's prosecution, stating that "it requires the clearest relevancy, and most convincing probation."[51] He was also highly critical of the way witchcraft trials had been conducted in Scotland, having direct experience of the practices used through his involvement as a justice depute in the great witch-hunt of 1661–1662. Mackenzie was particularly reproachful of the torture and starvation of suspects, who would often provide false confessions through fear and desperation.[52] His skepticism as to the guilt of many of the individuals accused of witchcraft, which had also been growing among his judicial colleagues, goes some way towards explaining why, in 1662, the Justiciary Court, Scotland's central criminal court, virtually refrained from adjudicating witchcraft trials.[53] From this point on, prosecutions for witchcraft declined in Scotland and the proportion of those acquitted rose—a change which Levack attributes more to legalistic changes, such as greater central control of trials and insistence on strict standards of proof, than to any abatement in witchcraft beliefs. Indeed, the idea that witchcraft was an impossible crime did not take hold in Scotland until long after its formal decriminalization in 1736.[54]

The situation in England was analogous in that prosecutions declined long before the statute decriminalizing witchcraft was introduced. From the 1660s onwards, the number of witchcraft trials fell and convictions were extremely rare. Though support for prosecutions continued in some circles, stricter controls on the admissibility of evidence and changes in judicial attitude expedited the demise of witchcraft as an indictable felony.[55] A notable example of changing judicial attitudes is Sir Matthew Hale, who presided over the trial and conviction of Amy Denny and Rose Cullender for witchcraft at Bury St. Edmunds in 1662. Hale's decision to admit, and avoid summarizing, questionable evidence would come to be regarded as an unfortunate blemish on his otherwise distinguished character and career. In the course of his jury directions, and in writing about witchcraft days after the trial, Hale was clear that biblical authority, including the story of Saul and the witch of Endor, confirmed the existence of witches and his comments can be read as indicating that he was satisfied with the outcome of the trial.[56] Yet, there are suggestions, such as the dearth of commentary justifying the law against witchcraft in his *Historia Placitorum Coronae*, that he might later have undergone change of heart.[57]

Eventually, both the Scottish and English Acts against witchcraft would be repealed by an Act of 1736, according to which pretended witchcraft or sorcery was punishable with imprisonment, pillorying, and providing sureties for good behavior. By targeting those who pretended to tell fortunes, the Act, which aimed to protect "ignorant persons" from being deluded or defrauded, signaled increasing concerns over vagrancy and other threats to private property. Indeed, the nomenclature of witchcraft gradually came to be used as a metaphor for petty theft.[58] In an abstracted way, this change in the nature of wrongdoing with which witchcraft was associated indicates not only shifting concerns over the foundations of social order but also the complex and variegated process by which belief in witchcraft declined, at least within public communications by intellectual and social elites.[59] At the end of the early modern period, however, these transformations were, at most, nascent and the structures of thought within which traditional beliefs about witchcraft made sense were yet to disappear.[60]

SEXUAL WRONGS

[Magistrates should prosecute] common whoremongers, and common whores; for (by good opinion) adultery and bawdry is an offence temporal, as well as spiritual, and is against the peace of the land.[61]

The absence of a distinct boundary between sin and crime, and the shifting cultural and legal meanings of wrongdoing, is further illustrated by sexual wrongs. These included an extensive range sexual misconduct, from rape and sodomy to adultery, whoring, fornication, and other forms of lewdness. Such offenses could be dealt with in different ways, including informal social discipline, shaming rituals in local parish courts, and prosecution in the royal courts. Fornication, whoredom, adultery, or uncleanness were condemned in religious tracts sermons as well as in legislation but as the quotation from Dalton suggests, the terms did not distinguish clearly between specific types of sexual wrongdoing so much as between chastity and unchastity.[62] A common underlying theme was the desire to limit sexual contact outside of marriage and even in certain instances to regulate the approved forms of sexual contact within marriage. Daniel Defoe, for example, in his treatise *Conjugal Lewdness*, described even sexual relations within marriage that were not for the purposes of procreation as "nothing but Whoring under the shelter or cover of the Law."[63] Illicit sex, that is to say sex before or outwith marriage, was seen as corrupting to the individuals involved as well as to the broader community that permitted such conduct. It could lead to the spread of venereal disease; adultery or unwanted pregnancies could threaten social relations and the orderly succession of property; and because of its corrupting influences on character, illicit sex was believed to have the potential to lead to further crime or immorality.[64] The regulation of sex was thus seen as a matter of legitimate public concern and loomed large in early modern thought about social order.

In general, the regulation of sexual conduct was linked to the institution of marriage. The Catholic Church had long sought to instill sexual discipline in its followers, proscribing forms of sexual conduct outwith marriage. However, the regulation of sex intensified with the Reformation as Protestant reformers sought not only to purify the church, but also the souls of ordinary people.[65] Homilies against fornication and whoredom were read from the pulpits of churches across the country. Brothels were closed down, notorious whores were expelled from towns and fornicators were flogged or put in the stocks. Sexual offenders were brought before the parish or civil magistrates to be judged and could be subjected to punishments such as whipping or confinement in a house of correction. The actions of women were singled out for particular condemnation as female sexuality was regarded as a male possession, and the role of the good husband or father was to protect the honor of his wife and daughters.[66] The campaign against unchastity was also manifested in efforts to tighten moral discipline and in new laws to strengthen ecclesiastical justice where it was seen as ineffective. Central to this were the repeated attempts to extend secular jurisdiction over adultery and fornication from the 1540s onwards.[67] This produced legislation in 1576, empowering justices to punish the parents—particularly the mothers—of children born out of wedlock, and there is evidence that the courts punished those who had facilitated fornication by aiding pregnant women or single mothers.[68] An Act of 1610 provided a penalty of one year's confinement in the house of correction, and in 1624 a law was passed providing the death penalty for women who delivered illegitimate children who were found dead. This process culminated in the Act of 1650 "For the suppressing of the abominable and crying sins of Incest, Adultery and Fornication, wherewith this Land is much defiled, and Almighty God highly displeased"[69] (cf. Act of 1563 in Scotland criminalizing "notour" or notorious adultery). Under the Act, incest and adultery were made into capital felonies—though once again sanctions were directed primarily at woman. Adultery was defined as a married woman having sexual intercourse with any man other than her husband; intercourse of a married man with a single woman was the lesser offense of fornication. Bawds or brothel keepers were to be whipped and branded with the letter B and this was made capital for a second offense.

Although it is often seen as a watershed in the state regulation of sexual conduct, the Act was widely regarded—even at the time—as unworkable. The indictment had to be filed within twelve months of the alleged offense; the penalty did not apply to a man who did not know that the woman was married; the confession of one party could not be accepted as evidence against the other; and married partners could not testify against each other.[70] On the restoration of the monarchy in 1660, the Act lapsed and was not renewed. Much of the business of regulating sexual conduct reverted to the ecclesiastical courts; however, their declining role in this period reflected a broader cultural shift in attitudes towards sexual misconduct. This was exemplified in the well-known extra-marital relationships of King Charles II and the looser sexual morality of his court, but the shift in attitudes is also well illustrated by Samuel Pepys' recording of diverse sexual encounters without fear of prosecution. Although some moralists continued to call for the renewed criminalization and more effective punishment of adultery, illicit sex was increasingly viewed as a private matter. It was still recognized to be against religious teaching and morals, but its enforcement was a matter for individual conscience and no longer seen as a matter for the criminal law. By the 1730s, prosecutions for adultery had virtually ceased in London and marital infidelity was coming to be viewed as a private vice, rather than a matter of public concern. The focus of the law moved from fornication generally to specific offenses, such as public prostitution and its disorderly consequences.[71] The concern was thus no longer fornication as such but forms of sexual conduct that could be linked directly to other forms of social disorder.

These changes were also broadly reflected in the legal definition of more serious sexual wrongs such as rape and sodomy. Rape was regarded as an extremely serious felony, condemned in the strongest of terms by the writers of legal treatises, and was punishable by death, without benefit of clergy. But the very seriousness of an allegation of rape could, in practice, operate as a barrier to successful prosecution: the consequences were so severe that the courts required clear evidence of the use of extraordinary violence and of the impeccable character of the victim.[72] Rape was formally defined as "when a man hath carnal knowledge of a woman by force and against her will,"[73] requiring both penetration and emission and the use of force. However, the understanding of the crime was broader, shaped by older beliefs that rape was a kind of forcible taking[74] as well as the general social condemnation of fornication. Although rape and abduction were formally recognized as separate crimes in 1487 (3 Hen.VII c.2), the connection between the two lingered in an association with the taking of property. This can be seen in the belief that the law protected virtue or chastity as a property of the unmarried woman that was damaged by rape. It was also reflected in the belief that honor could be restored if the woman subsequently married her attacker. Hale, for example, discussed the situation in which a marriage which was voidable because of an initial rape might be ratified by the subsequent consent of the woman.[75] This also makes sense of Hale's notorious assertion that a wife could not be raped by her husband;[76] virtue had a different meaning in the context of marriage. Given the general social condemnation of fornication, a woman complaining of rape would need to be of unimpeachable virtue if she was to displace the suspicion that her accusation was designed to divert attention from the fact that she was of loose morals or that she was trying to engineer marriage or secure financial compensation. The association with property was thus also reflected in the reality that the law was more readily enforced where the victim was of good repute or had property or a good family name to protect. In other cases the crime was hard to prove with women and servants regarded as unreliable witnesses, particularly where the allegation was made against a man of high social standing.[77] Rape thus encompassed sexual behavior but, like sexual wrongs more generally, its meaning was understood in terms of institutions of property, marriage, and the family.[78]

Sodomy was likewise regarded as a crime of the utmost seriousness and its incidence as a measure of social corruption and godlessness, as illustrated by the biblical story of Sodom and Gomorrah. It was made into a common law felony by a statute of 1534, which took the jurisdiction over the crime away from ecclesiastical courts (25 Hen VIII c.6 (1533–4)).[79] The offense was defined broadly as carnal knowledge between two men, between human and animal or "unnaturally" between a man and a woman. Yet the proof required for conviction meant that it was difficult to prosecute: it required proof of anal penetration, but where sexual contact was consensual and took place in private there would rarely be a witness to this. In practice, in the seventeenth century, sodomy was prosecuted where the victim was a minor and there was no consent.[80] It was linked to rape because it involved "carnal knowledge" and raised similar issues of evidence and proof; but, as with rape, while the crime was defined in terms of sexual acts, they did not exhaust its definition in practice.[81] It was described as a crime against nature and, as a Plea of the Crown, it fell within the class of crimes which posed a serious threat to social order. As scholars have argued, there was general cultural acceptance of sexual relations between males, which were routinely satirized in early modern drama.[82] When sodomy was prosecuted in the seventeenth century this was usually because it was linked to some other threat posed by a particular individual or because the sexual activity signified an underlying social disorder:

> The danger of the sodomite was not that the focus of his attention was a man, but that his desires had no focus; they ran in indiscriminate streams that undermined allegedly categorical boundaries between men and women, humans and animals, nobles and commoners. (Herrup 1999: 33)

This explains the logic of conflating bestiality and sodomy in a category of buggery. It was against the order of nature, but the nature here was not heterosexuality "it was organisation born of moderation."

BLASPHEMY AND DISORDERLY SPEECH

The government of the tongue, or the control of disorderly speech, was central to the understanding of wrongdoing in early modern England.[83] The tongue was understood as giving voice to the inward thoughts of the heart, and so at one level disorderly speech was taken as evidence of weak or corrupt character or a lack of self-control. However, while the individual sinner would be judged before God, the unruly tongue was also a matter of concern for the civil magistrate, as words were seen as weapons that might inflict injury on individuals or a community. Robert Burton, for example, identified words as potential causes of melancholy, as a sharp tongue could inflict deep wounds: "A bitter jest, a slander, a calumny, pierceth deeper than any loss, danger, bodily pain, or injury whatsoever."[84] Disorderly speech was capable of spreading, like a disease or a poison, to corrupt or infect others and to undermine both religious and civil authority. Early modern authors drew on biblical authority, such as Exodus (22. 28) ("Thou shalt not revile the gods, nor curse the ruler of thy people") or Ecclesiastes (10. 20) ("curse not the king, no not in thy thought") to condemn heretical, blasphemous, and seditious speech. As with the regulation of sex, the control of disorderly speech was seen as central to the work of ordering families and communities and there were a range of mechanisms for punishing defamatory, blasphemous, licentious, and seditious speech. Parish courts could deal with minor wrongdoings through shaming punishments, such as the punishment of scolds, but to speak ill of someone in authority was to breach spiritual duties, such as

FIGURE 7.4 Woman wearing a scold's bridle. Ralph Gardiner, *England's Grievance Discovered* (1655). Source: Wellcome Library, London.

the fifth commandment (to honor thy father and mother), and to imperil the political establishment. It is interesting to note in this connection that Mackenzie, in his discussion of the law of blasphemy in Scotland, referred to the cursing of parents as a sub-species of the crime.[85] There were accordingly a range of legal wrongs, ascending in order of seriousness from defamation to *scandalum magnatum* (slandering those in authority) to sedition and treason where words were understood as conduct which undermined social and political institutions.

Heresy and blasphemy merit particular attention, as their separation into distinct spiritual and temporal offenses demonstrates how the law was changing towards the end of the early modern period. Between the fifteenth and seventeenth centuries, heresy was governed by the notorious statute *De Haeretico Comburendo* ("on the burning of heretics"), which was passed in 1401 (2 Hen IV c.15) and made the offense a capital crime enforced by the ecclesiastical courts. Heresy was understood as a crime against God, consisting in the denial of essential doctrines of Christianity or the expression of "erroneous opinions"—though what was understood as erroneous changed over time. Although prosecutions were initially directed against the Lollards, the crime of heresy became a tool in the religious conflicts of the sixteenth and seventeenth centuries as the church asserted the power to punish heretics by burning, with or without the consent of the monarch.[86] In 1558 (1 Eliz c.1) this power was removed from the ecclesiastical courts and given to the Court of High Commission, which retained an authority to investigate and punish heresy under the authority of the Crown until its abolition in 1640. The writ itself was not formally abolished until 1677, although the last execution for heresy had taken place in 1612.[87] Blasphemy, by contrast, was not formally recognized in the criminal law until the mid-seventeenth century. The condemnation of blasphemy (like adultery and fornication) had its origins in biblical law (Leviticus 24.16 "he that blasphemeth the name of the Lord, he shall surely be put to death") and the authority of Leviticus was frequently appealed to in the period of the Commonwealth by those seeking either stiffer punishments or more rigorously enforced laws against religious dissent or the expression of religious heterodoxy. The interregnum had freed a vast explosion of radical and dissenting religious ideas and sects, and a number of attempts were made to regulate dissenting or irreligious speech as damaging to the Commonwealth. These included statutes of 1648 ("An Ordinance for the punishing of blasphemies and heresies") and 1650 ("An Act against several Atheistical, Blasphemous and Execrable Opinions derogatory to the honour of God and destructive to humane society"), which were directed against radical antinomian sects such as the Ranters, who advocated free love. In spite of the strong language, the 1650 Act imposed a sentence of only six months' imprisonment for a first offense; thus while the Acts regulated conduct in a similar way to the crime of heresy, blasphemy was a much less serious offense. Like other Acts of the Commonwealth, the 1650 Act lapsed with the restoration of the monarchy in 1660. A similar pattern was followed in Scotland. A general law against heresy, passed in 1425, was at first enforced by ecclesiastical courts but then, after the Reformation, the Royal courts began to punish heresy which, by then, was seen as an offense against the Crown. The crime of blasphemy was not introduced until a statute of 1649 and, although it was a capital offense, only one person, Thomas Aitkenhead, is known to have been executed under the law.[88]

These conflicts over the dangers of irreligious speech came to a head in the Restoration period, as questions over the acceptability of religious dissent and the place of toleration were debated in the 1670s. At this time, there were a number of failed attempts to criminalize atheism, blasphemy, and profaneness[89] but the most significant change was the development of more clearly defined crime of blasphemy that could be prosecuted in the common law courts. Two cases can be regarded as of particular importance in shaping this new crime. The first was *Sedley's Case* in 1663 (17 St. Tr. 156; Pepys, July 1st 1663). Sedley had appeared drunk and naked on the balcony of a house in Covent Garden before abusing the crowd below by, among other things, preaching blasphemy, washing his penis in a glass of wine and drinking it in a toast to the king. He was indicted at common law for his conduct and the court held that in the absence of the Court of Star Chamber, the Court of King's Bench was the guardian of the morals *(custos morum)* of the King's subjects and could punish such conduct. They then went on to hold that "profane actions committed against all modesty," or indecent conduct which was derogatory of Christianity, was punishable at common law, and fined Sedley the sum of £500. The second case was *R v Taylor* (1676 3 Keble 607),[90] which raised more directly the question of how the criminal law should deal with religious dissent. Taylor, a member of the radical sect the "Sweet Singers of Israel," was charged with having made various public statements alleging that Christ was a whoremaster and that religion was a cheat. His case eventually came before the Court of King's Bench where the Lord Chief Justice, Sir Matthew Hale, stated that:

> such kind of wicked and blasphemous words were not only an offence against God and religion, but a crime against the law, State and government; and, therefore, punishable in this court; that to say "religion is a cheat" is to dissolve all those obligations whereby civil societies are preserved, and Christianity being parcel of the laws of England, therefore, to reproach the Christian religion is to speak in subversion of the law.

Taylor was accordingly found guilty and ordered to pay a fine of 1,000 marks. As part of his punishment, he was also to be imprisoned until he found sureties for good conduct for life and placed in the pillory wearing a paper bearing the words "For Blasphemous Words and tending to the subversion of all government."

As a result of these two cases, conduct (whether indecent or blasphemous) which would previously have been dealt with in the ecclesiastical courts could now be treated as common law misdemeanours. Hale, moreover, did not assert that the laws of England were founded on scripture, conflating religion and state, but that the common law was a means of preserving civil order and that the content of the laws drew on Christian beliefs.[91] The way the offense of blasphemy was defined thus left a certain amount to the individual conscience. The wrong did not consist in holding particular beliefs (as a form of sin), but expressing them in a way that threatened those bonds which held civil society together. As later commentators have noted, there was a strong analogy between seditious and blasphemous libel in this period because both crimes were focused on the tendency of certain forms of conduct to subvert civil institutions.[92] The idea of disorderly speech as a form of spiritual wrongdoing, directed against God and established religion, was transformed into the idea of disorderly speech as a form of civic wrongdoing, which consisted in conduct that threatened the morals and institutions of society.

CONCLUSION

The picture that we have outlined in this chapter is one in which discrete wrongs gradually appeared out of more general categories of misconduct and burgeoning distinctions between spiritual and temporal delinquencies started to solidify. By a process of secularization, wrongs that were considered indistinguishable from sins came to be regarded as wrongs against society at large: its order, ethos, and institutions. Naturally, a central aspect of this metamorphosis was the changing relationship between church and state but this should not obscure the deeper, and connected, transformation between the individual and society that was also occurring. At the start of the early modern period there were few conceptual distinctions in the realm of wrongdoing. Wrongs were sins and sins were harmful to the collective social order. This harm need not have been physical, for the threat feared was to the establishment and maintenance of godly society on earth. Both religious and secular authorities were accordingly concerned with the close and continuous regulation of individuals, their actions and those actions' broader import. Indeed there was a continuity between the government of the individual, the family, and polity, with the godly city and the salvation of the individual soul being closely linked. Slips or failings in one area required swift and effective repression, lest they spread into other areas of social life and undermine the project of holistic governance.

By the end of the period, however, a new mode of governance was emerging. Some forms of wrongdoing, such as witchcraft, were disappearing and others, such as adultery, were coming to be seen as private matters rather than targets for state intervention. The fact that conduct contravened a rule in scripture or divine law was no longer seen in itself as reason for legal intervention. As a consequence, a distinction began to emerge between crimes and sins, with crimes coming to be considered more explicitly in terms of their harmful social consequences. Certain areas of individual life—sexual conduct and religious belief, for example—were increasingly seen as personal matters. As long as they did not overtly threaten civil institutions, they were matters of individual conscience or morals. A more individualistic society was thus materializing and the more ambitious plans to achieve divine order on earth, which required an aggregated conception of wrongdoing, began to fade from view.

CHAPTER EIGHT

The Legal Profession

Tudor Lawyers in an Age of Litigation

DOMINIQUE GOY-BLANQUET

The Tudor age began on the battlefield. A king was killed, another king picked up his crown and climbed the throne. Was he legitimate? Victory made him so. After this dubious beginning, Henry VII took great care to keep on the right side of the law. He sometimes visited the Inns of Court and attended festivities there.[1] Within days of his arrival in London, he issued writs of summons for a parliament, who dutifully agreed that he had come to the throne by just title of inheritance and God's judgment in battle. The attainders against the Lancasters were cancelled or reversed, the most fervent surviving Yorkists attainted, and the Statute *Titulus Regius* declaring his future wife Elizabeth of York illegitimate, repealed.[2]

THE LEGAL MACHINE

In Edward Hall's chronicle, the first Tudor begins, as did Geoffrey of Monmouth's Welsh kings, by establishing profitable laws.[3] Henry VII did not attempt to replace the judges of his predecessors, though he sold some of the appointments for a high price.[4] Their first mission was to restore royal authority after the civil wars of the last Plantagenet reigns. The king's "over-mighty" subjects were put under restraint by laws against livery and maintenance designed to prevent them from setting up private armies. Traditionally, the middle class of country gentlemen, burgesses and lawyers were the monarchy's best allies against both arrogant nobility and unruly commons: in exchange, they were allowed a share in the executive government at central or local levels. Only a few common lawyers gained influence on the Privy Council or at court under the Tudors, to rise and fall as Fortune's wheel moved, but many became prominent as county justices of peace or town recorders. These amateur judges, who often had but a slight legal education, were also involved in complex local networks of affinities almost of necessity since they were virtually unpaid.[5] The Gloucestershire scenes of Shakespeare's *Henry IV*, like rural Windsor or the Dogberried Messina of his *Much Ado About Nothing*, provide a good example of how early modern England was governed on a daily basis, at fairly safe distance from the royal court. With the growth of administration, the numbers and the authority of justices of the peace were considerably increased, as were the instructions they received from the government. Royal proclamations told subjects where to apply for redress in case of abuses, placing justice more firmly under the king's control.

In the common law courts, standard practice comprised an adversarial representation of a case by advocates before a supposedly impartial judge or a jury. The trial by jury, combined with popular litigiousness and the bureaucracy of everyday life, made a number of legal concepts familiar to a large section of society. It certainly set the mode for the Elizabethan dramatic *agon*, as well as setting common law courts against all others. A teeming world of clerks, notaries, attorneys, scriveners and their paraphernalia figure in the margins of the Elizabethan stage, employed in varied daily tasks, though only on rare occasions do they come to the forefront, like the scrivener of *Richard III*, to expose distortions of justice. Various legal historians impute to lawyers the making of the Tudor state and the unmaking of the Stuart one. Recent studies tend to qualify the theory that Elizabethan Parliaments were filled with malcontents who would at length manage to unseat monarchy, but generally agree that they played a major role in the Tudor revolutions. In Wilfrid Prest's view, the bar included some of the Crown's most valuable servants as well as sharp critics of government policies; roles that were not mutually exclusive. In Tudor and early Stuart England the lawyers "played an essential role in the consolidation of centralized monarchical rule, advising both government and their subjects, whose lives were increasingly regulated by judicial tribunals, old and new, and by an ever-expanding body of statutory legislation."[6]

The Westminster courts grew and multiplied from the medieval three of King's Bench, Common Pleas, and Exchequer to become a panoply of specialized Tudor courts. Henry VII's highly unpopular Council Learned in the Law, formed around 1499 to deal with fiscal issues and to enforce payment of debts, was abolished after his death in 1509. For the most part he preserved the legal system he had found on his accession, but his son Henry VIII undertook a number of innovations. Four financial courts were created at the time of the dissolution of the monasteries. By the Submission of the Clergy Act 1533 (25 Hen 8 c 19), canons not repugnant to the royal prerogative or to laws and customs of the realm were permitted to remain on a provisional basis. Several ineffectual projects to revise canon law then followed. In 1556, during the reign of Henry VIII's son Edward VI, a commission led by Cranmer was set up to devise a comprehensive *Reformatio legum ecclesiasticarum*, but it failed in Parliament. Mary repealed the religious Acts of her father and revived the old heresy laws, which were overturned again by her sister. Again, the 1559 Act of Unity and Supremacy ruled that canon law was valid only where not repugnant to the laws of the realm. Common law did not suppress or grow at the expense of ecclesiastical law, Peter Goodrich points out, but absorbed it in a newly united civil and ecclesiastical commonwealth.[7] In the meantime, after the abrogation of the teaching of canon law at Oxford or Cambridge by Henry VIII, the "civilians" had taken over what remained of the ecclesiastical courts.

EQUITY VERSUS COMMON LAW

The religious changes caused upsets in other more material areas. Queen Mary proved unable to restore its properties to the church. Too many private interests were involved. When Elizabeth came to the throne, the Commons, their lawyers, and businessmen were kept busy for weeks by a number of conflicting claims over church lands, some of them existing prior to Mary's reign. One of the most complex cases was that pertaining to the Winchester lands. A warrant given by Mary to Bishop White had cancelled all the deeds of his predecessor Ponet, creating a dangerous precedent. If records could be destroyed and nullified, the possessions and inheritance of all men "may come to such dowte and question" that no one could know for certain who was the rightful owner.[8] On the other hand, if grants could be invalidated at the beginning of each new reign, there could be no security of tenure. In this case, time's charters were treated with due regard. Where the Marian bishop had obtained his rights by confiscation from a deprived predecessor, the claimant won. If he came without such history he lost.[9]

Most of the land in England was held by use. The birth pangs of the Statute of Uses, aimed to prevent the escape from payment of feudal dues, reveal the legal profession's ambivalent relations with the Crown. Undoubtedly the Statute of Uses "was forced upon an extremely unwilling Parliament by an extremely strong-willed King,"[10] but "this strong-willed King was obliged first to frighten and then to conciliate the common lawyers in order to get the statute through the House of Commons."[11] Henry VIII took the opportunity of their Supplication against Ordinaries to warn the Commons that he would "search out the extremity of the law" if they placed obstacles in the way of his legislative will. Increasingly, significant fields of litigation in which common law could not or would not operate were abandoned to Chancery. Wolsey had extended its jurisdiction, and developed the principle of equity in English law, causing Thomas Audley in his reading of 1526 at Inner Temple to argue that Chancery was a potential threat to the common law. The Statute gave the person or body in use, possession of the full title to the land, contrary to the doctrine set up by the court of Chancery that distinguished the seisin, or legal estate, from the use, or beneficial estate.

Another court of original jurisdiction, the Star Chamber began as an extension of the king's council. The Act Pro Camera Stellata of 1487 empowered it to control abuses of the judicial system.[12] To Chancellor Morton, its first concern was the offender's soul: "I know that an executor who fraudulently misapplies the goods and does not make restitution will be damned in Hell, and to remedy this is in accordance with conscience as I understand it."[13] Neither he nor Henry VII foresaw how deeply common lawyers would come to resent this "court of conscience," and not just on matters of principles. The legal profession had begun a steep decline during the civil wars. King's Bench and Common Pleas at the end of the fifteenth century conducted only half the business they had attained fifty years earlier, "for the common-law courts had failed to move with the times."[14] The product of an age of force rather than cunning, common law was poorly armed against such devious practices as fraud, perjury, corruption, and deliberate delay. As a result, the bulk of profitable litigation relating to real property went to equity courts. Chancery and the Star Chamber were able by writs of subpœna to deal more rapidly with cases of property settlement, titles to land, mercantile debts or undue imprisonment.

The equity courts developed under the royal prerogative to provide relief in cases for which the strict rules and forms of the common law provided no adequate remedy, making equity a "judicial art of bending formal constraints without breaking them."[15] Writing *In Praise of the Laws of England* Sir John Fortescue had celebrated the English legal system and its nursery, the Inns of Court. Seen from the shores of another island, the laws of Tudor England were not so praiseworthy. Thomas More in his fictional island of *Utopia* mentions a whole store of them "not made according to equity." Reporting a discussion at the home of More's first mentor, Cardinal Morton, the dialogue stigmatizes the inequity of the English system that allows the abuses of landlords, creates poverty with enclosures and hangs poor desperate trespassers. Since most chancellors before More had no legal training, their decisions could vary significantly from one case to the next, one of the reasons that made equity "A Roguish thing" in the eyes of common lawyers.[16] Young barristers had no qualms about pleading before equity courts, but the older ones watched with a jaundiced eye the encroachments on their jurisdiction.

Should chancellors, acting under royal prerogative, continue to remedy the whole gamut of defects in the legal system? Arguments made due reference to Aristotle and Aquinas, echoes of which can be heard in Portia's remonstrances to Shylock on justice and mercy in Shakespeare's *The Merchant of Venice*,[17] albeit echoes that distort the flexibility of equity into something more strict.[18] In his *Summa*, Aquinas had put the case for equity in the lawyerly form of a *pro et contra* dispute, later repeated in endless debates: is equity a vice or a virtue? Is it a part of justice? The *pro* quoted Aristotle on *epieikeia*, the need to interpret the mind of the legislator and protect the rights of individuals within, or against, the common weal. The *contra* stressed the risks of arbitrariness. All the shades of meaning given to "equity," the need to mitigate or amend the law, implied that justice was inadequate, too harsh, unfair. There were hesitations over the meaning of "equity": Morton's "conscience as I understand it," a very flexible one in his own case, or a sort of consensus, broadly based on principles of English law? The growth of equity courts under the Tudor reigns shoved "conscience" from the offender's to the judge's place, till Selden dismissed the notion in his *Table Talk*: "For Law we have a measure, know what to trust to. Equity is according to the conscience of him that is Chancellor, and as that is larger or narrower, so is Equity."[19] As the length of a chancellor's foot varies, so does his conscience.

THE KING'S GREAT MATTER

The Tudor lawyers' fortunes received support from a conflict between their monarch's will to remain under the law and his longing for freedom, when a private worry began to trouble Henry VIII: he is in great scruple of conscience, Hall writes, for diverse learned divines have told him secretly he lives in adultery. Teams of advisors worked hard for several years, looking for precedents to procure a canonical annulment of his marriage to Catherine of Aragon. Several methods were tried, and many books written, until Thomas Cromwell, of Gray's Inn, solved the king's dilemma. The strategy decided upon was to make imperial kingship a reality through Parliament, "imperial" no longer meaning what it did originally, a rule over several kingdoms, but asserting total independence from "the authority of any foreign potentates."[20] The "Reformation Parliament" met in Blackfriars' hall where Wolsey's legatine court had first met, and continued with eight sessions from 1529 to 1536. The Commons were packed not so much with the king's supporters as with a strongly anti-clerical laity.[21] While few of them dared oppose, many actively assisted England's break with Rome.[22] They welcomed its accompanying benefits, the expropriation of church land and the reduction of privileges. The redistribution of national wealth was larger than anything since the land settlement of the Norman conquest. The purchasers were peers and commoners, country esquires, London merchants, lawyers, civil servants. Against such a wide range of interests, Mary would find it impossible to reorganize religious life on its former basis.

Among the lawyers recruited in the service of Henry VIII's anti-clerical cause Christopher Saint-German, utter barrister of Middle Temple, was the loudest.[23] So loud that in 1536 he was one of those whose heresies the "northern rebels" wanted destroyed.[24] His first concern was not Henry's marital divorce but the harmonization of legal systems and jurisdictions; the coincidence of his anticlericalism with the royal team's personal objects was only partial and temporary.[25] His two *Dialogues in English*, *betweene a Doctor of Divinity and a Student in the Laws of England* infuriated Thomas More, who demurely thought that abuse of the clergy should be confined to Latin. After his resignation, More officially kept silence about the king's religious policy, but under color of answers to Saint-German his *Apologye* and *Debellation of Salem and Bizance* vigorously criticized Protestant theology. Both men thought that equity should be part of the common law.[26] Where they disagreed was over the legal independence of the church. More insisted that canon law, the common law of Christendom, stood above any local code in Europe, while Saint-German wanted uniform civil principles. He was in full sympathy with the Commons' Supplication against the Ordinaries in 1532, that "canon law itself was inimical to the common law of England and that the independence of the church courts was insupportable."[27]

After years of procrastination, Henry's Great Matter was settled at high speed. The Act in Restraint of Appeals drafted by Cromwell was passed on April 7, 1533, prohibiting any appeal from the archbishop's court. On May 23, the marriage to Catherine was formally declared invalid *ab initio*. On the 28th, Cranmer validated Henry's secret marriage to Anne Boleyn. The first Succession Act, passed in the spring session, regularized the marriage and its consequences. A Second Act in 1536 reflected the latest changes in Henry's family. The Act of Supremacy gave him the authority to disband monasteries and confiscate their properties. It was now well established through the religious settlements that the king-in-Parliament reigned supreme. How far the king's power could extend out of Parliament was a gray area left for the next dynasty to explore.

STATE TRIALS

The debates of the early 1530s grew increasingly one-sided in the course of the decade. From April 1535, a series of government letters addressed to bishops and lay officers gave them strict instructions to enforce the law and detect suspected opponents. Long sets of articles composed under Cromwell's supervision provided them with correct preaching material. A letter of June 1535 informed the justices of assizes of "the treasons traitorously committed against us and our laws by the late bishop of Rochester and Sir Thomas More," although More had not been tried yet.[28] Cromwell's good services were not rewarded with a proper trial when a charge of treason was brought against him. The instrument of his destruction was the machinery he had helped set up, especially the extension of treason laws. After 1534, by a bill of attainder the person accused of serious crimes like treason, felony, or misprision was declared guilty without benefit of a trial.[29] It took the form of a petition from both Houses, begging the king to punish the offenders, as if the whole realm were clamoring for their blood from a too merciful prince. "No man ought to be condemned without answer," Coke wrote in discussing Cromwell's attainder.[30] The readings of the attainder passed with the clerk's mention *"nemine discrepante,"* no one disagreeing.[31] Probably because, as the judges would answer Coke, "it was a dangerous question."

The dramatic reversals of fortune continued under Henry's successors, whose adherence to fair rule of law was at best intermittent. Their insistence on legality, based on historical precedents and trials, set teams of jurists to work at crucial turning points. The lawyers who were told to execute Edward VI's will barring his sisters from the succession had replied it would be treason, but soon surrendered, then found themselves in the dock when the "nine-day Queen" Lady Jane was overthrown. Seymours, Dudleys, Howards, Greys fell under the ax by attainder without undue fuss, but Archbishop Cranmer and

Mary Queen of Scots were treated to a full-scale trial, although in both cases there could be little doubt about the verdict.

"The execution of the Scottish Queen is of necessitie," Thomas Norton of the Middle Temple declared to the Commons, reassuring them "it lawfully maie be done."[32] Like Henry's, the Elizabethan think tank and Parliament explored several tracks before they took the awful step. At first Mary Stuart was to be judged for her crimes, adultery and murder.[33] The next plan was to bar her from the succession: though next of blood to Her Majesty, Mary is a stranger, Ralph Sadler argued.[34] At that point, Edmund Plowden was approached for a learned opinion, and wrote a *Treatise* developing his doctrine of the King's two bodies.[35] In his argument, the common law rule against alien inheritance does not apply to the crown. The crown is passed by succession, not by inheritance or descent, though the successor is in general determined by proximity of blood: this is applicable wherever the next of blood was born.[36]

Requests for Mary's head came fast and early. Paul Wentworth neatly sums up the dilemma with his question, "whither wee should call for an axe or an acte." To Norton, the peril at hand justifies all extremes: "The Scottish Queen, which is termed the sonne risinge, is but a comet, which doth pronosticate the overthrowe of this realme." Thomas Hussey of the Middle Temple recalls the contention of York and Lancaster, "betweene two kings as this is betweene two queenes."[37] The bill to remove Mary from the succession was passed by Commons on June 24, 1572 without any negative voice, two days later by the Lords, and vetoed by Elizabeth. It would be another fifteen years before Mary was tried, sentenced, and executed.

THE INNS OF COURT: THE NURSERIES OF LAW

The Inns' proximity to the law courts and to Westminster Hall made them attractive hosts for committee meetings. In October 1566, days after the opening of Parliament, a moot at Lincoln's Inn had rejected the claims of Mary Stuart on the grounds that she was a foreigner. This led to the imprisonment of the Reader of the Inn, William Thornton.[38] At least three of the men who were about to emerge as insurgent MPs, James Dalton, William Lambarde, and Robert Monson, were alumni of that Inn.[39] Ben Jonson dedicated *Every Man Out of His Humour* to the "noblest nourceries of Humanity, and Liberty, in the Kingdom; the Inns of Court."[40] One of Thomas Lodge's characters defines them as "a place of abode for our English gentrie, and the onely nurserie of true lerning."[41] This positive image of the Inns is one largely of their own making. In rehearsing the distinctive features of the English legal system, Fortescue's *Praise* offers the first extended portrait of a place unique in Europe, of "continual peace and perfect amity," where England's good laws are taught, the perfect education for young nobility.[42] His idealization of the body politic and its sinews, *nervi*, the law binding it together, owes much to its actual context, the Wars of the Roses. Shakespeare's choice to set the first act of that great civil strife in the Temple Garden of the Inns of Court is uncannily apt. An Edenic haven in the midst of destructive disorder, Fortescue's Inns stand as a model common weal, united by a love of justice, regulated by courtly manners and strict rules.

The earliest surviving literary portraits of the Inns were less glamorous. Chaucer's corrupt "manciple of a Temple" is probably drawn from life. His Serjeant-at-Law is a man of fame, learning, and high position, yet "All was fee-simple to his strong digestion."[43] Shakespeare's legal personnel seem hardly more appealing, ranging as they do from "mad" Shallow (*2 Hen 6*) to the round-bellied judge of *As You Like It*, with only one legal figure of awesome dignity: the Lord Chief Justice who replaces the unruly Falstaff as mentor to Prince Hal. Although rule of law was meant to guarantee "right or justice" to all,[44] the rallying cry of Jack Cade's mob, "let's kill all the lawyers" (2 *Hen* 6) is perhaps more revealing of popular attitudes towards the legal breed.

At the onset of the Tudor dynasty, the Inns had acquired most of their enduring features. Still, they were not quite the nursery of nobility, the Athens of the law or the third university that Fortescue's followers advertized them to be. Many records deplore, and a former alumnus of Gray's Inn like William Cecil acknowledges, the lack of student guidance. The study of common law did not have a classic pedigree like Roman or canon law, and was not taught at the universities. No educational prerequisites were needed for admission at the Inns. To the first generation of humanists, lawyers were a barbarous set armed with rude Latin and no Greek.

The Inns were ruled by "benchers" or "governors" with most "anciency." How efficiently remains dubious. Their sumptuary edicts, for instance, had to be frequently reiterated, in both house rules and Royal Proclamations. French dress and styles were banned.[45] The students were supposed not to wear weapons or long beards. They had to be in their houses by six o'clock, and to keep commons (both the meal they ate and the dining hall where it was served) thereby upholding Fortescue's corporate spirit. The exercises continued after meals through mooting or putting of cases. These were argued by "Utter Barristers," since the Inner Barristers (the younger men yet to be called to the bar) "for lack of learning, and continuance, are not able to argue and reason in these Motes," but two of them sit with the Utter Barristers on the "formes which they call the barr" in the midst of the Hall, and recite by heart the pleading of the moot case, "the one of them taking the part of the plaintiff, and the other the part of the defendant."

No trace is found of compulsory exercises before the 1440s, and no clear set of qualifications for professional practice emerges until the last quarter of Elizabeth's reign. By then, it was necessary to perform in moots, and deliver a set of lectures to be recognized as an advocate. No one could be made a Serjeant unless he had read, and only Serjeants became judges of the King's Bench or Common Pleas. Only professors could become leaders of the bar and judges.[46] The readings took place twice a year, in Lent and August, and followed a chronological cycle of statutory texts.[47] Readers were expected to do little more than repeat the work of their predecessors, continuing the chapters of statutes they had begun. The readings, like the moot books, seem to have generally avoided open reference to contemporary events or biting statutes. Edward Hall's reading at Gray's in 1541 dealt with the liberties of the church under Henry IV.

The vital part of exercises was the contradictory debate that made a legal trial the forum for testing the advocates' eloquence by a form of rhetorical duel. Court proceedings were mimicked in moots where students performed pleas for opposing parties, while manuals recreated the atmosphere of the classroom through exchanges between master and pupil. The matter taught, both in content and shape, was consistently theatrical, as a number of essays have shown since Finkelpearl's groundbreaking study of Marston's plays.[48] Books being scarce, the learning exercises were mainly oral, especially the mock trials modelled on the procedures of Common Pleas. Some moot cases recorded allude to actual cases, others were purely hypothetical exercises. These family romances more than matched the beauty of the playwrights' most complex fictions. The "Case called *the little rose*, or *FitzJohn*" discusses a Lear-like share of inheritance between three daughters, in which "the younger daughter is ousted, the youngest gets possession of the whole rent." Others oppose bastard and legitimate sons, twins, children in their nonage and maternal uncles, ravished wards, villains, women kept like minors under the authority of an abbot or a husband, clerks between two jurisdictions.⁴⁹ The intricacies of divorce, dowries, waste, disseisin, wills, tenancies, leases, chattels real and personal, gambling and dice playing, widowhood, bailiffs, expulsions, property of denizens, aliens, foreigners, are all deployed ... mostly in the strange mixture of Norman and English known as law French, which was still used in the report of proceedings and in legal treatises.

As a barrister must accept his client or an actor his part, so a mooter could not choose his side but had to defend the party entrusted to him. Elizabethan mootmen could seek assistance from the collection of 376 moot points put together by Plowden that had circulated in manuscript long before its publication.⁵⁰ Exercises *in utramque partem* used guides like the *Progymnasmata* of Aphthonius, whom Erasmus recommends in his list of teaching authorities along with Pliny and Cicero.⁵¹ Its model for invective borrows Demosthenes' oration against Philip of Macedonia, a precedent Norton would follow in his *Oration of Arsanes*.⁵² In pathetic characterizations, the student must imagine what Hecuba would say after the sack of Troy, or tearful Niobe on the death of her children, as does Hamlet when ruing his lack of active response to his father's murder. One easily sees what protocols for *prosopopeia* (personification), arguments *pro et contra*, characterization and slanging match trainee lawyers would draw from such models, not to mention the benefits to chroniclers like Edward Hall, playwrights like Norton and Sackville or Gascoigne and the many parliamentarians who had received an education in the Inns.

GATES TO HIGH PLACES

The Inns compensated for their alleged lack of classical learning with an enviable position at the heart of the realm's activities. Tudor Holborn was still a quiet suburban village, but its proximity to Westminster enabled the Inns to play up the ambivalence of their name, advertising their close relationship with the royal Court and the courts of law. Students could learn the courtly *trivium* of fencing, dancing, and music, if they were prepared to pay for extra tuition, and practise social graces at the revels held every Saturday night from All Saints' Day to Candlemas, or at feasts offered by the Societies of Inns members.

Legal expertise was needed in many areas beside administration. As first landowner of the realm, the Crown was frequently involved in land disputes, leases, property forfeited by attainders, royal prerogatives on goods, mining underground, forests, waters, boundaries of the British seas, all of which required the services of lawyers. On a less lofty plane, legal practice offered a variety of profitable side-lines, from money-lending to purchase of landed property. To Wilfrid Prest, it was probably the continuing decline in prestige and authority of the church, the first learned profession, that gave lawyers their great chance, and made the Inns the most promising gateway to upward mobility in early modern England.⁵³ The admissions boom began around 1550, and peaked under Elizabeth when Gray's Inn especially, thanks to its aristocratic image, attracted a large share of the entrants. A 1586 census shows a total of 356 members for Gray's against 200 for each of the other three Inns, much less altogether than the estimated 3,000 of Oxford plus Cambridge at the time.⁵⁴ Hardly any domestic records exist of the Inns of Chancery. Fortescue's *De laudibus* mentions ten, nine of which are recorded under Henry VIII, but only eight survived to receive a mention in Coke's *Reports*. For a long while the minor Inns of Chancery functioned as junior or preparatory Inns for the Inn of Court to which they were attached. It was the threat that Middle Temple might gain control over Lyon's

Inn that prompted the Inner Templars to run for help to Robert Dudley, Earl of Leicester, and to thank him in due course with the splendid revels of 1561.

The government's close interest in the running of the Inns appears in surveys and enquiries ordered by the Privy Council. First of its kind, a report of 1540 to Henry VIII gives an elaborate description of their parts and degrees.[55] A survey in 1574 shows a total of 761, distributed among 408 chambers, while 132 had to find lodgings outside.[56] Another survey ordered by the Privy Council in 1577, hard on the heels of the first Douai missions, examined the religious conformity of the Inns, which were thought to be "greatlie infected with poperie." The eight surveyors listed 180 Catholics, approximately one member in five.

On the eve of the Civil War, the poet Milton would accuse lawyers of having hindered the establishment of the Elizabethan church, through "the great Places and Offices executed by Papists, the Judges, the Lawyers, the Justices of the Peace for the most part Popish."[57] Historians of the Inns generally agree that they were a nest of papists, a chief target of the Jesuit missionaries, and a community so tightly knit that all government attempts to enforce conformity were deflected. This view was largely shared by the Privy councilors. Parmiter's study of recusancy shows that the government's suspicions were justified, yet the Inns were treated with extraordinary leniency.[58] Why? The usual answer is that the Privy Council were baffled by the lack of cooperation from the Inns' governors; that the professional solidarity, the old tradition of liberties, were stronger than religious feelings.

What happened in the 1580s between the Court and the Inns of Court looks more like a gentlemen's tacit agreement. The Elizabethan Council could not afford to antagonize the legal body by harassing members of the Inns, but made it clear to them where their best interests lay. If Catholicism was not a complete bar to the profession, it could still hinder a career. Recusants were left to their work, taking regular if slower steps up the ladder of honors. Thomas Egerton of Lincoln's Inn, listed a recusant in 1569, made poor progress until he conformed. He was eventually appointed Lord Chancellor, and became a prominent enforcer of anti-Catholic penal laws.[59] The legal profession had no other martyrs of eminence after Thomas More of Lincoln's Inn. He may have been an admired icon, his colleagues under Elizabeth may have had a tolerant eye for their fellow members' waywardness, but the fact remains that they did not rise as a body to denounce injustice, illegal procedures, or the process of treason by words. Being but men before the almighty machine of state security, not cut for martyrdom, they thought it wiser to keep their silence.

Despite their suspected papistry, the Inns were a nursery for Parliament, with a membership steadily rising from just over a quarter of all MPs in 1563 to more than a third in 1584, which explains the government's close interest in their business. The Inns were quite as interested in the government's politics. Law students sneaked into the Commons, and debates on the bills spilled out into classes at the Inns. Queen Elizabeth herself complained "that she hard how Parlyment matters was the common table talk at ordinaryes, which was a thing against the dignitie of the Howse."[60] In April 1571, a bill for the burgesses was read and committed, "the same beinge apoynted to be dyscoursed at the Temple the Saterday folowinge."[61] The same month, two young Inner Templars who sneaked into the House were expelled.[62] In 1576, one Charles Johnson of Inner Temple was found out "having sit in the parliament howse one houer and a halfe being none of the same," thus endangering the validity of the proceedings.[63]

REVELS AND ENTERTAINMENTS

"What a blessing it would be for the world, if magistrates like More were everwhere put in office by sovereigns!" Erasmus exclaims in portraying Sir Thomas More to a humanist friend.[64] The medieval ideal of "good counsel" to the Prince permeated political thought, resounding still in the Tudor Parliaments and theaters. John of Salisbury's considerations on the role of the Senate in Roman history reappear in Fortescue's lessons to Prince Edward, in Thomas Elyot's *Governor*, and again in *Gorboduc*'s warnings to Elizabeth, or in Lodge's *Wounds of Civil Wars*. The Inns, Paul Raffield argues, behaved as custodians of common law against mounting claims of absolute kingship, using classical models of limited authority and republican virtue. Besides the lawyers' pamphlets, lobbying, think tanks and committees, the Inns' entertainments made serious political statements in the guise of courtly masques. Edward Hall reports how John Roo's play at Gray's Inn on Christmas 1526 was highly praised of everybody except Cardinal Wolsey who thought he could recognize himself under the guise of its evil Lord Governance.[65] Roo was deprived of his coif and sent to the Fleet prison until he was delivered by the means of friends. Against Henry VIII's propagandists who argued that "the king makes the law," Inns men like Roo replied with Bracton that the law makes the king.

The dividing line between work and entertainment at the Inns was a porous one. Moots and bolts were reproduced in ironical or inverted mode in the masques performed on feast days, many of which ended with the burlesque trial of a fanciful case. Plays and masques were modelled on courtly events, and like them enriched by Burgundian fashions. The feasts offered by the Inns to celebrate the accession of Henry VIII followed earlier practices: in Edward IV's reign, during the negotiations for the marriage of his sister Margaret to Charles the Bold, each Inn supplied armed men for the king's guard, and contributed to the cost of scaffoldings for a tournament between Anthony Woodville Lord Scales and Antoine, Grand Bastard of Burgundy: once the king was seated in his throne, "the mayor of London, with the aldermen and men of law, entered the lists, the sword held before him."[66]

Feasts were costly events, and occasionally rowdy ones, which sometimes led benchers to suspend or suppress them. Christmas festivities, when they did take place, could be solemn affairs, designed as a compulsory part of the students' education. At the first benchers' meeting of November, special officers were appointed, who "for the most part are such as are exercised in the King's Highness's house, and other noblemen, and this is done only to the intent that they should in time come to know how to use themselves."[67] When Middle Temple kept Christmas, a Steward, Marshal, Butler, Master of the Revels, Constable of the Tower, Marshal's Constable were designated. The Steward was a barrister, often the Reader designated for the next vacation, which further points to the Christmas revels as a sort of dress rehearsal for later practice. The other offices were filled by junior members. These rituals seem to have been scorned by many young men who were fined for non-attendance. The records of Lincoln's Inn show that some were disbarred for not dancing on Candlemas day in the presence of Judges, "according to the antient Order of this Society." John Donne would have to pay the customary fine of 26s 8d in 1593 for having declined to act as Steward of Christmas.[68]

The lawyers' taste for and share in royal entertainments, the presence of the theater in political ceremonies, the double plots, moral saws, and versification of these revels continue throughout the Tudor reigns, along with fitful attitudes towards their foreign sources. Some Inns members would carry them to the stage, like Marston of Middle Temple, whose *Parasitaster, or The Fawn*, performed the same year as Shakespeare's *Measure for Measure*, has many references to intramural matters at the Inns.[69] Its hero Duke Hercules disguises himself as a courtier, the Fawn, to enter the court of Duke Gonzago and observe his son's behavior. Under the protection of his alias, Hercules witnesses the lechery of the courtiers and the vanity of their master. At the play's conclusion, he holds a symbolic Court of Cupid, in which all the more foolish folk are arrested for their crime against love and good sense.

In 1551, as young Edward VI worried over the condemnation of his uncle the Duke of Somerset, it was thought a good idea to cheer him up with some entertainment, devised by the lawyer poet George Ferrers "of Lincolnes Inne, being Lord of the merry Disports all the 12 dayes, who so pleasantly and wisely behaved himselfe, that the King had great delight in his pastimes."[70] The feast went with a swing, enjoyed by everybody and "best of all by the yoong king himselfe," at the end of which, "Christmas being thus passed with much mirth and pastime" that appeased the minds and ears of murmurers, "it was thought now good to proceed to the execution of the iudgment given against the duke of Summerset."[71] Holinshed does not indicate here that Ferrers would fight for the Queen in the Wyatt rebellion, write part of the *Mirror for Magistrates*, nor that he had translated Magna Carta into English, and been the hero of a case for Parliamentary privilege, a typically magnificent instance of a Tudor lawyer's infinite variety.

The tradition of "Good Counsel" through entertainment induced a group of young Inns members to continue Lydgate's *Fall of Princes*, itself adapted from Boccaccio, via the French translation of Laurent de Premierfait, with "Tragedies" drawn from Hall's chronicle. Their first attempt at publication was censured by Mary's Chancellor, Archbishop Gardiner. The *Mirror for Magistrates* first appeared in the year of Elizabeth's accession, and was soon followed by new enlarged editions. Its stories are told by the ghosts of fallen British Statesmen who return from Hades, one of its many Senecan features, to visit the narrator Baldwin. Where Boccaccio's tales depict accidents of fortune, most of their woes are the deserved punishment of some grievous fault. Each stresses the inevitability of divine retribution on those who betray their office: "For here as in a loking glass you shall see (if any vice be in you) how the like hath been punished heretofore." Out of the complex, amoral, raw matter of history emerges a highly pedagogic concatenation of deeds. Saluted as the ideal humanist synthesis, the *Mirror for Magistrates* inspired a long list of poems and plays. Sidney gives it a place in his *Defence* between Chaucer and the Earl of Surrey's lyrics, accounting it "meetly furnished of bewtiful partes," a few lines above his critical review of *Gorboduc*.

TRANSLATING EUROPE

One foreign import in particular raised hostility: language. A Statute of Pleading in 1362 directed—in Anglo-Norman French—that pleas in all courts of justice should be pleaded and judged in English, because French was "trope desconnue en ledit realme" ("largely unknown in the said realm").[72] Law French had become so alien to non-professionals that lexicons had to be devised when Henry VII ordered the publication of statutes in English. His son followed suit by having the complete body of statutes translated. Protests were made to Henry VIII against the continued use of law French, "as therby ys testyfied our subjectyon to the Normannys,"[73] yet the use of English in law courts would not be obligatory until George II. Foreign laws and languages had helped the Conqueror's barony take possession of the land. One of the popular charges against lawyers was their use of a hermetic foreign idiom, a prejudice voiced in Jack Cade's demagogic puns on "tongue": Lord Saye "can speak French, and therefore he is a traitor," for he "speaks with the tongue of an enemy."[74] If the Inns stood at the hub of the Tudor translation workshop, it was originally for practical, not to say chauvinistic reasons.

In the preface to his 1519 translation of medieval statutes, John Rastell explains that William's Norman counselors had judged the native language too rude for their laws, but Henry VII, "worthye to be called the seconde Solomon," found it marvelously amended: learned men have lately translated "many noble works into our English tongue," making "our vulgar tongue so amplified and sufficient of itself to expound many laws or ordinances."[75] His *Expositiones terminorum legum anglorum*, compiled around 1525, provided parallel texts in English and French.[76] Baker thinks that in the long term his efforts promoted the use of English for legal purposes, especially in the 1530s when he printed George Ferrers' full translation of the medieval statutes, but that in its own day his glossary served only to emphasize the continued primacy of law French.[77] Rastell's biography is itself a tale emblematic of the period. A Middle Templar turned printer, he specialized in printing legal works and stage plays, some of which he wrote himself, like the *Interlude of the Four Elements*, and had a little theater built on his home grounds. Having opposed the Act of Supremacy, he ended in prison, where he died a few months after the execution of his brother-in-law, Thomas More.

Accomplishments and languages were necessary for high employments at Court or in diplomacy. During his years at Inner Temple, Robert Ashley would study Spanish, Italian, Dutch, and French. Some of the well-travelled young men were torn between love of the classics and love of the nation. Thomas Phaer of Lincoln's Inn explains that his purpose in translating the *Æneid* is "the defence of my countrey language (which I have heard discommended of many, and estemyd of some to bee more than barbarous)."[78] At the end of the Elizabethan era, Camden would praise the virtues of English like so many chips on the shoulder, declaring the clear native language of the realm now "as fluent as the Latine, as courteous as the Spanish, as court-like as the French, and as amorous as the Italian."[79] The antiquary Richard Carew, of Middle Temple, closed the century with *An Epistle concerning the Excellencies of the English Tongue*.

In the first half of Elizabeth's reign, the Inns of Court virtually monopolized translations classic and modern.[80] From roughly 1550 to 1575, Finkelpearl asserts, they formed the literary centre of England, through a group of serious young men intent on making the Reformation in England humanistic, and its government secure. While at Inner Temple, Thomas Norton made the first English translation of Calvin's *Institutio*. It was in the *Institutes* that he first used blank verse, to translate the passages of Virgil's *Æneid* that Calvin had quoted in the original.[81] Theatrical university performances until the late sixteenth century were usually in Latin, whereas the Inns performed plays in English. The community of writers and translators that developed there found it an ideal way of advertising themselves to prospective patrons and of publishing their views of the *res publica*. The works of Inns members show "the natural bias of law students looking to the state services for their future" as well as genuine concern for the immediate future of the realm.[82]

GHOSTLY VOICES

In his Preface to *Thyestes*, Jasper Heywood is visited by the ghost of Seneca, who wants him to translate more of his work, but he modestly directs his visitor to the Inns of Court where "finest witts doe swarme." Of the eight young men he cites as deserving praise for their works of poetry and translation, six were Inns members.[83] Drama, through dialogues and debating jousts, had always featured prominently in the Inns' exercises. From its earliest days, law and legal issues furnished the stage with both matter and form. The method of argument *in utramque partem* had behind it a long history of moral and philosophical education, perfecting the dialogue in dialectics that allowed a progressive unveiling of the truth.

The works of Inns members are in every sense educational exercises. Choruses are given extra lines to stress premonitions and perils. Heroic deeds, human sufferings, the weight of power, the torments of Hell, also receive their shares of additional stanzas. These expansions require the old fourteener, redolent with alliteration, to do them justice[84]:

O Kyng of Dytis dungeon darke, and grysly Ghosts of hell,
That in the deepe and dredfull Denne, of blackest Tartare dwell.
(*Thyestes*, V.iv.1–2)

As to the matter itself, the authors' main dilemma is to combine Senecan vengeance, cruel fortune, and blind fate with divine retribution and justice. Here again, occasional twists and additions give the last word to Christian judges. Norton and Sackville's *Gorboduc*, "clyming to the height of Seneca his style" in Sidney's tepid praise, closely imitates his five-act structure, chorus, and political meditations. So will its follower, *Gismond of Salerne*, authored by five gentlemen of the Inner Temple.

Seneca had failed as a tutor, but lived through four successive emperors before dying victim to the tyranny of the fifth,[85] and witnessed at close range all the horrors he depicted: "Exile, murder, incest, the threat of poverty and a hideous death, and all the savagery of fortune were the very texture of his career."[86] His plays had political relevance in his own days. With a little mending they could be translated into the present turmoils of Tudor monarchy, and act as "glasses of governance." Where could the law apprentices find better informed, more resilient lessons on the mutability of court life? These ambitious young men were ready to revive the humanist hopes of sharing in the government of the realm. Queen Elizabeth was fully awake to the lawyers' earnest wish to guide her political steps with Senecan *exempla*. The enmity between brothers that launches the action of *Thyestes* makes the core of *Gorboduc*, and of many ensuing plays, from *Jocasta* to *As You Like It*, *Hamlet*, or *The Tempest*. With the potential threat of rival claimants to the throne the theme was again relevant. The Inns made theatrical history in 1561 at Inner Temple, weaving drama, law, and politics, when two of their members composed the first Elizabethan tragedy in blank verse, to urge a settlement of the succession by Parliament, stigmatize foreign threats, and promote their patron Leicester, elected for the occasion "Mightye Palaphilos Prince of Sophie," as the most suitable spouse for the Queen. *Gorboduc*, or *The Tragidie of Ferrex and Porrex*, was part of the Christmas revels of 1561–2 at Inner Temple, and followed by a performance at court in January. On both occasions, the play went with a masque of Beauty and Desire, a tale of chivalric wooing crowned by a marriage in the temple of Pallas.[87]

The frontier between the early Elizabethan political and stage arenas was of the flimsiest. Norton and Sackville both sat in Elizabeth's first Parliament. Shortly after the Queen's illness, in January 1563, Norton was one of the commission appointed "to drawe artycles of peticion for the Quenes mariage and Succession,"[88] and as their spokesman it was he who read their petition to the House. Seen in retrospect as the father of history plays, *Gorboduc*'s most significant steps were the dramatization of an episode from the

British chronicles, the insertion of dumb shows, and the use of blank verse. Seen on its own merits, the play has worse faults than those Sidney found damnable. Its didactic aim overwhelms all artistic considerations.[89] No interaction, no suspense is allowed to interfere with the political lessons, which the dumb shows and choruses stress redundantly, in case the audience failed to get the points argued at exhaustive length by the characters.[90] As in any trial, the pleas and plays of the period aimed at a specific immediate issue, while working within the frame of enduring rules and precedents to stress the three elements of mixed monarchy, king, council, Parliament.[91]

We have T. S. Eliot's word that "No author exercised a wider or deeper influence upon the Elizabethan mind or upon the Elizabethan form of tragedy than did Seneca."[92]

FIGURE 8.1 Drawing by Robert Beale in his official report on "the trial and execution of Mary Queen of Scots." "The trial," Add. 48027, f. 569*. Source: British Library, London, UK / © British Library Board. All Rights Reserved / Bridgeman Images.

FIGURE 8.2 Another drawing in Beale's report, "The execution." Add. 48027, f. 650*. Source: British Library, London, UK / © British Library Board. All Rights Reserved / Bridgeman Images.

He wastes no thought on Euripides, though *Troades* makes the basis of *Troas*, the first of Heywood's translations, and *Phœnissae* is behind Seneca's *Thebais*. Little interest so far has been spent on the one "Greek" play in English Shakespeare undoubtedly knew, *Jocasta*. It was originally presented as "A Tragedie written in Greeke by *Euripides*, translated and digested into Acte by George Gascoygne and Francis Kinwelmersh of Grayes Inne, and there by them presented, 1566."[93] "Digested" is the operative word, for in actual fact this *Jocasta* is a close rendering of an Italian version of *Phœnissae*, published in 1549, by Lodovico Dolce.[94] If Shakespeare had access in his youth to half a dozen English tragedies at best, then this would have been the one closest to his early leanings. *Jocasta* has many elements that would be refined in the histories, most prominently in *Henry VI*: fatal curses, revenge, ghosts, and stichomythia—all of which were Greek before they turned Senecan—oath breaking, prophecies and soothsayers, and strong feminine figures (Jocasta, like Queen Margaret, survives her husband's fall). The servant's speech on "The glittering mace, the pompe of swarming traine" paid for by heavy cares ushers in Shakespeare's sleepless kings. If the Inns had no other claim to cultural significance, their gifts to the Elizabethan stage should be enough to make them proud.

FIGURE 8.3 Anonymous colored woodcut, is entitled "The Seven Ages of Man, From a Black Print in the British Museum" colored woodcut, originally inserted in a printed copy of Nicolaus de Lyra's *Moralia super Bibliam*, c. 1460, reproduced under the title "The Seven Ages of Man" in *Archæologia*, vol. XXXV, 1853, plate XVII, p. 188. Source: British Library, London, UK / © British Library Board. All Rights Reserved / Bridgeman Images.

NOTES

Preface

1. Laurence Rosen. *Law as Culture: An Invitation*. Princeton: Princeton University Press, 2006, pp. 199–200.
2. Pierre Legrand. *Fragments on Law-as-Culture*. Deventer: W.E.J. Tjeenk Willink, Schoordijk Institute, 1999, p. 5.
3. Malcolm Andrews. *Landscape and Western Art* (Oxford History of Art). Oxford: Oxford University Press, 1999, p. 53.

Introduction

1. Piero Valeriano, *Hieroglyphica sive de sacris Aegyptorum literis commentarii*. Basle, 1550, 237 recto. For further elaboration in probiscodology and legality see P. Goodrich, "Proboscations: Excavations in Comedy and Law" 2017. 43(2) *Critical Inquiry* 361–388.
2. Desiderius Erasmus, *Ciceronianus*. a reliable translation is available in Izora Scott (ed.), *Controversies over Cicero* Davis, CA: Hermagoras Press, 1991, II, p. 20.
3. *Hulcote v Ingleton* (1493), 115 Selden Soc. 138—"il ne voet luy oyer a arguer a c'est conceit, pur ceo est merement encontre nostre auncient commen erudycyon et est a ore en maner un principle."
4. Ottavio Scarlattini. *Homo et eius partes* (1695 edn), p. 80.
5. Isidore of Seville, *Etymologies*, pp. 232, 234.
6. Piyel Haldar, "The Tongue and the Eye: Eloquence and Office in Renaissance Emblems" in *Genealogies of Legal Vision*, ed. Peter Goodrich and Valérie Hayaert. Abingdon: Routledge, 2015.
7. Haldar, "Tongue," p. 162.
8. Claude Paradin, *Devises heroiques* (1551), p. 78.
9. On organic architecture, dating back to Alberti, see David Evans, "The Theatre of Deferral" 1999. 10(1) *Law and Critique* 14–15. And on the latter expression, from John Cowell's *Interpreter* of 1607, see Bradin Cormack, *A Power to Do Justice*. Chicago: Chicago University Press, 2005.
10. J. H. Baker (ed.), *Spelman's Reports*, vol. 2. London: Selden Society, 1978, pp. 159ff.
11. Dyer, cited in Sir John Doderidge, *The English Lawyer*. London: I. More, 1631, p. 154.
12. Doderidge, *English Lawyer* 162, citing to Joachim Hopper, *Tractatus de iuris arte* (1584): *Principia externa proprié vocamus ea quae in Communi hominium vita versantur & ab experientibus & prudentibus animadvertuntur.*
13. *Boswel's Case* (1606) 77 Eng.Rep. 326.
14. *Boswel's Case*, 327 (meaning that it was a question of popular perception).
15. *Boswel's Case.*
16. *Boswel's Case.*
17. *Boswel's Case*, referencing Seneca, Traged. Fo. 55. Medea, 195.
18. On the theological roots of this concept, see John M. Kelly, "Audi Alteram Partem" (1964) 84 *Natural Law Forum* 103.

19. Ian Maclean, *Interpretation and Meaning in the Renaissance*. Cambridge: Cambridge University Press, 1992. Chapter 3 provides an invaluable discussion of the term and its context in contemporary theories of interpretation.
20. Bartholomaeus Caepolla, *De Interpretatione legis extensiva*. Venice: 1557, fol. 7.
21. Selden. *Table Talk* [1689]. London: Murray (1868 edn.), p. 20.
22. Selden, *Table Talk*, 31. The discussion of Philologie as "this great Lady of Learning" is in *Historie of Tithes*. London: n.p., 1618, p. xix.
23. Selden, *Historie of Tithes*, pp. xix–xx.
24. Sir Robert Wiseman, *The Law of Laws: or, the Excellency of the Civil Law above all humane laws whatsoever* [1656]. London: Royston, 1664, fol. A 3 b.
25. On the latter borrowings from the civilians, see A. W. B. Simpson, "Innovation in 19th Century Contract Law" in *Legal Theory and Legal History: Essays on the Common Law*. Oxford: Clarendon Press, 1987, p. 171; James Gordley, *The Philosophical Origins of Modern Contract Doctrine*. Oxford: Oxford University Press, 1991.
26. Jacques Lacan, *The Other Side of Psychoanalysis*. London: Norton, 2007, p. 36.
27. See, in particular, G. Bennington and J. Derrida, *Circumfessions*. Chicago: Chicago University Press, 1993.
28. Sir Thomas More, *The Apologye of Sir Thomas More Knyght*. London: Rastell, 1533; More, *The Deballacyon of Salem and Bizance*. London: Rastell, 1533; St. German, *Salem and Bizance*. London: Berthelet, 1533; St. German, *A Treatise Concerning the Division between the Spirituality and the Temporality*. London: Redman, 1534; William Tyndale, *An Answer unto Tomas Mores Dialogue*. London: n.p., 1530.
29. John Jewel, *An Apologie or Answere in Defence of the Churche of England*. London: n.p., 1562; John Jewel, *A Defence of the Apologie of the Churche of England*. London: Fleetstreet, 1567.
30. *Digest* 22.4.1. (Paulus ... *et ideo tam testimonia quam personae instrumentorum loco habentur*.)
31. Jewel, *Apologie*, p. Aiiiv.
32. Jewel, *Defence*, p. 55.
33. Jewel, *Defence*, p. 204. Also noting Chrysostom to the effect that *in Figuris literarum, an in intellectu sensuû*, the form of the words is nothing compared to the understanding of their meaning.
34. Jewel, *Defence*, p. 479.
35. St German, *Doctor and Student* [1528]. London: Selden Society, 1974; Thomas Starkey, *A Dialogue between Reginald Pole and Thomas Lupset* [1535]. London: Chatto and Windus, 1945; Thomas Hobbes, *A Dialogue between a Phylospher and a Student of the Common Laws of England* [1681]. Oxford: Oxford University Press, 1985. One might add here the anonymous dialogue, *The English Courtier, and the Cùtry-gentleman: A pleasant and learned Disputation*. London: Jones, 1586 as an instance of the founding dialogue of honor and morals, of gentility and manners, that make up the civility in civil law. The model is Italian, translated by Thomas Hoby, as Baldesar Castilio, *The Courtyer*. London: n.p., 1561.
36. Sir John Fortescue, *De Laudibus legum Angliae* [1470]. Cambridge: Cambridge University Press, 1997.
37. Whitehouse, *Fortescutus illustratus, or a Commentary on that Nervous Treatise* De Laudibus Legum Angliae. London: Roycroft, 1663, p. 2.
38. St German, *Doctor and Student*, 2 *principia sive fundamenta legum anglie*.
39. Sir John Fortescue, "De natura legis naturae" in Thomas Fortescue (ed.), *The Works of Sir John Fortescue*. London: Private Circulation, 1869 edn, p. 192. The sentiment is reiterated

throughout the early modern period, perhaps most directly by William Fulbeck, *A Parallele or Conference of the Civil law, the Canon law, and the Common Law of this Realme of England*. London: Society of Stationers, 1618.

40. M. M. Bakhtin, *Speech Genres and Other Late Essays*. Austin: University of Texas Press, 1986, p. 92. Further elaboration can be found in M. M. Bakhtin, *The Dialogic Imagination*. Austin: Texas University Press, 1981, ch. 4 and particularly the discussion of heteroglossia.
41. Bakhtin, *Speech Genres*, p. 170.
42. Andrea Alciato, *Emblemata*. Antwerp: Plantin, p. 500.
43. Democritick is from Blount's *Glossographia*. London: Newcomb, 1656: "mocking, jeering, laughing at everything."

Chapter 1

1. My deep gratitude goes to Peter Goodrich and Vanessa Paumen who helped smooth the English and enriched the first draft of this text.
2. See two articles by Hugo Van der Velden: "Cambyses for Example: The Origins and Function of an *exemplum iustitiæ* in Netherlandish Art of the Fifteenth, Sixteenth and Seventeenth Centuries" and "Cambyses Reconsidered: Gerard David's *exemplum iustitiæ* for Bruges Town Hall" 1995. 23 *Simiolus* 5–39 and 40–62.
3. Hugo van der Velden. "Cambyses for Example" at 30–39.
4. Juan de Horozco y Covarrubias, *Emblemas morales*. Segovia: n.p. 1589, emblem XXIII.
5. Plutarch, *Morals (Isis and Osiris, or of the Ancient Religion and Philosophy of Egypt)*. Vol. 4.13, ed. William Baxter, W. Goodwin. New York: Athenaeum Society, 1905. See also Erasmus, *Adagia* 2601, Scarabaeus aquilam quaerit [A dung-beetle hunting an eagle].
6. Andrea Alciato, *Emblèmes*. Lyon: Macé Bonhomme for Guillaume Rouille, 1549, p. 176. Depending on the edition chosen, the figure does not always depict severed hands.
7. Étienne Pasquier, *La Main ou Œuvres poétiques faits sur la Main d'E. Pasquier aux Grands Jours de Troyes*. 1583. Edition used: *Les oeuvres d'Estienne Pasquier*, vol. 2 Amsterdam, 1723.
8. Étienne Pasquier, *La Main*, p. 1031.
9. Saavedra Fajardo, *Idea principis christiano-politici*. Brussels: Jean Mommaert, 1649, symbolum LIII, p. 374.
10. Johann Theodor de Bry, *Proscenium vitæ humanæ, sive Emblematum secularium, jucundissima et artificiosissima varietate vitæ humanæ* ... Frankfurt: G. Fitzer, 1611 (1st edn. 1596), II, p. 10.
11. "Omnis qui recte judicat, stateram in manu gestat, et in utroque penso justitiam et misericordiam portat; sed per justitiam reddit peccatis sententiam, per misericordiam peccantis temperat pœnam, ut justo libramine quædam per æquitatem corrigat, quædam vero per misericordiam indulgeat."
12. Christoph Haunold, *Controversiarum de Justitia et Jure privatorum universo nova et theorica methodo*. tomus primus. Ingolstadt: Joannes Simon Knab, 1671.
13. Jean Carbonnier, *Flexible droit. Textes pour une sociologie du droit sans rigueur*. Paris: Librairie générale de droit et de jurisprudence, 1969.
14. Juan de Solorzano Pereira, *Emblemata regio politica in centuriam unam redacta*. Garcia Morràs: 1653, "Statera Regum," emblema LXII, pp. 449–507.
15. Seneca, *Medea*, Act II, sc. 2, v. 199–200.
16. Quentin Skinner, *Reason and Rhetoric in the Philosophy of Hobbes*. Cambridge: Cambridge University Press, 1996, pp. 15–16.
17. Juan Solorzano Pereira, *Emblemas regio-politicos* (1st edn., Madrid, 1653), ed. J. M. Gonzàlez de Zàrate. Madrid: Ediciones Tuero, 1987.

18. Honoratus Draco, *Elementa juris seu Institutiones imperiales in Carmen contractæ*. Lyon: Thibaut Payen, 1551.
19. Matteo Gribaldi Mofa, *De methodo ac ratione studendi libri III*. Cologne: n.p. 1553, p. 9 (Preface). See more in Valérie Hayaert, *"Mens emblematica" et humanisme juridique*. Geneva: Droz, 2008, pp. 173–175.
20. Étienne Forcadel, *Sphæra legalis*, ed. and trans. Anne Teissier-Ensminger, Classiques Garnier, 2011. Lyon: Jean de Tournes, 1549; *Cupido jurisperitus*. Lyon: Jean de Tournes, 1553.
21. Étienne Forcadel, *Cupido jurisperitus*, 1595 edn., p. 398.
22. Mirabeau, Honoré-Gabriel de Riqueti, Comte de, *Des Lettres de Cachet et des Prisons d'État*. Ouvrage posthume, composé en 1778, Hambourg, s.n., 1782.
23. Florentius Schoonhovius, *Emblemata partim moralia partim etiam civilia*. Gouda: Andreas Burier, 1618. Edition used: Amsterdam, Jean Jansonius, 1648, emblem LV "Juste fiunt quæ a Deo," pp. 163–165.
24. Hugo Grotius, *De Jure Praedæ*. mss. 1st Latin edn., HG Hamaker, 1868. (Commentary on the Law of Prize and Booty), Ch. II *Prolegomena, Including Nine Rules and Thirteen Laws*. Rule 1.
25. Pierre Coustau, *Pegma cum narrationibus philosophicis*. Lyon: Macé Bonhomme, 1555, emblem "Ad statuam Jovis et Themidos. Justa a Deo roganda," pp. 12–14.
26. Cesare Ripa, *Iconologia*. Padua: 1611, p. 201.
27. The reference to the blindfolded Christ is Mark 14.65 and Luke 22.64.
28. Josse Damhoudere, *Praxis rerum criminalium*. Anvers, 1556, 2nd edn., ch. 149, pp. 560–563 and the engraving, p. 561.
29. Robert Jacob, *Images de la Justice. Essai sur l'iconographie judiciaire du Moyen-Âge à l'âge classique*. Paris: Le Léopard d'or, 1994, pp. 78–79.
30. Musée municipal de Cambrai, sculpture section, nos. 57 and 58.
31. Charles de Bovelles, *Géométrie praticque* (1st edn in French, 1511). Paris: Denise Cavellat, 1605, pp. 201–203; The broom image is available at: www.erara.ch/zut/content/pageview/2702780.
32. Michel Foucault, *Discipline and Punish: The Birth of the Prison*. London: Penguin, 1977.
33. Heinrich Oraeus, *Viridarium hieroglyphico-morale: in quo virtutes et vitia … illustrantur*. Frankfurt: Jacques de Zetter, 1619, pp. 52–53. Jacob de Zetter had first used the eighty-eight emblematic plates for another emblem book, Andreas Friedrich, *Emblemata Nova*, Frankfurt 1617. The text was not in neo-Latin but in German. See Christophe Martin, *Les Emblèmes nouveaux d'Andreas Friedrich* [1617] (Critical edition and commentary), coédition Presses Universitaires François Rabelais, Tours, Presses Universitaires de Rennes, 2013.

Chapter 2

1. Aalt Willem Heringa and Philipp Kiiver, *Constitutions Compared: An Introduction to Comparative Constitutional Law*. 3rd edn., Cambridge: Intersentia, 2012, pp. 2–3. Contemporary debates regarding the socio-cultural foundations of constitutions focus on their nature: rigid or flexible, "natural growths" or "works of conscious art" (James Bryce, *Constitutions*. Holmes Beach, FL: Gaunt, 1997, p. 6.), contracts or coordination mechanisms (Tom Ginsburg, "Constitutions as Contract, Constitutions as Charters" in *Social and Political Foundations of Constitutions*. Eds. ed. Denis J. Galligan and Mila Versteeg. Cambridge:

Cambridge University Press, 2013, pp. 182–204; Russell Hardin, "Why a Constitution?" in *Social and Political Foundations of Constitutions*, ed. Denis J. Galligan and Mila Versteeg. Cambridge: Cambridge University Press, 2013, pp. 51–72) and even a reading of the documents as "holistic mission statements" (Jeff King, "Constitutions as Mission Statements" in *Social and Political Foundations of Constitutions*, ed. Denis J. Galligan and Mila Versteeg. Cambridge: Cambridge University Press, 2013, pp. 73–102 at p. 81).

2. Antonio de Nebrija, *Vocabulario español-latino*. Salamanca: Impresor de la Gramática castellana, 1495.
3. Sebastián de Covarrubias Orozco, *Tesoro de la lengua castellana o española*. Madrid: Castalia, 1994 [1611]. Here and in what follows, unless otherwise noted all translations are my own.
4. Fergus Kelly, *A Guide to Early Irish Law*. Dublin: Dublin Institute for Advanced Studies, 1998, p. 95.
5. Lawrence H. Tribe, *American Constitutional Law*. 2nd edn. Mineola, NY: The Foundation Press, 1988, 1.
6. J. R. Tanner, *Tudor Constitutional Documents A.D. 1485–1603 with an Historical Commentary*. Cambridge: Cambridge University Press, 1940, v.
7. Russell Hardin, *Why a Constitution?*, p. 52.
8. For an explanation of formal versus broad constitutions see Heringa and Kiiver, *Constitutions Compared*, pp. 2–5. As will be made clear in what follows, there are multiple written documents that form what Heringa and Kiiver refer to as the "working" or "broader constitution" in the making (4). An earlier Spanish written constitution issued by a provisional government following the 1868 Revolution did not survive the political winds of the day.
9. Walton, Clifford Stevens. 2002. *The Civil Law in Spain and Spanish-America*. Clark, NJ: The Lawbook Exchange, Ltd., v.
10. The word *fueros* translates as books of law, founding charter or, read broadly, constitution[s]. During the Reconquest of the Peninsula from the eighth to fifteenth centuries, a reconquered town would be granted its *fuero*. Each had its own particular character, and provided specific rights. For the reflection of those legal texts in the *Cantar de mío Cid* and *Libro de buen amor*, see Eduardo de Hinojosa, "El derecho en el *Poema del Cid*" in *Homenaje a Menéndez y Pelayo*. 2 vols. Madrid: Librería general de Victoriano Suárez, 1899.; Rafael Lapesa, "Notas etimológicas y semánticas." *Annexes des Cahiers de linguistique hispanique médiévale* 1988. 7 469–476. Susan Byrne, "¿Por qué una niña de nuef años?: la edad de razón y la razón del poeta del CMC." 2002. 31(1) *La corónica* 5–17.
11. For Aragon's legal history, see López de Haro and for the full peninsula's governance systems during the time, Tomás y Valiente. With the marriage of Ferdinand and Isabel in 1469, and the accession of the former to the throne of Aragon in 1479, the dynasties of the peninsula's two biggest reigns were united. However, Aragon, Valencia and the Principality of Catalonia, which together constituted the Crown of Aragon, each retained the rights to their own *fueros* and constitutions. I follow Elliott in using "Crown of Aragon" to identify this three-part political federation from the simple "Aragon" for the kingdom alone (J. H. Elliott, *The Revolt of the Catalans: A Study in the Decline of Spain*. Cambridge: Cambridge University Press, 1963, p. 4, n. 1). See also Garrido Arredondo for how the reception and role of Justinian's concept of *ius commune* differed from reign to reign on the Iberian Peninsula from the twelfth century onward (José Garrido Arredondo, "*Quod principi placuit legis habet vigorem*. Su recepción en la corona de Castilla" in *Fvndamenta Ivris*: Terminología, principios e *interpretatio*, ed. Pedro Resina Sola. Almería: Editorial Universidad de Almería, 2012, pp. 339–354, 344–354).

12. *Cortes de los antiguos reinos de León y de Castilla.* 5 vols. Madrid: Real Academia de la Historia; Rivadeneyra, 1864.
13. Here and in what follows, I cite to book, title, and law of the 1640 facsimile edition, abbreviating as *Recop.* in subsequent citations: Spain. 1982. *Recopilación de las leyes destos reynos.* Edition fac. Valladolid: Lex Nova, 1640.
14. The speaker is King Ferdinand, as recorded in a notarial document, responding to a request from the Queen of Navarre that certain lawbreakers be detained (Antonio de la Torre, ed., *Documentos sobre relaciones internacionales de los Reyes Católicos.* 13 vols. Barcelona: CSIS, 1966, XIII, pp. 391–392).
15. Alfonso de Valdés, *Diálogo de las cosas acaecidas en Roma*, ed. Rosa Navarro Durán. Madrid: Cátedra, 2007, p. 163.
16. Hugo de Celso, *Repertorio universal de las leyes de todos los reynos de Castilla.* Alcalá de Henares: Juan de Brocar, 1540, f. 84r.
17. José Antonio Maravall, *Teatro y literatura en la sociedad barroca.* Madrid: Seminarios y Ediciones, 1972, pp. 219–220.
18. Susan Byrne, *Law and History in Cervantes' Don Quixote.* Toronto: University of Toronto Press, 2012, pp. 62–74.
19. James Bryce, *Constitutions.* Holmes Beach, FL: Gaunt, 1997, p. vii.
20. Denis J. Galligan and Mila Versteeg, "Theoretical Perspectives on the Social and Political Foundations of Constitutions" in *Social and Political Foundations of Constitutions*, ed., Denis J. Galligan and Mila Versteeg. Cambridge: Cambridge University Press, 2013, pp. 3–48, 4.
21. Pérez Martín notes that although Alphonse X himself was the "formal author" of the Partidas, Jacobo de las Leyes was, undoubtedly, the "principal material author" of the collection (Antonio Pérez Martín, "Jacobo de las Leyes: Ureña tenía razón" 2008. 26 *Anales de Derecho* (Universidad de Murcia) 251–273).
22. Kelley quotes Tony Honoré to call Gaius "the true architect of Justinian's collection," then adds that in this fashion, Gaius was the model for later national collections like the Siete Partidas and the Code Napoléon (Donald R. Kelley, "Gaius Noster: Substructures of Western Social Thought" 1979. 84 *The American Historical Review* 619–648, 620).
23. Gaspar de Baeza, undated. Handwritten gloss on last folio of *Ordenamiento reales.* Real Biblioteca de El Escorial. ms.Z.I.10.
24. See Byrne, *Law and History in Cervantes' Don Quixote* for the *mos hispanicus*; Goodrich for *mos britannicus* (Peter Goodrich, "Intellection and Indiscipline" 2009. 36 *Journal of Law & Society* 460–480) and *mos piraticus* (Peter Goodrich, "*Mos piraticus:* On the Haunting and Infesting of the Seas." *Piracy and Jurisprudence: An Interdisciplinary Workshop.* 21–22 June 2013, Centre for Law, Ethics and Globalization, University of Southampton Law School, University of Southampton, England).
25. Eva Botella-Ordinas, "Exempt from Time and from its Fatal Change: Spanish Imperial Ideology, 1450–1700" 2012. 26 *Renaissance Studies* 580–604.
26. The influence of Ficino's writings on Erasmus, Thomas More, and Machiavelli has been studied. See Eric Nelson, *The Greek Tradition in Republican Thought.* Cambridge: Cambridge University Press, 2004; James Hankins, "Religion and the Modernity of Renaissance Humanism" in *Interpretations of Renaissance Humanism*, ed. Antelo Mazzocco. Leiden: Brill, 2006, pp. 137–153; Cesare Vasoli, *Ficino, Savonarola, Machiavelli: Studi di storia della cultura.* Turin, Nino Aragno, 2006; Peter G. Bietenholtz, *Encounters with a Radical Erasmus: Erasmus' Work as a Source of Radical Thought in Early Modern Europe.* Toronto: University of Toronto Press, 2009, pp. 114–133. For the influence of those texts on governance issues in creative Spanish

writings of the period, see Susan Byrne, *Ficino in Spain*. Toronto: University of Toronto Press, 2015, pp. 188–213.

27. Magna Carta. British Library. Available at: www.bl.uk/magna-carta/articles/magna-carta-english-translation.

28. Tom Ginsburg, "Constitutions as Contract, Constitutions as Charters" in *Social and Political Foundations of Constitutions*, ed. Denis J. Galligan and Mila Versteeg. Cambridge: Cambridge University Press, 2013, pp. 182–204, 184. Describing constitutions as "elite bargains," Ginsburg references Burton and Higley (Michael G. Burton and John Higley, "Elite Settlements" 1987. 52 *American Sociological Review* 295–307) who begin their study with England in the later part of the early modern period (1688–1689).

29. The ancient Greeks, of course, read the term differently. For Plato, justice is the harmony that results from each person fulfilling himself, an internal balance that leads to social harmony and rule by the best men. The same dictionaries referenced above for their definitions of constitutions offer "equity" as the first definition of justice, reading equity as both commutative and distributive justice.

30. I cite to law number and page of the five-volume 1864 edition of *Cortes de los antiguos reinos de León y de Castilla*, abbreviating the title as *Cortes*.

31. Jacob Grimm, "Von der Poesie im Recht" *Zeitschrift für geschichtliche Rechtswissenschaft*, 1816, pp. 25–99 at 27.

32. Eduardo de Hinojosa, "Las relaciones entre la poesía y el derecho." *Discurso leído ante S.M. El Rey Don Alfonso XIII*. Madrid: Real Academia Española, 1904, pp. 7–41, 7–8.

33. Samuel Taylor Coleridge, *Biographia Literaria*, 2004 [1817]. Project Gutenberg. Available at: www.gutenberg.org/files/6081/6081-h/6081-h.htm#link2HCH0014, ch. XIV.

34. William Egginton, *The Man Who Invented Fiction: How Cervantes Ushered in the Modern World*. New York: Bloomsbury, 2016, pp. xvii–xix.

35. Writing on nationalisms and "imagined communites," Andersen notes changes in concepts of time, with a "simultaneity ... marked ... by temporal coincidence" becoming evident in the eighteenth century in "the novel and the newspaper" (Benedict Richard O'Gorman Andersen, *Imagined Communities: Reflections on the Origin and Spread of Nationalism*. rev. edn. London: Verso, 1991. pp. 24–25). He illustrates with later writings but those studied here, and particularly a creative text like Cervantes' Don Quijote, offer earlier developments along those same lines of readers as "imagined communities" to whom an author writes with a surprising level of "ironical intimacy" (28).

36. Byrne, *Law and History in Cervantes' Don Quixote*, pp. 8–9. Published in three different editions in three different cities in 1554, the idea of a probable earlier edition is accepted although no extant copy has ever been found. The identity of the anonymous author is much debated in critical circles.

37. *Celestina comentada*. 2002. Eds. Louise Fotherfill-Payne, Enrique Fernández Rivera, and Peter Fothergill-Payne. Salamanca: Ediciones Universidad de Salamanca. This mixing of law and creative writing is, of course, not restricted to Spanish texts: see Howard Bloch. 1977. *Medieval French Literature and Law*. Berkeley: University of California Press; Justin Steinberg. 2013. *Dante and the Limits of the Law*. Chicago: University of Chicago Press; Ian Ward. 1999. *Shakespeare and the Legal Imagination*. London: Butterworths. For a recent look at Shakespeare and the Law, a title first used by Sir Dunbar Plunkett Barton in 1929, see Bradin Comack, et al., eds. 2013. *Shakespeare and the Law: A Conversation about Disciplines and Professions*. Chicago: University of Chicago Press. Gustavo Illades Aguiar (Gustavo Illades Aguiar. 2013. "El carácter delictivo de los personajes celestinescos a la luz de *Las siete partidas*" 37 *Celestinesca* 87-100) studies the resonance of the *Siete*

Partidas in the *Celestina*, and notes that the legal collection was reprinted following the 1981 coup d'etat by Spain's Guardia Civil. Javier Cerca's 2009 *Anatomía de un instante* offers a brilliant look at this latter moment in Spanish history.

38. The related section of the *Partidas* begins by separating persons into three groups: free, slave or indentured (4.23.preamble), then further distinguishing between those already born and those about to be born. The same section (4.23) continues with further classifications according to the criteria listed above for status and condition. Spain. *Siete Partidas*. Salamanca: Domingo de Portonarijs Ursino, 1576
39. Francisco Rico, ed., *Lazarillo de Tormes*. Madrid: Cátedra, 2002, pp. 99–100.
40. Ibid., p. 102.
41. Ibid., p. 94
42. Francisco Rico notes the episode as critical commentary on forms of address in vogue in the Court (*Lazarillo*, pp. 100–101, n. 131).
43. Miguel de Cervantes Saavedra. 2005. *El ingenioso hidalgo Don Quijote de la Mancha*. Eds. Celina Sabor de Cortazar and Isaías Lerner, 2 vols. Buenos Aires: Eudeba. Pragmatics (laws) regulating forms of address were promulgated in 1586, 1593, 1598, 1600, 1604, 1611, and 1623 (Faustino Gil Ayuso. 1935. *Textos y disposiciones legales de los reinos de Catilla impresos en los siglos XVI y XVII*. Madrid: Aguirre. number 172.1). For Sancho's use of the term and subsequent attempts by modern editors to edit it out of the text as an *errata*, see Byrne *Law and History in Cervantes' Don Quixote* 96.
44. Fray Tomás de Mercado, *Summa de tratos y contratos*. Seville: Hernando Díaz, 1571. I cite from the 1571 revised edition of this work first published in 1569 by a member of the sixteenth-century School of Salamanca. Folio numbers refer to the second series of folios, which begin with 1 at Book 4, after having reached folio number 162 in the first series, at the close of Book 3. For recent scholarship on the School of Salamanca, see www.salamanca.adwmainz.de/informationen.html.
45. Melveena McKendrick, *Theatre in Spain 1490–1700*. Cambridge: Cambridge University Press, 1992, p. 86.
46. Pablo José Abascal Monedero, *La infidelidad y el adulterio en España (estudios histórico-legal)*. Córdoba: Universidad de Córdoba, 2009, pp. 107–108.
47. Jerónimo de Barrionuevo, *Avisos (1654–1658)*. 4 vols. Madrid: Tello, 1892, IV, p. 103.
48. Abascal Monedero notes this "right to revenge" in relation to the Roman *Lex Julia*, with the difference that the Roman code post-Julia involves public sentencing whereas the Visigothic code allows private retribution (67).
49. See Peter Dunn, "Honour and the Christian Background in Calderón" 1960. 37(2) *Bulletin of Hispanic Studies* 75–105, and Melveena McKendrick, "Calderón and the Politics of Honour" 1993. 70(1) *Bulletin of Hispanic Studies* 135–146. Novelist María de Zayas puts the same thematic concerns into a series of short stories featuring female protagonists, most commonly titled *Desengaños amorosos*.
50. Pablo José Abascal Monedero, *La infidelidad y el adulterio en España (estudios histórico-legal)*. Córdoba: Universidad de Córdoba, 2009, pp. 85–87.
51. Hernando Díaz de Valdepeñas, *Summa de notas copiosas muy sustanciales y compendiosas*. Toledo: Hernando Díaz y Juan de Medina, 1544, f. 42r.
52. Francisco de Quevedo, *Obras de Francisco de Quevedo Villegas*. 3 vols. Amberes: Henrico y Cornelio Verdussen, 1699, p. 535.
53. Abascal Monedero, *La infidelidad y el adulterio en España*, p. 15.
54. For the history of these laws and later developments, see Saúl Martínez Bermejo, "Beyond Luxury: Sumptuary Legislation in 17th-Century Castile" in *Making, Using, and Resisting the*

Law in European History, ed. Günther Lottes, et al. Pisa: Plus-Pisa University Press, 2008, pp. 93–108, who includes comparisons to contemporary sumptuary legislation in England.
55. Miguel de Cervantes Saavedra, *El ingenioso hidalgo Don Quijote de la Mancha*. 2 vols., ed. Celina Sabor de Cortazar and Isaías Lerner. Buenos Aires: Eudeba, 2005, II, pp. 10, 526.
56. Lope de Vega, *El peregrino en su patria*, ed. Juan Bautista Avalle-Arce. Madrid: Castalia, 1973, p. 388.
57. Cervantes Saavedra, 2005, II, 30, p. 662.
58. Ibid., II, 16, p. 561.
59. Luis Cabrera de Córdoba, *Relaciones de las cosas sucedidas en la Corte de España, desde 1599 hasta 1614*. Madrid: J. Martín Alegra, 1857, January 5, 1602.
60. Ruth Lee Kennedy,"Certain Phases of the Sumptuary Decrees and Their Relation to Tirso's Theatre" 1942. 10(2) *Hispanic Review* 91–115, 95.
61. Marcelo Martínez Alcubilla, *Diccionario de la administración española, peninsular y ultramarina*. 2nd ed. 12 vols. Madrid: A. Peñuelas, 1869, vol. 8, p. 889.
62. Cervantes Saavedra, 2005, II, 31, p.668.
63. Ibid., II, 32, p. 676.
64. Ibid., II, 34, p. 690.
65. Spain. *Cortes de Madrid*, Quaderno de las leyes y pregmáticas que su Magestad mandó hazer en las cortes que tuuo y celebró en la villa de Madrid, el año de D.lxiii. Alcalá de Henares: Andrés de Angulo, 1563, chapter 124.
66. Cervantes Saavedra, 2005, II, 34, p. 690.
67. Spain. *Fuero Juzgo*, Madrid: RAE, Ibarra, 1815, 3.4.18.
68. Spain. *Siete Partidas*, 1576. Salamanca: Domingo de Portonarijs Ursino, 1.3.21 and 22.
69. Juan María Marín dedicates a section of his introduction to the politics in the play (Vega, *Fuenteovejuna*, 40 and ff.). See also Javier Herrero. "The New Monarchy: A Structural Reinterpretaion of *Fuenteovejuna*" 1970–1971. 36 *Revista Hispánica Moderna* 173–85.
70. Vega, *Fuenteovejuna*, 43.
71. For "the people" as well as their representation in and relationship with a constitution, see Denis J. Galligan, "The People, the Constitution, and the Idea of Representation" in *Social and Political Foundations of Constitutions*, ed. Denis J. Galligan and Mila Versteeg. Cambridge: Cambridge University Press, 2013, pp. 134–156. Regarding evolving interpretations of the phrase "We the People" of the U.S. Constitution, see Bruce Ackerman, *We the People*. 2 vols. Cambridge, MA: Harvard University Press, 1991.
72. Spain. *Quaderno de las leyes y premáticas reales*. Madrid, 1528. In Collected volume ms., Biblioteca Nacional Española, R/14090, f. 41r.
73. Antonio Peña. undated ms. *Tratado de los juicios*. Biblioteca Nacional Española. MSS/6379. I thank Professor Augustín Redondo of the Sorbonne for having alerted me to the existence of this manuscript.
74. This law predates the 1568 *Recopilación*, and is also found in the 1518 *Quaderno de las leyes*, as Title 4, law 1 of that collection.
75. Marco Salón de Pace, *Ad leges Taurinas insignes comentarij*. Pinciae: Franciscum Ferdinand Cordubensis, 1568, f. 59a.
76. Adrián Celaya Ibarra, *Selección de estudios jurídicos: En especial sobre el País Vasco*. Bilbao: Universidad de Deusto, 1999, p. 355.
77. For the play's astrological references, see Frederick de Armas, "Segismundo/Philip IV: The Politics of Astrology in *La vida es sueño*" 2001. 53 *Bulletin of the Comediantes* 83–100, and Jorge Brioso, "¿Cómo hacer cosas con los enigmas?: *La vida es sueño* o el drama del desengaño" 2004. 56 *Bulletin of the Comediantes* 55–75.

78. For the political importance of Poland and its portrayal in the play, including details on hereditary versus elective monarchies, see G. A. Davies, "Poland, Politics, and *La vida es sueño*" 2001. 70 *Bulletin of Hispanic Studies* 147–163, who also notes the resonance of political events closer to home, as regards the privados (court favorites). The bitter polemic regarding the *privados* and power struggles at the courts of Phillip III and Phillip IV has been studied for its resonance in the drama of the day, and specifically in Calderón: see Antonio Carreño-Rodríguez, *Alegorías del poder: crísis imperial y comedia nueva (1598–1659)*. Woodbridge, Suffolk: Tamesis, 2009; Frederick de Armas, *Cervantes, Raphael, and the Classics*. Cambridge: Cambridge University Press, 1998; Julio Juan Ruiz, "La tradición medieval y el realismo político modern en el teatro de Calderón de la Barca" 2013. 46 *Acta Literaria* 127–141; Margaret Greer, *The Play of Power*. Princeton: Princeton University Press, 1991; Julio Vélez-Sainz. "Anatomía áulica y política de *Fieras afemina amor* de Calderón" 2011. 161 *Hispanófila* 1–17. Christoph Strosetzki, "La filosofís política, el tacitismo español y Calderón" in *Calderón y el pensamiento ideológico y cultural de su época: XIV Coloquio Anglogermano sobre Calderón*. Heidelberg, de julio de 24–28 2005, ed. Madred Tietz y Gero Arnscheidt. Stuttgart, 2008: Steiner reviews the themes of war, treason, and tyranny in four Calderón plays, and Pérez-Magallón studies subsequent use of Calderón as a political icon for conservative politics.

79. Teresa Ferrer Valls, *Nobleza y espectáculo teatral (1535–1622): Estudio y documentos*. Ser. Textos Teatrales Hispánicos del siglo XVI. Valencia: UNED; Universidad de Sevilla; Universitat de Valencia, 1993, p. 345.

80. Sir William Blackstone, *Commentaries on the Laws of England*. Vol. 1. Dublin: printed for John Exshaw, Henry Saunders, Boulter Grierson, and James Williams, 1769, pp. 270, 249.

81. When Navarre was incorporated into the Crown of Castile in 1515, it retained the rights to its own Cortes and other institutions (Elliott (1963) 2, n. 1). For modern readings of the fractious history of Navarre, see Pedro Esarte Muniain, *Represión y reparto del Estado navarro (siglos XVI y XVII): La nación vasca, expolio franco-español*. Navarra: Nabarralde, 2007; Javier Gallastegui Ucin, *Navarra a través de la correspondencia de los virreyes (1598–1648)*. Navarra: Gobierno de Navarra, 1990; Departamento de Educación, Cultura y Deporte; and Alfredo Floristán, ed., *1512, conquista e incorporación de Navarra: Historiografía, derecho y otros procesos de integración en la Europa renacentista*. Barcelona: Ariel, Planeta, 2012.

82. Jerónimo Zurita, *Anales de la coróna de Aragón*. 9 vols, ed. Ángel Canellas López. Zaragoza: Instituto Fernando el Católico, 1967–1985, III, p. 538.

83. The naming of a foreigner as viceroy in Aragon had polemical precedent: in 1482, Fernando II had done so, but following a "tense standoff" was force to to retract that choice and select a "natural son" of Aragon. Enrique Solano Camón, "La institución virreinal en Aragón durante la Edad Moderna" in *El mundo de los virreyes en las monarquías de España y Portugal*, ed. Pedro Cardim and Joan-Lluís Palos. Madrid: Iberoamericana, 2012, pp. 149–172, 150–151. For other appointments under Charles V and Phillip II leading up to the 1590 legal suit, see Solano Camón, pp. 150–153, who asserts that en 1588 Phillip II acted with intent to provoke the lawsuit.

84. Valencia, *Alegaciones de derecho, del licenciado Valencia*. Zaragoza: Lorenço de Robles, 1590.

85. Kilcullen identifies *Princeps legibus solutus est* as "the origin of the term absolutism." John Kilcullen, "Medieval Political Philosophy." *The Stanford Encyclopedia of Philosophy*, 2014, n. 33.

86. For the history of the affirmation *Quod principi placuit ...* as well as its reception in Spain, see Garrido Arredondo, who notes Stoic thought regarding the king as a divine being among men, Hellenistic perception of a monarch as "law incarnate" (for Cicero: *principem legem ese loquentem*), later readings such as Caracalla's "*Si libet, licet*," and Isidore of Seville's Christian reformulation of the concept as it would then be transmitted through the Visigoths' *Fuero Juzgo* (pp. 341–344).
87. The introductory pages are unnumbered, and I use folio to indicate which; page numbers begin with the legal response, and I indicate those with just the number.
88. Pedro Luis Martínez, *Discvrso y alegaciones de derecho del licenciado Pedro Lvis Martínez, en que trata y declara el origen, y principio del nobilíssimo y fidelíssimo Reyno de Aragón...* Zaragoza: Lorenço de Robles, 1591, f. 2r.
89. There is an echo of this complaint in one of the U.S. Declaration's complaints against England's King George: "He has made judges dependent on his Will alone." Available at: www.archives.gov/exhibits/charters/declaration_transcript.html.
90. See above, re Ferdinand II's frustrated attempt to make such an appointment. López de Haro offers full details on the development of Aragon's constitutions.
91. Cabrera de Córdoba (1857), p. 141.
92. J. H. Elliott, *The Revolt of the Catalans: A Study in the Decline of Spain*. Cambridge: Cambridge University Press, 1963; Luis R. Corteguera, *For the Common Good: Popular Politics in Barcelona, 1580–1640*. New York: Cornell University Press, 2002.
93. Susan Byrne, *Ficino in Spain*. Toronto: University of Toronto Press, 2015, pp. 128–129.
94. The *Fuero Juzgo* had allowed a full thirty years for denounciation of false testimony (2.4.7–8).
95. Aaron M. Kahn. "Moral Opposition to Phillip II in Pre-Lopean Drama" 2006. 74 *Hispanic Review* 227–250 at 228.
96. Watson, Anthony. 1972. *Juan de la Cueva and the Portuguese Succession*. London: Tamesis.
97. Alfredo Hermenegildo, *El tirano en escena: siglo XVI*. Madrid: Biblioteca Nueva, 2002; Frederick de Armas, *Cervantes, Raphael, and the Classics*. Cambridge: Cambridge University Press, 1998; Aaron M. Kahn, "Moral Opposition to Phillip II in Pre-Lopean Drama" 2006. 74 *Hispanic Review* 227–250; Willard King, "Cervantes' *La Numancia* and Imperial Spain" 1979. 94 *MLN* 200–221; Stephen Rupp, *Heroic Forms: Cervantes and the Literature of War*. Toronto: University of Toronto Press, 2014.
98. Byrne, *Law and History in Cervantes' Don Quixote*.
99. Cervantes, *El ingenioso hidalgo Don Quijote de la Mancha*, II, 60, p. 861.
100. Ibid.
101. Cervantes (2005), II, 61.
102. Jover Zamora (José María Jover Zamora, ed., *Historia de la cultura española "Menéndez Pidal": El siglo del* Quijote, *1580–1680*. 2 vols. Madrid: Espasa, 1996, II, pp. 231–233) points out that in Aragon, Valencia and Mallorca, the term *bandolero* was directly related to the formation of bands or factions of family groups waging battles against each other on a regular basis throughout the fourteenth and fifteenth centuries. With a gradual lessening of these clashes in the sixteenth century, the fighters found themselves without a means of earning a living, and turned to a more general lawlessness (II, pp. 231–233).
103. Miguel de Cervantes Saavedra, *La cueva de Salamanca. Entremeses*, ed. Eugenio Asensio. Madrid, Castalia, 1970, pp. 185–199, 189.
104. Miguel de Cervantes Saavedra, *Los trabajos de Persiles y Sigismunda*, ed. Carlos Rumero Muñoz. Madrid: Cátedra, 2003, III, 12, p. 564.
105. Tirso de Molina, *Cigarrales de Toledo*, ed. Luis Vázquez Fernández. Madrid: Castalia, 1996, pp. 314–315.

106. James Bryce, *Constitutions*. Holmes Beach, FL: Gaunt, 1997, p. 4.
107. Spain. *Cortes de Madrid*, 1579. 1588. Madrid: Querino Gerardo, n.4, f. 3v.
108. Kuhn notes a quite literal transfer of those idealist texts, in that Vasco de Quiroga used Thomas More's *Utopia* as a model for "central-American settlements" (Heinrich C. Kuhn, "Ideal Constitutions in the Renaissance: Sizes, Structures, Dynamics, Continuities and Discontinuities" in *Ideal Constitutions in the Renaissance. Papers from the Munich February 2006 Conference*, ed. Heinrich C. Kuhn and Diana Stanciu. Frankfurt am Main: Peter Lang, 2009 pp. 9–27, 12).
109. Susan Byrne, *Ficino in Spain*. Toronto: University of Toronto Press, 2015, pp. 188–191.
110. Ibid., pp. 191–203. See also Eric Nelson, *The Greek Tradition in Republican Thought*. Cambridge: Cambridge University Press, 2004, for the topic of equity in sixteenth-century English writings.
111. Byrne, *Ficino in Spain*, pp. 203–206.
112. Jerónimo Castillo de Bobadilla, *Política para corregidores*. Barcelona: Gerónymo Margarit, 1616, 2.16.74. I cite by book, chapter, and paragraph.
113. Castillo de Bobadilla (1616) 2.16.72.
114. Castillo de Bobadilla (1616) 2.16.74.
115. Miguel de Cervantes Saavedra, *La elección de los alcaldes de Daganzo. Entremeses*, ed. Eugenio Asensio. Madrid, Castalia, 1970, pp. 103–126. Alvar Ezquerra (Alfredo Alvar Ezquerra. "Los entremeses de Cervantes, leídos por un historiador" 1995. 29 *Torre de los Lujanes* 137–157) finds in this insistence on an exam an echo of contemporary debates regarding merit versus intellectual capacity in the awarding of administrative posts. Alvar Ezquerra and Montcher study and contextualize Cervantes' political use of history (2014).
116. Cascardi 2012, and Byrne, *Ficino in Spain*, pp. 188–213.
117. For a recent review of the socio-political implications of Sancho's governorship, see Luis R. Corteguera, "Sancho Panza Wants an Island: Cervantes and the Politics of Peasant Rulers" 1995. 2 *Romance Quarterly* 261–270. I maintain the term *ínsula*, in the Latin as used by Cervantes, because a literal translation into "island" does not describe the land-bound town governed by Sancho.
118. Cervantes (2005), II, 3, p. 487.
119. Ibid., II, 43, p. 740.
120. Ibid., II, 32, pp. 680–681.
121. Ibid., II, 45, p. 755.
122. Ibid., II, 53, p. 813.
123. Ibid., II, 51, p. 802.
124. In his introduction to an 1883 edition of Morton's work, titled *New Canaan*, Charles Francis Adams offers all the details of Morton's experiences with Standish, and it is a wonderful read. Morton was twice arrested by Standish and sent back to England, where he was acquitted of all charges. He would eventually die in Maine in 1647 (Hovey in Morton I, pp. 176–177). Thomas Morton, *New English Canaan*. In *The Heath Anthology of American Literature*, vol. 1, ed. Paul Lauter, et al. Lexington, MA: D.C. Heath and Co., 1990, pp. 176–187.
125. See Garrido Ardila (J. A.Garrido Ardila, ed., *The Cervantean Heritage: Reception and Influence of Cervantes in Britain*. London: Legenda, 2009) for the resonance of Cervantes in Britain from 1605–2000. Schmidt has noted the chronological coincidence of the first modern novel and the "birth of the modern nation state" (Rachel Schmidt, *Forms of Modernity: Don Quixote and the Modern Theories of the Novel*. Toronto: University of Toronto Press, 2011, p. 9).

126. Hardin, 2013, p. 68.
127. For late twentieth-century historiographical debates regarding the political theory of Locke in the American revolution, and for the American founders' expressions of Platonic principles and ideas in their own writings, see Nelson (pp. 201–233).
128. Robert B. Winans, "Bibliography and the Cultural Historian: Notes on the Eighteenth-Century Novel" in *Printing and Society in Early America*, ed. William L. Joyce, et al. Worcester: American Antiquarian Society, 1983, p. 178.
129. Stanley T. Williams, *The Spanish Background of American Literature*. 2 vols. Hamden, CT: Archon Books, 1968, p. 17.
130. T. J. Holmes, *Cotton Mather: A Bibliography of His Works*. 3 vols. Cambridge, MA: Harvard University Press, 1940, I, p. 208.
131. Holmes (1940) II, 497.
132. Williams, *The Spanish Background of American Literature*, p. 15.
133. Libraries in Colonial Virginia. *The William and Mary Quarterly* 2 (1894), pp. 169–175.
134. Richard Beale Davis, *Intellectual Life in the Colonial South, 1585–1763*. 3 vols. Knoxville, TN: Knoxville University Press, 1978.
135. Stanley T. Williams, *The Spanish Background of American Literature*. 2 vols. Hamden, CT: Archon Books, 1968, I, p. 329, n.67 to chapter 2.
136. Available at: http://memory.loc.gov/cgi-bin/ampage?collId=rbpe&fileName=rbpe17/rbpe178/17800500/rbpe17800500.db&recNum=0&itemLink =D?rbpebib:11:./temp/~ammem_2lii::&linkText=0.
137. Cervantes (2005), II, pp. 58, 836.
138. See http://avalon.law.yale.edu/18th_century/patrick.asp.
139. The Monticello website dedicates a page to Jefferson's references to Don Quijote. Available at: www.monticello.org/site/research-and-collections/don-quixote-novel.
140. Jefferson to Mary Jefferson, April 11, 1790, is at PTJ 16:331; Mary Jefferson to Jefferson, May 23, 1791, PTJ 16: 436. See Papers of Thomas Jefferson. Available at: http://founders.archives.gov/content/volumes#Jefferson.
141. Wood, Sarah, *Quixotic Fictions of the USA 1792–1815*. Oxford: Oxford University Press, 2005, p. 3.
142. Gardoqui to George Washington, November 9, 1787, Founders Online, National Archives. Available at:http://founders.archives.gov/documents/Washington/04-05-02-0386. Wood notes that, from the condition of the two copies, Washington apparently read the work in English.
143. Franklin to William Strahan, December 4, 1781, Franklin Papers, Founders Online, National Archives. Available at: http://founders.archives.gov/documents/Franklin/01-36-02-0124.
144. John Quincy Adams to Elizabeth Smith Shaw, March 29, 1786, Founders Online, National Archives. Available at: http://founders.archives.gov/documents/Adams/04-07-02-0035.
145. Jefferson to Edmond Randolph, August 18, 1799 (PTJ 31: 170–171).
146. Nathaniel Irwin to James Madison, March 31, 1801. Available at: http://founders.archives.gov/documents/Madison/02-01-02-0078.
147. James Monroe's Account of a Conversation with Thomas Jefferson, 30 November 1809. Available at: http://founders.archives.gov/documents/Jefferson/03-02-02-0026-0003.
148. John Quincy Adams to Louisa Catherine Johnson Adams, November 15, 1814. Available at: http://founders.archives.gov/documents/Adams/99-03-02-2667.

149. William Jackson to John Adams, October 26, 1781. Available at: http://founders.archives.gov/documents/Adams/04-04-02-0159.
150. Manuel, Durán and Fay Rogg, eds., *Fighting Windmills: Encounters with Don Quijote*. New Haven, CT: Yale University Press 2006; Wood, *Quixotic Fictions of the USA 1792–1815*.
151. Bryce, *Constitutions*, p. 4.
152. Denis J. Galligan and Mila Versteeg eds. *Social and Political Foundations of Constitutions*. Cambridge: Cambridge University Press, 2003, p. 8.

Chapter 3

1. Repertories of the Court of Aldermen, London Metropolitan Archive. All further references to the Repertories are from this collection. COL/CA/01/01/17, 414v.
2. May 6, 1562 Paul L. Hughes and James F. Larkin, *Tudor Royal Proclamations: The Later Tudors (1553–1587)*, vol. 2. New Haven and London: Yale University Press, 1969, pp. 187–192.
3. The population of London is hard to estimate in this period. Scholars have used various different sources to estimate figures, and have thus produced substantially different results. For the best summary of these estimates, see Vanessa Harding, "The Population of London, 1550–1700: A Review of the Published Evidence," 1990. 15(2) *The London Journal* 111–128.
4. Brian Dietz, "Overseas Trade and Metropolitan Growth," in *London 1500–1700: The Making of the Metropolis*, ed. A. L. Beier and Roger Finlay. London and New York: Longman, 1986, pp. 115–140.
5. A. L. Beier, "Engine of Manufacture: The Trades of London," *London 1500–1700*, pp. 141–167.
6. Richard Wunderli, "Evasion of the Office of Alderman in London, 1523–1672" 1990. 15(1) *The London Journal*, 3–18.
7. John Earle, *Microcosmographie, or a Peece of the World Discovered* (1622), part 5, as cited in Robert Tittler, *The Face of the City: Civic Portraiture and Civic Identity in Early Modern England*. Manchester and New York: Manchester University Press, 2007, p. 120.
8. For more on clothing as a "material memory" and store of identity, see Jones and Stallybrass, *Renaissance Clothing and the Materials of Memory*. Cambridge: Cambridge University Press, 2000.
9. "livery, n." OED Online. September 2015. Oxford University Press. Available at: www.oed.com/view/Entry/109344?rskey=safFH7&result=1&isAdvanced=false.
10. Peter Stallybrass, "Worn Worlds: Clothes and Identity on the Renaissance Stage," in *Subject and Object in Renaissance Culture*, ed. Margreta De Grazia, Maureen Quilligan, and Peter Stallybrass. Cambridge: Cambridge University Press, 1996, p. 289.
11. Ian W. Archer, *The Pursuit of Stability: Social Relations in Elizabethan London*. Cambridge: Cambridge University Press, 1991, pp. 18–57, 100–148.
12. COL/CA/01/01/19, 330v.
13. COL/CA/01/01/17, 78.
14. John Bulwer, *Anthropometamorphosis: Man Transform'd: Or, the Artificiall Changling Historically Presented, in the Mad and Cruell Gallantry, Foolish Bravery, Ridiculous Beauty, Filthy Finenesse, and Loathsome Loveliness of Most Nations, Fashioning and Altering Their Bodies from the Mould Intended by Nature; with Figures of Those Transfigurations. To Which Artificiall and Affected Deformations Are Added, All the Native and Nationall Monstrosities That Have Appeared to Disfigure the Humane Fabrick. With a Vindication of the Regular Beauty and Honesty of Nature. And an Appendix of the Pedigree of the English Gallant*. London: William Hunt, 1653, pp. 542–543.

15. For example, Lisa Jardine, *Worldly Goods: A New History of the Renaissance*. New York: Doubleday, 1996); Lorna Weatherill, *Consumer Behaviour and Material Culture in Britain, 1660–1760*. London: Routledge, 1996; Jan De Vries, *The Industrious Revolution: Consumer Behavior and the Household Economy, 1650 to the Present*. Cambridge: Cambridge University Press, 2008; John Brewer and Roy Porter, *Consumption and the World of Goods*. Routledge, 1993; Maxine Berg, *Luxury and Pleasure in Eighteenth-Century Britain*. Oxford: Oxford University Press, 2005 for an exhibition that explored such claims, see Victoria Avery, Melissa Calaresu, and Mary Laven, eds., *Treasured Possessions from the Renaissance to the Enlightenment*. London: Philip Wilson Publishers, 2015.
16. Catherine Kovesi Killerby, *Sumptuary Law in Italy 1200–1500*. Oxford and New York: Oxford University Press, 2002, p. 69; Kent Roberts Greenfield, *Sumptuary Law in Nürnberg: A Study in Paternal Government*. Baltimore: The Johns Hopkins University Press, 1918, p. 109.
17. 1559, 1562 x 3, 1566, 1574, 1577, 1580 1588, 1597 x 2, 1597 as in Hughes and Larkin, *Tudor Royal Proclamations: The Later Tudors (1553–1587)*; Paul L. Hughes and James F. Larkin eds., *Tudor Royal Proclamations: The Later Tudors (1588–1603)*, vol. 3. New Haven and London: Yale University Press, 1969.
18. 1572, 1573, 1570, 1575, 1590, 1597 as in Hughes and Larkin, *Tudor Royal Proclamations: The Later Tudors (1553–1587)*; Hughes and Larkin, *Tudor Royal Proclamations: The Later Tudors (1588–1603)*; The November 19, 1595 proclamation enforcing statutes on hats and caps is not included in Hughes and Larkin, but is identified in Frederic A. Youngs, *The Proclamations of the Tudor Queens*. Cambridge: Cambridge University Press, 1976, p. 259.
19. Alan Hunt, *Governance of the Consuming Passions: A History of Sumptuary Law*. New York: St. Martin's Press, 1996, pp. 320–321.
20. June 15, 1574 in Hughes and Larkin, *Tudor Royal Proclamations: The Later Tudors (1553–1587)*, II, pp. 381–386.
21. Youngs, *The Proclamations of the Tudor Queens*, p. 25.
22. For more on these efforts in 1566, 1571, 1575, 1589, and 1597–8 see ibid., p. 162.
23. T. E. Hartley, ed., *Proceedings in the Parliaments of Elizabeth I*, Volume I: *1558–1581*. Leicester: Leicester University Press, 1981, pp. 454–456.
24. Hooper, "The Tudor Sumptuary Laws," pp. 448–449; Harte, "State Control of Dress and Social Change in Pre-Industrial England," pp. 148–150; Vincent, *Dressing the Elite*, pp. 118–119.
25. COL/CC/01/01/29/01, 161r-162v.
26. COL/CC/01/01/29/01, 186r.
27. "little-ease, n." OED Online. December 2015. Oxford University Press. Available at: www.oed.com/view/Entry/109252?redirectedFrom=little+ease (accessed January 23, 2016).
28. COL/CC/01/01/29/01, 161r-162v.
29. Ulinka Rublack, *Dressing Up: Cultural Identity in Renaissance Europe*. Oxford: Oxford University Press, 2010, p. 265.
30. G. R. Elton, *The Parliament of England 1559–1581*. Cambridge, 1986, pp. 273, 253 and Lawrence Stone, *The Crisis of the Aristocracy 1558–1641*. Oxford, 1965, p. 566 as in Vincent, *Dressing the Elite*, p. 117.
31. Daniel Roche, *The Culture of Clothing: Dress and Fashion in the Ancien Régime*, originally published in French as *La Culture des apparences*, 1989. First published in England in 1994 (Cambridge University Press, 1996), 56.
32. Hunt, *Governance of the Consuming Passions*, pp. 12–14.

33. Alan Hunt, "The Governance of Consumption: Sumptuary Laws and Shifting Forms of Regulation" in *The Consumption Reader*, ed. David B. Clarke, Marcus A. Doel, and Kate M. L. Housiaux. London: Routledge, 2003, p. 62.
34. Kovesi Killerby, *Sumptuary Law in Italy 1200–1500*; Emanuela Zanda, *Fighting Hydra-like Luxury: Sumptuary Regulation in the Roman Republic*. London: Bloomsbury, 2013.
35. Hooper, "The Tudor Sumptuary Laws"; Frances Elizabeth Baldwin, *Sumptuary Legislation and Personal Regulation in England*. Baltimore: Johns Hopkins University Press, 1923; Syliva A. Miller, "Old English Laws Regulating Dress," 20 (2) *Journal of Home Economics*, 89–94; Clifford R. Bell and Evelyn Ruse, "Sumptuary Legislation and English Costume: An Attempt to Assess the Effect of an Act of 1337," 1972, 6(1) *Costume* 22–31; Harte, "State Control of Dress and Social Change in Pre-Industrial England"; Vincent, *Dressing the Elite*, pp. 117–152; Maria Hayward, *Rich Apparel: Clothing and the Law in Henry VIII's England*. Farnham: Ashgate, 2009; Hilary Doda, "'Saide Monstrous Hose': Compliance, Transgression and English Sumptuary Law to 1533," *Textile History*, 45 (2), 2014, 171–191.
36. This study offers an excellent example of how sumptuary legislation can be closely connected to clothing, although sadly no guardainfante survive, so the study lacks extant examples: Amanda Wunder, "Women's Fashions and Politics in Seventeenth-Century Spain: The Rise and Fall of the Guardainfante," *Renaissance Quarterly*, 68 (1), 2015, 133–186.
37. Barnabe Barnes, *Foure Bookes of Offices: Enabling Privat Persons for the Speciall Seruice of All Good Princes and Policies*. London: A. Islip, 1606, p. 15.
38. N. B. Harte, *The New Draperies in the Low Countries and England, 1300–1800*. Oxford: Oxford University Press, 1997.
39. For an image of the doublet, hose, and canions, while on loan to the Victoria and Albert Museum see Madeleine Ginsburg, Avril Hart, and Valerie Mendes, *Four Hundred Years of Fashion*, ed. Natalie Rothstein. London: V&A Publications, 1992, p. 144. Note the voluminous shape of the hose.
40. For the terms of the proclamation, see May 6, 1562 Hughes and Larkin, *Tudor Royal Proclamations: The Later Tudors (1553–1587)*, II, pp. 187–192.
41. The Lord Mayor's jurisdiction covered an area that extended beyond London's ancient walls. The city boundary was marked with bars, one of which Temple Bar. Those who dwelt or traded outside of the City's jurisdiction (i.e., without Temple Bar) were regulated by other authorities. For a sense of the cultural impact of such divisions, see Joseph P. Ward, *Metropolitan Communities: Trade Guilds, Identity, and Change in Early Modern London*. Stanford: Stanford University Press, 1997, in particular pp. 7–26.
42. Foreigners here refers to those who were not members of the London livery companies and dwelt outside London jurisdiction. British Library MS Lansdowne 8. art 64. As transcribed in Henry Ellis, ed., *Original Letters, Illustrative of English History: Including Numerous Royal Letters; from Autographs in the British Museum, and One or Two Other Collections*, vol. 2. London: Harding and Lepard, 1827, pp. 306–307; also quoted in Hooper, "The Tudor Sumptuary Laws," pp. 442–443.
43. Nancy Cox, *Retailing and the Language of Goods, 1550–1820*. Farnham: Ashgate, 2015, pp. 17–22.
44. John Marston, *Jacke Drum's Entertainment: Or The Comedie of Pasquill and Katherine As It Hath Bene Sundry Times Plaide by the Children of Powles*. London: Richard Olive, 1601, Act IV; Robert Greene, *A Quip for an Vpstart Courtier: Or, A Quaint Dispute Betvveen Veluet Breeches and Cloth-Breeches Wherein Is Plainely Set Downe the Disorders in All Estates and Trades*. London: John Wolfe, 1592, C3v.

45. Phillip Stubbes, *The Anatomie of Abuses Contayning A Discouerie, or Briefe Summarie of Such Notable Vices and Imperfections, as Now Raigne in Many Christian Countreyes of the Worlde: But (especiallie) in a Verie famous Iilande Called Ailgna: Together, with Most Fearefull Examples of Gods Iudgementes, Executed Vpon the Wicked for the Same, Aswell in Ailgna of Late, as in Other Places, Elsewhere. Verie Godly, to Be Read of All True Christians, Euerie Where: But Most Needefull, to Be Regarded in Englande*. London: John Kingston for Richard Jones, 1583, BVII.
46. Greene, *A Quip for an Vpstart Courtier*, A4v–B1r.
47. Ibid., B1r.
48. For more on *Quip* and the links between plain cloth and English identity, see Hilary M. Larkin, *The Making of Englishmen: Debates on National Identity 1550–1650*. Leiden and Boston: Brill, 2014, pp. 40–43, 90; Roze Hentschell, *The Culture of Cloth in Early Modern England: Textual Constructions of a National Identity*. Aldershot: Ashgate, 2008, pp. 103–128.
49. 16 February 1577, printed by R. Jugge (London, 1577).
50. 6 May 1562, as in Hughes and Larkin, *Tudor Royal Proclamations*, pp. 187–194.
51. Stubbes, *The Anatomie of Abuses*, CII V.
52. "An Homily Against Excess of Apparel," Church of England, *Sermons or Homilies Appointed to Be Read in Churches in the Time of Queen Elizabeth of Famous Memory*. Oxford: Clarendon Press, 1802, p. 260.
53. Peter Goodrich, "Signs Taken for Wonders: Community, Identity, and 'A History of Sumptuary Law,'" 1998, 23(3) *Law & Social Inquiry* 709.
54. For the foundational text on the emergence of Puritanism and the vestiarian constrovery's role in this development, see Patrick Collinson, *The Elizabethan Puritan Movement*. London: Jonathan Cape, 1967.
55. For more on the "vestiarian controversy," see John Henry Primus, *The Vestments Controversy: An Historical Study of the Earliest Tensions within the Church of England in the Reigns of Edward VI and Elizabeth*. Kampen: J. H. Kok, 1960; Leo F. Solt, *Church and State in Early Modern England, 1509–1640*. New York and Oxford: Oxford University Press, 1990 pp. 83–85; Hilary Doda, "Rounde Heades in Square Cappes: The Role of the Vestments in the Vestiarian Controversy," 2013, 39(2) *Dress* 93–110.
56. As quoted in Solt, *Church and State in Early Modern England, 1509–1640*, pp. 83–84.
57. Robert Crowley, *A Briefe Discourse against the Outwarde Apparell and Ministring Garmentes of the Popishe Church*. Emden: Egidius van der Erve, 1566, A iiii r–v.
58. Anthony Gilby, *To My Louynge Brethren That Is Troublyd About the Popishe Apparell, Two Short and Comfortable Epistels*. Emden: Egidius van der Erve, 1566, Ciir.
59. Brett Usher, *William Cecil and Episcopacy, 1559–1577*. Aldershot: Ashgate, 2003, pp. 128–129.
60. May 6, 1562 in Hughes and Larkin, *Tudor Royal Proclamations: The Later Tudors (1553–1587)*, II, p. 439.
61. Henry Machyn, *The Diary of Henry Machyn, Citizen and Merchant-Taylor of London, from A. D. 1550 to A. D.1563*, ed. John Gough Nichols. New York: AMS Press, 1968, pp. 280–281.
62. For Machyn's biography, which suggests he had Catholic tendencies, see Ian Mortimer "Machyn, Henry (1496/1498–1563)," Ian Mortimer in *The Oxford Dictionary of National Biography*, ed. H. C. G. Matthew and Brian Harrison. Oxford: Oxford University Press, 2004; online, ed. Lawrence Goldman, January 2008. Available at: www.oxforddnb.com/view/article/17531.

63. For more about this phenomenon in England, see Julie Crawford, *Marvelous Protestantism: Monstrous Births in Post-Reformation England*. Baltimore: Johns Hopkins University Press, 2005. Similar phenomena were recorded across Protestant Europe. See, e.g. Jennifer Spinks, *Monstrous Births and Visual Culture in Sixteenth-Century Germany*. Abingdon: Routledge, 2016.
64. John Hayward, *Annals of the First Four Years of the Reign of Queen Elizabeth*, ed. John Bruce, vol. 7, Camden Society 1. New York: Johnson Reprint Corp., 1968, 242v; as quoted in Crawford, *Marvelous Protestantism*, p. 46.
65. 12 February 1580, as in Hughes and Larkin, *Tudor Royal Proclamations: The Later Tudors (1553–1587)*, II, p. 462.
66. Stubbes, *The Anatomie of Abuses*, DVIIv.
67. John Stow, *Annales, or a General Chronicle of England*, ed. Edmund Howes (1631), pp. 868–869; For more on women and the starching industry, see Natasha Korda, *Labors Lost: Women's Work and the Early Modern English Stage*. Philadelphia: University of Pennsylvania Press, 2011, pp. 93–143.
68. Alastair Bellany, "Mistress Turner's Deadly Sins: Sartorial Transgression, Court Scandal, and Politics in Early Stuart England," *Huntington Library Quarterly*, 1995, 58 (2), 179–210; Jones and Stallybrass, *Renaissance Clothing and the Materials of Memory*, pp. 59–86; Ann Rosalind Jones and Peter Stallybrass, "'Rugges of London and the Diuell's Band': Irish Mantles and Yellow Starch as Hybrid London Fashion," in *Material London, Ca. 1600*, ed. Lena Cowen Orlin. Philadelphia: University of Pennsylvania Press, 2000, pp. 128–149.
69. Ayesha Mukherjee, *Penury Into Plenty: Dearth and the Making of Knowledge in Early Modern England*. London and New York: Routledge, 2015 pp. 165–166.
70. A quarter was approximately eight bushels, although quantity varied according to different localities and what was being measured. "quarter, n." OED Online. December 2015. Oxford University Press. Available at: www.oed.com/view/Entry/156027?rskey=P6swwo&result=1&isAdvanced=false; Joan Thirsk, *Economic Policy and Projects: The Development of a Consumer Society in Early Modern England*. Oxford: Clarendon Press, 1978, p. 92.
71. Lansdowne MS. 42. 73 as cited in Mukherjee, *Penury into Plenty*, p. 166; Thirsk, *Economic Policy and Projects*, p. 89.
72. Richard H. Tawney and Eileen Power, eds., *Tudor Economic Documents: Being Select Documents Illustrating the Economic and Social History of Tudor England*, vol. 2. London: Longmans, Green and Co., 1953, p. 124.
73. John Evelyn, *Tyrannus, Or, The Mode in a Discourse of Sumptuary Lawes*. London: G. Bedel, T. Collins, and J. Crook, 1661.
74. June 15, 1574 in Hughes and Larkin, *Tudor Royal Proclamations: The Later Tudors (1553–1587)*, II, pp. 381, 383–384.
75. 13 Eliz. I, c.19 (1571) as in Harte, "State Control of Dress and Social Change in Pre-Industrial England," p. 138.
76. The Act mentions fifteen specialists involved in the "capping" trade: carders, knitters, wool parters, forcers, thickers, dressers, walkers, dyers, buttelers, shearers, pressers, edgers, liners, bandmakers, and other exercisers, see Jane Malcolm-Davies and Hilary Davidson, "'He Is of No Account … if He Have Not a Velvet or Taffeta Hat': A Survey of Sixteenth Century Knitted Caps," *NESAT* XII (2015), p. 224.
77. 1572, 1573, 1570, 1575, 1590, 1597 Hughes and Larkin, *Tudor Royal Proclamations: The Later Tudors (1553–1587)*; Hughes and Larkin, *Tudor Royal Proclamations: The Later Tudors (1588–1603)*; The November 19, 1595 proclamation enforcing statutes on hats and caps is not included in Hughes and Larkin, but is identified in Youngs, *The Proclamations of the Tudor Queens*, p. 259.

78. April 28, 1573 in Hughes and Larkin, *Tudor Royal Proclamations: The Later Tudors (1553–1587)*, II, p. 369.
79. Malcolm-Davies and Davidson, "He Is of No Account … if He Have Not a Velvet or Taffeta Hat" p. 227.
80. No comprehensive survey has been done of these hats, but they appear in collections across British, Irish, and North American institutions, including the Victoria and Albert Museum and the Metropolitan Museum of Art.
81. As in Kate Pogue, *Shakespeare's Family*. London: Praeger, 2008, p. 28.
82. Laws in Venice and Switzerland, for example, lasted until the end of the eighteenth century, Hunt, *Governance of the Consuming Passions*, pp. 28–38.
83. Harte, "State Control of Dress and Social Change in Pre-Industrial England" p. 147; for Baldwin's claims, see Baldwin, *Sumptuary Legislation and Personal Regulation in England*, especially pp. 117–118, 314.
84. Hunt, *Governance of the Consuming Passions*, pp. 326–327.
85. The May 7, 1562 proclamation blamed the "negligence of officers" for the increase in offenses against the "good laws and orders for redress of many enormities," Hughes and Larkin, *Tudor Royal Proclamations: The Later Tudors (1553–1587)*, II, p. 192.
86. May 6, 1562 in ibid., p. 188.
87. Hooper, "The Tudor Sumptuary Laws" p. 439.
88. There were 110 parishes in London. COL/CA/01/01/18, 13v and in ibid., 444.
89. COL/CA/01/01/17, 414v and in ibid., 443.
90. COL/CA/01/01/17, 414v (their appearance is recorded on 415v).
91. COL/CA/01/01/17, 415r.
92. COL/CA/01/01/17, 416v.
93. COL/CA/01/01/17, 416v.
94. COL/CA/01/01/17, 420v.
95. COL/CC/01/01/22, 206v.
96. COL/CC/01/01/22, 210v.
97. William Allyn to Lord Burghley, November 1, 1571, The National Archives, State Papers 12/83 f.5. Accessed though State Papers Online.
98. March 8, 1579, in "Watch and Ward" *Analytical Index to the Series of Records Known as the Remembrancia. Preserved among the Archives of the City of London, A.D. 1579–1664. Prepared by the Authority of the Corporation of London, under the Superintendence of the Library Committee*. London: E. J. Francis & Co., 1878, pp. 549–550.
99. May 5, 1580 in "Costume" ibid., p. 117.
100. John Roche Dasent, *Acts of the Privy Council of England*, vol. 22. (London: H.M. Stationery Office, 1901, p. 175.
101. As quoted in Vincent, *Dressing the Elite*, p. 142.
102. British Museum (now in British Library collections) Stowe MS. 554 fo. 48v as in Joan Kent, "Attitudes of Members of the House of Commons to the Regulation of 'Personal Conduct in Late Elizabethan and Early Stuart England," *Historical Research*, 46, 113 1973, 51.
103. COL/CA/01/01/17, 83v.
104. For more on the exuberance and challenges of young men in London, see Amanda Bailey, *Flaunting: Style and the Subversive Male Body in Renaissance England*. Toronto: University of Toronto Press, 2007; Paul Griffiths, *Youth and Authority: Formative Experiences in England, 1560–1640*. Oxford: Clarendon Press, 1996.
105. Francis Lenton, *The Young Gallants Whirligigg; or, Youth Reakes*. London, 1629, B3, as quoted in Bailey, *Flaunting*, p. 31.

106. Henry Smith, *Sermons*. London, 1591, p. 231 as quoted in Ian W. Archer, "Material Londoners?" in *Material London*, p. 178.
107. Nathaneall Cannon, *The Cryer. A Sermon Preached at Pauls Crosse*. London: Felix Kingston, 1613, p. 30.
108. Sir John Harington, *The Epigrams of Sir John Harington*, ed. Gerard Kilroy. Surrey: Ashgate, 2009, p. 183.
109. Chamberlain to Carleton, January 25, 1620, in *Letters of John Chamberlain*, ed. Norman E. McClure. Philadelphia, 1939, 2, pp. 286–287 as in Bellany, "Mistress Turner's Deadly Sins," p. 205.
110. Chamberlain to Carleton, March 11, 1620, in *Letters*, 2, p. 294 as in ibid., p. 206.
111. The tale correlates with an account of the Flemish painter Lucas de Heere, a Protestant refugee who lived in England in the 1560s and 1570s. Karel van Mander, a student of de Heere's, recounted a commission to paint the gallery of the Lord High Admiral Edward Clinton, "in which he [De Heere] had to paint all the costumes or clothing of the nations. When all but the Englishman were done, he painted him naked and set beside him all manner of cloth and silk materials, and next to them the tailor's scissors and chalk. When the Admiral saw this figure he asked Lucas what he meant by it. He answered that he had done that with the Englishman because he did not know what appearance or kind of clothing he should give him because they varied so much from day to day; for if he had done it one way today the next day it would have to be another—be it French or Italian, Spanish or Dutch," Karel van Mander, ed. H. Miedema, J. Pennial-Boer and trans. C. Ford, *The Lives of the Illustrious Netherlandish and German Painters*. Doornspijk, 1994, p. 281 as quoted in Michael Gaudio, "'Counterfeited According to the Truth': John White, Lucas de Heere, and the Truth in Clothing," in *European Visions: American Voices*, ed. Kim Sloan. London: The British Museum, 2009, pp. 24–32.
112. "An Homily Against Excess of Apparel," in *Certain Sermons or Homilies Appointed to Be Read in Church in the Time of the Late Queen Elizabeth of Famous Memory*. Oxford: Oxford University Press, 1840, 278.
    In fact, the naked countryman was something of a trope. Ulinka Rublack refers to a naked German in Wilhelm IV of Bavaria's *Book of Court Costumes* (Hofkleiderbuch), in Rublack, *Dressing Up*, p. 145.
113. "An Homily Against Excess of Apparel" p. 278.
114. Joan Thirsk, "The Fantastical Folly of Fashion: The English Stocking Knitting Industry, 1500–1700," in *The Rural Economy of England*. London: The Hambledon Press, 1984, pp. 235–258.
115. Evelyn Welch and Juliet Claxton, "Easy Innovation in Early Modern Europe," in *Fashioning the Early Modern: Dress, Textiles, and Innovation in Europe, 1500–1800*, ed. Evelyn Welch. Oxford: Oxford University Press, 2017, pp. 87–110.
116. Courtbooks of the Court of London Bridewell 7, 377v as in Griffiths, *Youth and Authority*, p. 224.
117. Kay Staniland, "Thomas Deane's Shop in the Royal Exchange," in *The Royal Exchange*, ed. Ann Saunders. London: The London Topographical Society, 1997, pp. 59–67.
118. Shrewsbury Papers MS.697 Folio 47, Lambeth Palace Archives.
119. "mockado, n.1 and adj." OED Online. December 2015. Oxford University Press. Available at: www.oed.com/view/Entry/120532?rskey=lBdayV&result=1&isAdvanced=false (last accessed January 23, 2016).
120. PRO SP 14/89/55 as cited in Griffiths, *Youth and Authority*, p. 227.

121. For brief summaries of these attempts, see Kent, "Attitudes of Members of the House of Commons to the Regulation of 'Personal Conduct' in Late Elizabethan and Early Stuart England" pp. 63–64; Harte, "State Control of Dress and Social Change in Pre-Industrial England" p. 816.
122. COL/CC/01/01/29/01 119r, 161r-162v, 186r.
123. "Bodies" or a "pair of bodies" were stiffened supportive undergarments, designed to shape the body, from which the term "bodice" is derived.
124. *The Letters and Life of Francis Bacon*, ed. J. Spedding. 7 vols, 1862–1874, vi, 74, as in Kent, "Attitudes of Members of the House of Commons to the Regulation of 'Personal Conduct' in Late Elizabethan and Early Stuart England" p. 57.
125. *Journals of the House of Lords*, XII, 228 as quoted in Vincent, *Dressing the Elite*, p. 126.
126. See, e.g. Larkin and Hughes, *Stuart Royal Proclamations*, Vol. 1: *Royal Proclamations of King James I 1603–1625*. Oxford: Clarendon Press, 1973 pp. 545–548, 581.
127. "Charles II, 1666: An Act for Burying in Woollen onely" in *Statutes of the Realm*: Vol. 5, 1628–80, ed. John Raithby. s.l: Great Britain Record Commission, 1819, p. 598, accessed February 6, 2016. Available at: www.british-history.ac.uk/statutes-realm/vol5/p598a.
128. Adam Smith, *The Wealth of Nations* (ed. E. Cannan, 1904), p. 328, as cited in N. B. Harte, "Silk and Sumptuary Legislation in England," in *La Seta in Europa*, Sec. XIII-XX, ed. Simonetta Cavaciocchi. Florence: Le Monnier, 1993), p. 802.
129. Evelyn presented his pamphlet at Arundel House on December 7, 1661, and on October 18, 1666 he noted he had "sometime before" presented it to the King to read. John Evelyn, *The Diary of John Evelyn*, II, pp. 180, 262; Evelyn, *Tyrannus, Or, The Mode in a Discourse of Sumptuary Lawes*, p. 14.
130. October 8, 1666, Robert Latham and William Matthews, eds., *The Diary of Samuel Pepys: 1666*, vol. 7. Berkeley and Los Angeles: University of California Press, 1974, p. 315.
131. Some credit Charles's fashion with originating the three-piece suit. For more on Charles II and the vest, see Vincent, *Dressing the Elite*, pp. 1–4; David Kuchta, *The Three-Piece Suit and Modern Masculinity: England, 1550–1850*. Berkeley and London: University of California Press, 2002, pp. 1–2.
132. COL/CA/01/01/19, 78v.

Chapter 4

1. No modern edition of this text exists. For an online facsimile of the second edition (1697), see: http://gallica.bnf.fr/ark:/12148/bpt6k55297429.r=. For the biography of Domat, see: Paul Nourrisson, *Un ami de Pascal, Jean Domat*. Paris: Sirey, 1939; Nicola Matteucci, *Jean Domat, un magistrato giansenista*. Bologne: Il Mulino, 1959; Ernst Holthöfer, "Domat, Jean," *Juristen: ein biographisches Lexikon; von der Antike bis zum 20. Jahrhundert*, Michael Stolleis (ed.), 2nd edn. Munich: C. H. Beck, 2001, p. 180.
2. On the Jansenist movement, the references are: Augustin Gazier, *Histoire générale du mouvement janséniste depuis ses origines jusqu'à nos jours*. 2 vols. Paris: Honoré Champion, 1924; Jean-Pierre Chantin, *Le jansénisme*. Paris: CERF, 1996; William Doyle, *Jansenism: Catholic Resistance to Authority from the Reformation to the French Revolution*. New York: St. Martin's Press, 1999.
3. Jean Domat, *Les lois civiles*, p. 72.
4. On the role of Racine in the Jansenist movement, see Lucien Goldmann, *Le Dieu caché. Étude sur la vision tragique dans les Pensées de Pascal et dans le théâtre de Racine*. Paris: Gallimard, 1955; Marie-Florine Bruneau, *Racine. Le jansénisme et la modernité*. Paris: José Corti, 1986.

5. Jean Racine, "Les plaideurs," *Œuvres complètes. I. Théâtre, poésie*, ed. Georges Forestier. Paris: Gallimard, 1999. On the place of *Les plaideurs* in Racine's life, see Georges Forestier,. *Jean Racine*. Paris: Gallimard, 2006.
6. The reference reproduction of *Le contrat de mariage* is featured in the *catalogue raisonné* of Watteau's oeuvre edited by Jean Ferré: *Watteau*, ed. Jean Ferré. 4 vols. Madrid: Athena, 1972. On Watteau in general, read Guillaume Glorieux, *Watteau*. Paris: Citadelles et Mazenod, 2011.
7. For *L'accordée de village*, see Jean Martin et Charles Masson, *Catalogue raisonné de l'œuvre peint et dessiné de Jean-Baptiste Greuze, suivi de la liste des gravures exécutées d'après ses ouvrages*. Paris: 1908. On Greuze, read Camille Mauclair, *Greuze et son temps*. Paris: Albin Michel, 1935.
8. Cf. Denis Diderot, *Salons*, ed. Michel Delon. Paris: Gallimard, 2008.
9. On the role of Domat in the elaboration of the French Civil Code, see André-Jean Arnaud, *Les origines doctrinales du Code civil français*. Paris: LGDJ, 1969; Jacques Ghestin, "Jean Domat et le Code civil français," *Scritti in onore di Rodolfo Sacco. La comparazione giuridica alle soglie del 3e millennio*, ed. Paolo Cendon. t. I. Milan: Giuffrè, 1994, pp. 533 *et seq.*
10. Pierre Choderos de Laclos. *Les liaisons dangereuses*. Catriona Seth (ed.) Paris: Gallimard, 2011. See also Jean-Paul Bertaud. *Choderlos de Laclos, l'auteur des "Liaisons dangereuses."* Paris: Fayard, 2003.
11. Giacomo Casanova, *Histoire de ma vie*, ed. Gérard Lahouati and Marie-Françoise Luna. 3 vols. Paris: Gallimard, 2013–2015.
12. Donatien Antoine François de Sade, "Les cent vingt journées de Sodome, ou l'école du libertinage," *Oeuvres*, ed. Michel Delon. t. I. Paris: Gallimard, 1990. On the relationship between Sade and the law, see François Ost, *Sade et la loi*. Paris: Odile Jacob, 2005; Bernard Edelman, *Sade, le désir et le droit*. Paris: L'Herne, 2014.
13. Cf. Gilles Deleuze, *Présentation de Sacher-Masoch. Le froid et le cruel*. Paris: Minuit, 1969. For a commentary, see Laurent de Sutter, *Deleuze, la pratique du droit*. Paris: Michalon, 2009.
14. On this tradition, see Jean Terrel, *Les théories du pacte social. Droit naturel, souveraineté et contrat de Bodin à Rousseau*. Paris: Seuil, 2001.
15. Jean-Jacques Rousseau, *Du contrat social, ou principes de droit politique*, ed. Gérard Mairet. Paris: LGF, 1996. For commentaries, see Robert Derathé, *Jean-Jacques Rousseau et la politique de son temps*. Paris: PUF, 1950; Louis Althusser, *Sur le contrat social* (1967); Patrick Hochart, *Houilles*, Paris: Manucius, 2008; Louis Althusser, *Cours sur Rousseau* (1972), ed. Yves Vargas. Paris: Le Temps des Cerises, 2012.
16. On this history, see the monumental work of Michael Stolleis, *Geschichte des öffentlichen Rechts in Deutschland*. 4 vols. Munich: C. H. Beck, 1988–2012. See also Olivier Jouanjan, *Une histoire de la pensée juridique allemande (1800–1918). Idéalisme et conceptualisme chez les juristes allemands du 19e siècle*. Munich: PUF, 2005.
17. Cf. Deleuze, *Présentation de Sacher-Masoch*.
18. Immanuel Kant, *Akademie*-Textausgabe. Band 4, *Kritik der reinen Vernunft (1. Aufl. 1781); Prolegomena; Grundlegung zur Metaphysik der Sitten; Metaphysische Anfangsgründe der Naturwissenschaften*. Berlin: de Gruyter, 1978. For a commentary, see Simone Goyard-Fabre, *La philosophie du droit de Kant*. Paris: Vrin, 1996.
19. Robert-Joseph Pothier, *Traité des obligations*, ed. Jean-Louis Halpérin. Paris: Dalloz, 2011. See Arnaud, *Les origines doctrinales du Code civil français*; Robert-Joseph Pothier, *d'hier à aujourd'hui*, ed. Joël Monéger. Paris: Economica, 2001.
20. On Pothier, read Jean-Louis Sourioux, "Pothier ou le sphinx d'Orléans" 2004. 30 *Droits* 69–75.

21. Harold J. Berman, *Law and Revolution II: The Impact of the Protestant Reformations on the Western Legal Tradition*. Cambridge, MA: The Belknap Press, 2006.
22. Blaise Pascal, *Les provinciales*, ed. Michel Le Guern. Paris: Gallimard, 1987. On the context of this controversy, see Gérard Ferreyrolles, *Les Provinciales de Pascal*. Paris: PUF, 1984; Pierre Cariou, *Pascal et la casuistique*, Paris: PUF, 1993.
23. Excerpts from Suárez' *Tractatus* are available in English in Francisco Suárez, *Selections from Three Works by Francisco Suárez, S.J.: "De legibus, ac deo legislatore," 1612; "Defensio fidei catholicae, et apostolicae adversus anglicanae sectae errores," 1613; "De triplici virtute theologica, fide, spe, et charitate,"* 1621, trans. Gwladys L. Williams, Ammi Brown, and John Waldron. Buffalo, NY: WS Hein, 1995. For a commentary, see Jean-François Courtine, *Nature et empire de la loi. Études suaréziennes*. Paris: Vrin, 1999.
24. On all this, see Susan Byrne, *Law and History in Cervantes' Don Quixote*. Toronto, University of Toronto Press, 2012. See also Laurent de Sutter, "The Quixote Principle, or Cervantes as a Critique of Law" 2014. 26(1) *Law and Literature* 117.
25. William Shakespeare, *The Merchant of Venice*, ed. John Drakakis. London: Methuen, 2011. Cf. *Shakespeare and the Law*, ed. Paul Raffield and Gary Watt. Oxford: Hart Publishing Ltd, 2009; *The Law in Shakespeare*, ed. Constance Jordan and Karen Cunningham. Basingstoke: Palgrave Macmillan, 2010; François Ost, *Shakespeare. La comédie de la loi*. Paris: Michalon, 2012; *Shakespeare and the Law: A Conversation among Disciplines and Professions*, ed. Bradin Cormack, Martha C. Nussbaum and Richard Streier. Chicago: University of Chicago Press, 2013.
26. Samuel Johnson, "Debtor's Prisons," *The Major Works*, ed. Donald Greene. 2nd edn. Oxford: Oxford University Press, 2000, pp. 285 *et seq.*
27. Ibid., p. 285.
28. Ibid.
29. Ibid., p. 286.
30. Ibid., p. 285. On Johnson and his biographical relationship to debt, read Peter Martin, *Samuel Johnson: A Biography*. Cambridge, MA: The Belknap Press, 2008.
31. On this painting, read David Bomford and Ashok Roy, "Hogarth's 'Marriage à la mode'" *National Gallery Technical Bulletin*, no. 6, 1982, pp. 45 *et seq.* More generally, see Ronald Paulson, *William Hogarth*. 3 vols. New Brunswick, NJ: Rutgers University Press, 1991–1993.
32. Christopher Marlowe, *The Complete Works of Christopher Marlowe*, Volume 2: *Doctor Faustus*, ed. Roma Gill (ed.)., Oxford: Oxford University Press, 1990.
33. Laurence Sterne, *The Life and Opinions of Tristram Shandy, Gentleman*, ed. Melvyn and Joan New. London: Penguin, 2003. On the place of *Tristram Shandy* in Sterne's life, see Arthur H. Cash, *Laurence Sterne*. 2 vols. London: Methuen, 1975–1986.
34. John Locke, *The Clarendon Edition of the Works of John Locke: An Essay Concerning Human Understanding*, ed. Peter H. Nidditch. London: Clarendon, 1975. For a guide, see Jonathan Lowe, *Locke on Human Understanding*. London: Routledge, 1995. On the influence of Locke on Sterne, read *Laurence Sterne's Tristram Shandy: A Casebook*, ed. Thomas Keymer. Oxford: Oxford University Press, 2006; and *The Cambridge Companion to Laurence Sterne*, ed. Thomas Keymer. Cambridge: Cambridge University Press, 2009.
35. Laurence Sterne, *The Life and Opinions of Tristram Shandy*, p. I, 15.
36. Roland Barthes, "L'effet de réel" *Oeuvres complètes*, t. III, *1968–1971*, ed. Eric Marty. Paris: Le Seuil, 2002, pp. 25 *et seq.*
37. On this point, see Laurent de Sutter, "Legal Shandeism: The Law in Laurence Sterne's *Tristram Shandy*" 2011. 23(2) *Law and Literature* 224.
38. Cf. Roland Barthes, *Sade, Fourier, Loyola*, in *Oeuvres complètes*, t. III, *1968–1971*, pp. 699 *et seq.*

39. Cf. Jean Terrel, *Les théories du pacte social*.
40. On this tradition, read *La contre-révolution. Origines, histoire, postérité*, ed. Jean Tulard. Paris: Perrin, 1990.

Chapter 5

1. John Doderidge, *The English Lawyer*. London: Moore, 1631, p. 32. See also Thomas Wilson, *The Rule of Reason Containing the Arte of Logicke*. London: Richard Grafton, 1551.
2. William Fulbecke, for example, objected to the ornaments of rhetoric in law yet advocated following the examples provided by Cicero. See William Fulbecke, *Directive or Preparative to the Study of Law* 1600. London: W.T. Clarke (1829 edn). For the broader terms of anti-Ciceronian rhetoric see Petrus Ramus, *Brutinae Questiones*. Carole Newlands tr. Davis CA: Hermagoras Press, 1993.
3. Elizabeth Eisenstein, *The Printing Press as an Agent of Change: Communication and Cultural Transformations in Early Modern Europe*. Cambridge: Cambridge University Press, 1982.
4. *Ramus, Method and the Decay of Dialogue*. Chicago: University of Chicago Press, 1985. Walter Ong, *Orality and Literacy; The Technologizing of the Word*. London: Routledge, 2002.
5. See Shaun McVeigh, "Postmodernism and Common Law" in Reza Banakar and Max Travers, eds., *An Introduction to Law and Social Theory*. Oxford: Hart Publishing, 2002, pp. 267–283.
6. Bartolus de Saxoferrato, *De Insigniis et armis* (1358) in Evan John Evans, ed., *Medieval History*. Cardiff: Lewis, 1943.
7. Gerard Legh, *The Accedens of Armory*. London: Richard Totell, 1562; Abraham Fraunce, *Insignia, Armorum, Emblematum, Hieroglyphicum et Sumbolorum*. London: Orwin, 1588.
8. Peter Goodrich, *Legal Emblems and the Art of Law: Obiter Depicta as the Vision of Governance*. Cambridge: Cambridge University Press, 2015.
9. Michel Foucault, "What is Enlightenment?" in *The Foucault Reader*, ed. Paul Rabinow. New York: Pantheon 1985, p. 38.
10. Claude Mignault, "A Treatise on Symbols, on the Theory of Coats of Arms and Figures which are Commonly called Insignia or Family Badges, and on Emblems" in *Emblematum Liber*, ed. Andreas Alciato. Antwerp: Plantin, 1577, p. 43.
11. Ibid. at p. 43. See also Quintilian, *Institutio Oratoria*, H. E. Butler tr. Oxford: Loeb 2.4 27.
12. The allusions are, of course, to Shakespeare's *King John* (the quotations are taken from *King John*, ed. W. Braunmuller. Oxford: Oxford University Press, 2008 IV).
13. Alciato, *Emblematum Liber*, n. 13.
14. Valérie Hayaert, *Mens Emblematica et Humanism Juridique*. Droz, 2008. For further analyses on the relationship between law and emblems see Dennis Drysdall, *Hieroglyphs, Speaking, Pictures and the Law: The Context of Alciato's Emblems*. Glasgow: Emblem Studies, 2013, and Peter Goodrich, *Legal Emblems*.
15. Henry Peacham, *Manuscript Emblem Books*, ed. Alan Young and Peter Daly. Toronto: University of Toronto Press, 1999.
16. Thomas Murner, *Logica Memorativa* (1509). Leiden: E. J. Brill, 1967. See also Walter Ong, *Orality and Literacy*, p. 91.
17. Robert Burton, *Anatomy of Melancholy*. London: Dent, 1932.
18. Gerard Gennette, *Paratext*. Cambridge: Cambridge University Press, 2010.
19. See Burton, *Anatomy of Melancholy*.
20. Ibid., at p. 8.
21. John Manning, *Emblems*. London: Reaktion, 2002.
22. Cicero., *Murder Trials*. Dover: Thrift, 1990.

23. Ludwig Wittgenstein, *Tractatus Logico-Philosophicus*. D. F Pears and B. F. McGuiness tr. London: Routledge, 1961 at 5.123.
24. Alan Watson, ed., *The Digest of Justinian*. Philadelphia: University of Pennsylvania Press 1998, 1.1.1.
25. *Digest*, 1.1.3.
26. Ibid., at 1.1.2.
27. It might be objected that the visuality of texts, particularly legal texts, was not unknown to medieval legal science. Laws and the epistolary decretals of the papal courts were, of course, highly ornate pieces of legal material and they were not without their own frames. For the glossators, the presentation of the main seat of these ornate texts would be surrounded by extravagant commentary, annotations, and new interpretations of the original law. Surrounding a copy of the *corpus iuris civilis* or a papal decretal with glosses certainly provided a frame of sorts but such a frame must be distinguished from those surrounding emblems. For the glossators, it was the host text sitting imperiously in the centre of the page that determined everything. See Herman Kantorowicz, *Studies in the Glossators of the Roman Law: Newly Discovered Writings of the Twelfth Century*. Cambridge: Cambridge University Press, 1938.
28. Gabrielle Rollenhagen, *Nucleus Emblematum selectissimorum*. Cologne: Crispiani Passaei, 1611; George Wither, *A Collection of Emblems*. Leden: Plantyn, 1586.
29. George Whitney, *Choice of Emblems*. Leden: Plantyn, 1586. Emblem 122. The image is taken from Barthélemy Aneau, *Picta Poesis*. Lyon: France, Bonhommie, 1552 at p. 49. For a discussion of Aneau's image see Goodrich, *Legal Emblems* n. 8 at p. 89.
30. Georg Stengel, *Ova Paschalia; Sacra emblemate inscripta descriptaque*. Munich: Henricus, 1634.
31. This theme is treated more substantially by Goodrich. See Goodrich, *Legal Emblems*, pp. 89–124.
32. See Markus Dubischar. "Typology of Philological Writing" in Franco Montanary, *Brill's Companion to Ancient Greek Scholarship*, ed. Franco Montanary, Stephanos Matthaios and Antonios Rengakos. Vol 1. Boston: Brill, 2015, pp. 545–599.
33. Cicero, *On Duties*. M. T. Griffin and E. M. Atkins tr. Cambridge: Cambridge University Press, 2001, at 1:28.
34. Cicero, *Offices*, at 1.iv.
35. See Piyel Haldar, "The Tongue and the Eye" in Peter Goodrich and Valérie Hayaert eds., *Genealogies of Legal Vision*. Abingdon: Routledge, 2015. See also Piyel Haldar, "Equity as a Question of Decorum and Manners: Conscience as Vision" 2016. Polemos 311–327.
36. Erasmus, *The Adages of Erasmus*, ed. William Barker. Toronto: University of Toronto Press, 2001, at i.ii.15.
37. George Puttenham, *Art of English Poesie*. Cambridge: Cambridge University Press, 1936, at 3.5.
38. Ernst Kantorowicz, *The King's Two Bodies: A Study in Medieval Political Theology*. Princeton: Princeton University Press, 1957.
39. Andreas Alciato, "Praetermissa," 1518 in *Opera Omnia* (Basle, 1557 ed.). 4.1 at 403.
40. Andrea Alciato, "Avignon Oration" In *Nature, Self and History in the Works of Guillaumé Budé, Andreas Alciato and Ulrich Zazius: A Study of the Role of Legal Humanism in Western Natural Law*, ed. Susan Longfield Karr. Chicago: University of Chicago Press, 2008, at p. 209.
41. Junius Hadrianus, *Emblemata*. Antwerp: Christophe Plantin, 1565, Emblem v ("*Vita Mortalium vigila*").

42. Peter Goodrich, *Legal Emblems*, p. 243.
43. Ernst Kantorowicz, "The Sovereignty of the Artist" in *Selected Studies*. Locus Valley, NY: J.J. Augustin, 1965, pp. 352–365.
44. Ibid. See also, Milton C. Nahm, "The Theological Background of the Artist as Creator" 1947. 8(3) *Journal for the History of Ideas* 363–372.
45. Cicero, *On the Nature of Gods*, H. Rackham tr. Oxford: Loeb, 1933, at 2.5.
46. In a letter to Zwinger (May 14, 1579), Alciato writes: "Our religious disputes are so heated, that I would rather keep aloof for quite some time than hear and watch distressing, unfair things every day; the external sensitivities slow down my writing completely." Cited in Arnoud Visser, "Escaping the Reformation in the Republic of Letters: Confessional Silence in Latin Emblem Books" 2008. 88(2) *Church History and Religious Culture* 139–167.
47. Cicero, *On Duties*, 31 2.14.51
48. Chaim Perelman, *Justice, Law and Argument: Essays on Moral and Legal Reasoning*. Dordrecht: Reidel, 1980, p. 163.
49. Puttenham, *Art of English Poesie*, at 3.4.
50. Calvin Rom 9:2 cited in Jurislav Pelikan, *The Christian Tradition: A History of the Development of Doctrine. Reformation of Church and Dogma*. Chicago: University of Chicago Press, 1985, at p. 231.
51. Henry Peacham, *Minerva Britannica or a Garden of Heroical Devices* (1612). Available at: https://archive.org/details/minervabritannao00peac.
52. Puttenham, *Art of English Poesie*, at 25.3
53. William Bullein, *A Dialogue against Fever Pestilence* (1564). London: Early English Texts, 1888.
54. Thomas Wilson, *The Arte of Rhetorique* (1553), ed. Thomas Derrick. New York: Garland, 1982, p. 6. preface sig. A3v.
55. St. Augustine, *On Christian Doctrine*. New York: Dover Publications, 2009, p. 102.
56. Nicholas de Cusa, *On Learned Ignorance*. Paul Wilpert, Ernest Hoffmann and Raymond Klibansky tr. Minneapolis: Arthur J. Banning, 1981.
57. William Harrison, *The Difference of Hearers*. London. T. Creed, 1614, at p. 20.
58. Ralph Lever, *The Art of Reason, Rightly trermed witcraft teaching a perfect way to argue and dispute*. London: Bynnemann, 1573.
59. Ibid., at p. 17.
60. Ibid., at p. 23.
61. Thomas Wright, *Passions of the Mind in General*, 1601. New York: Garland Press, 1986, at p. 45.
62. Chaim Perelman and Lucie Obrechts-Tytreca, *The New Rhetoric: A Treatise on Argumentation*. Notre Dame, IN: University of Notre Dame Press, 1991.
63. Pierre Legendre, "The Dogmatic Value of Aesthetics" 2008. 14(4) *Parallax* 10, 17.
64. Peter Goodrich, "Spectres of Law: Why the History of Legal Spectacle Has Not Been Written" 2011. 1(3) *UC Irvine Law Review* 773.

Chapter 6

1. T. W. Adorno and M. Horkheimer, *The Dialectic of Enlightenment*, trans. J. Cumming. London: Verso, 2010, p. 7.
2. N. Davidson, "Marx and Engels on the Scottish Highlands" 2001. *Science & Society* 286–326; P. M. Sweezy, and M. Dobb, "The Transition from Feudalism to Capitalism" 1950. *Science & Society* 134–167; the most recent interventions into this debate at time of

writing are S. Dimmock, *The Origins of Capitalism in England, 1400–1600*. Leiden: Brill, 2014 and A. Anievas and K. Nisancioglu, *How the West Came to Rule*. Chicago: University of Chicago Press, 2015.

3. G. Caffentzis and S. Federici, "Commons against and beyond Capitalism" 2014. 49(1) *Community Development Journal* 92–105.
4. D. Willis, "Shakespeare's Tempest and the Discourse of Colonialism" 1989. 29(2) *Studies in English literature, 1500–1900* 277–289; J. D. Rea, "A Source for the Storm in The Tempest" 1919. 17(5) *Modern Philology* 279–286. For a class analysis of the characters in the play, see P. Linebaugh and M. Rediker, *The Many-Headed Hydra*. Boston: Beacon, 2000, pp. 14–32.
5. *The Tempest*, 2.1, ll. 851–868.
6. Ibid., 2.1, ll. 869–874.
7. "Dreamer and cynics" as Edgell Rickword and Jack Lindsay put it: *Spokesmen for Liberty*. London: Lawrence and Wishart, 1941, p. 103.
8. S. Greenblatt, "Shakespeare's Montaigne" in S. Greenblatt and P. Platt, *The Florio Translation of the Essays*. New York: New York Review Books Classics, 2014, pp. ix–xxxiii. Also see P. Mack, *Reading and Rhetoric in Montaigne and Shakespeare*, 2010; A. T. Vaughan and V. M. Vaughan, *Shakespeare's Caliban: A Cultural History*, 1993; A. Harman, "How Great Was Shakespeare's Debt to Montaigne?" 1942. French original in F. Lestringant ed., *Le Brésil de Montaigne*. Paris: 2005, p. 103.
9. S. Greenblatt and P, Platt, *The Florio Translation of the Essays*. New York: New York Review of Books Classics, 2014, p. 61.
10. M. Koskenniemi, "Colonization of the 'Indies': The Origin of International Law" *La Idea de América en el Pensamiento ius Internacionalista del Siglo XXI*. Universidad de Zaragoza, 2010, pp. 43–64.
11. H. Yoran, *Between Utopia and Dystopia: Erasmus, Thomas More, and the Humanist Republic of Letters*. Lexington: Lexington Books, 2010.
12. T. More, *Utopia*, in *The Complete Works of St. Thomas More*. Vol. 4. Princeton: Yale University Press, 1965, p. 107: See the discussion in J. Phillips, *English Fictions of Communal Identity, 1485–1603*. Farnham: Ashgate, 2010, p. 44.
13. *The Works of Gerrard Winstanley, with an Appendix of Documents Related to the Digger Movement*, ed. George H. Sabine. New York: Russell and Russell, 1941/1965, p. 270.
14. O. Langholm, "The German Tradition in Late Medieval Value Theory" 2008. 15(4) *The European Journal of the History of Economic Thought* 555–570.
15. M. Tronti, *La politica al tramonto*. Turin: Einaudi, 1998, p. 9.
16. T. Herzog, "Colonial Law and 'Native Customs': Indigenous Land Rights in Colonial Spanish America" 2013. 69(3) *The Americas* 303–321.
17. For the purposes of this work, we omit here the bondage of serfs, which was a technically contractual relation for labor services, and not a law of property, even if it approximated it.
18. T. D. Morris, *Southern Slavery and the Law, 1619–1860*. Chapel Hill: University of North Carolina Press, 1996, p. 41.
19. Ibid., p. 39.
20. V. Carey, R. Bogdan, and E. A. Walsh (eds.), *Voices for Tolerance in an Age of Persecution*. Washington: Folger Shakespeare Library, 2004, p. 103.
21. D. Booy, ed., *Personal Disclosures: An Anthology of Self-Writings from the Seventeenth Century*. Aldershot: Ashgate, 2002, p. 309.
22. R. Brenner, *Merchants and Revolution: Commercial Change, Political Conflict and London's Overseas Traders, 1550–1653*. London: Verso, 2003, p. 164.

23. In the eighteenth century a new body of law would develop through precedent to confront the problems of that unusual quality of these objects, their sexual reproduction.
24. Morris, *Southern Slavery and the Law*, pp. 4, 19–20.
25. D. R. Roediger, *The Wages of Whiteness: Race and the Making of the American Working Class*. New York: Verso, 1999, pp. 29–30.
26. J. B. Felt, *A Memoir of Defence of Hugh Peters*. Boston: C.C.P. Moody, 1851, p. 32. See also, A. Fitzmaurice, *Sovereignty, Property and Empire, 1500–2000*. Cambridge: Cambridge University Press, 2014.
27. R. Ligon, *A True and Exact History of the Island of Barbados*. Indianapolis: Hackett, 2011, p. 59.
28. Ibid., p. 64.
29. Reference is made here to Rachel Speght's (1597) *A Mouzell for Melastomus*. London, 1617.
30. See C. Fell, *Women in Anglo-Saxon England and the Impact of 1066*. Bloomington: Indiana University Press, 1984, pp. 56–59.
31. M. De Grazia, M. Quilligan, and P. Stallybrass, eds., *Subject and Object in Renaissance Culture*. Cambridge: Cambridge University Press, 1996. See also W. Coyle, "Common Law Metaphors of Coverture: Conceptions of Women and Children as Property in Legal and Literary Contexts" 1992. 1 *Texas Journal of Women and the Law* 315.
32. See S.P. Menefee, *Wives for Sale: An Ethnographic Study of British Popular Divorce*. Oxford: Basil Blackwell, 1981, pp. 21–59.
33. See the detailed analysis by M. de Grazia, "The Ideology of Superfluous Things: *King Lear* as Period Piece" in *Subject and Object in Renaissance Culture*, ed. de Grazia, Quilligan and Stallybrass, pp. 17–42; quotation at p. 21.
34. E. Cary, *The Tragedy of Mariam, Faire Queene of Jewry* (3.3, 227–38).
35. T. Stretton, *Women Waging Law in Elizabethan England*. Cambridge: Cambridge University Press, 1998, p. 47.
36. B. S. Travitsky and A. L. Prescott, eds., "The Lawes Resolutions of Women's Rights," in *Legal Treatises*. 3 vols. *The Early Modern Englishwoman: A Facsimile Library of Essential Works, Series III. Essential Works for the Study of Early Modern Women: Part I*. Aldershot: Ashgate, 2005.
37. R. Speght, *A mouzell for Melastomus, the cynicall bayter of, and foule mouthed barker against Euahs sex*. London: Printed by Nicholas Okes for Thomas Archer, 1617, p. 15.
38. J. Greenberg, "The Legal Status of the English Woman in Eighteenth-century Common Law and Equity" 1974. 4 *Studies in Eighteenth-century Culture* 178.
39. L. Gowing, *Domestic Dangers: Women, Words, and Sex in Early Modern London*. Oxford: Oxford University Press, 1996, p. 178. See T. Stretton. *Women Waging Law in Elizabethan England*. Cambridge: Cambridge University Press, 1998, p. 34.
40. See M. MacCurtain and M. O'Dowd, eds., *Women in Early Modern Ireland*. Dublin: Wolfhound Press, 1992, and R. R. Davies, "Property Interests in the Classical Welsh Law of Women," in *The Welsh Law of Women: Studies Presented to Professor Daniel A. Binchy on his 80th Birthday*, ed. D. Jenkins and M. E. Owen. Cardiff: University of Wales Press, 1980; F. Kelly, *A Guide to Early Irish Law*. Dublin: Dublin Institute for Advanced Studies, 1988; and A. Laurence. "Women and the Transmission of Property: Inheritance in the British Isles in the 17th Century" 2009. 244(3) *Dix-septième siècle* 435–450.
41. Ibid. See also for the wider context, H. S. Turner, ed., *The Culture of Capital: Property, Cities, and Knowledge in Early Modern England*. New York: Routledge, 2002.

42. M. Chan and N. E. Wright, "Marriage, Identity, and the Pursuit of Property in Seventeenth-century England: The Cases of Anne Clifford and Elizabeth Wiseman" in Wright, Ferguson and Buck, 2004, pp. 165–168.
43. Anne Clifford, Great Books, Claim and Title (Hothfield Manuscripts on file with the Cumbria Record Office, Kendal Archive Center; WD/Hoth/A988/10). See C. Spivack, "Law, Land, Identity: The Case of Lady Anne Clifford" 2012. 87(2) *Women's Legal History: A Global Perspective* 393.
44. P. Salzman, "Early Modern (Aristocratic) Women and Textual Property" in Wright, Ferguson and Buck, 2004, p. 285. See also P. Brand. "'Deserving' and 'Undeserving' Wives: Earning and Forfeiting Dower in Medieval England" 2001. 22 *Legal History* 1–20.
45. As quoted in J. P. Ingram, *Idioms of Self-Interest—Credit, Identity and Property in Renaissance Literature*. New York/London: Routledge, 2006, p. 2. See also, Andrew Zurcher, *Spenser's Legal Language—Law and Poetry in Early Modern England*. Cambridge: Cambridge University Press, 2007.
46. Ibid., p. 91.
47. Ibid. See also B. K. Lewalski, "Re-Writing Patriarchy and Patronage: Margaret Clifford, Anne Clifford, and Aemilia Lanyer" 1991. 21 *The Yearbook of English Studies* 104–106; and P. Hammons, "Rethinking Women and Property in Sixteenth and Seventeenth-Century England" 2006. 3(6) *Literature Compass* 1386–1407.
48. See B. Lemire, *The Business of Everyday Life: Gender, Practice and Social Politics in England, c. 1600–1900*. Manchester: Manchester University Press, 2005.
49. N. Korda, *Shakespeare's Domestic Economies: Gender and Property in Early Modern England*. Pennsylvania: Pennsylvania University Press, 2008, p. 8.
50. Ibid.
51. "I will be master of what is mine own.
    She is my goods, my chattels. She is my house,
    My house-hold stuff, my field, my barn,
    My horse, my ox, my ass, my anything": 3.3.100–3.
52. Korda, *Shakespeare's Domestic Economies*, p. 175.
53. See F. E. Dolan, "Home-Rebels and House-Traitors: Murderous Wives in Early Modern England" 1992. 4 *Yale Journal of Law & the Humanities* 25–27; and F. E. Dolan, "Gender, Moral Agency, and Dramatic Form in a Warning for Fair Women" 1989. 29 *Studies in English Literature* 201–218; and B. S. Travitsky, "Husband-Murder and Petty Treason in English Renaissance Tragedy" 1990. 21 *Renaissance Drama*, new series 171–198; and D. Underdown, "The Taming of the Scold: The Enforcement of Patriarchal Authority in Early Modern England" in Anthony Fletcher and John Stevenson (eds.), *Order and Disorder in Early Modern England* Cambridge: Cambridge University Press, 1985, pp. 116–136.
54. F. E. Dolan, "Home-Rebels and House-Traitors" at p. 7; quoting C. Z. Wiener, "Is a Spinster an Unmarried Woman?" 1976. 20(1) *American Journal of Legal History* 30.
55. As well as Dolan's articles above, see P. Stallybrass, "Patriarchal Territories: The Body Enclosed" in *Rewriting the Renaissance: The Discourses of Sexual Difference in Early Modern Europe*, ed. M. W. Ferguson, M. Quilligan, and N. J. Vickers. Chicago: University of Chicago Press, 1986, pp. 123–142.
56. See C. Jordan, "Woman's Rule in Sixteenth-century British Political Thought" 1987. 40(3) *Renaissance Quarterly* 435; and M. E. Doggett, *Marriage, Wife-Beating and the Law in Victorian England*. London: Weidenfeld & Nicolson, 1992; and N. E. Wright,

M. W. Ferguson and A. R. Buck, eds., *Women: Property and the Letters of the Law in Early Modern England*. Toronto: University of Toronto Press, 2004; and R. Hillman and P. Ruberry-Blanc, eds., *Female Transgression in Early Modern Britain: Literary and Historical Explorations*. Farnham: Ashgate, 2014, p. 196.

57. S. Federici, *Caliban and the Witch*, Autonomedia, pp. 85–87, 171.
58. *Henry V*, 5.2.39–60. See the analysis of J. R. Siemon, "Landlord Not King: Agrarian Change and Interarticulation" in Burt and Archer, 2004, pp. 17–33.
59. Ibid., p. 19.
60. J. G. Harris, "This is Not a Pipe: Water Supply, Incontinent Sources and the Leaky Body Politic" in *Enclosure Acts—Sexuality, Property and Culture in Early Modern England*, ed. R. Burt and J. M. Archer. Ithaca/London: Cornell University Press, 1994, p. 203.
61. Ibid., p. 203; Song of Songs 4.12 (Geneva Bible).
62. See, for instance, the analysis of A. Marvell's "Nature" in C. Rees, *The Judgment of Marvell*. London: Pinter, 1989, pp. 142–143 and the discussion from which we drew inspiration in J. Rogers, "The Enclosure of Virginity: The Poetics of Sexual Abstinence in the English Revolution," in *Enclosure Acts—Sexuality, Property and Culture in Early Modern England*, ed. R. Burt and J. M. Archer. Ithaca/London: Cornell University Press, 1994, pp. 229–250.
63. A. Marvell, *The Poems and Letters of Andrew Marvell*, ed. H. M. Margoliouth, vol. 1. Oxford: Clarendon Press, 1971, "Upon Appleton House," stanza 59. See the analysis in C. Malcolmson. "The Garden Enclosed/The Woman Enclosed: Marvell and the Cavalier Poets," in Burt and Archer, 1994, pp. 261–266.
64. See P. Seed, *Ceremonies of Possession in Europe's Conquest of the New World, 1492–1640*. Cambridge: Cambridge University Press, 1995.
65. Ibid., pp. 18–19.
66. Ibid., pp. 20–21.
67. Ibid., pp. 32–33.
68. The English terms "commons" and "communing" have been widely employed by Antonio Negri and Michael Hardt, who derive the terms from E. P. Thompson and his research colleagues at Warwick in the 1970s, most notably Janet Neeson and Peter Linebaugh. See also K. Eden, *Friends Hold All Things in Common*. New Haven/London: Yale University Press, 2001.
69. See on this the central influence of E. P. Thompson's *Customs in Common*. London: Merlin Press, 1991, chapter 3 as well as P. Collinson's *De Republica Anglorum: or, History with the Politics Put Back*. Cambridge: Cambridge University Press, 1989.
70. A. Wood, "The Place of Custom in Plebeian Political Culture: England 1550–1800" 1997. 22(1) *Social History* 46–60 at 47. See also, A. Kiralfy, "Custom in Medieval English Law" 1988. 9(1) *Journal of Legal History* 26 at 33–34.
71. See G. C. Comninel, "English Feudalism and the Origins of Capitalism" 2000. 27(4) *The Journal of Peasant Studies* 1–53 at 4.
72. On the development of early modern property rights see D. Seipp, "The Concept of Property in the Early Common Law" 1994. 12 *Law and History Review* 29–91; in particular, as to the late-sixteenth and crucial seventeenth century see M. Sampson, "'Property' in Seventeenth-century English Political Thought" in *Religion, Resistance and Civil War: Papers Presented at the Folger Institute Seminar*, ed. G. Schochet, P. Tatspaugh and C. Brobeck. Washington, 1990, pp. 259–275.
73. Ibid., p. 38. See also generally A. W. B. Simpson, *A History of the Land Law*. 2nd edn. Oxford: Oxford University Press, 1986.

74. See F. Bacon, *The Essays, or Counsels Civil and Moral* (1587; 1882 edn.), pp. 219–220 and as discussed in Wood, *The Place of Custom*, p. 48. See also, on the way custom affected the definition of property in law, G. Aylmer, "The Meaning and Definition of 'Property' in Seventeenth-century England" 1980. 86 *Past and Present* 87.
75. See, for instance, J. C. Davis, "Radicalism in a Traditional Society: The Evaluation of Radical Thought in the English Commonwealth 1649–60" 1982. 3(2) *History of Political Thought* 193–213, and A. Randall, *Before the Luddites: Custom, Community and Machinery in the English Woollen Industry 1776–1809*. Cambridge: Cambridge University Press, 1991. See further, H. R. French, "The Common Fields of Urban England: Communal Agriculture and the 'Politics of Entitlement', 1500–1750" in *Custom, Improvement and the Landscape in Early Modern England*, ed. R.W. Hoyle. Ashgate, 2011, pp. 149–175.
76. See J. G. A. Pocock, *The Ancient Constitution and the Feudal Law: A Study of English Historical Thought in the Seventeenth Century. A Reissue with Retrospect*. Cambridge: Cambridge University Press, 1987, pp. 42–47.
77. Wood, *The Place of Custom*, p. 56. On the protests and conflicts see, for instance, S. Hondle, "Persuasion and Protest in the Caddington Common Enclosure Dispute, 1635–1639" 1998. 158(1) *Past and Present* 37–78, and S. Hipkin, "Sitting on his Penny Rent: Conflict and Right of Common in Faversham Blean, 1595–1610" 2000. 11(1) *Rural History* 1–35; B. McDonagh, "Subverting the Ground: Private Property and Public Protest in the Sixteenth-century Yorkshire Wolds" 2009. 57(2) *Agricultural History Review* 191–206.
78. M. McKeon, "Historicizing Patriarchy: The Emergence of Gender Difference in England, 1660–1760" 1995. 28(3) *Eighteenth-century Studies* 295–322 at 299.
79. See J. A. Guy, *The Cardinal's Court: The Impact of Thomas Wolsey in Star Chamber*. Hassocks: Harvester, 1977.
80. B. McDonagh, "Making and Breaking Property: Negotiating Enclosure and Common Rights in Sixteenth-century England" 2013. 76 *History Workshop Journal* 32–56 at 35–36.
81. Ibid. Other forms of direct action involved, for instance, hedge breakings, mass trespasses, and impounding animals. See also, B. Sharp, *In Contempt of all Authority: Rural Artisans and Riot in the West of England, 1586–1660*. Berkeley: University of California Press, 1980, and N. Whyte, *Inhabiting the Landscape: Place, Custom and Memory, 1500–1800*. Oxford: Windgather Press, 2009.
82. Brenner, *Merchants and Revolution*, p. 105.
83. Ibid., p. 618, *our emphasis*.
84. Ibid., p. 507.
85. C. Hill, *The Century of the Revolution*. 2nd edn. London: Routledge, 1980, p. 161.
86. C. Hill, *Winstanley "The Law of Freedom" and Other Writings*. Cambridge: Cambridge University Press, 2006, p. 97.
87. M. McKeon, *The Secret History of Domesticity: Public, Private, and the Division of Knowledge*. Baltimore: Johns Hopkins University Press, 2009: also see the discussion in A. Johns, *The Nature of the Book: Print and Knowledge in the Making*. Chicago: University of Chicago Press, 1998.
88. R. Atkyns, *The Original and Growth of Printing, Collected Out of History and the Records of this Kingdom*. London: 1664. Available at: http://quod.lib.umich.edu/cgi/t/text/text-idx?c=eebo;idno=A26139.0001.001 (last accessed November 10, 2015).
89. J. H. Baker. *Oxford History of the Laws of England*, Volume 6: *1483–1558*. Oxford: Oxford University Press, 2003, p. 569. For the class struggle over the poaching of deer

in enclosed royal forests, see, of course, E. P. Thompson, *Whigs and Hunters*. London: Penguin Books, 1975.
90. Atkyns, *The Original and Growth of Printing*, p. 18.

Chapter 7

1. Cynthia Herrup, "Law and Morality in Seventeenth Century England" 1984. 106 *Past & Present* 102–123.
2. Tessa Watt, *Cheap Print and Popular Piety, 1550–1640*. Cambridge: Cambridge University Press, 1993.
3. J. A. Sharpe, "'Last Dying Speeches': Religion, Ideology and Public Execution in Seventeenth-Century England" 1985. 107 *Past and Present* 144–167; Lincoln B Faller, *Turned to Account: The Forms and Functions of Criminal Biography in Late Seventeenth and Early Eighteenth-Century England*. Cambridge: Cambridge University Press, 1987.
4. Watt, *Cheap Print and Popular Piety*; Michael Bath, *Renaissance Decorative Painting in Scotland*. Edinburgh: NMS Publishing, 2003; Malcolm Jones, *The Print in Early Modern England: An Historical Oversight*. New Haven, CT; London: Yale University Press, 2010.
5. Arlette Zinck, "Dating the Spiritual Warfare Broadsheet" *The Recorder: Newsletter of the International John Bunyan Society*, 2010, pp. 3–4.
6. Richard H. Helmholz, *The Oxford History of the Laws of England: The Canon Law and Ecclesiastical Jurisdiction from 597 to the 1640s*. Oxford: Oxford University Press, 2004, chapter 4.
7. R. B. Outhwaite, *The Rise and Fall of the English Ecclesiastical Courts, 1500–1860*. Cambridge: Cambridge University Press, 2007, p. 81.
8. Leah Leneman and Rosalind Mitchison, *Sexuality and Social Control: Scotland, 1660–1780*. Oxford: Basil Blackwell, 1989, p. 27; Brian P. Levack, "The Prosecution of Sexual Crimes in Early Eighteenth-Century Scotland" 2010. 89(2) *Scottish Historical Review* 172–193.
9. Dickson, David and Vannet, Alfred D. 2008. "Criminal Procedure." In *The Laws of Scotland: Stair Memorial Encyclopaedia*, Reissue: paragraphs 4–25.
10. James A. Sharpe, *Crime in Early Modern England 1550–1750*. London and New York: Longman, 1999, pp. 30–40.
11. Frederick W. Maitland and Frederick Pollock, *A History of English Law Before the Time of Edward I*. Cambridge: Cambridge University Press, [1898] 1968, p. 453.
12. T. G. Barnes, "The Making of the English Criminal Law (2). Star Chamber and the Sophistication of the Criminal Law" 1977. *Criminal Law Review* 316.
13. William Holdsworth, *History of English Law* (3rd edn, vol. 4). London: Methuen & Co., 1945, pp. 501–503.
14. Stuart Clark, *Thinking with Demons: The Idea of Witchcraft in Early Modern Europe*. Oxford: Oxford University Press. 1999, pp. 607–608.
15. Olivia Robinson, "Law, Morality and Sir George Mackenzie." I *Miscellany VI* (vol. 54), ed. Hector L. MacQueen. Edinburgh: Stair Society, 2009, p. 14.
16. Sharpe, *Crime in Early Modern England 1550–1750*, p. 9; Kenneth McK. Norrie, "The Intentional Delicts" in *A History of Private Law in Scotland* (vol. 2), ed. Kenneth Reid and Reinhard Zimmermann. Oxford: Oxford University Press, 200, p. 477.
17. Francis Charles Stroud Milsom, *Historical Foundations of the Common Law*. London: Butterworths, 1969, chapter 13.
18. Norrie , 'Intentional Delicts'.

19. Hector MacQueen, and W. D. H. Sellar, "Negligence" in *A History of Private Law in Scotland* (vol. 2), ed. Kenneth Reid and Reinhard Zimmermann. Oxford: Oxford University Press, 2000.
20. Milsom, *Foundations*, pp. 332–344; Ian Maclean, *Interpretation and Meaning in the Renaissance: The Case of Law*. Cambridge: Cambridge University Press, 1992, pp. 186–202.
21. John Blackie, "Defamation" in *A History of Private Law in Scotland* (vol. 2), ed. Kenneth Reid and Reinhard Zimmermann Oxford: Oxford University Press, 2000.
22. Clark, *Thinking with Demons*, chapter 33.
23. Ibid., chapter 2; Charles Zika, *The Appearance of Witchcraft: Print and Visual Culture in Sixteenth Century Europe*. London: Routledge, 2007; William de Blécourt, "Sabbath Stories: Towards a New History of Witches' Assemblies" in *The Oxford Handbook of Witchcraft in Early Modern Europe and Colonial America*, ed. Brian P. Levack. Oxford: Oxford University Press, 2013.
24. Levack, *Oxford Handbook*, p. 483.
25. Malcolm Gaskill, *Crime and Mentalities in Early Modern England*. Cambridge: Cambridge University Press, 2000, p. 70.
26. Brian P. Levack, "Introduction" in *The Oxford Handbook of Witchcraft in Early Modern Europe and Colonial America*. Oxford, ed. Brian Levack. Oxford University Press, 2013, p. 4.
27. Norman James, "Defining Superstitions: Treasonous Catholics and the Act against Witchcraft of 1563" in *State, Sovereigns and Society in Early Modern England*, ed. Charles Carlton et al. Stroud: Sutton Publishing, 1998.
28. Julian Goodare, "The Scottish Witchcraft Act" 2005. 74(1) *Church History* 39–67.
29. Paula Hughes, "Witch-Hunting in Scotland, 1649–1650" in *Scottish Witches and Witch-Hunters*, ed. Julian Goodare. Basingstoke: Palgrave Macmillan, 2013, p. 86.
30. P. G. Maxwell-Stuart, "King James's Experience of Witches and the 1604 English Witchcraft Act" in *Witchcraft and the Act of 1604*, ed. John Newton and Jo Bath. Leiden; Boston: Brill, 2008, p. 38.
31. Gibson. 2008., "Applying the Act of 1604: Witches in Essex, Northamptonshire and Lancashire." In John Newton and Jo Bath (eds.), *Witchcraft and the Act of 1604*. Leiden; Boston: Brill.
32. Brian P. Levack, *Witch-Hunting in Scotland: Law, Politics and Religion*. New York: Routledge, 2008, pp. 21–30.
33. George Mackenzie, *The Laws and Customes of Scotland, in Matters Criminal Wherein is to be Seen How the Civil Law, and the Laws and Customs of Other Nations Do Agree with, and Supply Ours*. Edinburgh: James Glen, 1678, p. 88.
34. Helmholz, *The Oxford History of the Laws of England*, p. 634; David M. Walker, *A Legal History of Scotland* (vol. 3). Edinburgh: T&T Clark, 1995, p. 478.
35. Levack, *Witch-Hunting in Scotland*, pp. 30–32.
36. Ibid., chapter 4.
37. Malcolm Gaskill, "Fear Made Flesh: The English Witch-Panic of 1645–1647" in *Moral Panics, the Media and the Law in Early Modern England*, ed. David Lemmings and Claire Walker. Basingstoke: Palgrave Macmillan, 2009, p. 80.
38. Chris Brooks, "Witchcraft and Stage Spectacle: Spectacular Witches after 1604" in *Witchcraft and the Act of 1604*, ed. John Newton and Jo Bath. Leiden; Boston: Brill, 2008.
39. Peter Elmer, "Towards a Politics of Witchcraft in Early Modern England" in *Languages of Witchcraft: Narrative, Ideology and Meaning in Early Modern Culture*, ed. Stuart Clark. Basingstoke: Macmillan, 2001, p. 108.
40. Levack, *Oxford Handbook*, 2013b, p. 482.

41. David J. Parkinson, "'The Legend of the Bischop of St. Androis Lyfe' and the Survival of Scottish Poetry" 2003. 9(1) *Early Modern Literary Studies* pp. 1–24.
42. John L. Teall, "Witchcraft and Calvinism in Elizabethan England: Divine Power and Human Agency" 1962. 23(1) *Journal of the History of Ideas* 21–36.
43. Mary Chan, "The Witch of Endor and Seventeenth-Century Propaganda" 1980. 34 *Musica Disciplina* 205–214.
44. James Kirkton, *The Secret and True History of the Church of Scotland*. Edinburgh: James Ballantyne and Co., 1817, pp. 126–127; Brian P. Levack, "The Great Scottish Witch Hunt of 1661–1662" 1980. 20(1) *Journal of British Studies* 90–108.
45. Edward Coke, *The Third Part of the Institutes of the Laws of England: Concerning High Treason, and Other Pleas of the Crown, and Criminall Causes*. London: Printed by M. Flesher, for W. Lee, and D. Pakeman, 1644, p. 45.
46. Mackenzie, *The Laws and Customes of Scotland*, p. 82.
47. Zika, *The Appearance of Witchcraft*, p. 162.
48. Coke, *The Third Part of the Institutes of the Laws of England: Concerning High Treason, and Other Pleas of the Crown, and Criminall Causes*, pp. 44–45.
49. Mackenzie, *The Laws and Customes of Scotland*, p. 82.
50. Goodare 'The Scottish Witchcraft Act'.
51. Mackenzie, *The Laws and Customes of Scotland*, p. 85.
52. Ibid., pp. 85–87.
53. Levack, *Witch-Hunting in Scotland*, p. 94.
54. Ibid., pp. 131–134.
55. Gaskill. 2013., "Witch Trials in England." In Brian Levack (ed.), *The Oxford Handbook of Witchcraft in Early Modern Europe and Colonial America*. Oxford: Oxford University Press.
56. Gilbert Geiss and Ivan Bunn, *A Trial of Witches: A Seventeenth-Century Witchcraft Prosecution*. London: Routledge, 1997, pp. 101, 157–158.
57. Ibid., p. 166.
58. Owen Davies, "Decriminalising the Witch: The Origin and Response to the 1736 Witchcraft Act" in *Witchcraft and the Act of 1604*, ed. John Newton and Jo Bath. Leiden; Boston: Brill, 2008, pp. 221–222.
59. Gaskill, *Crime and Mentalities in Early Modern England*, chapter 3.
60. Stuart Clark, *Thinking with Demons*, postscript.
61. Michael Dalton, *The Countrey Justice: Conteyning the Practise of the Justices of the Peace Out of Their Sessions, Gathered for the Better Helpe of Such Justices of Peace as Have Not Beene Much Conversant in the Studie of the Lawes of this Realme*. London: Company of Stationers, 1618.
62. David M.Turner, *Fashioning Adultery: Gender, Sex and Civility in England 1660–1740*. Cambridge: Cambridge University Press, 2002, p. 27.
63. Daniel Defoe, *Conjugal Lewdness: Or Matrimonial Whoredom*. London: T. Warner, 1727, p. 165.
64. Faramerz Dabhoiwala, "Lust and Liberty" 2010. 207 *Past & Present* 89–179.
65. Faramerz Dabhoiwala, *The Origins of Sex: A History of the First Sexual Revolution*. New York: Oxford University Press, 2012, pp. 11–16.
66. B. Capp, "The Double Standard Revisited: Plebeian Women and Male Sexual Reputation in Early Modern England" 1999. 162 *Past & Present* 70–100.
67. Keith Thomas, "The Puritans and Adultery: The Act of 1650 Reconsidered" in *Puritans and Revolutionaries*, ed. Donald Pennington and Keith Thomas. Oxford: Oxford University Press, 1978.

68. R. H. Helmholz. "Harboring Sexual Offenders: Ecclesiastical Courts and Controlling Misbehavior" 1998. 37 *Journal of British Studies* 258–268.
69. Charles Harding Firth and Robert Sangster Rait, eds., *Acts and Ordinances of the Interregnum, 1642–1660*. London: HMSO, 1911, pp. 387–389.
70. Keith Thomas, "The Puritans and Adultery: The Act of 1650 Reconsidered" 278–280.
71. Turner, *Fashioning Adultery: Gender, Sex and Civility in England 1660–1740*, p. 5.
72. Garthine Walker, "Rereading Rape and Sexual Violence in Early Modern England" 1998. 10 *Gender & History* 1–25; N. Bashar, "Rape in England between 1550 and 1700." in *The Sexual Dynamics of History*, ed. The London Feminist History Group. London: Pluto, 1983.
73. Coke, *The Third Part of the Institutes of the Laws of England: Concerning High Treason, and Other Pleas of the Crown, and Criminall Causes*, p. 60.
74. Henry De Bracton, *Bracton on the Laws and Customs of England*. Trans. S. E. Thorne. Cambridge, MA: Harvard University Press, 1968, p. 415.
75. Sir Matthew Hale, *Pleas of the crown, or, A methodical summary of the principal matters relating to that subject*. London: Printed by the assigns of Richard Atkyns and Edward Atkyns Esquires, for William Shrewsbury, 1698; Cynthia Herrup, *A House in Gross Disorder: Sex, Law and the 2nd Earl of Castlehaven*. Oxford: Oxford University Press, 1999, pp. 151–152.
76. Hale, *Pleas of the Crown*, p. 628.
77. Bashar, *Rape in England*; Walker, *Rereading Rape*; Anna Clark, *Women's Silence, Men's Violence*. New York: Pandora, 1987.
78. Herrup, *A House in Gross Disorder*, pp. 37–38; Dabhoiwala, *The Origins of Sex*, chapter 3.
79. Pollock and Maitland, *A History of English Law before the Time of Edward I*, pp. 556–557.
80. Bruce R. Smith, *Homosexual Desire in Shakespeare's England: A Cultural Poetics*. Chicago: Chicago University Press, 1991.
81. Herrup, *A House in Gross Disorder*, pp. 33–37.
82. Stephen Orgel, *Impersonations: The Performance of Gender in Shakespeare's England*. Cambridge: Cambridge University Press, 1996.
83. David Cressy, *Dangerous Talk: Scandalous, Seditious and Treasonable Speech in Pre-Modern England*. Oxford: Oxford University Press, 2010, chapters 1 and 2.
84. Robert Burton, *The Anatomy of Melancholy*. New York: NRYB Classics, 2001, pp. i, 341.
85. Mackenzie, *The Laws and Customes of Scotland*, pp. 25–33.
86. James Fitzjames Stephen, *A History of the Criminal Law of England* (3 vols). London: Macmillan, 1883, vol. ii, chapter 25; Gerald Dacre Nokes, *A History of the Crime of Blasphemy*. London: Sweet & Maxwell, 1928, chapter 1.
87. Stephen, *A History of the Criminal Law of England*, vol. ii, 461–469.
88. Alastair J. Mann, "The Law of the Person: Parliament and Social Control" in *The History of the Scottish Parliament: Parliament in Context*, ed. Keith M. Brown and Alan R. Macdonald. Edinburgh: Edinburgh University Press, 2010, p. 198.
89. Julian Hoppit, *Failed Legislation 1660–1800: Extracted from the Commons and Lords Journals*. London: Hambledon, 1997.
90. Eliot Visconsi, "The Invention of Criminal Blasphemy: *Rex v Taylor* (1676)" 2008. 103 *Representations* 30–52.
91. Visconsi, pp. 42–43.
92. Nokes, *A History of the Crime of Blasphemy*, pp. 66–67.

Chapter 8

1. Frederick A. Inderwick, *A Calendar of the Inner Temple Records*. London: H. Sotheran and Co., 1896–98, pp. xxxvii–xl.
2. This Statute declared Edward IV's children illegitimate and gave the crown to their uncle Richard. Henry VII ordered all copies destroyed. Only one survived, in the Croyland Chronicle, where George Buc, one of Richard's early vindicators, found it a century later.
3. Henry Ellis, ed., *The union of the two noble and llustre famelies of Lancastre and Yorke*. London, 1809.
4. See Eric W. Ives, *The Common Lawyers of Pre-Reformation England: Thomas Kebell, a Case Study*. Cambridge: Cambridge University Press, 1983, pp. 85–86. S. J. Gunn, "The Courtiers of Henry VII", 1993, 108(426) *EHR* 45–46.
5. Lambarde lists their functions in *Eirenarcha: or of the office of the iustices of the peace*. London, 1582.
6. Wilfrid R. Prest, *The Rise of the Barristers: A Social History of the English Bar 1590–1640*. Oxford: Clarendon Press, 1986, p. 49.
7. Peter Goodrich, *Œdipus Lex: Psychoanalysis, History, Law*. Berkeley: California University Press, 1995, pp. 70–1, 78–83.
8. House of Lords Records Office, Original Acts, 1 Eliz. I no. 34, in Norman L. Jones, *Faith by Satute: Parliament and the Settlement of Religion 1559*. London: HLRO, 1982, p. 106.
9. Jones, *Faith by Statute*, p. 112.
10. Frederick W. Maitland, *Equity, Also the Forms of Action at Common Law*. Cambridge: Cambridge University Press, 1910, p. 35.
11. William S. Holdsworth, *A History of English Law*. London: Methuen, 1924, vol. 4, p. 461.
12. "Select Cases before the King's Council in the Star Chamber Commonly Called the Court of Star Chamber, A.D. 1477–1509" in *Publications of the Selden Society*, ed. I. S. Leadman. London, 1902, XVI, I, ix.
13. T. F. T. Plucknett, *Studies in English Legal History*. London: Hambledon Press, 1983, pp. 613–14.
14. John Guy, "Law, Lawyers and the English Reformation" 1985. 35(11) *History Today* 16–22.
15. Gary Watt, *Equity Stirring: The Story of Justice beyond Law*. Oxford: Hart Publishing, 2012, p. 88.
16. Samuel H. Reynolds, ed., *The Table Talk of John Selden*, ed. Samuel H. Reynolds. Oxford: Clarendon, 1892, 37, p. 61.
17. See Richard H. Weisberg, *Poethics: And Other Strategies of Law and Literature*. Columbia: Columbia University Press, 1992, pp. 94–104. Julia Lupton, *Citizen-Saints: Shakespeare and Political Theology*, University of Chicago Press, pp. 75–99. Lorna Hutson, *The Usurer's Daughter*. Abingdon: Routledge: 2007.
18. Watt, *Equity Stirring*, p. 81.
19. Reynolds, *The Table Talk of John Selden*, p. 49.
20. Preamble to Act in Restraint of Appeals.
21. Geoffrey de Clifton Parmiter, *The King's Great Matter: A Study of Anglo-Papal Relations 1527–1534*. London: Longmans, 1967, p. 125–129.
22. William S. Holdsworth, *Influence of the Legal Profession on the Growth of the English Constitution*. Oxford, Creighton Lecture, 1924.
23. Pearl Hogrefe, "The Life of Christopher Saint German" 1937. 13(52) *RES* 402–404.
24. *Letters and Papers, Henry VIII*, vol. 11, p. 1246.

25. Guy, "Thomas More and Christopher St. German: The Battle of the Books" in *Politics, Law and Counsel in Tudor and Early Stuart England*. Aldershot: Ashgate, 2000, 8, pp. 95–120. Henry A. Kelly, "Thomas More on Inquisitorial Due Process" 2018. 123(503) *HER* 847-894.
26. On More's arguments with common law judges over injunctions, see William Roper, *The Lyfe of Sir Thomas Moore, Knighte*, ed. Elsie V. Hitchcock. Oxford: Oxford University Press, 1935, p. 23.
27. Newe Addicions, in *Doctor and Student*, ed. Plucknett and J. L. Barton, London, Selden Society, 1974, p. 332.
28. *Letters and Papers, Henry VIII*, vol. 8, p. 921 [i].
29. Stanford E. Lehmberg, "Parliamentary Attainder in the Reign of Henry VIII" 1975. 18(4) *The Historical Journal* 684.
30. In *The Fourth Part of the Institutes of the Laws of England: Concerning the Jurisdiction of Courts*, 1644, printed for E. and R. Brooke. London, 1797, pp. 37–38.
31. *Lords' Journal*, I, 145–46, in Lehmberg, p. 694.
32. *Proceedings in the Parliaments of Elizabeth I*, May 15, 1572, ed. T. E. Hartley. Leicester: Leicester University Press, 1981, I, p. 326.
33. They were part of the dossier Buchanan sent to Cecil in June 1568, *A Detection of the doings of Mary Queen of Scots, touching the murder of her husband, and her conspiracy, and pretended marriage* ... John Guy, *Queen of Scots: The True Life of Mary Stuart*. New York: Mariner Books, 2005, pp. 386–419, 453.
34. *Proceedings*, I, 87,89. The speech, undated, is included by Hartley in the debates of 1563.
35. "Edmund Plowden, A Treatise on Mary, Queen of Scots, 1566" in *Early Modern Catholicism: An Anthology of Primary Sources*, ed. Robert S. Miola. Oxford: Oxford University Press, 2007, pp. 55–57.
36. See Marie Axton, "The Influence of Edmund Plowden's Succession Treatise" 1974. 37(3) *Huntington Library Quarterly* 209-226.
37. *Proceedings*, I, pp. 376, 325, 374.
38. *A Collection of State Papers ... left by William Cecil Lord Burghley*, ed. Samuel Haynes and William Murdin. London: William Bowyer, 1740–59, vol. 2, p. 762.
39. Mortimer Levine, *Early Elizabethan Succession Question 1558–1568*. Stanford: Stanford University Press, 1966, p. 170.
40. "Dedication to the Folio" *Every Man Out of His Humour*, ed. Helen Ostovich. Manchester: Manchester University Press, 2001, Appendix C, p. 383. See also Introd. "The Inns of Court Milieu," pp. 28–38.
41. Epistle addressed to "my curteous friends, the Gentlemen of the Innes of Court." *An Alarum against Usurers, Containing tryed experiences against worldly abuses*, in *A Defence of Poetry, Music, and Stage-Plays*. London. Shakespeare Society, 1853, p. 36.
42. On the community of the Inns and its symbolic associations, see Paul Raffield, *Images and Cultures of Law in Early Modern England: Justice and Political Power, 1558–1660*. Cambridge: Cambridge University Press, 2004, pp. 9–48.
43. Chaucer, *The Canterbury Tales*, trans. Nevill Coghill. London: Penguin, 1951, Prologue, p. 25.
44. "To no one will we sell, to no one deny or delay, right or justice," Magna Carta, 1215, art. 40.
45. On these "melancholy" regulations, see Goodrich, *Œdipus Lex*, pp. 3, 87–88.
46. John H. Baker, *The Third University of England: The Inns of Court and the Common-Law Tradition*. London: Selden Society, 1990.

47. Samuel E. Thorne, "The Early History of the Inns of Court with Special Reference to Gray's Inn" in *Essays in English Legal History*. London: Hambledon Press, 1985, ch. 10, pp. 137–154.
48. *John Marston of the Middle Temple: An Elizabethan Dramatist in his Social Setting*. Cambridge, MA, Harvard University Press, 1969. See, for instance, the works of W. R. Elton, Anthony Arlidge, Peter Goodrich, I.A. Shapiro, Luke Wilson, Lorna Hutson, Paul Raffield, Gary Watt, Andrew Zurcher, Constance Jordan, Karen Cunningham, Wilfrid Prest, Oliver Arnold.
49. *Moots and Readers' Cases*, p. 29 no. 42, 49 no. 4, 242 no. 56, 18 no. 5b, 145 no. 33, 251 no. 68, 54 no. 5, 293 no. 139, 279 no. 110.
50. His *Commentaries, or Reports* were published in October 1571 by Richard Tottel. *Les Quaeres des Mounsieur Plowden* was printed only in 1620.
51. In his letter *"De ratione studii"* to Petrus Viterius, *On the Method of Study*, trans. Brian McGregor. *Collected Works of Erasmus*. Toronto: University of Toronto Press, 1978, vol. 24.
52. *Oration, of Arsanes agaynst Philip the trecherous kyng of Macedone*. Amsterdam: Da Capo Press, 1970.
53. Prest, *The Rise of the Barristers*, p. 323.
54. Prest, *The Inns of Court*, pp. 12–35.
55. Thomas Denton, Nicholas Bacon, and Robert Cary, "Henry VIII's Royal Commission on the Inns of Court," in *Origines Juridiciales*, ed. D. S. Bland, printed by Dugdale, pp. 183–194.
56. "A survey of the Chambers and societies of all the Innes of Courte," in *State Papers, Domestic, Elizabeth*, 1574, vol. xcv, Art. 91.
57. John Milton, *Of Reformation Touching Church Discipline in England, and the Causes that Hitherto have Hindred It*, 1641, p. 15.
58. G. Parmiter, *Elizabethan Popish Recusancy in the Inns of Court*, Bulletin of the Institute of Historical Research, Special Supplement, no. 11, London, 1976, pp. 19–30.
59. *Black Books of Lincoln's Inn*, vol. 1, pp. 372, 381. *Acts of the Privy Council of England*, London, 1905, vol. 8, p. 160.
60. Anonymous Journal, March 1585, *Proceedings*, II, p. 118.
61. Hooker's Journal, *Proceedings*, I, p. 247.
62. April 5, 1571, Thomas Clarke and Anthony Bull, *Proceedings*, I, pp. 200, 478.
63. February 13, 1576, *Proceedings*, I, p. 478.
64. L. 999 to Ulrich Von Hutten, in *La Correspondance d'Erasme*, ed. Aloïs Gerlo, Brussels, Éditions de l'Université de Bruxelles, 1969–84.
65. Hall's *Chronicle*, p. 719.
66. *Les mémoires de messire Olivier de la Marche*. Paris. Foucault, 1825, Bk I, ch. 37, p. 261. See his hour by hour account in Bk II, ch. 4, pp. 299–391.
67. Denton's report, "Henry VIII's Royal Commission," p. 188.
68. I. A. Shapiro, "John Donne and Lincoln's Inn," *Times Literary Supplement*, October 16 and 23, 1930.
69. Finkelpearl, *John Marston*, pp. 30–32.
70. John Stow, *Annals*, quoted in Dawson, *Christmas*, pp. 117–118.
71. *Holinshed's Chronicles of England, Scotland and Ireland*, ed. Henry Ellis, vol. 3, 1399–1553, London, 1807–8, vol. 3, p. 1032. Somerset was executed on January 22, 1552.
72. W. M. Ormrod, "The Use of English: Language, Law, and Political Culture in Fourteenth-Century England" 2003. 78(3) *Speculum* 750–787.

73. In Kathleen Lambley, *The Teaching and Cultivation of the French Language in England during Tudor and Stuart Times*. Manchester: Manchester University Press, 1920, p. 22.
74. Starkey, *A Dialogue between Reginald Pole and Thomas Lupset*, ed. K. Burton. London, 1948, p. 82. Shakespeare, *2 Henry VI*, IV, ii, ll. 156–161.
75. *The Abbreviacion of Statutes translated out of French into English by John Rastell*, 1519, A1 r-v.
76. See J. H. Baker, "John Rastell and the Terms of the Law" in *Language and the Law: Proceedings of a Conference*, ed. Marlyn Robinson. Buffalo: W. S. Hein, 2003.
77. Baker, *The Oxford History of the Laws of England*, vol. 6: *1483–1556*, Oxford University Press, 2003, p. 26.
78. Postface to *The Seven First Bookes of the Eneidos of Virgill*. London, 1558, p. 81.
79. William Camden, *Remaines of a Greater Worke Concerning Britaine*, 1605, p. 20.
80. C. H. Conley, *The First English Translators of the Classics*. New Haven: Yale University Press, 1927.
81. Michael A. R. Graves, *Thomas Norton, the Parliament Man*. Oxford: Blackwell, 1994, p. 45.
82. H. B. Charlton, *The Senecan Tradition in Renaissance Tragedy*. Manchester: Manchester University Press 1946 (1921), p. 163.
83. "The Preface," in *Jasper Heywood and His Translations of Seneca*, ed. H. De Vocht. Louvain: A. Uystpruyst, 1913, pp. 97–104.
84. In *Thyestes*, the decasyllable is reserved to the Chorus, the other characters speak in fourteeners. Their lines being too long for the page, Berthelet printed them as two lines of eight and six.
85. Winston, "Seneca," p. 4.
86. C. J. Herington, "Senecan Tragedy" 1966. 5 *Arion* 430.
87. See Gerard Legh's description in *Accedens of Armorie* (1562). London: J. Jaggard, 1612. Marie Axton, *The Queen's Two Bodies: Drama and the Elizabethan Succession*. London: Royal Historical Society, 1977, pp. 39–48, reconstructs the masque from his account.
88. *Commons Journals*, I, p. 63.
89. Paul White and Norman Jones, "*Gorboduc* and Royal Marriage Politics: An Elizabethan Playgoer's Report of the Premiere Performance" 1966. 26(1) *English Literary Renaissance* 3–16. Axton, *The Queen's Two Bodies*, pp. 38–48. Graves, *Norton*, pp. 91–99.
90. Henry James and Greg Walker, "The Politics of *Gorboduc*" 1995. 110(435) *EHR* 119.
91. Stephen Alford, *The Early Elizabethan Polity: William Cecil and the British Succession Crisis, 1558–1569*. Cambridge: Cambridge University Press, 1998, pp. 100–102.
92. "Seneca in Elizabethan Translation" in *Elizabethan Dramatists*. London: Faber & Faber, 1963, p. 11.
93. *Supposes; And Jocasta: Two plays translated from the Italian the first by Geo. Gascoigne, the second by Geo. Gascoigne and F. Kinwelmersh*, ed. John W. Cunliffe. Boston: D. C. Heath & Co., 1906.
94. *Giocasta*, tragedia di M. Lodovico Dolce, Vinegia, Figliuoli d'Aldo, Aldi filii, 1549. See Ronnie H. Terpening, *Lodovico Dolce: Renaissance Man of Letters*. Toronto: University of Toronto Press, 1997.

BIBLIOGRAPHY

Abascal Monedero, Pablo Jose. 2009. *La infidelidad y el adulterio en España (estudios históricolegal)*. Córdoba: Universidad de Córdoba.
Ackerman, Bruce. 1991. *We the People*, 2 vols. Cambridge, MA: Harvard University Press.
Adorno, T.W. and Horkheimer, M. 2010. *The Dialectic of Enlightenment*. Translated by J. Cumming. London: Verso.
Aeschylus. 1991. *Oresteia*. Translated by Richard Lattimore. In David Grene and Richard Lattimore (eds.), *The Complete Greek Tragedies*, vol. 1. Chicago: University of Chicago Press.
Aeschylus. 2011. *The Complete Aeschylus, Volume 1: The Oresteia* (Greek Tragedy in New Translations). Translated and edited by Peter Burian and Alan Shapiro. Oxford: Oxford University Press.
Aguiar, Gustavo Illades. 2013. "El carácter delictivo de los personajes celestinescos a la luz de *Las siete partidas*" 37 *Celestinesca* 87–100.
Albanese, Bernardo. 1987. *Il processo privato romano delle legis actiones*. Palermo: Palumbo.
Alciato, Andrea. 1531. *Emblemata*. Antwerp: Plantin.
Alciato, Andrea. 1557 (edn.). "Praetermissa." In *Opera Omnia*. 1582. Bâle: Thomas Guiran.
Alciato, Andrea. 2008. "Avignon Oration." In Susan Longfield Karr (ed.), *Nature, Self and History in the Works of Guillaumé Budé, Andreas Alciato and Ulrich Zazius: A Study of the Role of Legal Humanism in Western Natural Law*. Chicago: University of Chicago Press.
Alcubilla, Marcelo Martinez. 1869. *Diccionario de la administración española, peninsular y ultramarina*, 12 vols. 2nd edn. Madrid: A. Peñuelas, vol. 8.
Alford, Stephen. 1998. *The Early Elizabethan Polity: William Cecil and the British Succession Crisis, 1558–1569*. Cambridge: Cambridge University Press.
Allen, Danielle. 2005. "Greek Tragedy and Law." In Michael Gagarin and David Cohen (eds.), *The Cambridge Companion to Ancient Greek Law*. New York: Cambridge University Press.
Alt, Albrecht. 1966. *The Origins of Israelite Law: Essays on Old Testament History and Religion*. Translated by Robert A. Wilson. Garden City, NY: Doubleday.
Althusser, Louis. 1967. *Sur le contrat social*. Paris: Le Marteau sans Maître.
Althusser, Louis. 2012. *Cours sur Rousseau (1972)*. Edited by Yves Vargas. Paris: Le Temps des Cerises.
Amsterdam, Anthony and Bruner, Jerome. 2000. *Minding the Law*. Cambridge, MA: Harvard University Press.
Andersen, Benedict. 1991. *Imagined Communities: Reflections on the Origin and Spread of Nationalism*. rev. edn. London: Verso.
Ando, Clifford. 2011. *Law, Language, and Empire in the Roman Tradition*. Philadelphia: University of Pennsylvania Press.
Ando, Clifford. 2015a. "Fact, Fiction, and Social Reality in Roman Law" 110 *Law and Philosophy Library* 295–324.
Ando, Clifford. 2015b. *Roman Social Imaginaries: Language and Thought in Contexts of Empire*. Toronto, Buffalo, London: University of Toronto Press.

Andrews, Malcolm. 1999. *Landscape and Western Art* (Oxford History of Art). Oxford: Oxford University Press.

Aneau, Barthélemy. 1552. *Picta Poesis*. Lyon: France, Bonhommie.

Anievas, A. and Nisancioglu, K. 2015. *How the West Came to Rule*. Chicago: University of Chicago Press.

Ankum, Hans. 1985. "La *captiva adultera*. Problèmes concernant l'*accusatio adulterii* en droit Romain classique" 32 *Revue Internationale des Droits de l'Antiquité* 153–205.

Annas, Julia. 2010. "Virtue and law in Plato." In Christopher Bobonich (ed.), *Plato's Laws: A Critical Guide*. New York: Cambridge University Press.

Antaki, Mark. 2014. "No Foundations?" 11 *No Foundations: An Interdisciplinary Journal of Law and Justice* 61–77.

Arcangeli, Alessandro. 2012. *Cultural History: A Concise Introduction*. London and New York: Routledge.

Archer, Ian W. 1991. *The Pursuit of Stability: Social Relations in Elizabethan London*. Cambridge: Cambridge University Press.

Archi, Gian Gualberto. 1958. "Il concetto della proprietà nei diritti del mondo antico" 4(1) *Rivista trimestrale di diritto e procedura civile*, fasc 1201–1216.

Aristophanes. 1978. *The Knights*. Translated by Alan Sommerstein. London: Penguin.

Aristotle. 1996. *The Politics and the Constitution of Athens*. Edited by Stephen Everson. New York: Cambridge University Press.

Aristotle. 2002. *Nicomachean Ethics*. Translated by Joe Sachs. Newburyport, MA: Focus Publishing.

Arnaud, Andre-Jean. 1969. *Les origines doctrinales du Code civil français*. Paris: LGDJ.

Arredondo, Jose Garrido. 2012. "*Quod principi placuit legis habet vigorem*. Su recepción en la corona de Castilla." In Pedro Resina Sola (ed.), *Fvndamenta Ivris: Terminología, principios e interpretatio*. Almería: Editorial Universidad de Almería.

Atkison, Larissa M. 2016. "*Antigone*'s Remainders: Choral Ruminations and Political Judgment" 44 *Political Theory* 219–239.

Atkyns, R. 1664. *The Original and Growth of Printing, Collected Out of History and the Records of this Kingdom*. London. Available at: http://quod.lib.umich.edu/cgi/t/text/text-idx?c=eebo;idno=A26139.0001.001 (last accessed November 10, 2015).

Augustine, St. 2009. *On Christian Doctrine*. New York: Dover Publications.

Avery, Victoria, Calaresu, Melissa and Laven, Mary, ed. 2015. *Treasured Possessions from the Renaissance to the Enlightenment*. London: Philip Wilson Publishers.

Axton, Marie. 1974. "The Influence of Edmund Plowden's Succession Treatise" 37(3) *Huntington Library Quarterly* 209–226.

Axton, Marie. 1977. *The Queen's Two Bodies: Drama and the Elizabethan Succession*. London: Royal Historical Society.

Aylmer, G. 1980. "The Meaning and Definition of 'Property' in Seventeenth-century England" 86 *Past and Present* 87.

Ayuso, Faustino Gil. 1935. *Textos y disposiciones legales de los reinos de Catilla impresos en los siglos XVI y XVII*. Madrid: Aguirre.

Bablitz, Leanne. 2007. *Actors and Audience in the Roman Courtroom*. Abingdon and New York: Routledge.

Bacon, Francis. 1882 (edn.). *The Essays, or Counsels Civil and Moral 1587*. London: Macmillan & Co.

Badian, Ernst. 2000. "The Road to Prominence." In Ian Worthington (ed.), *Demosthenes: Statesman and Orator*. London: Routledge.

Bahrani, Zainab. 2003. *The Graven Image: Representation in Babylonia and Assyria.* Philadelphia: University of Pennsylvania.

Bailey, Amanda. 2007. *Flaunting: Style and the Subversive Male Body in Renaissance England.* Toronto: University of Toronto Press.

Baker, J.H. 1978. *Spelman's Reports*, vol. 2. London: Selden Society.

Baker, J.H. 1990. *The Third University of England: The Inns of Court and the Common-Law Tradition.* London: Selden Society.

Baker, J.H. 2003a. *Oxford History of the Laws of England, Volume 6: 1483–1558.* Oxford: Oxford University Press.

Baker, J.H. 2003b. "John Rastell and the Terms of the Law." In Marlyn Robinson (ed.), *Language and the Law: Proceedings of a Conference.* Buffalo: W. S. Hein.

Bakhtin, M.M. 1981. *The Dialogic Imagination.* Austin: Texas University Press.

Bakhtin, M.M. 1986. *Speech Genres and Other Late Essays.* Austin: University of Texas Press.

Baldwin, Frances E. 1923. *Sumptuary Legislation and Personal Regulation in England.* Baltimore: Johns Hopkins University Press.

Balkin, Jack M. 1994. "Understanding Legal Understanding: The Legal Subject and the Problem of Legal Coherence" 103 *Yale Law Journal* 105–176.

Balot, Ryan. 2001. *Greed and Injustice in Classical Athens.* Princeton, NJ: Princeton University Press.

Barnes, Barnabe. 1606. *Foure Bookes of Offices: Enabling Privat Persons for the Speciall Seruice of All Good Princes and Policies.* London: A. Islip.

Barnes, T.G. 1977. "The Making of the English Criminal Law (2). Star Chamber and the Sophistication of the Criminal Law" *Criminal Law Review* 316.

Barthes, Roland. 2002. "L'effet de réel." In Eric Marty (ed.), *Oeuvres complètes*, t. III, *1968–1971.* Paris: Le Seuil.

Bartor, Assnat. 2010. *Reading Law as Narrative: A Study in the Casuistic Laws of the Pentateuch.* Atlanta, GA: Society of Biblical Literature.

Bashar, N. 1983. "Rape in England between 1550 and 1700." In The London Feminist History Group (ed.), *The Sexual Dynamics of History.* London: Pluto.

Bath, Michael. 2003. *Renaissance Decorative Painting in Scotland.* Edinburgh: NMS Publishing.

Bauman, Richard A. 1983. *Lawyers in Roman Republican Politics: A Study of the Roman Jurists in their Political Setting, 316-82 BC.* Munich: C. H. Beck.

Bauman, Richard A. 1985. *Lawyers in Roman Transitional Politics: A Study of the Roman Jurists in their Political Setting in the Late Republic and Triumvirate.* Munich: C. H. Beck.

Bauman, Richard A. 1989. *Lawyers and Politics in the Early Roman Empire: A Study of Relations between the Roman Jurists and the Emperors from Augustus to Hadrian.* Munich: C. H. Beck.

Bauman, Richard A. 1996. *Crime and Punishment in Ancient Rome.* London and New York: Routledge.

Beard, Mary. 2015. *SPQR: A History of Ancient Rome.* New York: Liveright.

Behrends, O. 1976. "Die Wissenschaftslehre im Zivilrecht des Q. Mucius Scaevola pontifex" 7 *Nachrichten der Akademie der Wissenschaften in Göttingen, Philologisch-historische Klasse* 263–304.

Behrends, Okko, Mommsen, Theodor, Krüger, Paul, and Apathy, Peter, eds. 1995. *Corpus Iuris Civilis: Text und Übersetzung. Bd. 2, Digesten 1-10.* Müller: Heidelberg.

Beier, A.L. "Engine of Manufacture: The Trades of London." In A.L. Beier and Roger Finlay (eds.), *London 1500–1700: The Making of the Metropolis.* London and New York: Longman.

Bell, Clifford R. and Ruse, Evelyn. 1972. "Sumptuary Legislation and English Costume: An Attempt to Assess the Effect of an Act of 1337" 6(1) *Costume* 22–31.

Bellany, Alastair. 1995. "Mistress Turner's Deadly Sins: Sartorial Transgression, Court Scandal, and Politics in Early Stuart England" 58(2) *Huntington Library Quarterly* 179–210.

Bennington, G. and Derrida, J. 1993. *Circumfessions*. Chicago: Chicago University Press.

Berg, Maxine. 2005. *Luxury and Pleasure in Eighteenth-Century Britain*. Oxford: Oxford University Press.

Berger, Harry Jr. 2015. *The Perils of Uglytown: Studies in Structural Misanthropology from Plato to Rembrandt*. New York: Fordham University Press.

Berkowitz, Beth A. 2006. *Execution and Invention: Death Penalty Discourse in Early Rabbinic and Christian Cultures*. New York: Oxford University Press.

Berman, Harold J. 2006. *Law and Revolution II: The Impact of the Protestant Reformations on the Western Legal Tradition*. Cambridge, MA: The Belknap Press.

Berman, Joshua. 2013. "Historicism and its Limits: A Response to Bernard M. Levinson and Jeffrey Stackert" 4 *Journal of Ancient Judaism* 297–309.

Bermejo, Saul Martinez. 2008. "Beyond Luxury: Sumptuary Legislation in 17th-Century Castile." In Günther Lottes, et al. (ed.), *Making, Using, and Resisting the Law in European History*. Pisa: Plus-Pisa University Press.

Bertaud, Jean-Paul. 2003. *Choderlos de Laclos, l'auteur des "Liaisons dangereuses."* Paris: Fayard.

Bietenholtz, Peter G. 2009. *Encounters with a Radical Erasmus: Erasmus' Work as a Source of Radical Thought in Early Modern Europe*. Toronto: University of Toronto Press.

Binder, Guyora and Weisberg, Robert. 2000. *Literary Criticisms of Law*. Princeton, NJ: Princeton University Press.

Birks, Peter and Grant, McLeod. 1987. "Introduction." In Peter Birks and Grant McLeod (eds.), *Justinian's Institutes*. Ithaca, NY: Cornell University Press.

Birks, Peter, Rodger, Alan, and Richardson, John S. 1984. "Further Aspects of the 'Tabula Contrebiensis'" 74 *The Journal of Roman Studies* 45–73.

Black, Jeremy and Green, Anthony, eds. 1992. *Gods, Demons and Symbols of Ancient Mesopotamia: An Illustrated Dictionary*. Illustrated by Tessa Rickards. London: The British Museum Press.

Blackie, John. 2000. "Defamation." In Kenneth Reid and Reinhard Zimmermann (eds.), *A History of Private Law in Scotland*, vol. 2. Oxford: Oxford University Press.

Blackstone, Sir William. 1769. *Commentaries on the Laws of England*, vol. 1. Dublin: printed for John Exshaw, Henry Saunders, Boulter Grierson, and James Williams.

Blass, Friedrich. 1893. *Die attische Beredsamkeit, Book 3:1, Demosthenes*. Leipzig: Teubner.

Bleicken, Jochen. 1974. *In provinciali solo dominium populi Romani est vel Caesaris: zur Kolonisationspolitik der ausgehenden Republik und frühen Kaiserzeit*. Frankfurt am Main: Johann Wolfgang Goethe-Universität.

Bloch, Howard. 1977. *Medieval French Literature and Law*. Berkeley: University of California Press.

Blount, Thomas. 1656. *Glossographia*. London: Newcomb.

Bomford, David and Roy, Ashok. 1982. "Hogarth's 'Marriage à la mode'" *National Gallery Technical Bulletin*, no. 6.

Bonner, Robert J. 1905. *Evidence in Athenian Courts*. Chicago: University of Chicago.

Bonner, Robert J. 1926. *Lawyers and Litigants in Ancient Athens: The Genesis of the Legal Profession*. Chicago: University of Chicago.

Booy, D., ed. 2002. *Personal Disclosures: An Anthology of Self-Writings from the Seventeenth Century*. Aldershot: Ashgate.

Botella-Ordinas, Eva. 2012. "Exempt from Time and from its Fatal Change: Spanish Imperial Ideology, 1450–1700" 26 *Renaissance Studies* 580–604.

Bottéro, Jean. 1992. *Mesopotamia: Writing, Reasoning, and Theogony*. Chicago: The University of Chicago Press.

Bowersock, Glen W. 2015. "Inside the Emperor's Clothes" 62(20) *New York Review of Books*, December 17, 2015. Available at: www.nybooks.com/articles/2015/12/17/rome-inside-emperors-cothes/.

Boyarin, Daniel. 1990. "The Politics of Biblical Narratology: Reading the Bible like/as a Woman" 20(4) *Diacritics* 31–43.

Bracton, Henry De. 1968. *Bracton on the Laws and Customs of England*. Translated by S.E. Thorne. Cambridge, MA: Harvard University Press.

Brand, P. 2001. "'Deserving' and 'Undeserving' Wives: Earning and Forfeiting Dower in Medieval England" 22 *Legal History* 1–20.

Brenner, R. 2003. *Merchants and Revolution: Commercial Change, Political Conflict and London's Overseas Traders, 1550–1653*. London: Verso.

Brewer, John and Porter, Roy. 1993. *Consumption and the World of Goods*. London: Routledge.

Brioso, Jorge. 2004. "¿Cómo hacer cosas con los enigmas?: *La vida es sueño* o el drama del desengaño" 56 *Bulletin of the Comediantes* 55–75.

Brooks, Chris. 2008. "Witchcraft and Stage Spectacle: Spectacular Witches after 1604." In John Newton and Jo Bath (eds.), *Witchcraft and the Act of 1604*. Leiden and Boston: Brill.

Bruneau, Marie-Flroine. 1986. *Racine. Le jansénisme et la modernité*. Paris: José Corti.

Bruner, Jerome. 1991. "The Narrative Construction of Reality" 18 *Critical Inquiry* 1–21.

Bryce, James. 1997. *Constitutions*. Holmes Beach, FL: Gaunt.

Bryen, Ari Z. 2013. *Violence in Roman Egypt: A Study in Legal Interpretation*. Philadelphia: University of Pennsylvania Press.

Buckland, William Warwick. 1908. *The Roman Law of Slavery*. Cambridge: Cambridge University Press.

Bullein, William. 1888. *A Dialogue against Fever Pestilence (1564)*. London: Early English Texts.

Bulwer, John. 1653. *Anthropometamorphosis: Man Transform'd: Or, the Artificiall Changling Historically Presented, in the Mad and Cruell Gallantry, Foolish Bravery, Ridiculous Beauty, Filthy Finenesse, and Loathsome Lovelinesse of Most Nations, Fashioning and Altering Their Bodies from the Mould Intended by Nature; with Figures of Those Transfigurations. To Which Artificiall and Affected Deformations Are Added, All the Native and Nationall Monstrosities That Have Appeared to Disfigure the Humane Fabrick. With a Vindication of the Regular Beauty and Honesty of Nature. And an Appendix of the Pedigree of the English Gallant*. London: William Hunt.

Burckhardt, Jacob. [1860] 2004. *The Civilization of the Renaissance in Italy*. Translated by S.G.C. Middlemore with a new Introduction of Peter Burke and Notes by Peter Murray. Harmondsworth: Penguin.

Burckhardt, Jacob. [1872] 1998. *The Greeks and Greek Civilization*. Edited by Oswyn Murray and translated by Sheila Stern. New York: St. Martin's Press.

Burckhardt, Jacob. [1902] 1979. *Reflections on History*. Indianapolis: Liberty Classics.

Burke, Peter. 2004a. "Introduction: Jacob Burckhardt and the Italian Renaissance." In Jacob Burckhardt (ed.), *The Civilization of the Renaissance in Italy*. London: Penguin.

Burke, Peter. 2004b. *What Is Cultural History?* Cambridge, UK and Malden, MA: Polity Press.

Burke, Peter, Rubiés, Joan Pau, Calaresu, Melissa, and De Vivo, Filippo. 2010. *Exploring Cultural History: Essays in Honour of Peter Burke*. Farnham, Surrey, England and Burlington, VT: Ashgate.

Burt, R. and Archer, J.M., eds. 1994. *Enclosure Acts—Sexuality, Property and Culture in Early Modern England*. Ithaca and London: Cornell University Press.

Burton, Robert. 1932. *Anatomy of Melancholy*. London: Dent.

Burton, Robert. 2001. *The Anatomy of Melancholy*. New York: NRYB Classics.

Byrne, Susan. 2002. "¿Por qué una niña de nuef años?: la edad de razón y la razón del poeta del CMC" 31(1) *La corónica* 5–17.

Byrne, Susan. 2012. *Law and History in Cervantes' Don Quixote*. Toronto: University of Toronto Press.

Byrne, Susan. 2015. *Ficino in Spain*. Toronto: University of Toronto Press.

Caepolla, Bartholomaeus. 1557. *De Interpretatione legis extensiva*. Venice: Tridino Montisferrati.

Caffentzis, G. and Federici, S. 2014. "Commons against and beyond Capitalism" 49(1) *Community Development Journal* 92–105.

Cahen, R. 1923. "Examen de quelques passages du *Pro Milone*" 25(2) *Revue des Études Anciennes* 119–233.

Calasso, Francesco. 1967. *Il negozio giuridico*. 2nd edn. Milan: Giuffrè.

Calhoun, Gorge M. 1919. "Oral and Written Pleading in Athenian Courts" 50 *Transactions of the American Philological Association* 177–193.

Camden, William. 1605. *Remaines of a Greater Worke Concerning Britaine*. London: Simon Waserfon.

Camon, Enrique Solano. 2012. "La institución virreinal en Aragón durante la Edad Moderna." In Pedro Cardim and Joan-Lluís Palos (eds.), *El mundo de los virreyes en las monarquías de España y Portugal*. Madrid: Iberoamericana, 149–172.

Campbell, Brian. 2000. *The Writings of the Roman Land Surveyors: Introduction, Text, Translation and Commentary*. London: Society for the Promotion of Roman Studies.

Cannon, Nathaneall. 1613. *The Cryer. A Sermon Preached at Pauls Crosse*. London: Felix Kingston.

Cantarella, Eva. 1991. "Moicheia. Reconsidering a Problem." In Michael Gagarin (ed.), *Symposion 1990*. Cologne, Weimar and Vienna: Böhlau.

Capogrossi Colognesi, Luigi. 1969. *La struttura della proprietà e la formazione dei "iura praediorum" nell'età repubblicana*, Book 1. Milan: Giuffrè.

Capogrossi Colognesi, Luigi. 1976. *La struttura della proprietà e la formazione dei "iura praediorum" nell'età repubblicana*, Book 2. Milan: Giuffrè.

Capogrossi Colognesi, Luigi. 1978. *Storia delle istituzioni romane arcaiche*. Rome: Ricerche.

Capogrossi Colognesi, Luigi. 1981. *La terra in Roma antica: forme di proprietà e rapporti produttivi*. Rome: La Sapienza.

Capogrossi Colognesi, Luigi. 2014. *Law and Power in the Making of the Roman Commonwealth*. Translated by Laura Kopp. Cambridge: Cambridge University Press.

Capp, B. 1999. "The Double Standard Revisited: Plebeian Women and Male Sexual Reputation in Early Modern England" 162 *Past & Present* 70–100.

Carandini, Andrea. 2011. *Rome: Day One*. Princeton, NJ: Princeton University Press.

Carbonnier, Jean. 1969. *Flexible droit. Textes pour une sociologie du droit sans rigueur*. Paris: Librairie générale de droit et de jurisprudence.

Carey, Chris. 1994a. "Legal Space in Classical Athens" 41 *Greece & Rome* 172–186.

Carey, Chris. 1994b. "Artless Proofs in Aristotle and the Orators" 95–106.

Carey, Chris. 1995. "The Witness's *Exomosia* in the Athenian Courts" 45 *The Classical Quarterly* 114–119.

Carey, Chris. 1996. "*Nomos* in Attic Rhetoric and Oratory" 116 *The Journal of Hellenic Studies* 33–46.

Carey, V., Bogdan, R. and Walsh, E.A., eds. 2004. *Voices for Tolerance in an Age of Persecution*. Washington: Folger Shakespeare Library.
Cariou, Pierre. 1993. *Pascal et la casuistique*. Paris: PUF.
Carreno-Rodriguez, Antonio. 2009. *Alegorías del poder: crísis imperial y comedia nueva (1598–1659)*. Woodbridge, Suffolk: Tamesis.
Casanova, Giacomo. 2013–2015. *Histoire de ma vie*. Edited by Gérard Lahouati and Marie-Françoise Luna, 3 vols. Paris: Gallimard.
Cascio, Elio Lo. 1997. "Dall'affitto agrario al colonato tardoantico: continuità o frattura?" In Elio Lo Cascio (ed.), *Terre, proprietari e contadini dell'impero romano: dall'affitto agrario al colonato tardoantico*. Rome: NIS.
Cascio, Elio Lo. 2015. "The Imperial Property and Its Development." In P. Erdkamp, et al. (eds.), *Ownership and Exploitation of Land and Natural Resources in the Roman World*. Oxford: Oxford University Press.
Cascione, Cosimo. 2003. *Consensus. Problemi di origine, tutela processuale, prospettive sistematiche*. Naples: Editoriale Scientifica.
Cash, Arthur H. 1975–1986. *Laurence Sterne*, 2 vols. London: Methuen.
Catalano, Pierangelo. 1965. *Linee del sistema sovrannazionale romano*, vol. 1. Turin: Giappichelli.
Chan, Mary. 1980. "The Witch of Endor and Seventeenth-Century Propaganda" 34 *Musica Disciplina* 205–214.
Chan, M. and Wright, N.E. 2004. "Marriage, Identity, and the Pursuit of Property in Seventeenth-century England: The Cases of Anne Clifford and Elizabeth Wiseman." In N.E. Wright, M.W. Ferguson, and A.R. Buck (eds.), *Women: Property and the Letters of the Law in Early Modern England*. Toronto: University of Toronto Press.
Chantin, Jean-Pierre. 1996. *Le jansénisme*. Paris: CERF.
Charlton, H.B. 1946. *The Senecan Tradition in Renaissance Tragedy*. Manchester: Manchester University Press.
Charpin, Dominique. 2010. *Reading and Writing in Babylon*. Translated by Jane Marie Todd. Cambridge, MA: Harvard University Press.
Chaucer, Geoffrey. 1951. *The Canterbury Tales*. Translated by Nevill Coghill. London: Penguin.
Chiba, Masaji. 1993. "Legal Pluralism in Sri Lankan Society: Toward a General Theory of non-Western Law" 33 *Journal of Legal Pluralism* 197–212.
Cicero, Marcus Tullius. 1933. *On the Nature of Gods*. Translated by H. Rackham. Oxford: Loeb.
Cicero, Marcus Tullius. 1990. *Murder Trials*. Dover: Thrift.
Cicero, Marcus Tullius. 2000. *On the Republic*. Translated by Clinton Walker Keyes. Cambridge, MA: Harvard University Press.
Cicero, Marcus Tullius. 2001. *On Duties*. Translated by M.T. Griffin and E.M. Atkins. Cambridge: Cambridge University Press.
Civil, Miguel. 2011. "The Law Collection of Ur-Namma." In A.R. George (ed.), *Cuneiform Royal Inscriptions and Related Texts in the Schøyen Collection*. Bethesda, MD: CDL Press.
Clark, Anna. 1987. *Women's Silence, Men's Violence*. New York: Pandora.
Clark, Matthew. 2012. *Exploring Greek Myth*. Chichester, West Sussex and Malden, MA: Wiley-Blackwell.
Clark, Stuart. 1999. *Thinking with Demons: The Idea of Witchcraft in Early Modern Europe*. Oxford: Oxford University Press.

Cohen, David. 1991. *Law, Sexuality and Society. The Enforcement of Morals in Classical Athens*. Cambridge: Cambridge University Press.

Cohen, David. 1995. *Law, Violence and Community in Classical Athens*. Cambridge: Cambridge University Press.

Cohen, David. 2005. "Introduction." In Michael Gagarin and David Cohen (eds.), *The Cambridge Companion to Ancient Greek Law*. New York: Cambridge University Press.

Coke, Sir Edward. 1644. *The Third Part of the Institutes of the Laws of England: Concerning High Treason, and Other Pleas of the Crown, and Criminall Causes*. London: Printed by M. Flesher, for W. Lee and D. Pakeman.

Coleridge, Samuel Taylor. [1817] 2004. *Biographia Literaria*. Project Gutenberg. Available at: www.gutenberg.org/files/6081/6081-h/6081-h.htm#link2HCH0014, ch. XIV.

Colish, Marcia L. 2008. "Ambrose of Milan on Chastity." In Nancy Deusen (ed.), *Chastity: A Study in Perception, Ideals, Opposition*. Leiden and Boston, MA: Brill.

Collinson, P. 1989. *De Republica Anglorum: or, History with the Politics Put Back*. Cambridge: Cambridge University Press.

Comninel, G.C. 2000. "English Feudalism and the Origins of Capitalism" 27(4) *The Journal of Peasant Studies* 1–53.

Conley, C.H. 1927. *The First English Translators of the Classics*. New Haven, CT: Yale University Press.

Connerton, Paul. 1989. *How Societies Remember*. Cambridge: Cambridge University Press.

Connor, W. Robert. 1984. *Thucydides*. Princeton, NJ: Princeton University Press.

Cooper, Jerrold S. 1993. "Paradigm and Propaganda: The Dynasty of Akkade in the 21st Century BC." In Mario Liverani (ed.), *Akkad, The First World Empire. Structure, Ideology, Traditions*. Padova: Sargon.

Corbo, Chiara. 2013. *Constitutio Antoniniana: Ius Philosophia Religio*. Naples: M. D'Auria editore.

Coriat, Jean-Pierre. 2014. *Les constitutions des Sévères. Règne de Septime Sévère*, vol. 1. Rome: École Française de Rome.

Cormack, Bradin. 2005. *A Power to Do Justice*. Chicago: Chicago University Press.

Cormack, Bradin, Nussbaum, Martha C. and Streier, Richard, eds 2013. *Shakespeare and the Law: A Conversation about Disciplines and Professions*. Chicago: University of Chicago Press.

Cornell, Tim. 1995. *The Beginnings of Rome: Italy and Rome from the Bronze Age to the Punic Wars (c. 1000-264 BC)*. London and New York: Routledge.

Corteguara, Luis R. 1995. "Sancho Panza Wants an Island: Cervantes and the Politics of Peasant Rulers" 2 *Romance Quarterly* 261–270.

Corteguara, Luis R. 2002. *For the Common Good: Popular Politics in Barcelona, 1580–1640*. New York: Cornell University Press.

Cortes de los antiguos reinos de León y de Castilla. 1864, 5 vols. Madrid: Real Academia de la Historia; Rivadeneyra.

Cortes de Madrid. 1563. Quaderno de las leyes y pregmáticas que su Magestad mandó hazer en las cortes que tuuo y celebró en la villa de Madrid, el año de D.lxiii. Alcalá de Henares: Andrés de Angulo, chapter 124.

Cortes de Madrid. [1579] 1588. Madrid: Querino Gerardo.

Cotterrell, Roger. 2006. *Law, Culture and Society: Legal Ideas in the Mirror of Social Theory*. Aldershot, England and Burlington, VT: Ashgate.

Cotterrell, Roger. 2014. "A Concept of Law for Global Legal Pluralism?" In Seán P. Donlan and Lukas H. Urscheler (eds.), *Concepts of Law: Comparative, Jurisprudential and Social Science Perspectives*. Farnham: Ashgate.

Cottier, Michel and Corbier, Mireille. 2008. *The Customs Law of Asia*. Oxford and New York: Oxford University Press.

Cotton, A.K. 2014. *Platonic Dialogue and the Education of the Reader*. Oxford: Oxford University Press.

Courtine, Jean-Francois. 1999. *Nature et empire de la loi. Études suaréziennes*. Paris: Vrin.

Coustau, Pierre. 1555. *Pegma cum narrationibus philosophicis*. Lyon: Macé Bonhomme.

Cover, Robert M. 1983. "The Supreme Court 1982 Term. Foreword: Nomos and Narrative" 97(4) *Harvard Law Review* 4–68.

Cover, Robert M. 1992. *Narrative, Violence, and the Law: The Essays of Robert Cover*. Edited by Martha Minow, Michel Ryan and Austin Sarat. Ann Arbor: University of Michigan Press.

Cox, Nancy. 2015. *Retailing and the Language of Goods, 1550–1820*. Farnham: Ashgate.

Coyle, W. 1992. "Common Law Metaphors of Coverture: Conceptions of Women and Children as Property in Legal and Literary Contexts" 1 *Texas Journal of Women and the Law* 315.

Crawford, Michael H. 1996. *Roman Statutes*. London: Institute of Classical Studies, School of Advanced Study, University of London.

Cressy, David. 2010. *Dangerous Talk: Scandalous, Seditious and Treasonable Speech in Pre-Modern England*. Oxford: Oxford University Press.

Crook, J.A. 1995. *Legal Advocacy in the Roman World*. Ithaca, NY: Cornell University Press.

Crowley, Robert. 1566. *A Briefe Discourse against the Outwarde Apparell and Ministring Garmentes of the Popishe Church*. Emden: Egidius van der Erve.

Cunliffe, John W., ed. 1906. *Supposes; And Jocasta: Two plays translated from the Italian the first by Geo. Gascoigne, the second by Geo. Gascoigne and F. Kinwelmersh*. Boston: D. C. Heath & Co.

Cursi, Maria Floriana. 2013. "*Amicitia* e *societas* nei rapporti tra Roma e gli altri popoli del Mediterraneo" 41 *Index* 195–227.

Cursi, Maria Floriana. 2014. "*Bellum iustum* tra rito e *iustae causae belli*" 42 *Index* 569–585.

Dabhoiwala, Faramerz. 2010. "Lust and Liberty" 207 *Past & Present* 89–179.

Dabhoiwala, Faramerz. 2012. *The Origins of Sex: A History of the First Sexual Revolution*. New York: Oxford University Press.

Damhoudere, Josse. 1556. *Praxis rerum criminalium*. Anvers: Ioan Belleri.

Dasent, John Roche. 1901. *Acts of the Privy Council of England*, vol. 22. London: H.M. Stationery Office.

David, Jean-Michel. 1992. *Le patronat judiciaire au dernier siècle de la république romaine*. Rome: École Française de Rome.

Davidson, N. 2001. "Marx and Engels on the Scottish Highlands" 65(3) *Science & Society* 286–326.

Davies, G.A. 2001. "Poland, Politics, and *La vida es sueño*" 70 *Bulletin of Hispanic Studies* 147–163.

Davies, John. 2005. "The Gortyn Laws." In Michel Gagarin and David Cohen (eds.), *The Cambridge Companion to Ancient Greek Law*. New York: Cambridge University Press.

Davies, Owen. 2008. "Decriminalising the Witch: The Origin and Response to the 1736 Witchcraft Act." In John Newton and Jo Bath (eds.), *Witchcraft and the Act of 1604*. Leiden and Boston: Brill.

Davis, J.C. 1982. "Radicalism in a Traditional Society: The Evaluation of Radical Thought in the English Commonwealth 1649–60" 3(2) *History of Political Thought* 193–213.

Davis, Natalie Zemon. 1983. *The Return of Martin Guerre*. Cambridge MA: Harvard University Press.

Davis, Richard Beale. 1978. *Intellectual Life in the Colonial South, 1585–1763*, 3 vols. Knoxville, TN: Knoxville University Press.

Dawson, Richard. 2014. *Justice as Attunement: Transforming Constitutions in Law, Literature, Economics, and the Rest of Life*. Abingdon: Routledge.

de Armas, Frederick. 1998. *Cervantes, Raphael, and the Classics*. Cambridge: Cambridge University Press.

de Armas, Frederick. 2001. "Segismundo/Philip IV: The Politics of Astrology in *La vida es sueño*" 53 *Bulletin of the Comediantes* 83–100.

de Baeza, Gaspar. undated. Handwritten gloss on last folio of *Ordenamiento reales*. Real Biblioteca de El Escorial. ms.Z.I.10.

de Barrionuevo, Jeronimo. 1892. *Avisos (1654–1658)*, 4 vols. Madrid: Tello.

de Blecourt, William. 2013. "Sabbath Stories: Towards a New History of Witches' Assemblies." In Brian P. Levack (ed.), *The Oxford Handbook of Witchcraft in Early Modern Europe and Colonial America*. Oxford: Oxford University Press.

de Bobadilla, Jeronimo Castillo. 1616. *Política para corregidores*. Barcelona: Gerónymo Margarit.

de Bovelles, Charles. 1605. *Géométrie praticque*. Paris: Denise Cavellat.

de Bry, Johann Theodor. *Proscenium vitæ humanæ, sive Emblematum secularium, jucundissima et artificiosissima varietate vitæ humanæ ....* Frankfurt: G. Fitzer.

de Celso, Hugo. 1540. *Repertorio universal de las leyes de todos los reynos de Castilla*. Alcalá de Henares: Juan de Brocar.

de Cervantes Saavedra, Miguel. 1970. *La cueva de Salamanca. Entremeses*. Edited by Eugenio Asensio. Madrid: Castalia, 185–199.

de Cervantes Saavedra, Miguel. 2003. *Los trabajos de Persiles y Sigismunda*. Edited by Carlos Rumero Muñoz. Madrid: Cátedra.

de Cervantes Saavedra, Miguel. 2005. *El ingenioso hidalgo Don Quijote de la Mancha*. Edited by Celina Sabor de Cortazar and Isaías Lerner, 2 vols. Buenos Aires: Eudeba.

de Clifton Parmiter, Geoffrey. 1967. *The King's Great Matter: A Study of Anglo-Papal Relations 1527–1534*. London: Longmans.

de Clifton Parmiter, Geoffrey. 1976. *Elizabethan Popish Recusancy in the Inns of Court*. Bulletin of the Institute of Historical Research, Special Supplement, no. 11, London.

de Córdoba, Luis Cabrera. 1857. *Relaciones de las cosas sucedidas en la Corte de España, desde 1599 hasta 1614*. Madrid: J. Martín Alegra, January 5, 1602.

de Covarrubias Orozco, Sebastian. [1611] 1994. *Tesoro de la lengua castellana o española*. Madrid: Castalia.

de Cusa, Nicholas. 1981. *On Learned Ignorance*. Translated by Paul Wilpert, Ernest Hoffmann, and Raymond Klibansky. Minneapolis: Arthur J. Banning.

de Grazia, M., Quilligan, M. and Stallybrass, P., eds. 1996. *Subject and Object in Renaissance Culture*. Cambridge: Cambridge University Press.

de Hinojosa, Eduardo. 1899. "El derecho en el *Poema del Cid*." In *Homenaje a Menéndez y Pelayo*, 2 vols. Madrid: Librería general de Victoriano Suárez.

de Hinojosa, Eduardo. 1904. "Las relaciones entre la poesía y el derecho." In *Discurso leído ante S.M. El Rey Don Alfonso XIII*. Madrid: Real Academia Española.

de Horozco Y. Covarrubias, Juan. 1589. *Emblemas morales*. Segovia: n.p.

de La Torre, Antonio, ed. 1966. *Documentos sobre relaciones internacionales de los Reyes Católicos*, 13 vols. Barcelona: CSIS.

de Laclos, Pierre Choderos. 2011. *Les liaisons dangereuses*. Edited by Catriona Seth. Paris: Gallimard.

de Martino, Francesco. 1972. *Storia della costituzione romana*, vol. 1. 2nd edn. Naples: Jovene.
de Martino, Francesco. 1973. *Storia della costituzione romana*, vol. 2. 2nd edn. Naples: Jovene.
de Mercado, Fray Tomas. 1571. *Summa de tratos y contratos*. Seville: Hernando Díaz.
de Molina, Tirso. 1996. *Cigarrales de Toledo*. Edited by Luis Vázquez Fernández. Madrid: Castalia.
de Nebrija, Antonio. 1495. *Vocabulario español-latino*. Salamanca: Impresor de la Gramática castellana.
de Pace Salón, Marco. 1568. *Ad leges Taurinas insignes comentarij*. Pinciae: Franciscum Ferdinand Cordubensis.
de Quevedo, Francisco. 1699. *Obras de Francisco de Quevedo Villegas*, 3 vols. Amberes: Henrico y Cornelio Verdussen.
de Riqueti, Honore-Gabriel. 1782. *Des Lettres de Cachet et des Prisons d'État*. Ouvrage posthume, composé en 1778, Hambourg, s.n.
de Sade, Donatien Antoine Francois. 1990. "Les cent vingt journées de Sodome, ou l'école du libertinage." In Michel Delon (ed.), *Oeuvres*. t. I. Paris: Gallimard.
de Saxoferrato, Bartolus. 1943. *De Insigniis et armis (1358)* in Evans, John Evan (ed.), *Medieval History*. Cardiff: Lewis.
de Solorzano Pereira, Juan. 1653. *Emblemata regio politica in centuriam unam redacta*. Madrid: Garcia Morràs.
de Sutter, Laurent. 2009. *Deleuze, la pratique du droit*. Paris: Michalon.
de Sutter, Laurent. 2011. "Legal Shandeism: The Law in Laurence Sterne's *Tristram Shandy*" 23(2) *Law and Literature* 224.
de Sutter, Laurent. 2014. "The Quixote Principle, or Cervantes as a Critique of Law" 26(1) *Law and Literature* 117.
de Valdepeñas, Hernando Díaz. 1544. *Summa de notas copiosas muy sustanciales y compendiosas*. Toledo: Hernando Díaz y Juan de Medina.
de Valdes, Alfonso. 2007. *Diálogo de las cosas acaecidas en Roma*. Edited by Rosa Navarro Durán. Madrid: Cátedra.
de Vega, Lope. 1973. *El peregrino en su patria*. Edited by Juan Bautista Avalle-Arce. Madrid: Castalia.
De Vocht, H., ed. 1913. *Jasper Heywood and His Translations of Seneca*. Louvain: A. Uystpruyst.
de Vries, Jan. 2008. *The Industrious Revolution: Consumer Behavior and the Household Economy, 1650 to the Present*. Cambridge: Cambridge University Press.
Defoe, Daniel. 1727. *Conjugal Lewdness: Or Matrimonial Whoredom*. London: T. Warner.
Del Bene, Bartolomeo. 1609. *Civitas veri sive morum, Aristotelis de moribus doctrinam carmine et picturis complexa, et illustrata commentariis Th. Marcilii*. Paris: Ambroise et Jérôme Drouart.
Deleuze, Gilles. 1969. *Présentation de Sacher-Masoch. Le froid et le cruel*. Paris: Minuit.
DeLorme, Charles D., Isom, Stacey, and Kamerschen, David R. 2005. "Rent Seeking and Taxation in the Ancient Roman Empire" 37(6) *Applied Economics* 705–711.
Dening, Greg. 2002. "Performing on the Beaches of the Mind: An Essay" 41 *History and Theory* 1.24.
Derathe, Robert. 1950. *Jean-Jacques Rousseau et la politique de son temps*. Paris: PUF.
Dickson, David and Vannet. 2008. "Criminal Procedure." In *The Laws of Scotland: Stair Memorial Encyclopaedia*. London: LexisNexis.
Diderot, Denis. 2008. *Salons*. Edited by Michel Delon. Paris: Gallimard.
Diesselhorst, Malte. 1959. *Die Lehre des Grotius vom Versprechen*. Cologne-Graz: Böhlau.

Dietz, Brian. 1986. "Overseas Trade and Metropolitan Growth." In A.L. Beier and Roger Finlay (eds.), *London 1500–1700: The Making of the Metropolis*. London and New York: Longman.

Dilke, Oswald A.W. 1971. *The Roman Land Surveyors: An Introduction to the Agrimensores*. Newtonabbot: David and Charles.

Dimmock, S. 2014. *The Origins of Capitalism in England, 1400–1600*. Leiden: Brill.

Diósdi, György. 1970. *Ownership in Ancient and Preclassical Roman Law*. Budapest: Akadémiai Kiadó.

Doda, Hilary. 2013. "Rounde Heades in Square Cappes: The Role of the Vestments in the Vestiarian Controversy" 39(2) *Dress* 93–110.

Doda, Hilary. 2014. "'Saide Monstrous Hose': Compliance, Transgression and English Sumptuary Law to 1533" 45(2) *Textile History* 171–191.

Doderidge, Sir John. 1631. *The English Lawyer*. London: I. More.

Doggett, M.E. 1992. *Marriage, Wife-Beating and the Law in Victorian England*. London: Weidenfeld & Nicolson.

Dolan, F.E. 1989. "Gender, Moral Agency, and Dramatic Form in a Warning for Fair Women" 29 *Studies in English Literature* 201–218.

Dolan, F.E. 1992. "Home-Rebels and House-Traitors: Murderous Wives in Early Modern England" 4 *Yale Journal of Law & the Humanities* 25–27.

Dolganov, Anna. n.d. "Reichsrecht and Volksrecht in Theory and Practice: Roman Law and Litigation Strategy in the Province of Egypt (P. Oxy. II 237, P. Oxy. IV 706, SB XII 10929)." Available at: www.academia.edu/5896267/Reichsrecht_and_Volksrecht_in_Theory_and_Practice_Roman_Law_and_Litigation_Strategy_in_the_Province_of_Egypt_P._Oxy._II_237_P._Oxy._IV_706_SB_XII_10929_.

Dover, Kenneth J. 1968. *Lysias and the Corpus Lysiacum*. Berkeley: University of California.

Dover, Kenneth James. 1974. *Greek Popular Morality in the Time of Plato and Aristotle*. Oxford: Blackwell.

Doyle, William. 1999. *Jansenism: Catholic Resistance to Authority from the Reformation to the French Revolution*. New York: St. Martin's Press.

Draco, Honoratus. 1551. *Elementa juris seu Institutiones imperiales in Carmen contractæ*. Lyon: Thibaut Payen.

Drysdall, Dennis. 2013. *Hieroglyphs, Speaking, Pictures and the Law: The Context of Alciato's Emblems*. Glasgow: Emblem Studies.

Dubischar, Markus. 2015. "Typology of Philological Writing." In Franco Montanary, Stephanos Matthaios and Antonios Rengakos (ed.), *Brill's Companion to Ancient Greek Scholarship*, vol. 1. Boston, MA: Brill.

Dumézil, Georges. 1969. *Idées romaines*. Paris: Gallimard.

Dunn, Peter. 1960. "Honour and the Christian Background in Calderón" 37(2) *Bulletin of Hispanic Studies* 75–105.

Duran, Manuel and Rogg, Fay. 2006. *Fighting Windmills: Encounters with Don Quijote*. New Haven, CT: Yale University Press.

Earle, John. 1622. *Microcosmographie, or a Peece of the World Discovered*. Wurzburg: Konigshausen and Neumann.

Edelman, Bernard. 2014. *Sade, le désir et le droit*. Paris: L'Herne.

Eden, K. 2001. *Friends Hold All Things in Common*. New Haven and London: Yale University Press.

Egginton, William. 2016. *The Man Who Invented Fiction: How Cervantes Ushered in the Modern World*. New York: Bloomsbury.

Eichler, Barry L. 1987. "Literary structure in the laws of Eshnunna." In Francesca Rochberg-Halton (ed.), *Language, Literature and History: Philological and Historical Studies Presented to Erica Reiner*. New Haven, CT: American Oriental Society.

Eisenstein, Elizabeth. 1982. *The Printing Press as an Agent of Change: Communication and Cultural Transformations in Early Modern Europe*. Cambridge: Cambridge University Press.

Elliott, J.H. 1963. *The Revolt of the Catalans: A Study in the Decline of Spain*. Cambridge: Cambridge University Press.

Ellis, Henry, ed. 1809. *The Union of the Two Noble and Llustre Famelies of Lancastre and Yorke*. London: J. Johnson.

Ellis, Henry, ed. 1827. *Original Letters, Illustrative of English History: Including Numerous Royal Letters; from Autographs in the British Museum, and One or Two Other Collections*, vol. 2. London: Harding and Lepard.

Elmer, Peter. 2001. "Towards a Politics of Witchcraft in Early Modern England." In Stuart Clark (eds.), *Languages of Witchcraft: Narrative, Ideology and Meaning in Early Modern Culture*. Basingstoke: Macmillan.

Elton, G.R. 1986. *The Parliament of England 1559–1581*. Cambridge: Cambridge University Press.

Erasmus, Desiderius. 2001. *The Adages of Erasmus*. Edited by William Barker. Toronto: University of Toronto Press.

Erasmus, Desiderius. *Ciceronianus*. 1536. 1908 edn. New York: Columbia University Press.

Etxabe, Julen. 2010. "The Legal Universe after Robert Cover" 4(1) *Law & Humanities* 115–147.

Etxabe, Julen. 2013. *The Experience of Tragic Judgement*. Abingdon: Routledge.

Euben, J. Peter. 1997. *Corrupting Youth: Political Education, Democratic Culture, and Political Theory*. Princeton, NJ: Princeton University Press.

Euripides. 1991a. *Orestes*. Translated by William Arrowsmith. In David Grene and Richard Lattimore (eds.), *The Complete Greek Tragedies*, vol. 4. Chicago: University of Chicago Press.

Euripides. 1991b. *The Suppliant Women*. Translated by Frank William Jones. In David Grene and Richard Lattimore (eds.), *The Complete Greek Tragedies*, vol. 4. Chicago: University of Chicago Press.

Evans, David. 1999. "The Theatre of Deferral: The Image of the Law and the Architecture of the Inns of Court" 10(1) *Law and Critique* 1–25.

Evelyn, John. 1661. *Tyrannus, Or, The Mode in a Discourse of Sumptuary Lawes*. London: G. Bedel, T. Collins, and J. Crook.

Ewald, William. 1998. "The Jurisprudential Approach to Comparative Law: A Field Guide to 'Rats'" 46(4) *American Journal of Comparative Law* 701–707.

Ezquerra, Alfredo Alvar. 1995. "Los entremeses de Cervantes, leídos por un historiador" 29 *Torre de los Lujanes* 137–157.

Fajardo, Saavedra. 1649. *Idea principis christiano-politici*. Brussels: Jean Mommaert.

Falchi, Gian L. 1981. *Le controversie tra Sabiniani e Proculiani*. Milan: Giuffrè.

Faller, Lincoln B. 1987. *Turned to Account: The Forms and Functions of Criminal Biography in Late Seventeenth and Early Eighteenth-Century England*. Cambridge: Cambridge University Press.

Federici, Silvia. 2004. *Caliban and the Witch*. New York: Autonomedia.

Fell, C. 1984. *Women in Anglo-Saxon England and the Impact of 1066*. Bloomington: Indiana University Press.

Felt, J.B. 1851. *A Memoir of Defence of Hugh Peters*. Boston: C.C.P. Moody.

Ferrari, G.R.F. 2005. *City and Soul in Plato's Republic*. Chicago: University of Chicago Press.

Ferre, Jean. 1972. *Watteau*, 4 vols. Edited by Jean Ferré. Madrid: Athena.
Ferreyrolles, Gerard. 1984. *Les Provinciales de Pascal*. Paris: PUF.
Finkelpearl, Philip J. 1969. *John Marston of the Middle Temple: An Elizabethan Dramatist in his Social Setting*. Cambridge, MA: Harvard University Press.
Finkelstein, Jacob J. 1958. "Bible and Babel" 26(431) *Commentary* 44.
Finkelstein, Jacob J. 1966. "Sex Offenses in Sumerian Laws" 86(4) *Journal of the American Oriental Society* 355–372.
Finkelstein, Jacob J. 1981. "The Ox that Gored" 71(2) *Transactions of the American Philosophical Society* 1–89.
Finley, Moses. 1951. "Some Problems of Greek Law: A Consideration of Pringsheim on Sale" 9 *Seminar Jurist* 72–91.
Finley, Moses. 1966. "The Problem of the Unity of Greek Law." In *La Storia del Diritto nel Quadro delle Scienze Storiche. Atti del Primo Congresso Internazionale della Società Italiana di storia del Diritto*. Florence: Leo Olshki, 129–142.
Fiori, Roberto. 1996. *Homo sacer. Dinamica politico-costituzionale di una sanzione giuridico-religiosa*. Naples: Jovene.
Fiori, Roberto. 1998–1999. "*Ius civile, ius gentium, ius honorarium*: il problema della 'recezione' dei *iudicia bonae fidei*" *Bullettino dell'Istituto di Diritto romano "Vittorio Scialoja,"* 101–102:165–197.
Fiori, Roberto. 1999a. "*Sodales*. 'Gefolgschaften' e diritto di associazione in Roma arcaica (VIII-V sec. a.C.)." In *Societas-Ius. Munuscula di allievi a Feliciano Serrao*. Naples: Jovene.
Fiori, Roberto. 1999b. *La definizione della locatio conductio. Giurisprudenza romana e tradizione romanistica*. Naples: Jovene.
Fiori, Roberto. 2003a. "Il problema dell'oggetto del contratto nella tradizione civilistica." In *Modelli teorici e metodologici nella storia del diritto privato*, vol. 1. Naples: Jovene.
Fiori, Roberto. 2003b. *Ea res agatur. I due modelli del processo formulare repubblicano*. Milan: Giuffrè.
Fiori, Roberto. 2008. "*Fides* et *bona fides*. Hiérarchie sociale et catégories juridiques" 86 *Revue historique de droit français et étranger* 465–481.
Fiori, Roberto. 2011a. *Bonus vir. Politica filosofia retorica e diritto nel de officiis di Cicerone*. Naples: Jovene.
Fiori, Roberto. 2011b. "La struttura del matrimonio romano" 105 *Bullettino dell'Istituto di diritto romano Vittorio Scialoja* 197–234.
Fiori, Roberto. 2012. "The Roman Conception of Contract." In T.A.J. McGinn (ed.), *Obligations in Roman Law. Past, Present, and Future*. Ann Arbor: University of Michigan Press.
Fiori, Roberto. 2013. "La gerarchia come criterio di verità: *boni* e *mali* nel processo romano arcaico." In C. Cascione and C. Masi Doria (eds.), *Quid est veritas? Un seminario su verità e forme giuridiche*. Naples: Satura.
Fiori, Roberto. 2014a. "The *vir bonus* in Cicero's *de officiis*: Greek philosophy and Roman legal science." In *Aequum ius*. От друзей и коллег к 50-летию профессора Д.В. Дождева. Moscow: Statyt.
Fiori, Roberto. 2014b. "Rise and Fall of the Specificity of Contracts." In B. Sirks (ed.), *Nova ratione. Change of Paradigms in Roman Law*. Wiesbaden: Harrassowitz.
Firth, Charles Harding and Rait, Robert Sangster, eds. 1911. *Acts and Ordinances of the Interregnum, 1642–1660*. London: HMSO.
Fish, Stanley E. 1980. *Is there a Text in this Class? The Authority of Interpretive Communities*. Cambridge, MA: Harvard University Press.

Fish, Stanley E. 1989. *Doing What Comes Naturally: Change, Rhetoric, and the Practice of Theory in Literary and Legal Studies*. Durham, NC: Duke University Press.

Fitzmaurice, A. 2014. *Sovereignty, Property and Empire, 1500–2000*. Cambridge: Cambridge University Press.

Floristan, Alfredo. 2012. *1512, conquista e incorporación de Navarra: Historiografía, derecho y otros procesos de integración en la Europa renacentista*. Barcelona: Ariel, Planeta.

Forcadel, Etienne. [1549] 2011. *Sphæra legalis*. Edited by Anne Teissier-Ensminger. Classiques Garnier. Lyon: Jean de Tournes.

Forcadel, Etienne. 1553. *Cupido jurisperitus*. Lyon: Jean de Tournes.

Forestier, Georges. 2006. *Jean Racine*. Paris: Gallimard.

Forsdyke, Sara. 2009. "The Uses and Abuses of Tyranny." In Ryan Balot (ed.), *A Companion to Greek and Roman Political Thought*. Chichester: Wiley-Blackwell.

Forsythe, Gary. 2005. *A Critical History of Early Rome from Prehistory to the First Punic War*. Berkeley: University of California Press.

Fortescue, Sir John. [1470] 1997. *De Laudibus legum Angliae*. Cambridge: Cambridge University Press.

Fortescue, Thomas. 1869. *The Works of Sir John Fortescue*. London: Private Circulation.

Foster, Benjamin. 1995. "Social Reform in Ancient Mesopotamia." In K.D. Irani and Morris Smith (eds.), *Social Justice in the Ancient World*. Westport, CT: Greenwood Press.

Foster, Benjamin R., ed. and trans. 2001. *The Epic of Gilgamesh*. New York: Norton.

Foucault, Michel. 1977. *Discipline and Punish: The Birth of the Prison*. London: Penguin.

Foucault, Michel. 1985. "What is Enlightenment?" In Paul Rabinow (ed.), *The Foucault Reader*. New York: Pantheon.

Fraistat, Shawn. 2015. "The Authority of Writing in Plato's *Laws*" 43 *Political Theory* 657–677.

Frank, Jill. 2005. *A Democracy of Distinction: Aristotle and the Work of Politics*. Chicago: University of Chicago Press.

Frank, Jill. 2006. "The *Antigone*'s Law" 2 *Law, Culture, and the Humanities* 336–340.

Frank, Jill. 2007. "Wages of War: On Judgment in Plato's *Republic*" 35(4) *Political Theory* 443–467.

Frank, Jill. 2015. "On *Logos* and Politics in Aristotle." In Thornton Lockwood and Thanassis Samaras (eds.), *Aristotle's Politics: A Critical Guide*. Cambridge: Cambridge University Press.

Frank, Jill. 2017. *Poetic Justice: Rereading Plato's Republic*. Chicago: University of Chicago Press.

Frankenberg, Günther. 1985. "Critical Comparisons: Re-Thinking Comparative Law" 26(1) *Harvard International Law Journal* 411–455.

Frankenberg, Günther. 2014. "The Innocence of Method—Unveiled: Comparison as an Ethical and Political Act" 9(2) *Journal of Comparative Law* 222–258.

Fraunce, Abraham. 1588. *Insignium, Armorum, Emblematum, Hieroglyphicum et Symbolorum*. London: Orwin.

Freedman, Lawrence. 1990. "Some Thoughts on Comparative Legal Culture." In David Clark (ed.), *Comparative and Private International Law: Essays in Honor of John Henry Merryman on his Seventieth Birthday*. Berlin: Duncker and Humblot, 49–57.

French, H.R. 2011. "The Common Fields of Urban England: Communal Agriculture and the 'Politics of Entitlement', 1500–1750." In R.W. Hoyle (ed.), *Custom, Improvement and the Landscape in Early Modern England*. London: Routledge.

Friedrich, Andreas. 1617. *Emblemata Nova*. Frankfurt: Lucas Jennis.

Frier, Bruce W. 1985. *The Rise of the Roman Jurists: Studies in Cicero's* Pro Caecina. Princeton, NJ: Princeton University Press.

Fuero Juzgo. 1815. Madrid: RAE, Ibarra.

Fuhrmann, Christopher J. 2012. *Policing the Roman Empire: Soldiers, Administration, and Public Order*. New York: Oxford University Press.

Fulbecke, William. [1600] 1829 (edn.). *Directive or Preparative to the Study of Law*. London: W.T. Clarke.

Gadamer, Hans-Georg. [1960] 1989. *Truth and Method*. 2nd rev. edn. Translated by Joel Weinsheimer and Donald G. Marshall. New York: Continuum.

Gagarin, Michael. 1996. "The Torture of Slaves in Athenian Law" 91 *Classical Philology* 1–18.

Gagarin, Michael. 2005a. "The Unity of Greek Law." In Michael Gagarin and David Cohen (eds.), *The Cambridge Companion to Ancient Greek Law*. New York: Cambridge University Press.

Gagarin, Michael. 2005b. "Early Greek Law." In Michael Gagarin and David Cohen (eds.), *The Cambridge Companion to Ancient Greek Law*. New York: Cambridge University Press.

Gagarin, Michael, ed. 2011. *Speeches from Athenian Law*. Austin: University of Texas Press.

Gagarin, Michael and Cohen, David, eds. 2005. *The Cambridge Companion to Ancient Greek Law*. New York: Cambridge University Press.

Gagarin, Michael and Woodruff, Paul, eds. 1995. *Early Greek Political Thought from Homer to the Sophists*. New York: Cambridge University Press.

Galligan, Denis J. and Versteeg, Mila, eds. 2013. *Social and Political Foundations of Constitutions*. Cambridge: Cambridge University Press.

Gamauf, Richard. 1999. *Ad statuam licet confugere*. Frankfurt am Main: Peter Lang.

Gantz, Timothy. 1993. *Early Greek Myth*, vol. 1. Baltimore: Johns Hopkins University Press.

Garnsey, Peter. 1970. *Social Status and Legal Privilege in the Roman Empire*. Oxford: Oxford University Press.

Garrido Ardila, J.A. 2009. *The Cervantean Heritage: Reception and Influence of Cervantes in Britain*. London: Legenda.

Gaskill, Malcolm. 2000. *Crime and Mentalities in Early Modern England*. Cambridge: Cambridge University Press.

Gaskill, Malcolm. 2009. "Fear Made Flesh: The English Witch-Panic of 1645–1647." In David Lemmings and Claire Walker (eds.), *Moral Panics, the Media and the Law in Early Modern England*. Basingstoke: Palgrave Macmillan.

Gaskill, Malcolm. 2013. "Witch Trials in England." In Brian Levack (ed.), *The Oxford Handbook of Witchcraft in Early Modern Europe and Colonial America*. Oxford: Oxford University Press.

Gaudemet, Jean. 1967. *Institutions de l'Antiquité*. Paris: Sirey.

Gaudio, Michael. 2009. "'Counterfeited According to the Truth': John White, Lucas de Heere, and the Truth in Clothing." In Kim Sloan (ed.), *European Visions: American Voices*. London: The British Museum.

Gaughan, Judy E. 2010. *Murder Was Not a Crime: Homicide and Power in the Roman Republic*. Austin: University of Texas Press.

Gazier, Augustin. 1924. *Histoire Générale du mouvement janséniste depuis ses origines jusqu'à nos jours*, 2 vols. Paris: Honoré Champion.

Geertz, Clifford. 1973. *The Interpretation of Cultures*. New York: Basic Books.

Geertz, Clifford. 1983. *Local Knowledge: Further Essays in Interpretive Anthropology*. New York: Basic Books.

Geiss, Gilbert and Bunn, Ivan. 1997. *A Trial of Witches: A Seventeenth-Century Witchcraft Prosecution*. London: Routledge.

Gennette, Gerard. 2010. *Paratext*. Cambridge: Cambridge University Press.

German, St. [1528] 1974. *Doctor and Student*. London: Selden Society.

German, St. 1533. *Salem and Bizance*. London: Berthelet.

German, St. 1534. *A Treatise Concerning the Division between the Spirituality and the Temporality*. London: Redman.

Gernet, Louis. 1955. *Droit et société dans la Grèce Ancienne*. Paris: Sirey.

Ghestin, Jacques. 1994. "Jean Domat et le Code civil français." In Paolo Cendon (ed.), *Scritti in onore di Rodolfo Sacco. La comparazione giuridica alle sogliedel 3e millennio*. t. I. Milan: Giuffrè.

Gibson, M. 2008. "Applying the Act of 1604: Witches in Essex, Northamptonshire and Lancashire." In John Newton and Jo Bath (eds.), *Witchcraft and the Act of 1604*. Leiden and Boston: Brill.

Gilby, Anthony. 1566. *To My Louynge Brethren That Is Troublyd Abowt the Popishe Apparell, Two Short and Comfortable Epistels*. Emden: Egidius van der Erve.

Gill, Christopher. 2006. *The Structured Self in Hellenistic and Roman Thought*. Oxford: Oxford University Press.

Giltaij, Jacob. 2011. *Mensenrechten in het Romeinse recht?* Nijmegen: Wolf.

Giltaij, Jacob. 2013. "The Problem of the Content of the *lex Iulia iudiciorum publicorum*" 81(3/4) *Tijdschrift voor Rechtsgeschiedenis* 507–529.

Glanert, Simone, ed. 2014. *Comparative Law: Engaging Translation*. Abingdon: Routledge.

Glenn, Patrick H. 2010. *Legal Traditions of the World: Sustainable Diversity in Law*. 4th edn. Oxford and New York: Oxford University Press.

Glorieux, Guillaume. 2011. *Watteau*. Paris: Citadelles et Mazenod.

Goldhill, Simon. 2000. "Civic Ideology and the Problem of Difference: The Politics of Aeschylean Tragedy, Once Again" 120 *Journal of Hellenic Studies* 34–56.

Goldmann, Lucienn. 1955. *Le Dieu caché. Étude sur la vision tragique dans les Pensées de Pascal et dans le théâtre de Racine*. Paris: Gallimard.

Goodare, Julian. 2005. "The Scottish Witchcraft Act" 74(1) *Church History* 39–67.

Goodrich, Peter. 1995. *Œdipus Lex: Psychoanalysis, History, Law*. Berkeley: California University Press.

Goodrich, Peter. 1998. "Signs Taken for Wonders: Community, Identity, and 'A History of Sumptuary Law'" 23(3) *Law & Social Inquiry* 709.

Goodrich, Peter. 2011. "Spectres of Law: Why the History of Legal Spectacle Has Not Been Written" 1(3) *UC Irvine Law Review* 773.

Goodrich, Peter. 2013. "*Mos piraticus*: On the Haunting and Infesting of the Seas." *Piracy and Jurisprudence: An Interdisciplinary Workshop*. Centre for Law, Ethics and Globalization, University of Southampton Law School, University of Southampton, England.

Goodrich, Peter. 2014. *Legal Emblems and the Art of Law: Obiter Depicta as the Vision of Governance*. New York: Cambridge University Press.

Goodrich, Peter. 2017. "Proboscations: Excavations in Comedy and Law" 43(2) *Critical Inquiry* 361–388.

Goodrich, Peter and Hayaert, Valerie. 2015. *Genealogies of Legal Vision*. Abingdon: Routledge.

Gordley, James. 1991. *The Philosophical Origins of Modern Contract Doctrine*. Oxford: Oxford University Press.

Gordon, Peter. 2014. "Contextualism and Criticism in the History of Ideas." In Darrin McMahon and Samuel Moyn (eds.), *Rethinking Modern European Intellectual History*. Oxford and New York: Oxford University Press.

Gordon, William M. and Robinson, O.F. 1988. *The Institutes of Gaius*. Ithaca, NY: Cornell University Press.

Gowing, L. 1996. *Domestic Dangers: Women, Words, and Sex in Early Modern London*. Oxford: Oxford University Press.

Goyard-Fabre, Simone. 1996. *La philosophie du droit de Kant*. Paris: Vrin.

Graves, Michael A.R. 1994. *Thomas Norton, the Parliament Man*. Oxford: Blackwell.

Green, Anna. 2008. *Cultural History: History and Theory*. New York: Palgrave Macmillan.

Greenberg, J. 1974. "The Legal Status of the English Woman in Eighteenth-century Common Law and Equity" 4 *Studies in Eighteenth-century Culture* 178.

Greenberg, M. 1960. "Some Postulates of Biblical Criminal Law." In Menahen Haran (ed.), *Yehezkel Kaufmann Jubilee Volume*. Jerusalem: Magnes Press.

Greenblatt, S. 2014. "Shakespeare's Montaigne." In S. Greenblatt and P. Platt (eds.), *The Florio Translation of the Essays*. New York: New York Review Books Classics.

Greenblatt, S. and Platt, P. 2014. *The Florio Translation of the Essays*. New York: New York Review of Books Classics.

Greene, Robert. 1592. *A Quip for an Vpstart Courtier: Or, A Quaint Dispute Betvveen Veluet Breeches and Cloth-Breeches Wherein Is Plainely Set Downe the Disorders in All Estates and Trades*. London: John Wolfe.

Greenfield, Kent Roberts. 1918. *Sumptuary Law in Nürnberg: A Study in Paternal Government*. Baltimore: The Johns Hopkins University Press.

Greengus, Samuel. 1995. "Legal and Social Institutions of Ancient Mesopotamia." In Jack Sasson (ed.), *Civilizations of the Ancient Near East*. New York: Scribner's.

Greenidge, Abel Henry Jones. 1894. *Infamia: Its Place in Roman Public and Private Law*. Oxford: Clarendon.

Greer, Margaret. 1991. *The Play of Power*. Princeton, NJ: Princeton University Press.

Gribaldi Mofa, Matteo. 1553. *De methodo ac ratione studendi libri III*. Cologne: n.p.

Griffiths, Paul. 1996. *Youth and Authority: Formative Experiences in England, 1560–1640*. Oxford: Clarendon Press.

Grimm, Jacob. 1816. "Von der Poesie im Recht" 2 *Zeitschrift für geschichtliche Rechtswissenschaft* 25–99.

Grimme, Hubert. 1907. *The Law of Hammurabi and Moses: A Sketch*. Translated by William T. Pilter. London: Society for Promoting Christian Knowledge.

Grossi, Paolo. 1973. "La proprietà nel sistema privatistico della Seconda Scolastica." In P. Grossi (ed.), *La Seconda Scolastica nella formazione del diritto privato moderno*. Milan: Giuffrè.

Gruen, Erich. 1995. *The Last Generation of the Roman Republic*. Berkeley: University of California Press.

Gualandi, Giovanni. 1963. *Legislazione imperiale e giurisprudenza*, vol. 2. Milan: Giuffrè.

Guettel Cole, Susan. 1984. "Greek Sanctions Against Sexual Assault" 79(2) *Classical Philology* 97–113.

Gunn, S.J. 1993. "The Courtiers of Henry VII" 108(426) *EHR* 45–46.

Guy, John. 1985. "Law, Lawyers and the English Reformation" 35(11) *History Today* 16–22.

Guy, John. 2000. "Thomas More and Christopher St. German: The Battle of the Books." In *Politics, Law and Counsel in Tudor and Early Stuart England*. Aldershot: Ashgate.

Guy, John. 2005. *Queen of Scots: The True Life of Mary Stuart*. New York: Mariner Books.

Guy, John. 1977. *The Cardinal's Court: The Impact of Thomas Wolsey in Star Chamber*. Hassocks: Harvester.

Hadrianus, Junius. 1565. *Emblemata*. Antwerp: Christophe Plantin.

Hagemann, Matthias. 1998. *Iniuria. Von den XII-Tafeln bis zur Justinianischen Kodifikation*. Cologne, Weimar, Vienna: Böhlau.

Hahm, David E. 2009. "The Mixed Constitution in Greek Thought." In Ryan Balot (ed.), *A Companion to Greek and Roman Political Thought*. Chichester: Wiley-Blackwell.

Halbertal, Moshe. 1997. *Mahpekhot parshaniyot be-hithavutan: 'arakhim ke-shiḳulim parshaniyim be-midreshe halakhah*. Jerusalem: Magnes Press.

Haldar, Piyel. 2015. "The Tongue and the Eye." In Peter Goodrich and Valérie Hayaert (eds.), *Genealogies of Legal Vision*. Abingdon: Routledge.

Haldar, Piyel. 2016. "Equity as a Question of Decorum and Manners: Conscience as Vision" 10(2) *Polemos* 311–327.

Hale, Sir Matthew. 1698. *Pleas of the Crown, or, A Methodical Summary of the Principal Matters Relating to that Subject*. London: Printed by the assigns of Richard Atkyns and Edward Atkyns Esquires, for William Shrewsbury Cynthia Herrup, *A House in Gross Disorder: Sex, Law and the 2nd Earl of Castlehaven*. Oxford: Oxford University Press, 1999.

Halliwell, Stephen. 2009. "Theory and Practice of Narrative in Plato." In Jonas Grethlein and Antonios Rengakos (eds.), *Narratology and Interpretation: The Content of Narrative Form in Ancient Literature*. Berlin and New York: Walter De Gruyter.

Hammer, Dean. 2014. *Roman Political Thought: From Cicero to Augustine*. Cambridge: Cambridge University Press.

Hammons, P. 2006. "Rethinking Women and Property in Sixteenth and Seventeenth-Century England" 3(6) *Literature Compass* 1386–1407.

Hansen, Mogens H. 1991. *The Athenian Democracy in the Age of Demosthenes*. Oxford: Oxford University Press.

Harding, Vanessa. 1990. "The Population of London, 1550–1700: A Review of the Published Evidence" 15(2) *The London Journal* 111–128.

Harington, Sir John. 2009. *The Epigrams of Sir John Harington*. Edited by Gerard Kilroy. Surrey: Ashgate.

Harman, Alice. 2005. "How Great Was Shakespeare's Debt to Montaigne?" In F. Lestringant (ed.), *Le Brésil de Montaigne*. Paris: Chandeigne.

Harper, Kyle. 2015. "Landed Wealth in the Long Term: Patterns, Possibilities, Evidence." In Paul Erdkamp, Koenraad Verboven, and Arjan Zuiderhoek (eds.), *Ownership and Exploitation of Land and Natural Resources in the Roman World*. Oxford: Oxford University Press.

Harrell, Hansen C. 1936. *Public Arbitration in Athenian Law*. Columbia: University of Missouri.

Harries, Jill. 2006. *Cicero and the Jurists: From Citizen's Law to the Lawful State*. London: Duckworth.

Harries, Jill. 2007. *Law and Crime in the Roman World*. Cambridge: Cambridge University Press.

Harries, Jill. 2012. "Roman Law and Legal Culture." In Scott Johnson (ed.), *The Oxford Handbook of Late Antiquity*. Oxford: Oxford University Press.

Harris, Edward M. 1993. "*Apotimema*: Athenian Terminology for Real Security in Leases and Dowry Agreements" 43 *The Classical Quarterly* 73–95.

Harris, Edward M. 1994. "Law and Oratory." In Ian Worthington (ed.), *Persuasion: Greek Rhetoric in Action*. London: Duckworth.

Harris, Edward M. 2013. *The Rule of Law in Action in Democratic Athens*. Oxford: Oxford University Press.

Harris, J.G. 1994. "This is Not a Pipe: Water Supply, Incontinent Sources and the Leaky Body Politic." In R. Burt and J.M. Archer (eds.), *Enclosure Acts—Sexuality, Property and Culture in Early Modern England*. Ithaca and London: Cornell University Press.

Harrison, William. 1614. *The Difference of Hearers*. London: T. Creed.

Harte, N.B. 1993. "Silk and Sumptuary Legislation in England." In Simonetta Cavaciocchi (ed.), *La Seta in Europa*, Sec. XIII–XX. Florence: Le Monnier.

Harte, N.B. 1997. *The New Draperies in the Low Countries and England, 1300–1800*. Oxford: Oxford University Press.

Hartley, T.E., ed. 1981. *Proceedings in the Parliaments of Elizabeth I, Volume 1: 1558–1581*. Leicester: Leicester University Press.

Hartman, Geoffrey H. and Budick, Sanford, eds. 1986. *Midrash and Literature*. New Haven, CT: Yale University Press.

Haunold, Christoph. 1671. *Controversiarum de Justitia et Jure privatorum universo nova et theorica methodo*. tomus primus. Ingolstadt: Joannes Simon Knab.

Hayaert, Valérie. 2008. *Mens Emblematica et Humanisme Juridique*. Geneva: Droz.

Haynes, Samuel and Murdin, William, ed. 1740–1759. *Collection of State Papers … left by William Cecil Lord Burghley vol. 2*. London: William Bowyer.

Hayward, John. 1968. *Annals of the First Four Years of the Reign of Queen Elizabeth*, vol. 7. Edited by John Bruce, Camden Society 1. New York: Johnson Reprint Corp.

Hayward, Maria. 2009. *Rich Apparel: Clothing and the Law in Henry VIII's England*. Farnham: Ashgate.

Heitland, William Emerton. 1921. *Agricola: A Study of Agriculture and Rustic Life in the Greco-Roman World from the Point of View of Labour*. Cambridge: Cambridge University Press.

Helmholz, Richard H. 1998. "Harboring Sexual Offenders: Ecclesiastical Courts and Controlling Misbehavior" 37 *Journal of British Studies* 258–268.

Helmholz, Richard H. 2004. *The Oxford History of the Laws of England: The Canon Law and Ecclesiastical Jurisdiction from 597 to the 1640s*. Oxford: Oxford University Press.

Hendry, Jennifer. 2014. "Legal Comparison and the (Im)possibility of Translation." In Simone Glanert (ed.), *Comparative Law: Engaging Translation*. Abingdon: Routledge.

Heringa, Aalt Willem and Kiiver, Philipp. 2012. *Constitutions Compared: An Introduction to Comparative Constitutional Law*. 3rd edn. Cambridge: Intersentia.

Herington, C.J. 1973. "Review: *The Justice of Zeus* by Hugh Lloyd-Jones" 94(4) *The American Journal of Philology* 395–398.

Hermenegildo, Alfredo. 2002. *El tirano en escena: siglo XVI*. Madrid: Biblioteca Nueva.

Herodotus. 1987. *The History*. Translated by David Grene. Chicago: University of Chicago Press.

Herrup, Cynthia. 1984. "Law and Morality in Seventeenth Century England" 106 *Past & Present* 102–123.

Herzog, T. 2013. "Colonial Law and 'Native Customs': Indigenous Land Rights in Colonial Spanish America" 69(3) *The Americas* 303–321.

Hesiod. 1993. *Works and Days; and Theogony*. Translated by Stanley Lombardo; Introduction by Robert Lamberton. Indianapolis and Cambridge: Hackett Publishing.

Hill, C. 1980. *The Century of the Revolution*. 2nd edn. London: Routledge.

Hill, C. 2006. *Winstanley "The Law of Freedom" and Other Writings*. Cambridge: Cambridge University Press.

Hillman, R. and Ruberry-Blanc, P., eds. 2014. *Female Transgression in Early Modern Britain: Literary and Historical Explorations*. Farnham: Ashgate.

Hiltebeitel, Alf. 2011. *Dharma. Its Early History in Law, Religion, and Narrative*. Oxford: Oxford University Press.

Hipkin, S. 2000. "Sitting on his Penny Rent: Conflict and Right of Common in Faversham Blean, 1595–1610" 11(1) *Rural History* 1–35.

Hitz, Zena. 2009. "Plato on the Sovereignty of Law." In Ryan Balot (ed.), *A Companion to Greek and Roman Political Thought*. Chichester: Wiley-Blackwell.

Hitzig, Hermann Ferdinand. 1899. *Injuria. Beiträge zur Geschichte der injuria im griechischen und römischen Recht*. Munich: Ackermann.

Hobbes, Thomas. [1681] 1985. *A Dialogue between a Phylospher and a Student of the Common Laws of England*. Oxford: Oxford University Press.

Höbenreich, Evelyn. 1992. "À propos 'Antike Rechtsgeschichte': einige Bemerkungen zur Polemik zwischen Ludwig Mitteis und Leopold Wenger" 109 *Zeitschrift der Savigny-Stiftung für Rechtsgeschichte: romanistische Abteilung* 547–562.

Hochart, Patrick. 2008. *Houilles*. Paris: Manucius.

Hogrefe, Pearl. 1937. "The Life of Christopher Saint German" 13(52) *RES* 402–404.

Holdsworth, William. 1924a. *A History of English Law*. London: Methuen.

Holdsworth, William. 1924b. *Influence of the Legal Profession on the Growth of the English Constitution*. Oxford: Creighton Lecture.

Holdsworth, William S. 1945. *History of English Law*, vol. 4. 3rd edn. London: Methuen & Co.

Holmes, T.J. 1940. *Cotton Mather: A Bibliography of His Works*, 3 vols. Cambridge, MA: Harvard University Press.

Holthofer, Ernst. 2001. "Domat, Jean." In Michael Stolleis (ed.), *Juristen: ein biographisches Lexikon; von der Antike bis zum 20. Jahrhundert*. 2nd edn. Munich: C. H. Beck.

Homer. 1990. *The Iliad*. Translated by Robert Fagles; Introduction by Bernard Knox. New York: Penguin.

Homer. 1996. *The Odyssey*. Translated by Robert Fagles; Introduction by Bernard Knox. New York: Penguin.

Hondle, S. 1998. "Persuasion and Protest in the Caddington Common Enclosure Dispute, 1635–1639" 158(1) *Past and Present* 37–78.

Honig, Bonnie. 2013. *Antigone, Interrupted*. Cambridge and New York: Cambridge University Press.

Honoré, Tony. 1994. *Emperors and Lawyers: With a Palingenesia of Third-Century Imperial Rescripts 193-305 AD*. Oxford: Clarendon Press.

Hoppit, Julian. 1997. *Failed Legislation 1660–1800: Extracted from the Commons and Lords Journals*. London: Hambledon.

Hudson, Michael. 1993. "The Lost Tradition of Biblical Debt Cancellations." Available at http://michael-hudson.com/wp-content/uploads/2010/03/HudsonLostTradition.pdf.

Hudson, Michael. 2002. "Reconstructing the Origins of Interest-Bearing Debt and the Logic of Clean Slates." In Michael Hudson and Marc Van De Mieroop (eds.), *Debt and Economic Renewal in the Ancient Near East*. Bethesda, MD: CDL Press.

Hughes, Paul L. and Larkin, James F. 1969. *Tudor Royal Proclamations: The Later Tudors*. New Haven and London: Yale University Press.

Hughes, Paula. 2013. "Witch-Hunting in Scotland, 1649–1650." In Julian Goodare (ed.), *Scottish Witches and Witch-Hunters*. Basingstoke: Palgrave Macmillan.

Humbert, Michel. 2005. *Le dodici tavole: dai decemviri agli umanisti*. Pavia: IUSS Press.

Humphreys, Sally C. 1985. "Social Relations on Stage: Witnesses in Classical Athens" 1(2) *History and Anthropology* 313–369.

Hunt, Alan. 1996. *Governance of the Consuming Passions: A History of Sumptuary Law*. New York: St. Martin's Press.

Hunt, Alan. 2003. "The Governance of Consumption: Sumptuary Laws and Shifting Forms of Regulation." In David B. Clarke, Marcus A. Doel, and Kate M.L. Housiaux (eds.), *The Consumption Reader*. London: Routledge.

Hurowitz, Victor. 1994. *Inu Anum *s*irum: Literary Structures in the Non-Juridical Sections of Codex Hammurabi*. Philadelphia, PA: University Museum.

Husa, Jaakko. 2007. "About the Methodology of Comparative Law: Some Comments Concerning the Wonderland" 5 *Maastricht Faculty of Law Working Paper Series* 1–20.

Hutson, Lorna. 2007. *The Usurer's Daughter*. Abingdon: Routledge.

Hyamson, Moses. 1913. *Mosaicarum et Romanarum legum collatio*. Oxford: Oxford University Press.

Ibarra, Adrián Celaya. 1999. *Selección de estudios jurídicos: En especial sobre el País Vasco*. Bilbao: Universidad de Deusto, 355.

Ibbetson, David J. 2013. "Iniuria, Roman and English." In Eric Descheemaeker and Helen Scott (eds.), *Iniuria and the Common Law*. Oxford and Portland, OR: Hart.

Inderwick, Frederick A. 1896–1898. *A Calendar of the Inner Temple Records*. London: H. Sotheran and Co.

Ingram, J.P. 2006. *Idioms of Self-Interest—Credit, Identity and Property in Renaissance Literature*. New York and London: Routledge.

Isidore of Seville. 2008. *Etymologies*. Cambridge: Cambridge University Press.

Ives, Eric W. 1983. *The Common Lawyers of Pre-Reformation England: Thomas Kebell, a Case Study*. Cambridge: Cambridge University Press.

Jackson, John. 1937. *Tacitus: Annals. With An English Translation*. Cambridge, MA: Harvard University Press (Loeb Classical Library).

Jacob, Robert. 1994. *Images de la Justice. Essai sur l'iconographie judiciaire du Moyen-Âge à l'âge classique*. Paris: Le Léopard d'or.

Jacobsen, Thorkild. 1987. "The Graven Image." In Patrick D. Miller, Paul Hanson and S. Dean McBride (eds.), *Ancient Israelite Religion: Essays in Honor of Frank Moore Cross*. Philadelphia, PA: Fortress.

Jacotot, Mathieu. 2013. *Question d'honneur. Les notions d'honos, honestum et honestas dans la République romaine antique*. Rome: École Française de Rome.

Jaeger, Werner. 1938. *Demosthenes: The Origins and Growth of His Policy*. Berkeley: University of California.

Jakab, Eva. 2015. "Property Rights in Ancient Rome." In Paul Erdkamp, Koenraad Verboven, and Arjan Zuiderhoek (eds.), *Ownership and Exploitation of Land and Natural Resources in the Roman World*. Oxford: Oxford University Press.

James, Henry and Walker, Greg. 1995. "The Politics of *Gorboduc*" 110(435) *EHR* 119.

James, Norman. 1998. "Defining Superstitions: Treasonous Catholics and the Act against Witchcraft of 1563." In Charles Carlton, et al. (eds.), *State, Sovereigns and Society in Early Modern England*. Stroud: Sutton Publishing.

Jardine, Lisa. 1996. *Worldly Goods: A New History of the Renaissance*. New York: Doubleday.

Jenkins, D. and Owen, M.E., eds. 1980. *The Welsh Law of Women: Studies Presented to Professor Daniel A. Binchy on his 80th Birthday*. Cardiff: University of Wales Press.

Jewel, John. 1562. *An Apologie or Answere in Defence of the Churche of England*. London: n.p.

Jewel, John. 1567. *A Defence of the Apologie of the Churche of England*. London: Fleetstreet.

Johns, A. 1998. *The Nature of the Book: Print and Knowledge in the Making*. Chicago: University of Chicago Press.
Johnson, Samuel. 2000. "Debtor's Prisons." In Donald Greene (ed.), *The Major Works*. 2nd edn. Oxford: Oxford University Press.
Jones, Ann Rosalind and Stallybrass, Peter. 2000. "'Rugges of London and the Diuell's Band': Irish Mantles and Yellow Starch as Hybrid London Fashion." In Lena Cowen Orlin (ed.), *Material London, Ca. 1600*. Philadelphia: University of Pennsylvania Press.
Jones, Malcolm. 2010. *The Print in Early Modern England: An Historical Oversight*. New Haven, CT and London: Yale University Press.
Jones, Norman L. 1982. *Faith by Satute: Parliament and the Settlement of Religion 1559*. London: HLRO.
Jordan, Constance. 1987. "Woman's Rule in Sixteenth-century British Political Thought" 40(3) *Renaissance Quarterly* 435.
Jordan, Constance and Cunningham, Karen, ed. 2010. *The Law in Shakespeare*. Basingstoke: Palgrave Macmillan.
Jouanjan, Olivier. 2005. *Une histoire de la pensée juridique allemande (1800–1918). Idéalisme et conceptualisme chez les juristes allemands du 19e siècle*. Munich: PUF.
Jover Zamora, Jose Maria. 1996. *Historia de la cultura española "Menéndez Pidal": El siglo del Quijote, 1580–1680*, 2 vols. Madrid: Espasa, II.
Kahn, Aaron M. 2006. "Moral Opposition to Phillip II in Pre-Lopean Drama" 74 *Hispanic Review* 227–250.
Kahn, Paul W. 1999. *The Cultural Study of Law: Reconstructing Legal Scholarship*. Chicago: University of Chicago Press.
Kant, Immanuel. 1781. *Akademie-Textausgabe*. Band 4, *Kritik der reinen Vernunft*, in Kants Werke. Berlin: de Gruyter, 1978 edn.
Kant, Immanuel. 1783. *Prolegomena*, in Kants Werke. Berlin: de Gruyter, 1978 edn.
Kant, Immanuel. 1785. *Grundlegung zur Metaphysik der Sitten*, in Kants Werke. Berlin: de Gruyter, 1978 edn.
Kant, Immanuel. 1786. *Metaphysische Anfangsgründe der Naturwissenschaften*, in Kants Werke. Berlin: de Gruyter, 1978 edn.
Kantorowicz, Ernst. 1957. *The King's Two Bodies: A Study in Medieval Political Theology*. Princeton, NJ: Princeton University Press.
Kantorowicz, Ernst. 1965. "The Sovereignty of the Artist." In *Selected Studies*. Locus Valley, NY: J.J. Augustin.
Kantorowicz, Herman. 1938. *Studies in the Glossators of the Roman Law: Newly Discovered Writings of the Twelfth Century*. Cambridge: Cambridge University Press.
Kaser, Max. 1956. *Eigentum und Besitz im älteren römischen Recht*. Cologne: Böhlau.
Kaser, Max. 1972. *Das römische Privatrecht*. I. *Das altrömische, das vorklassische und klassische Recht*. 2nd edn. Munich: C. H. Beck.
Kaser, Max. 1975. *Das römische Privatrecht*. II. *Die nachklassischen Entwicklungen*. 2nd edn. Munich: C. H. Beck.
Kaser, Max and Hackl, Karl. 1996. *Das römische Zivilprozessrecht*. Munich: C. H. Beck.
Kehoe, Dennis P. 2015. "Property Rights over Land and Economic Growth in the Roman Empire." In Paul Erdkamp, Koenraad Verboven, and Arjan Zuiderhoek (eds.), *Ownership and Exploitation of Land and Natural Resources in the Roman World*. Oxford: Oxford University Press.
Keller, Timothy. 2002. "What is Biblical Justice?" Available at www.relevantmagazine.com/god/practical-faith/what-biblical-justice.

Kelley, Donald R. 1979. "Gaius Noster: Substructures of Western Social Thought" 84 *The American Historical Review* 619–648.
Kelly, Fergus. 1998. *A Guide to Early Irish Law*. Dublin: Dublin Institute for Advanced Studies.
Kelly, Henry A. 2018. "Thomas More on Inquisitorial Due Process" 123(503) *HER* 847–894.
Kennedy, Ruth Lee. 1942."Certain Phases of the Sumptuary Decrees and Their Relation to Tirso's Theatre" 10(2) *Hispanic Review* 91–115.
Kenneth, Reid and Zimmerman, Reinhard. 2000. *A History of Private Law in Scotland*, vol. 2. Edited by Kenneth Reid and Reinhard Zimmermann. Oxford: Oxford University Press.
Kent, Joan. 1973. "Attitudes of Members of the House of Commons to the Regulation of 'Personal Conduct in Late Elizabethan and Early Stuart England" 46 (113) *Historical Research* 51.
Keymer, Thomas, ed. 2006. *Laurence Sterne's Tristram Shandy: A Casebook*. Oxford: Oxford University Press.
Keymer, Thomas, ed. 2009. *The Cambridge Companion to Laurence Sterne*. Cambridge: Cambridge University Press.
Kilcullen, John. 2014. "Medieval Political Philosophy." In *The Stanford Encyclopedia of Philosophy*. Available at https://plato.stanford.edu/entries/medieval-political/.
Killerby, Catherine Kovesi. 2002. *Sumptuary Law in Italy 1200–1500*. Oxford and New York: Oxford University Press.
King, Leonard W. 1910. *A History of Sumer and Akkad: An Account of the Early Races of Babylonia from Prehistoric Times to the Foundation of the Babylonian Monarchy*. London: Chatto & Windus.
King, Willard. 1979. "Cervantes' *La Numancia* and Imperial Spain" 94 *MLN* 200–221.
Kiralfy, A. 1988. "Custom in Medieval English Law" 9(1) *Journal of Legal History* 26.
Kirkton, James. 1817. *The Secret and True History of the Church of Scotland*. Edinburgh: James Ballantyne and Co.
Kleinhans, Martha-Marie and MacDonald, Roderick. 1997. "What is a *Critical* Legal Pluralism?" 12 *Canadian Journal of Law and Society* 25–46.
Korda, N. 2008. *Shakespeare's Domestic Economies: Gender and Property in Early Modern England*. Pennsylvania: Pennsylvania University Press.
Koselleck, Reinhart. 1975. *Preußen zwischen Reform und Revolution. Allgemeines Landrecht, Verwaltung und soziale Bewegung von 1791 bis 1848*. 2nd edn. Stuttgart: Klett-Cotta.
Koskenniemi, M. 2010. "Colonization of the 'Indies': The Origin of International Law." In *La Idea de América en el Pensamiento ius Internacionalista del Siglo XXI*. Universidad de Zaragoza: Universidad de Zaragoza.
Kraus, Fritz R. 1984. *Königliche Verfügungen in Altbabylonischer Zeit*. Leiden: Brill.
Krause, Jens-Uwe. 2004. *Kriminalgeschichte der Antike*. Munich: C. H. Beck.
Krinstensen, Karen R. 2004. "Codification, Tradition and Innovation in the Law Code of Gortyn" 7 *DIKE Rivista di storia del diritto greco ed ellenistico* 135–168.
Krygier, Martin. 1986. "Law as Tradition" 5 *Law and Philosophy* 237–262.
Kuchta, David. 2002. *The Three-Piece Suit and Modern Masculinity: England, 1550–1850*. Berkeley and London: University of California Press.
Kunkel, Wolfgang. 1962. *Untersuchungen zur Entwicklung des römischen Kriminalverfahrens in vorsullanischer Zeit*. Munich: C. H. Beck.
Kunkel, Wolfgang. 1974. "Quaestio" 8 *Kleine Schriften* 33–110.
Kunkel, Wolfgang. 2001. *Die Römischen Juristen. Herkunft und soziale Stellung*. Cologne, Weimar, Vienna: Böhlau Verlag.
Kunkel, Wolfgang and Wittmann, Roland. 1995. *Staatsordnung und Staatspraxis der römischen Republik*, vol. 2. Munich: C. H. Beck.

Lacan, Jacques. 2007. *The Other Side of Psychoanalysis*. London: Norton.
LaCapra, Dominick. 1983. "Rethinking Intellectual History and Reading Texts." In *Rethinking Intellectual History: Texts, Contexts, Language*. Ithaca, NY: Cornell University Press.
Laks, André. 2010. "Plato's 'Truest Tragedy': *Laws* Book 7, 817a-d." In Christopher Bobonich (ed.), *Plato's Laws: A Critical Guide*. New York: Cambridge University Press.
Lambley, Kathleen. 1920. *The Teaching and Cultivation of the French Language in England during Tudor and Stuart Times*. Manchester: Manchester University Press.
Lane, Melissa. 2013a. "Founding as Legislating: The Figure of the Lawgiver in Plato's *Republic*." In Noburu Notomi and Luc Brisson (eds.), *Dialogues on Plato's Politeia (Republic): Selected Papers from the Ninth Symposium Platonicum*. Sankt Augustin: Academia Verlag.
Lane, Melissa. 2013b. "Platonizing the Spartan *Politeia* in Plutarch's *Lycurgus*." In Verity Harte and Melissa Lane (eds.), *Politeia in Greek and Roman Philosophy*. Cambridge: Cambridge University Press.
Lane, Melissa. 2014. *The Birth of Politics: Eight Greek and Roman Political Ideas and Why They Matter*. Princeton, NJ: Princeton University Press.
Langholm, O. 2008. "The German Tradition in Late Medieval Value Theory" 15(4) *The European Journal of the History of Economic Thought* 555–570.
Langlands, Rebecca. 2006. *Sexual Morality in Ancient Rome*. Cambridge: Cambridge University Press.
Lanni, Adriaan. 2006. *Law and Justice in the Courts of Classical Athens*. Cambridge: Cambridge University Press.
Lapesa, Rafael. 1988. "Notas etimológicas y semánticas." 7(2) *Annexes des Cahiers de linguistique hispanique medievale* 469–476.
Latham, Robert and Matthews, William, ed. 1974. *The Diary of Samuel Pepys: 1666*, vol. 7. Berkeley and Los Angeles: University of California Press.
Launaro, Alessandro. 2015. "The Nature of the Villa Economy." In Paul Erdkamp, Koenraad Verboven, and Arjan Zuiderhoek (eds.), *Ownership and Exploitation of Land and Natural Resources in the Roman World*. Oxford: Oxford University Press.
Laurence, A. 2009. "Women and the Transmission of Property: Inheritance in the British Isles in the 17th Century" 244(3) *Dix-septième siècle* 435–450.
Leadman, I.S., ed. 1902. *Publications of the Selden Society*. London: Seldon Society.
Lebow, Richard Ned. 2003. *The Tragic Vision of Politics: Ethics, Interests and Orders*. Cambridge: Cambridge University Press.
Leesen, Tessa G. 2010. *Gaius Meets Cicero: Law and Rhetoric in the School Controversies*. Leiden and Boston, MA: Martinus Nijhoff Publishers.
Legendre, Pierre. 2008. "The Dogmatic Value of Aesthetics" 14(4) *Parallax* 10–17.
Legh, Gerard. 1562. *The Accedens of Armory*. London: Richard Totell.
Legrand, Pierre. 1995. "Comparative Legal Studies and Commitment to Theory" 58 *The Modern Law Review* 262–273.
Legrand, Pierre. 1999. *Fragments on Law-as-Culture*. Deventer: W.E.J. Tjeenk Willink, Schoordijk Institute.
Legrand, Pierre. 2014. "Withholding Translation." In Simone Glanert (ed.), *Comparative Law: Engaging Translation*. Abingdon: Routledge.
Legrand, Pierre. 2016. *Le Droit Comparé*. 5th edn. Paris: Presses Universitaires de France.
Lehmberg, Stanford E. 1975. "Parliamentary Attainder in the Reign of Henry VIII" 18(4) *The Historical Journal* 684.
Lemire, B. 2005. *The Business of Everyday Life: Gender, Practice and Social Politics in England, c. 1600–1900*. Manchester: Manchester University Press.

Lenel, Otto. 2010. *Das edictum perpetuum*. 3rd edn. Aalen: Scientia.
Leneman, Leah and Mitchison, Rosalind. 1989. *Sexuality and Social Control: Scotland, 1660–1780*. Oxford: Basil Blackwell.
Lenton, Francis. 1629. *The Young Gallants Whirligigg; or, Youth Reakes*. London: Robert Bostocke.
Lentz, Tony. 1989. *Orality and Literacy in Hellenic Greece*. Carbondale: Southern Illinois University Press.
Lepschy, Giulio. 1992. "Subject and Object in the History of Linguistics" 1 *Journal of the Institute of Romance Studies* 1–15.
Levack, Brian P. 1980. "The Great Scottish Witch Hunt of 1661–1662" 20(1) *Journal of British Studies* 90–108.
Levack, Brian P. 2008. *Witch-Hunting in Scotland: Law, Politics and Religion*. New York: Routledge.
Levack, Brian P. 2010. "The Prosecution of Sexual Crimes in Early Eighteenth-Century Scotland" 89(2) *Scottish Historical Review* 172–193.
Levack, Brian P. 2013a. "Introduction." In Brian Levack (ed.), *The Oxford Handbook of Witchcraft in Early Modern Europe and Colonial America*. Oxford: Oxford University Press.
Levack, Brian P. 2013b. *The Oxford Handbook of Witchcraft in Early Modern Europe and Colonial America*. Oxford: Oxford University Press.
Lever, Ralph. 1573. *The Art of Reason, Rightly Trermed Witcraft Teaching a Perfect Way to Argue and Dispute*. London: Bynnemann.
Levin, B.M., ed. 1921. *Iggeret Rav Sherira Gaon*. Haifa: Golda-Itskovski.
Levine, Mortimer. 1966. *Early Elizabethan Succession Question 1558–1568*. Stanford, CA: Stanford University Press.
Levinson, Bernard. 2008. *"The Right Chorale": Studies in Biblical Law and Interpretation*. Tübingen: Mohr Siebeck.
Levinson, Bernard and Stackert, Jeffrey. 2013. "The Limitations of 'Resonance': A Response to Joshua Berman on Historical and Comparative Method" 4 *Journal of Ancient Judaism* 310–333.
Levy, Ernst. 1951. *West Roman Vulgar Law: The Law of Property*. Philadelphia, PA: American Philosophical Society.
Levy, Ernst. 1956. *Weströmisches Vulgarrecht. das Obligationenrecht*. Weimar: Böhlaus.
Lewalski, B.K. 1991. "Re-Writing Patriarchy and Patronage: Margaret Clifford, Anne Clifford, and Aemilia Lanyer" 21 *The Yearbook of English Studies* 104–106.
Liebs, Detlef. 2010. *Hofjuristen der römischen Kaiser bis Justinian: vorgetragen in der Sitzung vom 14. November 2008*. Munich: Verlag der Bayerischen Akademie der Wissenschaften.
Liebs, Detlef. 2015. *Das Recht der Römer und die Christen*. Tübingen: Mohr Siebeck.
Ligon, R. 2011. *A True and Exact History of the Island of Barbados*. Indianapolis: Hackett.
Linebaugh, P. and Rediker, M. 2000. *The Many-Headed Hydra*. Boston, MA: Beacon.
Lintott, Andrew William. 1992. *Judicial Reform and Land Reform in the Roman Republic: A New Edition, with Translation and Commentary, of the Laws from Urbino*. Cambridge: Cambridge University Press.
Lintott, Andrew William. 2009. "The Theory of the Mixed Constitution at Rome." In Richard Brooks (ed.), *Cicero and Modern Law*. Burlington: Ashgate.
Liverani, Mario. 2003. *Oltre la Bibbia. Storia antica di Israele*. Rome-Bari: Laterza.
Lloyd-Jones, Hugh. 1983. *The Justice of Zeus*. 2nd edn. Berkeley: University of California Press.
Locke, John. 1975. *The Clarendon Edition of the Works of John Locke: An Essay Concerning Human Understanding*. Edited by Peter H. Nidditch. London: Clarendon.

Loraux, Nicole 2002. *The Divided City: On Memory and Forgetting in Ancient Athens.* Translated by Corinne Pache with Jeff Fort. New York: Zone Books.

Lowe, Jonathan. 1995. *Locke on Human Understanding.* London: Routledge.

Lupton, Julia. 2005. *Citizen-Saints: Shakespeare and Political Theology.* Chicago: University of Chicago Press.

MacDonald, Roderick. 2006. "Here, There ... And Everywhere: Theorizing Legal Pluralism; Theorizing Jacques Vanderlinden." In Nicholas Kasirer (ed.), *Étudier et enseigner le droit: Hier, aujord'hui et demain. Études offertes à Jacques Vanderlinden.* Montréal: Éditions Yvon Blais.

MacDowell, Douglas M. 2009. *Demosthenes the Orator.* Oxford: Oxford University Press.

Machyn, Henry. 1968. *The Diary of Henry Machyn, Citizen and Merchant-Taylor of London, from A. D. 1550 to A. D. 1563.* Edited by John Gough Nichols. New York: AMS Press.

Mack, P. 2010. *Reading and Rhetoric in Montaigne and Shakespeare.*

Mackenzie, George. 1678. *The Laws and Customs of Scotland, in Matters Criminal Wherein is to be Seen How the Civil Law, and the Laws and Customs of Other Nations Do Agree with, and Supply Ours.* Edinburgh: James Glen.

Mackenzie, Roderick A.F. 1964. "The Formal Aspect of Ancient Near Eastern Law." In W. Stewart McCullough (ed.), *The Seed of Wisdom: Essays in Honor of TJ Meek.* Toronto: University of Toronto Press.

Maclean, Ian. 1992. *Interpretation and Meaning in the Renaissance: The Case of Law.* Cambridge: Cambridge University Press.

MacQueen, Hector and Sellar, W.D.H. 2000. "Negligence." In *A History of Private Law in Scotland*, vol. 2. Edited by Kenneth Reid and Reinhard Zimmermann. Oxford: Oxford University Press.

Maganzani, Lauretta. 2007. *Land Surveying for Legal Disputes: Technical Advice in Roman Law.* Naples: Jovene. Available at http://hdl.handle.net/10807/28616.

Magna Carta. British Library. Available at: www.bl.uk/magna-carta/articles/magna-carta-english-translation.

Maine, Henry Sumner. [1861] 1906. *Ancient Law: Its Connection with the Early History of Society and its Relation to Modern Ideas.* 10th edition with Introduction and notes by Frederick Pollock. London: John Murray.

Maine, Henry Sumner. 1871. *Village-Communities in the East and West: Six Lectures Delivered at Oxford.* London: John Murray.

Maine, Henry Sumner. 1886. *Dissertations on Early Law and Custom: Chiefly Selected from Lectures at Oxford.* New York: Henry Holt.

Maitland, Frederick. 1910. *Equity, Also the Forms of Action at Common Law.* Cambridge: Cambridge University Press.

Maitland, Frederick W. and Pollock, Frederick. [1898] 1968. *A History of English Law Before the Time of Edward I.* Cambridge: Cambridge University Press.

Malcolm-Davies, Jane and Davidson, Hilary. 2015. "'He Is of No Account ... if He Have Not a Velvet or Taffeta Hat': A Survey of Sixteenth Century Knitted Caps" 33 *NESAT* XII 223–232.

Mann, Alastair J. 2010. "The Law of the Person: Parliament and Social Control." In Keith M. Brown and Alan R. Macdonald (eds.), *The History of the Scottish Parliament: Parliament in Context.* Edinburgh: Edinburgh University Press.

Manning, John. 2002. *Emblems.* London: Reaktion.

Manthe, Ulrich. 2003. *Die Rechtskulturen der Antike: vom alten Orient bis zum Römischen Reich.* Munich: C. H. Beck.

Mara, Gerald. 1997. *Socrates' Discursive Democracy: Logos and Ergon in Platonic Political Philosophy*. Albany: SUNY Press.

Maravall, Jose Antonio. 1972. *Teatro y literatura en la sociedad barroca*. Madrid: Seminarios y Ediciones.

Maresch, Klaus. 2002. "Die Bibliotheke Enkteseon Im Römischen Ägypten Überlegungen Zur Funktion Zentraler Besitzarchive" 48(1) *Archiv Für Papyrusforschung Und Verwandte Gebiete* 233–246.

Marlowe, Christopher. 1990. *The Complete Works of Christopher Marlowe, Volume 2: Doctor Faustus*. Edited by Roma Gill. Oxford: Oxford University Press.

Marston, John. 1601. *Jacke Drum's Entertainment: Or the Comedie of Pasquill and Katherine As It Hath Bene Sundry Times Plaide by the Children of Powles*. London: Richard Olive.

Martin, Antonio Perez. 2008. "Jacobo de las Leyes: Ureña tenía razón" 26 *Anales de Derecho* (Universidad de Murcia) 251–273.

Martin, Peter. 2008. *Samuel Johnson: A Biography*. Cambridge, MA: The Belknap Press.

Martínez, Pedro Luis. 1591. *Discvrso y alegaciones de derecho del licenciado Pedro Lvis Martínez, en que trata y declara el origen, y principio del nobilíssimo y fidelíssimo Reyno de Aragón ...* Zaragoza: Lorenço de Robles.

Martino, P. 1986. *Arbiter*. Rome: CNR e Università di Roma "La Sapienza."

Marvell, A. 1971. "Upon Appleton House." In H.M. Margoliouth (ed.), *The Poems and Letters of Andrew Marvell*, vol. 1. Oxford: Clarendon Press.

Marvell, A. 1989. "Nature." In C. Rees (ed.), *The Judgment of Marvell*. London: Pinter.

Masi Doria, Carla. 2012. "*Libertorum bona ad patronos pertineant*: su Calp. Flacc. *decl. exc.* 14" 40 *Index* 313–325.

Masson, Charles, and Martin, Jean. 1908. *Catalogue raisonné de l'oeuvre peint et dessiné de Jean- Baptiste Greuze, suivi de la liste des gravures exécutées d'après ses ouvrages*. Paris: Rapilly.

Matteucci, Nicola. 1959. *Jean Domat, un magistrato giansenista*. Bologne: Il Mulino.

Mauclair, Camille. 1935. *Greuze et son temps*. Paris: Albin Michel.

Maxwell-Stuart, P.G. 2008. "King James's Experience of Witches and the 1604 English Witchcraft Act." In John Newton and Jo Bath (eds.), *Witchcraft and the Act of 1604*. Leiden and Boston: Brill.

Maza, Sarah. 2014. "Stephen Greenblatt, New Historicism, and Cultural History, or, What We Talk about When We Talk about Interdisciplinarity" 1(2) *Modern Intellectual History* 249–265.

McDonagh, B. 2009. "Subverting the Ground: Private Property and Public Protest in the Sixteenth-century Yorkshire Wolds" 57(2) *Agricultural History Review* 191–206.

McDonagh, B. 2013. "Making and Breaking Property: Negotiating Enclosure and Common Rights in Sixteenth-century England" 76 *History Workshop Journal* 32–56.

McGinn, Thomas A.J. 1998. *Prostitution, Sexuality and the Law in Ancient Rome*. Oxford: Oxford University Press.

McIlwain, Charles Howard. 1940. *Constitutionalism: Ancient and Modern*. Ithaca, NY: Cornell University Press.

McKendrick, Melveena. 1992. *Theatre in Spain 1490–1700*. Cambridge: Cambridge University Press.

McKendrick, Melveena. 1993. "Calderón and the Politics of Honour" 70(1) *Bulletin of Hispanic Studies* 135–146.

McKeon, M. 1995. "Historicizing Patriarchy: The Emergence of Gender Difference in England, 1660–1760" 28(3) *Eighteenth-century Studies* 295–322.

McKeon, M. 2009. *The Secret History of Domesticity: Public, Private, and the Division of Knowledge*. Baltimore: Johns Hopkins University Press.

McVeigh, Shaun. 2002. "Postmodernism and Common Law." In Reza Banakar and Max Travers (eds.), *An Introduction to Law and Social Theory*. Oxford: Hart Publishing.

Menefee, S.P. 1981. *Wives for Sale: An Ethnographic Study of British Popular Divorce*. Oxford: Basil Blackwell.

Menn, Stephen. 2006. "On Plato's *Politeia*." In John Cleary and Gary Gurtler (eds.), *Proceedings of the Boston Area Colloquium in Ancient Philosophy*, vol. 21. Leiden: Brill Academic Publishers.

Menski, Werner. 2006. *Comparative Law in a Global Context: The Legal Systems of Asia and Africa*. New York: Cambridge University Press.

Merry, Sally Engle. 1998. "Law, Culture, and Cultural Appropriation" 10 *Yale Journal of Law & the Humanities* 575–603.

Meyer, Elizabeth A. 2004. *Legitimacy and Law in the Roman World: Tabulae in Roman Belief and Practice*. Cambridge: Cambridge University Press.

Meyer, Elizabeth A. 2015. "Writing in the Roman Legal Contexts." In David Johnston (ed.), *The Cambridge Companion to Roman Law*. New York: Cambridge University Press.

Mezey, Naomi. 2001. "Law as Culture" 13 *Yale Journal of Law & the Humanities* 35–67.

Michaels, Ralf. 2006. "The Functional Method of Comparative Law." In Mathias Reimann and Reinhard Zimmermann (eds.), *The Oxford Handbook of Comparative Law*. New York: Oxford University Press.

Michalowski, Piotr. 1990. "Early Mesopotamian Communicative Systems: Art, Literature and Writing." In Ann Gunter (ed.), *Investigating Artistic Environments in the Ancient Near East*. Washington, DC: Smithsonian Institution.

Mignault, Claude. 1577. "A Treatise on Symbols, on the Theory of Coats of Arms and Figures which are Commonly called Insignia or Family Badges, and on Emblems." In Andreas Alciato (ed.), *Emblematum Liber*. Antwerp: Plantin.

Miller, Sylvia A. "Old English Laws Regulating Dress" 20(2) *Journal of Home Economics* 89–94.

Miller, Walter. 1913. *M. Tullius Cicero: On Duties. With An English Translation*. Cambridge, MA: Harvard University Press (Loeb Classical Library 30).

Milsom, Stroud Francis Charles. 1969. *Historical Foundations of the Common Law*. London: Butterworths.

Milton, John. 1641. *Of Reformation Touching Church Discipline in England, and the Causes that Hitherto have Hindred It*. London: Thomas Underhill.

Miola, Robert S., ed. 2007. *Early Modern Catholicism: An Anthology of Primary Sources*. Oxford: Oxford University Press.

Mirhady, David C. 1990. "Aristotle on the Rhetoric of Law" 31 *Greek, Roman, and Byzantine Studies* 393–410.

Mirhady, David C. 1991a. "Non-Technical *pisteis* in Aristotle and Anaximenes" 112 *American Journal of Philology* 5–28.

Mirhady, David C. 1991b. "The Oath-Challenge in Athens" 41 *Classical Quarterly* 78–83.

Mirhady, David C. 1996. "Torture and Rhetoric in Athens" 116 *The Journal of Hellenic Studies* 119–131.

Mirhady, David C. 2000. "Demosthenes as Advocate: The Private Speeches." In Ian Worthington (ed.), *Demosthenes: Statesman and Orator*. London: Routledge.

Mirhady, David C. 2002. "Athens' Democratic Witnesses" 56 *Phoenix* 255–274.

Mirhady, David C. 2007. "The Dikasts' Oath and the Question of Fact." In A. Sommerstein and J. Fletcher (eds.), *Horkos: The Oath in Greek Society*. Bristol: Bristol Classical Press.

Mitteis, Ludwig. 1891. *Reichsrecht und Volksrecht in den östlichen Provinzen des Römischen Kaiserreichs mit Beiträgen zur Kenntniss des griechischen Rechts und der spätrömischen Rechtsentwicklung*. Leipzig: Teubner.

Mommsen, Theodor, Krueger, Paul, and Watson, Alan, eds. 1985. *The Digest of Justinian*, 4 vols. Philadelphia: University of Pennsylvania Press.

Mommsen, Theodor. 1877. *Römisches Staatsrecht*, vol. 2, part 1. Leipzig: Hirzel.

Monedero, Pablo José Abascal. 2009. *La infidelidad y el adulterio en España (estudios histórico-legal)*. Córdoba: Universidad de Córdoba.

Monoson, S. Sara. 2000. *Plato's Democratic Entanglements: Athenian Politics and the Practice of Philosophy*. Princeton, NJ: Princeton University Press.

More, Sir Thomas. 1533a. *The Apologye of Sir Thomas More Knyght*. London: Rastell.

More, Sir Thomas. 1533b. *The Deballacyon of Salem and Bizance*. London: Rastell.

More, Sir Thomas. 1965. *Utopia, in The Complete Works of St. Thomas More*, vol. 4. Princeton, NJ: Yale University Press.

Morgan, Kathryn, ed. 2003. *Popular Tyranny: Sovereignty and its Discontents in Ancient Greece*. Austin: University of Texas Press.

Morris, T.D. 1996. *Southern Slavery and the Law, 1619–1860*. Chapel Hill: University of North Carolina Press.

Morrow, Glenn R. 1960. *Plato's Cretan City: A Historical Interpretation of the Laws*. Princeton, NJ: Princeton University Press.

Morton, Thomas. 1990. *New English Canaan in The Heath Anthology of American Literature*, vol. 1. Edited by Paul Lauter, et al. Lexington, MA: D.C. Heath and Co, 176–187.

Mossé, Claude. 2004. "How a Political Myth Takes Shape: Solon, 'Founding Father' of the Athenian Democracy." In P.J. Rhodes (ed.), *Athenian Democracy*. New York: Oxford University Press.

Mukherjee, Ayesha. 2015. *Penury into Plenty: Dearth and the Making of Knowledge in Early Modern England*. London and New York: Routledge.

Muniain, Pedro Esarte. 2007. *Represión y reparto del Estado navarro (siglos XVI y XVII): La nación vasca, expolio franco-español*. Navarra: Nabarralde.

Munn, Mark. 2000. *The School of History: Athens in the Age of Socrates*. Berkeley: University of California Press.

Murner, Thomas. [1509] 1967. *Logica Memorativa*. Leiden: E. J. Brill.

Murray, Augustus T., trans. 1936–1939. *Demosthenes III–V*. Cambridge, MA: Harvard University Press.

Murray, Oswyn. 1998. "Introduction." In Jacob Burckhardt (ed.), *The Greeks and Greek Civilization*. New York: St. Martin's Press.

Mustakallio, Katariina and Krötzl, Christian, eds. 2010. *De Amicitia: Friendship and Social Networks in Antiquity and the Middle Ages*. Rome: Institutum Romanum Finlandiae.

Nagy, Gregory. 1995. "Images of Justice in Early Greek Poetry." In K.D. Irani and Morris Smith (eds.), *Social Justice in the Ancient World*. Westport, CT: Greenwood Press.

Nahm, Milton C. 1947. "The Theological Background of the Artist as Creator" 8(3) *Journal for the History of Ideas* 363–372.

Nails, Debra. 1999. "Mouthpiece Schmouthpiece." In Gerald A. Press (ed.), *Who Speaks for Plato?* Lanham: Rowman and Littlefield.

Nelken, David. 2004: "Using the Concept of Legal Culture" 29 *Australian Journal of Legal Philosophy* 1–26.

Nelken, David. 2007. "Defining and Using the Concept of Legal Culture." In Esin Örücü and David Nelken (eds.), *Comparative Law: A Handbook of Comparative Law*. Oxford: Hart.

Nelken, David. 2012. *Using Legal Culture*. London: Wildy, Simmonds & Hill.

Nelson, Eric. 2004. *The Greek Tradition in Republican Thought*. Cambridge: Cambridge University Press.

Nightingale, Andrea. 1993. "Writing/Reading a Sacred Text: A Literary Interpretation of Plato's *Laws*" 88(4) *Classical Philology* 279–300.

Nokes, Gerald Dacre. 1928. *A History of the Crime of Blasphemy*. London: Sweet & Maxwell.

Nörr, Dieter. 1969. *Die Entstehung der longi temporis praescriptio; Studien zum Einfluss der Zeit im Recht und zur Rechtspolitik in der Kaiserzeit*. Cologne: Westdeutscher Verlag.

Nörr, Dieter. 1981. "The Matrimonial Legislation of Augustus: An Early Instance of Social Engineering" 16 *The Irish Jurist* 350–364.

Nörr, Dieter. 1994. "Innovare" 22 *Index* 61–86.

Nourrisson, Paul. 1939. *Un ami de Pascal, Jean Domat*. Paris: Sirey.

Ober, Josiah. 2001. *Political Dissent in Democratic Athens: Intellectual Critics of Popular Rule*. Princeton, NJ: Princeton University Press.

Olivelle, Patrick. 1993. *The Āśrama System: The History and Hermeneutics of a Religious Institution*. Oxford: Oxford University Press.

Ong, Walter J. 1985. *Ramus, Method and the Decay of Dialogue*. Chicago: University of Chicago Press.

Ong, Walter J. 2002. *Orality and Literacy; The Technologizing of the Word*. London: Routledge.

Oræus, Heinrich. 1619. *Viridarium hieroglyphico-morale: in quo virtutes et vitia … illustrantur*. Frankfurt: Jacques de Zetter.

Orgel, Stephen. 1996. *Impersonations: The Performance of Gender in Shakespeare's England*. Cambridge: Cambridge University Press.

Orlin, Lena Cowen, ed. 2000. *Material London, ca. 1600*. Philadelphia: University of Pennsylvania Press.

Ormrod, W.M. 2003. "The Use of English: Language, Law, and Political Culture in Fourteenth-Century England" 78(3) *Speculum* 750–787.

Ost, Francois. 2005. *Sade et la loi*. Paris: Odile Jacob.

Ost, François. 2009. *Traduire: défense et illustration du multilinguisme*. Paris: Fayard.

Ost, Francois. 2012. *Shakespeare. La comédie de la loi*. Paris: Michalon.

Ostovich, Helen, ed. 2001. *Every Man Out of His Humour*. Manchester: Manchester University Press.

Ostwald, Martin. 1969. *Nomos and the Beginnings of Athenian Democracy*. Oxford: Clarendon Press.

Ostwald, Martin. 1986. *From Popular Sovereignty to the Sovereignty of Law*. Berkeley: University of California Press.

Outhwaite, R.B. 2007. *The Rise and Fall of the English Ecclesiastical Courts, 1500–1860*. Cambridge: Cambridge University Press.

Pangle, Lorraine Smith. 2014. *Virtue is Knowledge*. Chicago: University of Chicago Press.

Paradin, Claude. 1551. *Devises Heroiques*. Paris: J. Millot.

Parker, Robert. 2005. "Law and Religion." In Michael Gagarin and David Cohen (eds.), *The Cambridge Companion to Ancient Greek Law*. New York: Cambridge University Press.

Parkinson, David J. 2003. "'The Legend of the Bischop of St. Androis Lyfe' and the Survival of Scottish Poetry" 9(1) *Early Modern Literary Studies* 5: 1–24.

Pascal, Blaise. 1987. *Les provinciales*. Edited by Michel le Guern. Paris: Gallimard.

Pasquier, Etienne. 1583. *La Main ou OEuvres poétiques faits sur la Main d'E. Pasquier aux Grands Jours de Troyes*. Paris: Michel Gadouleau.

Paul, Shalom M. 1970. *Studies in the Book of the Covenant in the Light of Cuneiform and Biblical Law.* Leiden: E.J. Brill.

Paulson, Ronald. 1991–1993. *William Hogarth*, 3 vols. New Brunswick, NJ: Rutgers University Press.

Peacham, Henry, 1612. *Minerva Britanna or a Garden of Heroical Devices.* Available at: https://archive.org/details/minervabritannao00peac.

Peacham, Henry. 1999. *Manuscript Emblem Books.* Edited by Alan Young and Peter Daly. Toronto: University of Toronto Press.

Pearson, Lionel. 1976. *The Art of Demosthenes.* Meisenheim am Glan: Anton Hain Verlag.

Pelikan, Jurislav. 1985. *The Christian Tradition: A History of the Development of Doctrine. Reformation of Church and Dogma.* Chicago: University of Chicago Press.

Perelman, Chaim. 1980. *Justice, Law and Argument: Essays on Moral and Legal Reasoning.* Dordrecht: Reidel.

Perelman, Chaim and Obrechts-Tytreca, Lucie. 1991. *The New Rhetoric: A Treatise on Argumentation.* Notre Dame, IN: University of Notre Dame Press.

Pfau, Thomas. 2013. *Minding the Modern: Human Agency, Intellectual Traditions and Responsible Knowledge.* Indiana: University of Notre Dame Press.

Phillips, J. 2010. *English Fictions of Communal Identity, 1485–1603.* Farnham: Ashgate.

Piccinelli, Ferdinando. 1980. *Studi e ricerche intorno alla definizione: Dominium est ius utendi et abutendi re sua, quatenus iuris ratio patitur.* Naples: Jovene.

Pitkin, Hanna. 1987. "The Idea of a Constitution" 37 *Journal of Legal Education* 167–169.

Plato. 1980. *The Laws of Plato.* Translated by Thomas Pangle. New York: Basic Books.

Plato. 1997. "Republic." In John M. Cooper and D.S. Hutchinson (eds.), *Complete Works.* Indianapolis and Cambridge: Hackett Publishing.

Plato. 2013. *The Republic.* Translated by Tom Griffith and edited by G.R.F. Ferrari. New York: Cambridge University Press.

Plucknett, T.F.T. 1983. *Studies in English Legal History.* London: Hambledon Press.

Plutarch. 1905. *Morals (Isis and Osiris, or of the Ancient Religion and Philosophy of Egypt)*, vol. 4. Edited by William Baxter and W. Goodwin. New York: Athenaeum Society.

Plutarch. 1998. *Greek Lives.* Translated by Robin Waterfield. Oxford: Oxford University Press.

Pocock, J.G.A. 1987. *The Ancient Constitution and the Feudal Law: A Study of English Historical Thought in the Seventeenth Century. A Reissue with Retrospect.* Cambridge: Cambridge University Press.

Pogue, Kate. 2008. *Shakespeare's Family.* London: Praeger.

Pollock, Frederick. 1906. *Introduction and Notes to Sir Henry Maine's, Ancient Law: Its Connection with the Early History of Society and its Relation to Modern Ideas.* London: John Murray.

Polybius. 1962. *The Histories of Polybius.* Translated by Evelyn Shuckburgh. Bloomington: Indiana University Press.

Popper, Karl. [1944] 2013. *The Open Society and its Enemies.* Princeton, NJ: Princeton University Press.

Pothier, Robert-Joseph. 2001. *d'hier à aujourd'hui.* Edited by Joel Monéger. Paris: Economica.

Pothier, Robert-Joseph. 2011. *Traité des obligations.* Edited by Jean-Louis Halpérin. Paris: Dalloz.

Pradeau, Jean-François. 2005. "L'irréalisable vérité de la *République* platonicienne: Remarques sur le statut et sur le contenu de la *politeia* de la *République*." In Mogens Hansen (ed.), *The Imaginary Polis.* Copenhagen: The Royal Danish Academy of Sciences and Letters.

Press, Gerald A. 2007. *Plato: Guide for the Perplexed.* New York: Bloomsbury.

Prest, Wilfrid R. 1986. *The Rise of the Barristers: A Social History of the English Bar 1590–1640*. Oxford: Clarendon Press.

Primus, John Henry. 1960. *The Vestments Controversy: An Historical Study of the Earliest Tensions within the Church of England in the Reigns of Edward VI and Elizabeth*. Kampen: J. H. Kok.

Prodi, Paolo. 2000. *Una storia della giustizia. Dal pluralismo dei fori al moderno dualismo tra coscienza e diritto*. Bologna: Il Mulino.

Pugliese, Giovanni. 1941. *Studi sull "iniuria."* Milan: Giuffrè.

Pugliese, Giovanni. 1962. *Il processo civile romano, I: Le legis actiones*. Rome: Edizioni Ricerche.

Puttenham, George. 1936. *Art of English Poesie*. Cambridge: Cambridge University Press.

Quaderno de las leyes y premáticas reales. Madrid, 1528. In Collected volume ms., Biblioteca Nacional Española, R/14090, f. 41r.

Raber, Fritz. 1969. *Grundlagen klassischer Injurienansprüche*. Vienna, Cologne and Graz: Böhlau.

Racine, Jean. 1999. "Les plaideurs." In *OEuvres complètes. I. Théâtre, poésie*. Edited by Georges Forestier. Paris: Gallimard.

Raffield, Paul. 2004. *Images and Cultures of Law in Early Modern England: Justice and Political Power, 1558–1660*. Cambridge: Cambridge University Press.

Raffield, Paul and Watt, Gary, eds. 2009. *Shakespeare and the Law*. Oxford: Hart Publishing Ltd.

Ramus, Petrus. 1993. *rutinae Questiones*. Translated by Carole Newlands. Davis, CA: Hermagoras Press.

Randall, A. 1991. *Before the Luddites: Custom, Community and Machinery in the English Woollen Industry 1776–1809*. Cambridge: Cambridge University Press.

Rawson, Elizabeth. 1983. *Cicero. A Portrait*. Bristol: Bristol Classical Press.

Rea, J.D. 1919. "A Source for the Storm in The Tempest" 17(5) *Modern Philology* 279–286.

Renger, Johannes. 2002. "Royal Edicts of the Old Babylonian Period—Structural Background." In Michael Hudson and Marc Van De Mieroop (eds.), *Debt and Economic Renewal in the Ancient Near East*. Bethesda, MD: CDL Press.

Resnik, Judith and Curtis, Dennis. 2011. *Representing Justice. Invention, Controversy, and Rights in City-States and Democratic Courtrooms*. New Haven, CT: Yale University Press.

Reynolds, Samuel H., ed. 1892. *The Table Talk of John Selden*. Oxford: Clarendon.

Rhodes, P.J. 2009. "Civic Ideology and Citizenship." In Ryan Balot (ed.), *A Companion to Greek and Roman Political Thought*. Chichester: Wiley-Blackwell.

Richardson, John S. 1983. "The *Tabula Contrebiensis*: Roman Law in Spain in the Early First Century B.C." 73 *The Journal of Roman Studies* 33–41.

Rickword, Edgell and Lindsay, Jack. 1941. *Spokesmen for Liberty*. London: Lawrence and Wishart.

Rico, Francisco. 2002. *Lazarillo de Tormes*. Madrid: Cátedra.

Ripa, Cesare. 1611. *Iconologia*. Padua. Padua: P.P Tozzi.

Robinson, Olivia. 2009. "Law, Morality and Sir George Mackenzie." In Hector L. MacQueen (ed.), *Miscellany VI*, vol. 54. Edinburgh: Stair Society.

Robson, Elenor. 2007. "Gendered Literacy and Numeracy in the Sumerian Literary Corpus." In G. Cunningham and J. Ebeling (eds.), *Analysing Literary Sumerian: Corpus-Based Approaches*. London: Equinox.

Roche, Daniel. 1996. *The Culture of Clothing: Dress and Fashion in the Ancien Régime*. Cambridge: Cambridge University Press.

Roediger, D.R. 1999. *The Wages of Whiteness: Race and the Making of the American Working Class*. New York: Verso.

Rollenhagen, Gabrielle. 1611. *Nucleus Emblematum selectissimorum*. Cologne: Crispiani Passaei.

Romm, James. 2014. *Dying Every Day: Seneca at the Court of Nero*. New York: Knopf.

Roper, William. 1935. *The Lyfe of Sir Thomas Moore, Knighte*. Edited by Elsie V. Hitchcock. Oxford: Oxford University Press.

Rosen, Lawrence. 2006. *Law as Culture: An invitation*. Princeton, NJ: Princeton University Press.

Rosenwein, Barbara H. 2010. "Problems and Methods in the History of Emotions" 1 *Passions in Context: International Journal of the History and Theory of Emotions* 1–32.

Rosen-Zvi, I. 2008. *ha-Ṭekes she-lo hayah: miḳdash, midrash u-migdar be-Masekhet Soṭah*. Jerusalem: Magnes.

Roth, Martha T. 1995. "Mesopotamian Legal Traditions and the Laws of Hammurabi" 71 *Chicago-Kent Law Review* 13–39.

Roth, Martha T. 1997. *Law Collections from Mesopotamia and Asia Minor*. 2nd edn. Atlanta, GA: Scholars Press.

Rousseau, Jean-Jacques. 1996. *Du contrat social, ou principes de droit politique*. Edited by Gérard Mairet. Paris: LGF.

Rowe, Christopher. 2010. "The Relationship of the *Laws* to Other Dialogues: A Proposal." In Christopher Bobonich (ed.), *Plato's Laws: A Critical Guide*. New York: Cambridge University Press.

Rubinstein, Lene. 2005. "Main Litigants and Witnesses in the Athenian Courts: Procedural Variations." In Michael Gagarin and Robert Wallace (eds.), *Symposion 2001, Vorträge zur griechischen und hellenistischen Rechtsgeschichte* (Evanston, IL, September 5–8, 2001). Vienna: Verlag der Österreichischen Akademie der Wissenschaften.

Rublack, Ulinka. 2010. *Dressing Up: Cultural Identity in Renaissance Europe*. Oxford: Oxford University Press.

Ruiz, Julio Juan. 2013. "La tradición medieval y el realismo político modern en el teatro de Calderón de la Barca" 46 *Acta Literaria* 127–141.

Rupp, Stephen. 2014. *Heroic Forms: Cervantes and the Literature of War*. Toronto: University of Toronto Press.

Rupprecht, Hans A. 2005. "Greek Law in Foreign Surroundings: Continuity and Development." In Michael Gagarin and David Cohen (eds.), *The Cambridge Companion to Ancient Greek Law*. New York: Cambridge University Press.

Ruschenbusch, Eberhard. 1965. "ΥΒΡΕΩΣ ΓΡΑΦΗ. Ein Fremdkörper im athenischen Recht des 4. Jahrhunderts v. Ch" 82 *Zeitschrift der Savigny-Stiftung für Rechtsgeschichte: Romanistische Abteilung* 302–309.

Ruschenbusch, Eberhard. 2010. *Solon: das Gesetzeswerk-Fragmente*. Stuttgart: Steiner.

Ruskola, Teemu. 2012. "The East Asian Legal Tradition." In Mauro Bussani and Ugo Mattei (eds.), *The Cambridge Companion to Comparative Law*. New York: Cambridge University Press.

Sabbatucci, Dario. 1981. "Il peccato cosmico." In *Le délit religieux dans la cité antique (Actes Rome 1978)*. Rome: École Française de Rome.

Sabine, George H., ed. 1941/1965. *The Works of Gerrard Winstanley, with an Appendix of Documents Related to the Digger Movement*. New York: Russell and Russell.

Sacco, Rodolfo. 1991. "Legal Formants: Dynamic Approach to Comparative Law" 39 *The American Journal of Comparative Law* 1–34 (installment I) and 343–401 (instalment II).

Salzman, P. 2004. "Early Modern (Aristocratic) Women and Textual Property." In N.E.Wright, M.W. Ferguson, and A.R. Buck (eds.), *Women: Property and the Letters of the Law in Early Modern England*. Toronto: University of Toronto Press.

Sampson, M. 1990. "'Property' in Seventeenth-century English Political Thought." In G. Schochet, P. Tatspaugh, and C. Brobeck (eds.), *Religion, Resistance and Civil War: Papers Presented at the Folger Institute Seminar*. Washington: The Folger Shakespeare Library.

Santucci, Gianni. 2014a. "*Legum inopia* e diritto privato. Riflessioni intorno ad un recente contributo." 80 *Studia et documenta historiae et iuris* 373–393.

Santucci, Gianni. 2014b. "Die *rei vindcatio* im klassischen römischen Recht—ein überblick" 2 *Fundamina: A Journal of Legal History* 833–846.

Scafuro, Adele. 1994. "Witnessing and False-Witnessing: Proving Citizenship and Kin Identity in Fourth-Century Athens." In Allan L. Boegehold and A.C. Scafuro (eds.), *Athenian Identity and Civic Ideology*. Baltimore: Johns Hopkins University Press.

Scarlattini, Ottavio. 1695. *Homo et eius partes*. Dillingen: Bencard.

Scheid, John. 1981. "Le délit religieux dans la rome tardo-républicaine." In *Le délit religieux dans la cité antique (Actes Rome 1978)*. Rome: École Française de Rome, 117–171.

Scheid, John. 2001. *La religione a Roma*. Rome-Bari: Laterza.

Scheid, John. 2013. *Les dieux, l'État et l'individu. Réflexions sur la religion civique à Rome*. Paris: Seuil.

Schiappa, Edward. 1991. *The Beginnings of Rhetorical Theory in Classical Greece*. New Haven, CT: Yale University Press.

Schiffman, Lawrence H. 2010. *Qumran and Jerusalem: Studies in the Dead Sea Scrolls and the History of Judaism*. Grand Rapids, MI: William B. Eerdmans.

Schiller, A. Arthur. 1971. "Jurist's Law." In A. Arthur Schiller (ed.), *An American Experience in Roman Law*. Gottingen: Vandenhoeck & Ruprecht.

Schmähling, Eberhard. 1938. *Die Sittenaufsicht der Censoren*. Stuttgart: Kohlhammer.

Schmidt, Rachel. 2011. *Forms of Modernity: Don Quixote and the Modern Theories of the Novel*. Toronto: University of Toronto Press.

Schneewind, Jerome B. 1998. *The Invention of Autonomy: A History of Modern Moral Philosophy*. Cambridge: Cambridge University Press.

Schofield, Malcolm. 1996. "Sharing in the Constitution" 49(4) *Review of Metaphysics* 831–858.

Schofield, Malcolm. 1999. *Saving the City: Philosopher-Kings and Other Classical Paradigms*. London and New York: Routledge.

Schofield, Malcolm. 2006. *Plato: Political Philosophy*. Oxford: Oxford University Press.

Schofield, Malcolm. 2010. "The *Laws*' Two Projects." In Christopher Bobonich (ed.), *Plato's Laws: A Critical Guide*. New York: Cambridge University Press.

Schoonhovius, Florentius. 1618. *Emblemata partim moralia partim etiam civilia*. Gouda: Andreas Burier.

Schrage, Eltjo. 2003. "Het proces Jezus" 52(5) *Ars Aequi* 355–364.

Schulz, Fritz. 1946. *History of Roman Legal Science*. Oxford: Clarendon Press.

Schulz, Fritz. 1951. *Classical Roman Law*. Oxford: Oxford University Press.

Schulz, Fritz. 1953. *Roman Legal Science*. 2nd edn. Oxford: Oxford University Press.

Schulz, Fritz. 1954. *Prinzipien des römischen Rechts*. Berlin: Duncker & Humblot.

Schulz, Fritz. 1963. *History of Roman Legal Science*. Oxford: Oxford University Press.

Scott, Izora. 1991. *Controversies over Cicero*. Davis, CA: Hermagoras Press.

Scott, Joan. 2014. "Gender: A Useful Category of Historical Analysis" 91(5) *American Historical Review* 1053–1075.

Scurlock, JoAnn. 1995. "Death and Afterlife in Ancient Mesopotamian Thought." In Jack Sasson (ed.), *Civilizations of the Ancient Near East*, vol. 3. New York: Charles Scribners' Sons.

Sealey, Raphael. 1994. *The Justice of the Greeks*. Ann Arbor: University of Michigan Press.

Seed, P. 1995. *Ceremonies of Possession in Europe's Conquest of the New World, 1492–1640*. Cambridge: Cambridge University Press.

Seipp, D. 1994. "The Concept of Property in the Early Common Law" 12 *Law and History Review* 29–91.

Selden, John. 1618. *Historie of Tithes*. London: n.p.

Selden, John. [1689] 1868. *Table Talk*. London: Murray.

Seneca, *Medea*. 1917 edn. Loeb Classical Library. London: Heinemann.

Serrao, Feliciano. 1973. "Legge (diritto romano)." In *Enciclopedia del diritto*, vol. 23. Milan: Giuffrè, 794–850.

Serrao, Feliciano. 1974. *Classi partiti e legge nella repubblica romana*. Pisa: Pacini.

Serrao, Feliciano. 2006. *Diritto privato economia e società nella storia di Roma*, vol. 1. 3rd edn. Naples: Jovene.

Shakespeare, William. 2011. *The Merchant of Venice*. Edited by John Drakakis. London: Methuen.

Shapiro, I.A. 1930. "John Donne and Lincoln's Inn." *Times Literary Supplement*, October 16 and 23.

Sharp, B. 1980. *In Contempt of all Authority: Rural Artisans and Riot in the West of England, 1586–1660*. Berkeley: University of California Press.

Sharpe, J.A. 1985. "'Last Dying Speeches': Religion, Ideology and Public Execution in Seventeenth-Century England" 107 *Past and Present* 144–167.

Sharpe, J.A. 1999. *Crime in Early Modern England 1550–1750*. London and New York: Longman.

Shaw, Brent D. 2015. "The Myth of the Neronian Persecution" 105 *Journal of Roman Studies* 73–100.

Siete Partidas. 1576. Salamanca: Domingo de Portonarijs Ursino, 1. 3.21and 22.

Simon-Shoshan, Moshe. 2012. *Stories of the Law: Narrative Discourse and the Construction of Authority in the Mishnah*. New York: Oxford University Press.

Simpson, A.W.B. 1986. *A History of the Land Law*. 2nd edn. Oxford: Oxford University Press.

Skinner, Quentin. 1996. *Reason and Rhetoric in the Philosophy of Hobbes*. Cambridge: Cambridge University Press.

Slanski, Kathryn E. 2003a. *The Babylonian Entitlement narus (kudurrus): A Study in their Form and Function*. Boston, MA: American Schools of Oriental Research.

Slanski, Kathryn E. 2003b. "Representation of the Divine on the Babylonian Entitlement Monuments (kudurrus)" 50 *Archiv für Orientforschung* 308–320.

Slanski, Kathryn E. 2007. "The Mesopotamian 'Rod and Ring': Icon of Righteous Kingship and Balance of Power between Palace and Temple." In Harriet Crawford (ed.), *Regime Change in the Ancient Near East and Egypt: From Sargon or Agade to Saddam Hussein*. New York: Oxford University Press.

Slanski, Kathryn E. 2012. "The Law of Hammurabi and Its Audience" 24(1) *Yale Journal of Law & the Humanities* 97–110.

Smith, Bruce R. 1991. *Homosexual Desire in Shakespeare's England: A Cultural Poetics*. Chicago: Chicago University Press.

Smith, Henry. 1591. *Sermons*. London: Richard Field.

Solt, Leo F. *Church and State in Early Modern England, 1509–1640*. New York and Oxford: Oxford University Press, 1990.

Sommerstein, Alan H. and Bayliss, Andrew J. 2013. *Oath and State in Ancient Greece*. Berlin: De Gruyter.

Sophocles. 1991. *Antigone*. Translated by David Grene. In David Grene and Richard Lattimore (eds.), *The Complete Greek Tragedies*, vol. 2. Chicago: University of Chicago Press.

Sourioux, Jean-Louis. 2004. "Pothier ou le sphinx d'Orléans" 30 *Droits* 69–75.

Speght, Rachel. 1617. *A mouzell for Melastomus, the cynicall bayter of, and foule mouthed barker against Euahs sex*. London: Printed by Nicholas Okes for Thomas Archer.

Spivack, C. 2012. "Law, Land, Identity: The Case of Lady Anne Clifford" 87(2) *Women's Legal History: A Global Perspective* 393.

Stackert, Jeffrey. 2014. *A Prophet like Moses: Prophecy, Law, and Israelite Religion*. Oxford and New York: Oxford University Press.

Stallybrass, P. 1986. "Patriarchal Territories: The Body Enclosed." In M.W. Ferguson, M. Quilligan, and N.J. Vickers (eds.), *Rewriting the Renaissance: The Discourses of Sexual Difference in Early Modern Europe*. Chicago: University of Chicago Press.

Stallybrass, P. 1996. "Worn Worlds: Clothes and Identity on the Renaissance Stage." In Margreta de Grazia, Maureen Quilligan, and Peter Stallybrass (eds.), *Subject and Object in Renaissance Culture*. Cambridge: Cambridge University Press.

Staniland, Kay. 1997. "Thomas Deane's Shop in the Royal Exchange." In Ann Saunders (ed.), *The Royal Exchange*. London: The London Topographical Society.

Starkey, Thomas. [1535] 1945. *A Dialogue between Reginald Pole and Thomas Lupset*. London: Chatto and Windus.

Stein, Peter. 1966. Regulae Iuris: *From Juristic Rules to Legal Maxims*. Edinburgh: Edinburgh University Press.

Steinberg, Justin. 2013. *Dante and the Limits of the Law*. Chicago: University of Chicago Press.

Stengel, Georg. 1634. *Ova Paschalia; Sacra emblemate inscripta descriptaque*. Munich: Henricus.

Stephen, James Fitzjames. 1883. *History of the Criminal Law of England*, 3 vols. London: Macmillan.

Stern, David. 1996. *Midrash and Theory: Ancient Jewish Exegesis and Contemporary Literary Studies*. Evanston, IL: Northwestern University Press.

Stern, David. 1998. "The Captive Woman: Hellenization, Greco-Roman Erotic Narrative, and Rabbinic Literature" 19 *Poetics Today* 91–127.

Sternberg, Meir. 1985. *The Poetics of Biblical Narrative: Ideological Literature and the Drama of Reading*. Bloomington: Indiana University Press.

Sterne, Laurence. 2003. *The Life and Opinions of Tristram Shandy, Gentleman*. Edited by Melvyn New and Joan New. London: Penguin.

Stolleis, Michael. 1988–2012. *Geschichte des öffentlichen Rechts in Deutschland*, 4 vols. Munich: C. H. Beck.

Stone, Lawrence. 1965. *The Crisis of the Aristocracy 1558–1641*. Oxford: Oxford University Press.

Stow, John. 1631. *Annales, or a General Chronicle of England*. Edited by Edmund Howes (ed.) London: Society of Stationers.

Stretton, T. 1998. *Women Waging Law in Elizabethan England*. Cambridge: Cambridge University Press.

Stubbes, Phillip. 1583. *The Anatomie of Abuses Contayning A Discouerie, or Briefe Summarie of Such Notable Vices and Imperfections, as Now Raigne in Many Christian Countreyes of the Worlde: But (especiallie) in a Verie famousIilande Called Ailgna: Together, with Most Fearefull*

Examples of Gods Iudgementes, Executed Vpon the Wicked for the Same, Aswell in Ailgna of Late, as in Other Places, Elsewhere. Verie Godly, to Be Read of All True Christians, Euerie Where: But Most Needefull, to Be Regarded in Englande. London: John Kingston for Richard Jones.

Suarez, Francisco. 1995a. *De triplici virtute theologica, fide, spe, et charitate 1621*. Translated by Gwladys L. Williams, Ammi Brown, and John Waldron. Buffalo, NY: WS Hein.

Suarez, Francisco. 1995b. *Defensio fidei catholicae, et apostolicae adversus anglicanae sectae errores 1613*. Translated by Gwladys L. Williams, Ammi Brown, and John Waldron. Buffalo, NY: WS Hein.

Suarez, Francisco. 1995c. *Selections from Three Works by Francisco Suárez, S.J. 1612: "De legibus, ac deo legislatore."* Translated by Gwladys L. Williams, Ammi Brown, and John Waldron. Buffalo, NY: WS Hein.

Suolahti, Jaakko. 1963. *The Roman Censors: A Study on Social Structures*. Helsinki: Suomalainen tiedeakatemia.

Surkis, Judith. 2014. "Of Scandals and Supplements: Relating Intellectual and Cultural History." In Darrin McMahon and Samuel Moyn (eds.), *Rethinking Modern European Intellectual History*. Oxford and New York: Oxford University Press.

Sweezy, P.M. and Dobb, M. 1950. "The Transition from Feudalism to Capitalism" *Science & Society* 134–167.

Talamanca, Mario. 1990. *Istituzioni di diritto romano*. Milan: Giuffrè.

Talamanca, Mario. 1997. "*Lex* ed *interpretatio* in Lab. 4 *post. a Iav. epit.* D, 19, 1, 50." In *Nozione formazione e interpretazione del diritto dall'età romana alle esperienze moderne. Ricerche F. Gallo*, vol. 4. Naples: Jovene.

Tanner, J.R. 1940. *Tudor Constitutional Documents A.D. 1485–1603 with an Historical Commentary*. Cambridge: Cambridge University Press.

Tawney, Richard H. and Power, Eileen, eds. 1953. *Tudor Economic Documents: Being Select Documents Illustrating the Economic and Social History of Tudor England*, vol. 2. London: Green and Co., Longmans.

Taylor, Charles. 1971. "Interpretation and the Sciences of Man" 25(1) *The Review of Metaphysics* 3–51.

Tellegen-Couperus, Olga and Tellegen, Jan W. 2013. "*Artes Urbanae*: Roman Law and Rhetoric." In Paul Du Plessis (ed.), *New Frontiers: Law and Society in the Roman World*. Edinburgh: Edinburgh University Press.

Terpening, Ronnie H. 1997. *Lodovico Dolce: Renaissance Man of Letters*. Toronto: University of Toronto Press.

Terrel, Jean. 2001. *Les théories du pacte social. Droit naturel, souveraineté et contrat de Bodin à Rousseau*. Paris: Seuil.

Teubner, Günther and Fischer-Lescano, Andreas. 2004. "Regime Collisions: The Vain Search for Legal Unity in the Fragmentation of Global Law" 25(4) *Michigan Journal of International Law* 999–1046.

Thalheim, Theodor. 1916. "'Ύβρεως γραφή." In Wilhelm Kroll (ed.), *Paulys Realencyclopädie der classischen Altertumswissenschaft (RE) 17, Band IX,1*. Stuttgart: Metzler.

Thirsk, Joan. 1978. *Economic Policy and Projects: The Development of a Consumer Society in Early Modern England*. Oxford: Clarendon Press.

Thirsk, Joan. 1984. "The Fantastical Folly of Fashion: The English Stocking Knitting Industry, 1500–1700." In *The Rural Economy of England*. London: The Hambledon Press.

Thomas, Keith. 1978. "The Puritans and Adultery: The Act of 1650 Reconsidered." In Donald Pennington and Keith Thomas (eds.), *Puritans and Revolutionaries*. Oxford: Oxford University Press.

Thomas, Rosalind. 2005. "Writing, Law, and Written Law." In Michael Gagarin and David Cohen (eds.), *The Cambridge Companion to Ancient Greek Law*. New York: Cambridge University Press.

Thompson, E.P. 1975. *Whigs and Hunters*. London: Penguin Books.

Thompson, E.P. 1991. *Customs in Common*. London: Merlin Press.

Thorne, Samuel E. 1985. "The Early History of the Inns of Court with Special Reference to Gray's Inn." In *Essays in English Legal History*. London: Hambledon Press.

Thucydides. 1972. *A History of the Peloponnesian War*. Revised edn. Translated by Rex Warner; Introduction by M.I. Finley. New York: Penguin Classics.

Thucydides. 1996. *History of the Peloponnesian War*. Translated by Richard Crawley. In Robert Strassler (ed.), *The Landmark Thucydides: A Comprehensive Guide to the Peloponnesian War*. New York: Touchstone.

Thür, Gerhard. 1977. *Beweisführung vor den Schwurgerichtshöfen Athens: Die Proklêsis zur Basanos*. Vienna: Verlag der Österreichischen Akademie der Wissenschaften.

Tierney, Brian. 1997. *The Idea of Natural Rights: Studies on Natural Rights, Natural Law and Church law 1150–1625*. Atlanta, GA: Scholars Press.

Tigay, Jeffrey H. 1996. *Deuteronomy = [Devarim]: The Traditional Hebrew Text with the New JPS Translation*. Philadelphia, PA: Jewish Publication Society.

Tirso de Molina. 1996. *Cigarrales de Toledo*. Edited by Luis Vázquez Fernández. Madrid: Castalia.

Tittler, Robert. 2007. *The Face of the City: Civic Portraiture and Civic Identity in Early Modern England*. Manchester and New York: Manchester University Press.

Todd, Stephen. 1991. "The Purpose of Evidence in Athenian Courts." In Paul Cartledge, Paul Millett, and Stephen Todd (eds.), *Nomos: Essays in Athenian Law, Politics and Society*. Cambridge: Cambridge University Press.

Todd, Stephen. 1993. *The Shape of Athenian Law*. Oxford: Oxford University Press.

Travitsky, B.S. 1990. "Husband-Murder and Petty Treason in English Renaissance Tragedy" 21 *Renaissance Drama*, new series 171–198.

Travitsky, B.S. and Prescott, A.L., eds. 2005. "The Lawes Resolutions of Women's Rights." In *Legal Treatises. 3 vols. The Early Modern Englishwoman: A Facsimile Library of Essential Works. Series III. Essential Works for the Study of Early Modern Women: Part I*. Aldershot: Ashgate.

Tribe, Lawrence H. 1988. *American Constitutional Law*. 2nd edn. Mineola, NY: The Foundation Press.

Tronti, M. 1998. *La politica al tramonto*. Turin: Einaudi.

Tulard, Jean, ed. 1990. *La contre-révolution. Origines, histoire, postérité*. Paris: Perrin.

Tuori, K. 2007. *Ancient Roman Lawyers and Modern Legal Ideals: Studies on the Impact of Contemporary Concerns in the Interpretation of Ancient Roman Legal History*. Frankfurt am Main: Klostermann.

Turner, David M. 2002. *Fashioning Adultery: Gender, Sex and Civility in England 1660–1740*. Cambridge: Cambridge University Press.

Turner, H.S., ed. 2002. *The Culture of Capital: Property, Cities, and Knowledge in Early Modern England*. New York: Routledge.

Turner, Victor. 1982. *From Ritual to Theatre: The Human Seriousness of Play*. New York: PAJ Publications.

Twining, William. 2006. "Glenn on Tradition: An Overview" 1(1) *Journal of Comparative Law* 107–115.

Twining, William. 2009. *General Jurisprudence: Understanding Law from a Global Perspective*. New York: Cambridge University Press.

Tyndale, William. 1530. *An Answer unto Tomas Mores Dialogue*. London: n.p.

Ucin, Javier Gallastegui. 1990. *Navarra a través de la correspondencia de los virreyes (1598–1648)*. Navarra: Gobierno de Navarra.

Underdown, D. 1985. "The Taming of the Scold: The Enforcement of Patriarchal Authority in Early Modern England." In Anthony Fletcher and John Stevenson (eds.), *Order and Disorder in Early Modern England*. Cambridge: Cambridge University Press, 116–136.

Usher, Brett. 2003. *William Cecil and Episcopacy, 1559–1577*. Aldershot: Ashgate.

Valencia. 1590. *Alegaciones de derecho, del licenciado Valencia*. Zaragoza: Lorenço de Robles.

Valeriano, Piero. 1550. *Hieroglyphica sive de sacris Aegyptorum literis commentarii*. Basle, n.p.

Valls, Teresa Ferrer. 1993. *Nobleza y espectáculo teatral (1535–1622): Estudio y documentos*. Ser. Textos Teatrales Hispánicos del siglo XVI. Valencia: UNED; Universidad de Sevilla: Universitat de Valencia.

Van De Mieroop, Mark. 2002. "A History of Near Eastern Debt?" In Michael Hudson and Marc Van De Mieroop (eds.), *Debt and Economic Renewal in the Ancient Near East*. Bethesda, MD: CDL Press.

Van der Velden, Hugo. 1995a. "Cambyses for Example: The Origins and Function of an *exemplum iustitiae* in Netherlandish Art of the Fifteenth, Sixteenth and Seventeenth Centuries" 23 *Simiolus* 5.

Van der Velden, Hugo. 1995b. "Cambyses Reconsidered: Gerard David's *exemplum iustitiae* for Bruges Town Hall" 23 *Simiolus* 5.

Vandendriessche, Sarah. 2006. *Possessio und Dominium im postklassischen römischen Recht: eine Überprüfung von Levy's Vulgarrechtstheorie anhand der Quellen des Codex Theodosianus und der Posttheodosianischen Novellen*. Hamburg: Kovac.

Vasoli, Cesare. 2006. *Ficino, Savonarola, Machiavelli: Studi di storia della cultura*. Turin: Nino Aragno.

Vaughan, A.T. and Vaughan, V.M. 1993. *Shakespeare's Caliban: A Cultural History*. Cambridge: Cambridge University Press.

Vegetti, Mario. 2013. "How and Why Did the *Republic* Become Unpolitical?" In Noburu Notomi and Luc Brisson (eds.), *Dialogues on Plato's Politeia (Republic): Selected Papers from the Ninth Symposium Platonicum*. Sankt Augustin: Academia Verlag.

Veldhuis, Niek. 2011. "Levels of Literacy." In Eleanor Robson and Karin Radner (eds.), *The Oxford Handbook of Cuneiform Culture*. Oxford: Oxford University Press.

Velez-Sainz, Julio. 2011. "Anatomía áulica y política de *Fieras afemina amor* de Calderón" 161 *Hispanófila* 1–17.

Vendryes, Joseph. 1918. "Les correspondances de vocabulaire entre l'indo-iranien et l'italoceltique" 20 *Mémoires de la Société Linguistique de Paris* 265–285.

Vermuele, Emily. 1966. "The Boston Oresteia Krater" 70(1) *American Journal of Archaeology* 1–22.

Vernant, Jean-Pierre and Vidal-Naquet, Pierre. 1988. *Myth and Tragedy in Ancient Greece*. Translated by Janet Lloyd. New York: Zone Books.

Veyne, Paul 1984. *Writing History: Essay on Epistemology*. Translated by Mina Moore-Rinvolucri. Middletown, CT: Wesleyan University Press.

Visconsi, Elliot. 2008. "The Invention of Criminal Blasphemy: *Rex v Taylor* (1676)" 103 *Representations* 30–52.

Visser, Arnoud. 2008. "Escaping the Reformation in the Republic of Letters: Confessional Silence in Latin Emblem Books" 88(2) *Church History and Religious Culture* 139–167.

Volkmann, Hans. 1969. *Zur Rechtsprechung im Principat des Augustus*. Munich: C. H. Beck.

von Benda-Beckmann, F. and von Benda-Beckmann, Keebet. 2010. "Why Not Legal Culture?" 5(2) *The Journal of Comparative Law* 104–117.

von Savigny, Friedrich Carl. 1840. *System des heutigen römischen Rechts*, vol. 1. Berlin: Veit und Comp.

Walker, David M. 1995. *A Legal History of Scotland*, vol. 3. Edinburgh: T&T Clark.

Walker, Garthine. 1998. "Rereading Rape and Sexual Violence in Early Modern England" 10 *Gender & History* 1–25.

Walton, Clifford Stevens. 2002. *The Civil Law in Spain and Spanish-America*. Clark, NJ: The Lawbook Exchange, Ltd.

Ward, Ian. 1999. *Shakespeare and the Legal Imagination*. London: Butterworths.

Ward, Joseph P. 1997. *Metropolitan Communities: Trade Guilds, Identity, and Change in Early Modern London*. Stanford, CA: Stanford University Press.

Waterfield, Robin. 2009. *Why Socrates Died: Dispelling the Myths*. London: Faber & Faber.

Watson, Alan. 1968. *The Law of Property in the Later Roman Republic*. Oxford: Clarendon Press.

Watson, Alan. 1974. *Legal Transplants: An Approach to Comparative Law*. Edinburgh: Scottish Academic Press.

Watson, Alan. 1983a. "Legal Change: Sources of Law and Legal Culture." *Scholarly Works*. Available at http://digitalcommons.law.uga.edu/fac_artchop/534.

Watson, Alan. 1983b. "Roman Slave Law and Romanist Ideology" 37(1) *Phoenix* 53–65.

Watson, Alan. 1993. *International Law in Archaic Rome: War and Religion*. Baltimore: Johns Hopkins University Press.

Watson, Alan. 1998a. *Ancient Law and Modern Understanding*. Athens: University of Georgia.

Watson, Alan, ed. 1998b. *The Digest of Justinian*. Philadelphia: University of Pennsylvania Press.

Watson, Alan, et al. 1985. *The Digest of Justinian. English translation with the Latin text edited by Theodor Mommsen with the aid of Paul Krueger*. Philadelphia: University of Pennsylvania Press.

Watson, Anthony. 1972. *Juan de la Cueva and the Portuguese Succession*. London: Tamesis.

Watt, Gary. 2012. *Equity Stirring: The Story of Justice beyond Law*. Oxford: Hart Publishing.

Watt, Gary. 2013. *Dress, Law and Naked Truth: A Cultural History of Fashion and Form*. London: Bloomsbury.

Watt, Tessa. 1993. *Cheap Print and Popular Piety, 1550–1640*. Cambridge: Cambridge University Press.

Weatherill, Lorna. 1996. *Consumer Behaviour and Material Culture in Britain, 1660–1760*. London: Routledge.

Webber, Jeremy. 2004. "Culture, Legal Culture, and Legal Reasoning: A Comment on Nelken" 29 *Australian Journal of Legal Philosophy* 27–36.

Weil, Simone. [1940–1941] 2003. *The Iliad or the Poem of Force: A Critical Edition*. Edited by James P. Holoka. New York: Peter Lang.

Weisberg, Richard H. 1992. *Poethics: And Other Strategies of Law and Literature*. Columbia: Columbia University Press.

Weiss, Roslyn. 2012. *Philosophers in the Republic: Plato's Two Paradigms*. Ithaca, NY: Cornell University Press.

Welch, Evelyn and Claxton, Juliet. 2017. "Easy Innovation in Early Modern Europe." In Evelyn Welch (ed.), *Fashioning the Early Modern: Dress, Textiles, and Innovation in Europe, 1500–1800*. Oxford: Oxford University Press.

Wells, Bruce and Magdalene, F. Rachel, eds. 2009. *Law from the Tigris to the Tiber: The Writings of Raymond Westbrook*, 2 vols. Winona Lake: Eisenbrauns.

Westbrook, Raymond. 1988. *Studies in Biblical and Cuneiform Law*. Cahiers de la Revue Biblique 26. Paris: Gabalda.

Westbrook, Raymond. 2003a. "Introduction: The Character of Ancient Near Eastern Law." In Raymond Westbrook (ed.), *A History of Ancient Near Eastern Law*, 2 vols. Leiden and Boston, MA: Brill.

Westbrook, Raymond. 2003b. "Old Babylonian." In Raymond Westbrook (ed.), *A History of Ancient Near Eastern Law*, vol. 1. Leiden: Brill.

Westbrook, Raymond. [1985] 2009a. "Biblical and Cuneiform Law Codes." In Bruce Wells and F. Rachel Magdalene (eds.), *Law from the Tigris to the Tiber: The Writings of Raymond Westbrook*. Winona Lake: Eisenbrauns.

Westbrook, Raymond. [1989] 2009b. "Cuneiform Law Codes and the Origins of Legislation." In Bruce Wells and F. Rachel Magdalene (eds.), *Law from the Tigris to the Tiber: The Writings of Raymond Westbrook*. Winona Lake: Eisenbrauns.

Westbrook, Raymond. [1995] 2009c. "Social Justice in the Ancient Near East." In Bruce Wells and F. Rachel Magdalene (eds.), *Law from the Tigris to the Tiber: The Writings of Raymond Westbrook*. Winona Lake: Eisenbrauns.

Westbrook, Raymond. 2009d. *Law from the Tigris to the Tiber: The Writings of Raymond Westbrook*, 2 vols. Edited by Bruce Wells and F. Rachel Magdalene. Winona Lake, IN: Eisenbrauns.

Westbrook, Raymond. 2015. *Ex oriente lex: Near Eastern Influences on Ancient Greek and Roman Law*. Edited by Deborah Lyons and Kurt Raaflaub. Baltimore: The Johns Hopkins University Press.

White, Hayden. 1973. *Metahistory: The Historical Imagination in Nineteenth-century Europe*. Baltimore and London: The Johns Hopkins University Press.

White, James Boyd. 1973. *The Legal Imagination: Studies in the Nature of Legal Thought and Expression*. Boston, MA: Little, Brown & Co.

White, James Boyd. 1984. *When Words Lose Their Meaning: Constitutions and Reconstitutions of Language, Character, and Community*. Chicago: The University of Chicago Press.

White, James Boyd. 1985. *Heracles' Bow: Essays on the Rhetoric and Poetics of Law*. Madison: The University of Wisconsin Press.

White, James Boyd. 1990. *Justice as Translation: An Essay in Cultural and Legal Criticism*. Chicago: The University of Chicago Press.

White, Paul and Jones, Norman. 1966. "*Gorboduc* and Royal Marriage Politics: An Elizabethan Playgoer's Report of the Premiere Performance" 26(1) *English Literary Renaissance* 3–16.

Whitehouse, Edward. 1663. *Fortescutus illustratus, or a Commentary on that Nervous Treatise De Laudibus Legum Angliae*. London: Roycroft.

Whitney, George. 1586. *Choice of Emblemes*. Leden: Plantyn.

Whyte, N. 2009. *Inhabiting the Landscape: Place, Custom and Memory, 1500–1800*. Oxford: Windgather Press.

Wieacker, Franz. 1973. "*Contractus* und *obligatio* im Naturrecht zwischen Spätscholastik und Aufklärung." In P. Grossi (ed.), *La Seconda Scolastica nella formazione del diritto privato moderno*. Milan: Giuffrè.

Willets, Ronald F. 1967. *The Law Code of Gortyn*. Berlin: de Gruyter.

Williams, Raymond. 1976. *Keywords: A Vocabulary of Culture and Society*. New York: Oxford University Press.

Williams, Stanley T. 1968. *The Spanish Background of American Literature*, 2 vols. Hamden, CT: Archon Books.

Willis, D. 1989. "Shakespeare's Tempest and the Discourse of Colonialism" 29(2) *Studies in English literature, 1500–1900* 277–289.

Wilson, Thomas. 1551. *The Rule of Reason Containing the Arte of Logicke.* London: Richard Grafton.

Wilson, Thomas. 1982. *The Arte of Rhetorique (1553).* Edited by Thomas Derrick. New York: Garland.

Wimpfheimer, Barry S. 2011. *Narrating the Law: A Poetics of Talmudic Legal Stories.* Philadelphia: University of Pennsylvania Press.

Wimsatt, William K. 1954. *The Verbal Icon: Studies in the Meaning of Poetry.* Lexington: University of Kentucky Press.

Winans, Robert B. 1983. "Bibliography and the Cultural Historian: Notes on the Eighteenth-Century Novel." In William L. Joyce, et al. (eds.), *Printing and Society in Early America.* Worcester: American Antiquarian Society.

Winter, Irene J. 1992. "Idols of the King" 6(1) *Journal of Ritual Studies* 13–42.

Winter, Irene J. 1996. "Sex, Rhetoric, and the Public Monument: The Alluring Body of Naram-Sîn of Agade." In Natalie Boymel Kampen (ed.), *Sexuality in Ancient Art: Near East, Egypt, Greece, and Italy.* Cambridge: Cambridge University Press.

Wiseman, Sir Robert. [1656] 1664. *The Law of Laws: or, the Excellency of the Civil Law above all humane laws whatsoever.* London: Royston.

Wither, George. 1586. *A Collection of Emblems.* Leiden: Plantyn.

Wittgenstein, Ludwig. 1961. *Tractatus Logico-Philosophicus.* Translated by D.F. Pears and B.F. McGuiness. London: Routledge.

Wittmann, Roland. 1974. "Die Entwicklungslinien der klassischen Injurienklage" 91 *Zeitschrift der Savigny-Stiftung für Rechtsgeschichte: Romanistische Abteilung* 285–359.

Wohl, Victoria. 2002. *Love among the Ruins: The Erotics of Democracy in Classical Athens.* Princeton, NJ: Princeton University Press.

Wolff, Joseph Georg. 2015. "Documents in Roman Practice." In David Johnston (ed.), *The Cambridge Companion to Roman Law.* New York: Cambridge University Press.

Wood, A. 1997. "The Place of Custom in Plebeian Political Culture: England 1550–1800" 22(1) *Social History* 46–60.

Wood, Sarah. 2005. *Quixotic Fictions of the USA 1792–1815.* Oxford: Oxford University Press.

Wright, David. 2009. *Inventing God's Law: How the Covenant Code of the Bible Used and Revised the Laws of Hammurabi.* Oxford: Oxford University Press.

Wright, N.E., Ferguson, M.W., and Buck, A.R., eds. 2004. *Women: Property and the Letters of the Law in Early Modern England.* Toronto: University of Toronto Press.

Wright, Thomas. [1601] 1986. *Passions of the Mind in General.* New York: Garland Press.

Wunder, Amanda. 2015. "Women's Fashions and Politics in Seventeenth-Century Spain: The Rise and Fall of the Guardainfante" 68(1) *Renaissance Quarterly* 133–186.

Wunderli, Richard. 1990. "Evasion of the Office of Alderman in London, 1523–1672" 15(1) *The London Journal* 3–18.

Xenophon. 1925. *Constitution of the Lacedaemonians.* Cambridge, MA: Harvard University Press.

Yadin-Israel, Azzan. 2004. *Scripture as Logos: Rabbi Ishmael and the Origins of Midrash.* Philadelphia: University of Pennsylvania Press.

Yadin-Israel, Azzan. 2014. *Scripture and Tradition: Rabbi Akiva and the Triumph of Midrash.* Philadelphia: University of Pennsylvania Press.

Yoran, H. 2010. *Between Utopia and Dystopia: Erasmus, Thomas More, and the Humanist Republic of Letters.* Lexington: Lexington Books.

Youngs, Frederic A. 1976. *The Proclamations of the Tudor Queens*. Cambridge: Cambridge University Press.

Zanda, Emanuela. 2013. *Fighting Hydralike Luxury: Sumptuary Regulation in the Roman Republic*. London: Bloomsbury.

Zica, Charles. 2007. *The Appearance of Witchcraft: Print and Visual Culture in Sixteenth Century Europe*. London: Routledge.

Zimmermann, Reinhard. 1996. *The Law of Obligations: Roman Foundations of the Civilian Tradition*. Oxford: Oxford University Press.

Zinck, Arlette. 2010. "Dating the Spiritual Warfare Broadsheet." *The Recorder: Newsletter of the International John Bunyan Society*.

Zuckert, Catherine. 2009. *Plato's Philosophers: The Coherence of the Dialogues*. Chicago: University of Chicago Press.

Zumbansen, Peer. 2010. "Transnational Legal Pluralism" 1(2) *Transnational Legal Theory*, 141–189.

Zumbansen, Peer. 2014. "Law & Society and the Politics of Relevance: Facts and Field Boundaries in 'Transnational Legal Theory in Context'" 11 *No Foundations: An Interdisciplinary Journal of Law and Justice* 1–37.

Zurcher, Andrew. 2007. *Spenser's Legal Language—Law and Poetry in Early Modern England*. Cambridge: Cambridge University Press.

Zurita, Jerónimo. 1967–1985. *Anales de la coróna de Aragón*, 9 vols. Edited by Ángel Canellas López. Zaragoza: Instituto Fernando el Católico.

Zweigert, Konrad and Kötz, Hein. 1998. *An Introduction to Comparative Law*. 3rd edn. Translated by Tony Weir. Oxford: Oxford University Press.

INDEX

abuse of power 48–52
Accursius 26
Adams, John Quincy 64
Adamson, Patrick 144–5
adultery 147–8
agreements 87–8
   bonds 92–8
   legal subject 94–5
   Marlowe's *Faust* 94
   marriage contract 88–90, 96–7, 127–8
   Shakespeare's *Merchant* 92–3
Aitkenhead, Thomas 151
Alciato, Andrea 4, 13, 16, 20, 25, 26, 102, 112, 113, 116–17
Alcock, George 60
Aldermen 67, 81, 86
allegories 20–1
Allyn, William 81
Alphonse V of León 42
Alphonse X of Spain 41
"amende honorable" 30–1
Amerindians 123–4, 125
Andrews, Malcolm xiv
Aneau, Barthélemy 103
Anglican Church 4, 11, 12
Anglo-Norman language 165–6
Anselm of Canterbury 106
Aquinas, Thomas 158
argumentation
   emblem tradition (*see* emblematic argumentation)
   logic 99, 100, 103
   rhetoric 99, 100, 102, 106
Aristotle 19, 33, 34, 37, 43, 158
Arnold, Janet 72
Atkyns, Richard 122, 131, 133–5
audite alteram partem 3–9, 16, 23, 25
Audley, Thomas 157
Augustine of Hippo 118
Aulus Gellius 28
Ausonius, Decimius Magnus 25
axioms 101, 106, 110, 111
Ayrault, Pierre 39

Bacon, Francis 85, 121, 131
Baeza, Gaspar de 41
Baker, J. H. 4, 166
Bakhtin, M. M. 16, 173
Baldwin, Frances 80
Baldwin, William 165
Ball, John 129
Barnes, Barnabe 72
Barnes, Robert 12
barristers 161–2
Barthes, Roland 95
Bartolus de Saxoferrato 100
Baskyn, Martyn 81
Berman, Harold 91, 92
blasphemy 30–1, 149–52
Blount, Thomas 103
Boccaccio, Giovanni 165
Bodin, Jean 33
Boethius 44, 107
Boissard, Jean-Jacques 111–12, 114
Boleyn, Anne 159
Bonaventura 12
bonds 92–8
Boswel, Lawrence 6, 7
Boswel's Case 9, 11
Botella-Ordinas, Eva 42
Bove, Jean de 31
Bovelles, Charles de 31–2, 33
Bradshaw, Thomas 86
Brandt, Sebastian 28
breeches 72–5
Brenner, Robert 135
Brent, Nathaniel 85
Brisson, Barnabé 11
Brooks, Chris 143
Bryce, James 41, 58
Budé, Guillaume 11
Bullein, William 117
Bulwer, John 68
Burghley, William Cecil, Lord Burghley 74, 78, 81–82, 161
Burke, Edmund 63, 96
Burton, Robert 103–5, 149

INDEX

Cabrera de Córdoba, Luis 46–7
Caepolla, Bartholomaeus 10
Calderón de la Barca, Pedro 45, 46, 51, 92
Callistratus 25
Calvin, Jean 166
Cambacérès, Jean-Jacques de 89
Cambyses 18, 19
Cannon, Nathaneall 83
canon law 10, 156, 159
caps 79–80
Carbonnier, Jean 23
Cary, Elizabeth 126
Casanova, Giacomo 89, 95
Castillo de Bobadilla, Jerónimo 58, 59
casuistry 91–2, 95
Catherine of Aragon 158, 159
Cecil, Sir William, Lord Burghley 74, 78, 81–2, 161
Celso, Hugo de 40, 52
censorship 57
Cervantes, Miguel de 41, 42, 44, 47, 57, 58–64, 92, 183
Chan, M. 128
Charles II of England 148
Charles V, Holy Roman Emperor 51, 55
Chaucer, Geoffrey 160
checks and balances 48
church-state tensions 41, 57, 153
Cicero 26, 104, 112, 113, 114, 162
Cid 42, 48
civic justice 34–7
civil law 1, 98
Clarke, John 60
class struggle 132
Claudian 27
clemency 19
Clifford, Anne 128
codification 89, 91, 92
Coke, Sir Edward 10, 12, 139, 145, 159
colonies 121, 125, 126, 130, 132, 135
common law 1, 4, 6, 7, 10–11, 14, 98, 122, 127
  versus equity 156–9
commons 121, 130–5, 200–1
Commonwealth 132, 151
constitutions
  collective protections 48–52
  individual protections 39, 41, 42, 43–8, 64
  Roman constitution 37
  Spain (*see* Spanish law)
  systems of governance 39, 48–52
  U. S. constitution 39, 48, 60, 61, 64

contracts. *See* agreements
court hierarchy 137–40, 155–6
Court of King's Bench 6, 152
Cousteau, Pierre 102, 114, 115
coverture 127
Cranmer, Thomas 156, 159
Crawford, Daniel 60
crime. *See* wrongs
Cromwell, Oliver 28, 30
Cromwell, Thomas 158, 159
Crowley, Robert 76
Cruikshank, Isaac 63
Cujas, Jacques 11
Cullender, Rose 146
cultural history xii–xiv
Cusa, Nicholas de 118
customary rights 131

d'Aguesseau, Henri-François 91
Dalton, James 147, 160
Damhoudere, Josse (Joos de Damhoudere) 18, 31
Dancye, Edmund 81
Danolle, Guillaume 31
David, Gerard 18
David, Jan (*Veredicus Christianus*) 7, 8
Davidson, Hilary 79
Davis, Richard Beale 60, 61
decorum 111–17
defamation 140
Defoe, Daniel 147
De Grazia, M. 126
De Heere, Lucas 190
Del Bene, Bartholomeo 34–6
Deleuze, Gilles 89, 90
Democritus 16
Demosthenes 54, 113, 162
Denny, Amy 146
Derrida. Jacques 9, 11
dialogue 14–16
dichotomies 100
Diderot, Denis 89
disorderly speech 149–52
distributive justice 33
divine harmony 25–6
Doda, Hilary 72
Doderidge (Doddridge), Sir John 4, 6, 10, 99
Dolan, F. E. 129
Domat, Jean 87, 88, 90–1
Don Juan 45
Donne, John 164
Donnelly, John Jr. xiii

Draco, Honoratus 26
dress codes. *See* sumptuary laws
Dudley, Robert, Earl of Leicester 163
Dürer, Albrecht 28

eadem lex est ubi eadem est ratio 7, 9
Earle, John 67
ears, judicial sense and 1–3
　audite alteram partem 3–9, 16, 23, 25
　dialogue 14–16
　etymologies 3
　priority over eyes 4
　subauditio 9–14
ecclesiastical courts 137–9, 140, 143
Edict of Nantes 31
Edward IV of England 164
Edward VI of England 156, 159, 165
Egerton, Thomas 163
Eisenstein, Elizabeth 99
elegance 26
Eliot, T. S. 168
Elizabeth I of England 69, 73, 76, 77, 144, 167
Elton, G. R. 71
emblematic argumentation
　alternative to oral performance 100–1
　application to modern legal arguments 119–20
　axioms 101, 106, 110, 111
　Burton's *Anatomy of Melancholy* 103–5
　concealment and revelation 101
　ethos: decorum of emblematic advocacy 111–17
　hypothesis 111
　logos: framing the argument 106–11
　maxims 101, 102, 107
　opposing arguments 104, 106
　pathos 101, 117–19
　print revolution 99–100, 102
　status 103
　visual argumentation 99–102, 119–20
enclosure 121, 130–5
English Civil War 122, 133, 135
English colonies 121, 125, 126, 130, 132, 135
Englishness 121
equity 19, 21, 23, 127, 156–9
Erasmus, Desiderius 1, 112, 162, 164
erotic literature 89
Estienne, Henri 100
ethos 111–17
Evelyn, John 79, 86
exempla justitiae 17–20, 37

fashion. *See* sumptuary laws
Faust 94
Federici, Silvia 129
Ferdinand of Aragon 55
　and Isabel 40, 41, 175
Ferrers, George 165, 166
Fichte, Johann Gottlieb 96
Ficino, Marsilio 42, 176–7
Finkelpearl, Philip J. 161, 166
Fitzherbert, Anthony 128
Forcadel, Étienne 26
Fortescue, Sir John 14, 15, 157, 160, 161, 162
Foster, Edmund 81
Foucault, Michel 72, 101
foundational texts 14–15
Fourier, Charles 95
Foxdayle, Thomas 82
Fra Angelico 28
Fraunce, Abraham 100
French Code Civil 89
Fuero Juzgo 43, 45, 46, 48, 49, 62
funeral rites 47
fustian 73, 74

Galligan, Denis J. 41
garden imagery xiv, 129–30
Gascoigne, George 162
Gellius, Aulus 28
Genette, Gérard 103
Geoffrey of Monmouth 155
geometry 33–4
Giglio, Cesare 20
Glanvill, Joseph 143, 144
Goodrich, Peter 76, 101, 103, 110, 156
governance systems 34–7, 39. *See also* constitutions
　Spain 48–52
Gratian 21
Green, John 60
Greene, Robert 74
Greuze, Jean-Baptiste 89, 96
Grimm, Jacob 43
Grotius, Hugo 27, 90, 96
Guy, John 206, 207

Hadrianus, Junius 113
Haldar, Piyel 4
Hale, Sir Matthew 139, 146, 148
Hall, Edward 155, 162
Hardin, Russell 39
Harding, Thomas 12
harmony 25–6

Harrington, Sir John 83
Harte, N. B. 80
Haunold, Christian 21–3
Hayaert, Valérie 7
Hayward, John 77
Hayward, Maria 72
Haywood, John 81
Hegel, Georg Wilhelm Friedrich 96
Heidegger, Martin 101
Henry, Patrick 63
Henry VII of England 155, 156
Henry VIII of England 156, 157, 158, 164
Heraclitus 16
heresy 151
Herodotus 18
Hesiod 25
Heywood, Jasper 166
Hobbes, Thomas 90, 96
Hoey, Jean de 20
Hogarth, William 93–4, 97
Holinshed, Raphael 165
Holy Roman Empire 42
honor 45–6
Hooker, John 208
Hooker, Richard 12, 13
Hopper, Joachim 5
Horozco, Juan de 18
Howard, Lord William 82
humane law 19
humanists 3–4, 6, 9, 10, 11, 25, 26, 42, 120
  legal profession 164, 165, 166
  print revolution 99–100, 102, 104
  Renaissance culture 99, 103, 107, 112, 114, 117, 118
human rights 39, 41, 42, 43–8, 64
Hunt, Alan 72, 80
hunting 47
Hutson, Lorna 206, 207
Huybrechts, Adriaen 32

Ibarra, Celaya 51
Iberian Peninsula. *See* Spanish law
ideona persona 6, 7
Ignatius of Loyola, St 95
images. *See* emblematic argumentation
"imagined communities" 177
Inns of Court 4, 10, 160–5, 166–7
Institutes of Justinian 9, 14, 26, 54
interpretation 10, 26
Irwin, Nathaniel 64
Isidore of Seville 3, 14, 21

Jackson, John 60
Jackson, William 64
Jacob, Robert 31
Jacob de Gheyn 28, 29
Jacobo de las Leyes 41
James I of England 71, 83, 85, 103, 141, 144
Jansenists 87, 88, 91–2
Jefferson, Thomas 51, 63, 64
Jesuits 87, 91–2, 95
Jewel, Bishop John 12
Jobson, Richard 125
John, King of England xii, xiii, 42
Johnson, Charles 163
Johnson, Samuel 93, 95
jointures 128
Jonson, Ben 160
Joos de Damhoudere (Josse Damhoudere) 18, 31
Juan II of Aragon 52
judge's damnation 17–20
Junta, Jacobo de 41
Justice 17
  "amende honorable" 30–1
  civic justice 34–7
  judge's damnation 17–20
  Jupiter and Themis 26–7
  Justitia's blindfold 28–30
  Lady Justice 20–1
  musical metaphors 25–6
  scales of Justice 21–5
  symbolic geometry 33–4
  trivial imagery: the broom 31–3
Justinian 9, 14, 41, 54, 107, 113, 176
Justitia 28–30

Kagan, Richard 57
Kant, Immanuel 90–1, 92, 96
Kantorowicz, Ernst 112, 113
Kantorowicz, Herman 195
King's Bench 6, 152
Knox, John 141
Korda, Natasha 128–9

Lacan, Jacques 11
Laclos, Choderlos de 89, 95
Lady Justice 20–1
Lambarde, William 160
Lancastre, John, Bishop of London 6
Lanyer, Aemilia 128
Last Judgement 17
Latinitas 11
Le Blon, Christian 103, 104

legal agreements. *See* agreements
legal profession
    court hierarchy 155–6
    dramatic works 166–70
    equity *versus* common law 156–9
    Inns of Court 4, 10, 160–5, 166–7
    political influence 162–3
    revels and entertainments 164–5
    use of French language 165–6
legal subject 94–5
Legendre, Pierre 119
Legh, Gerard 100, 103
Legrand, Pierre xiii
Le Moyne, Pierre 107, 109
Lenton, Francis 82
Levack, Brian P. 146
Levellers 132
Lever, Ralph 118
Ligon, Richard 126
linen 76, 77, 79
livery 67–8, 81
Locke, Hew xii–xiii
Locke, John 60, 94–5, 96
Lodge, Thomas 160
logic 99, 100, 103
logos 106–11
Loisel, Antoine 20
Lollards 151
London
    dress codes 65–6 (*see also* sumptuary laws)
    urban growth 66–7
Lope de Vega 45, 48–9
Louis XIV of France 91
Louis XV of France 91
Lydgate, John 165

McDonagh, B. 131
Machyn, Henry 77
Mackenzie, Sir George 139, 143, 145, 146, 151
Maclean, Ian 10
Madison, James 64
Magna Carta xii, xiii, 42, 49
Maistre, Joseph de 98
Malcolm-Davies, Jane 79
Mandeville, Bernard 85
Manning, John 104
Marcile, Théodore 34
Marguerite, Duchess of Savoy 34
Marín, María 48
Marlowe, Christopher 94
marriage contracts 88–90, 96–7, 127–8

Marston, John 74, 161
Martínez, Pedro Luis 54–5
Marvell, Andrew 130, 200
Marx, Karl 121
Mary, Queen of England 156
Mary Queen of Scots 160, 168, 169
Mather, Cotton 60
maxims 1, 7, 8, 9, 23, 101, 102, 104, 107
Mayflower 60
Mercado, Fray Tomás de 44
Merchant Adventurers 67, 134
Mignault, Claude 102
Milton, John 163
Mirabeau, Honoré de 26
Miranda, Diego de 56, 60
mockado 84–5
Mofa, Matteo Gribaldi 26
Molina, Tirso de 45, 57
Monroe, James 64
Monson, Robert 160
Montaigne, Michel de 1, 104, 113, 123, 124
moot cases 161–2
Mor, Antonis 66
morality
    legal agreements 95
    sexual transgressions 45–6, 47–8
    sin and crime 137 (*see also* wrongs)
    sumptuary laws 76–9, 83
More, Sir Thomas 11, 34, 124, 157, 159, 163, 164, 166
Morris, Robert 60
Morton, John (Lord Chancellor) 60, 157, 158, 182
Mortymer, John 81
Murner, Thomas 103
musical metaphors 25–6

Natalis, Michel 28
New World 123, 130
norms 107, 110
Norton, Thomas 160, 162, 166, 167
nose, juridical sense and 1

Obrechts-Tytreca, Lucie 119
Ong, Walter 99–100
Onslow, Richard 74
Oraeus, Heinrich 33–4

Palacios Rubios, Juan López de 123
Palmer, Thomas 104, 106, 112
Paradin, Claude 4, 5
pari ratione et jure 7, 9

Parker, Archbishop Matthew 76
Pascal, Blaise 87, 88, 91
Pasquier, Etienne 20
pathos 101, 117–19
Peacham, Henry 103, 111, 117
pelican 116–17
penance 30–1
Pepys, Samuel 148
Perelman, Chaim 114, 119
Perrière, Guillaume de la 102, 107, 108
Peters, Hugh 132
Petrarch 113
Phillip II of Spain 40, 46, 47, 48, 50, 51, 52, 57, 58
Phillip III of Spain 56
Phillip IV of Spain 45
picaresque novel 43
Plato 42, 177
Plautus 25
Plutarch 20
poetry 26
Poland 51, 180
Pole, William 81
polities 37
Polybius 37
Pothier, Robert-Joseph 91
Prest, Wilfrid 156, 162
print revolution 99–100, 102, 133–4
Privy Council 82, 141, 155, 163
property laws
    Amerindians 123–4, 125
    colonies 121, 125, 126, 130, 132, 135
    enclosure of the commons 121, 130–5
    Englishness 121
    garden imagery 129–30
    possession 121–2
    Shakespeare's *Tempest* 122–6
    slaves 121, 125–6
    women 126–30
Protestantism 76, 91, 92, 141, 143, 147, 159
Provoost, Jan 17
Puritanism 76, 132
Puttenham, George 117

Quevedo, Francisco 46
Quintilian 102

Racine, Jean 87–8
Raffield, Paul 164
Ramus, Petrus 100
Ranters 151
rape 148

Rastell, John 166
reason 7, 9
Reformers 12
Renaissance culture 99, 103, 107, 112, 114, 117, 118, 126
republics 42
revenge 46, 178
rhetoric 99, 100, 102, 106
Rhodiginus, Caelius 28
Ripa, Cesare 28
Roche, Daniel 72
Rollenhagen, Gabriel 102, 110
Roman constitution 37
Roman law 10, 12, 15, 20, 26, 41, 122
Roo, John 164
Rosen, Lawrence xiii
Rousseau, Jean-Jacques 90, 91, 96
Rublack, Ulinka 71
ruffs 76–9, 82

Sackville, Thomas 162, 167
Sade, Donatien de 89, 95
Saint-Germain, Christopher 11, 14, 15, 158–9
Salzman, P. 128
Sanders, Frans 17
satire 116
Savaron, Jean 11
scales of Justice 21–5
Scarlattini, Ottavio 3
scholasticism 4, 92, 95, 96
Schoonhovius, Florentinus 26
Scot, Reginald 141
Scottish courts 138, 140, 141–3, 145–6
secularization 140, 153
Selden, John 10, 11
Seneca 7, 9, 11, 25, 166, 167, 168
sexual transgressions 45–6, 47–8, 137, 140, 146–9
Shakespeare, William xii, 80
    As You Like It 160
    Henry IV 155, 160, 161
    Henry V 129, 132
    influence of Seneca 168–70
    King Lear 126, 128
    Measure for Measure 165
    Merchant of Venice 92–3, 158
    Much Ado About Nothing 155
    Richard III 156
    Taming of the Shrew 128–9
    Tempest 122–6
Sidney, Philip 165, 167
Siemon, J. R. 129

silk 46, 67, 68, 71, 74, 75, 79, 81, 84, 85
Skinner, Quentin 25
slaves 121, 125–6
Smith, Adam 85
Smith, Henry 83
Smith, Sir Thomas 79
social differentiation 72–5
social order 137, 140, 146, 153
sodomy 149
Solomon, judgment of 23
Solorzano de Pereira, Juan de 23–6
Spanish law 39–43
   Aragon's legal history 175
   censorship 57
   Fuero Juzgo 43, 45, 46, 48, 49, 52
   funeral rites 47
   honor 45–6
   hunting 47
   individual protections 41, 42, 43–8
   Military Orders 48, 49
   Navarre's legal history 180
   officials 58–64
   periphery *versus* central state 52–8
   property and the New World 123, 124
   relations between clergy and women 47–8
   sumptuary laws 46–7
   systems of governance and abuse of power 48–52
Speght, Rachel 127
Spenser, John 12
"Spiritual Warfare" 137, 138
Standish, Miles 60, 182
Star Chamber 39, 81, 139, 140, 157
Starkey, Thomas 14
state trials 159–60
Statute of Westminster 6, 7
Stengel, Georg 110
Sterne, Lawrence 94
Stone, Lawrence 72
Stow, John 77
Stubbes, Philip 74, 77
studia humanitatis 99, 102
Suarez, Francisco 92
subauditio 9–14
sumptuary laws 65–6
   attitudes to clothing 68–9
   breeches 72–5
   caps 79–80
   economic concerns 79–80
   enforcement 80–3
   English law 69–71
   innovations 83–5

   legacy 85–6
   livery 67–8, 81
   religious and moral concerns 76–9, 83
   ruffs 76–9
   social differentiation 72–5
   Spanish law 46–7
   sumptuary studies 71–2

Tanner, J. R. 39
textiles 67, 72. *See also* fustian; linen; silk; velvet; wool
Themis 26–7
Theodor de Bry, Johann 20–1
Thornton, William 160
torture 146
Townson, Robert 83
treason 39
trial by jury 156
Tudor age 155–70
Tyndale, William 12
typefaces 100

urban growth 66–7
U. S. Constitution 39, 48, 60, 61, 64
U. S. Declaration of Independence 43
utopian literature 34, 114, 122–3, 124, 135, 157

Valencia, attorney to Philip II 52–4
Valeriano, Piero 1, 2
Valerius Maximus 18
van de Passe, Crispijn 28, 29
van der Borcht, Peter (Peeter) 32
Vega, Lope de 45, 48–9
Vellert, Dirck 18, 19
velvet 46, 65, 68, 71, 72–4, 75, 81, 85
Vergil 3
Versteeg, Mila 41
vestiarian controversy 76
Villadiego, Alfonso 52
Visigoths 40, 52
visual mediation. *See* emblematic argumentation
Vitoria, Francisco de 123–4

Walweyn, Richard 65, 81
Washington, George 63
Watteau, Antoine 88, 89, 97
Weaver, Thomas 81
Whitehouse, Edward 15
Whitney, Geoffrey 103, 110
Wiener, C. Z. 129

Williams, Stanley T. 61
Wilson, Thomas 118
Winans, Robert B. 60
Winstanley, Gerrard 122, 131, 132–3, 135
Wiseman, Sir Robert 11
witchcraft 140–6
Wither, George 103, 110
Wittgenstein, Ludwig 106
Wolsey, Cardinal Thomas 157, 158, 164
women's rights 126–30, 147–9
Wood, Philip 82
wool 79–80, 84, 85
Wormeley, Ralph 60
Worsey, Robert 81
Wright, Thomas 118, 128

wrongs
   blasphemy 149–52
   criminal and civil 137, 139–40
   defamation 140
   ecclesiastical and secular authorities 137–9, 140
   law and morality 137
   sexual transgressions 45–6, 47–8, 137, 140, 146–9
   sin and crime 137, 147, 152–3
   witchcraft 140–6

Zaleucus of Locria 18–19
Zika, Charles 145
Zurita, Jerónimo 52